Lecture Notes in Computer Science 4398

Commenced Publication in 1973
Founding and Former Series Editors:
Gerhard Goos, Juris Hartmanis, and Jan van Leeuwen

T0223277

Stéphane Marchand-Maillet   Eric Bruno
Andreas Nürnberger   Marcin Detyniecki (Eds.)

Adaptive Multimedia Retrieval: User, Context, and Feedback

4th International Workshop, AMR 2006
Geneva, Switzerland, July 27-28, 2006
Revised Selected Papers

 Springer

Volume Editors

Stéphane Marchand-Maillet
Eric Bruno
University of Geneva
Viper Group on Multimedia Information Retrieval
24, rue du Général Dufour, 1211 Geneva 4, Switzerland
E-mail: {marchand, eric.bruno}@cui.unige.ch

Andreas Nürnberger
Otto-von-Guericke Universität Madgeburg
Fakultät für Informatik
Universitätsplatz 2, 39106 Magdeburg, Germany
E-mail: nuernb@iws.cs.uni-magdeburg.de

Marcin Detyniecki
Laboratoire d'Informatique de Paris 6, LIP6
8 rue du Capitaine Scott, 75015 Paris, France
E-mail: marcin.detyniecki@lip6.fr

Library of Congress Control Number: 2007923197

CR Subject Classification (1998): H.3, H.5.1, H.5.5, I.4, I.2

LNCS Sublibrary: SL 3 – Information Systems and Application, incl. Internet/Web
and HCI

ISSN   0302-9743
ISBN-10   3-540-71544-4 Springer Berlin Heidelberg New York
ISBN-13   978-3-540-71544-3 Springer Berlin Heidelberg New York

Springer is a part of Springer Science+Business Media

springer.com

© Springer-Verlag Berlin Heidelberg 2007
Printed in Germany

Typesetting: Camera-ready by author, data conversion by Scientific Publishing Services, Chennai, India
Printed on acid-free paper   SPIN: 12040261   06/3142   5 4 3 2 1 0

Preface

This book is an extended collection of revised contributions that were initially submitted to the International Workshop on Adaptive Multimedia Retrieval (AMR 2006). This workshop was organized during July 27-28, 2006 at the University of Geneva, Switzerland.

AMR 2006 was the fourth workshop in the series, following AMR2005 organized at University of Glasgow (*Lecture Notes in Computer Science* volume 3877). The series started in 2003 with a workshop during the 26th German Conference on Artificial Intelligence (KI 2003 – *Lecture Notes in Computer Science* volume 3094) and continued in 2004 as part of the 16th European Conference on Artificial Intelligence (ECAI 2004).

This year, the AMR workshop kept its focus on accommodating user needs via adaptive processes. A number of contributions investigated the utility of segmentation in the query and retrieval process. Adaptive definitions of similarity were also proposed in the papers contained in this volume. The invited contributions were intended to open on less-addressed topics in the community. This is the case for music information retrieval and distributed information retrieval (e.g., on P2P networks). Other contributions looked at more applicative aspects of IR.

We think that this book provides a good and conclusive overview of the current research in the area of adaptive information retrieval. We would like to thank all members of the Program Committee for supporting us in the reviewing process, the workshop participants for their willingness to revise and extend their papers for this book and all staff at Springer for their support in publishing this book. We extend a special thanks to our supporting institutions.

December 2006

Stéphane Marchand-Maillet
Eric Bruno
Marcin Detyniecki
Andreas Nürnberger

Organization

General Chair

Stéphane Marchand-Maillet   University of Geneva, Switzerland

Program Chairs

Eric Bruno   University of Geneva, Switzerland
Andreas Nürnberger   University of Magdeburg, Germany
Marcin Detyniecki   CNRS, Lab. d'Informatique de Paris 6,
                               France

Local Chairs

Nicolas Moënne-Loccoz   University of Geneva, Switzerland
Serhiy Kosinov   University of Geneva, Switzerland

Publicity Chair

Jana Kludas   University of Geneva, Switzerland

Program Committee

Kobus Barnard   University of Arizona, USA
Stefano Beretti   Università di Firenze, Italy
Susan Boll   University of Oldenburg, Germany
Jesper W. Schneider   Royal School of Library and Information
                               Science, Denmark
Arjen de Vries   CWI, Amsterdam, The Netherlands
Philippe Joly   Université Paul Sabatier, IRIT, Toulouse,
                               France
Gareth Jones   Dublin City University, Ireland
Joemon Jose   University of Glasgow, UK
R. Manmatha   University of Massachusetts, USA
Trevor Martin   University of Bristol, UK
José M. Martínez Sánchez   Universidad Autnoma de Madrid, Spain
Bernard Mérialdo   Institut Eurcom , France
Jan Nesvadba   Philips Research, The Netherlands
Stefan Rüger   Imperial College London, UK
Simone Santini   University of California, San Diego, USA

Raimondo Schettini   University of Milano Bicocca, Italy
Ingo Schmitt   University of Magdeburg, Germany
Nicu Sebe   University of Amsterdam, The Netherlands
Alan F. Smeaton   Dublin City University, Ireland
Xian-Sheng Hua   Microsoft Research, China

Sponsoring Institutions

University of Geneva, Switzerland (http://www.unige.ch)
The IM2 Swiss NCCR (http://www.im2.ch)
The SIMILAR EU Network of Excellence (http://www.similar.cc)
PHILIPS Research, The Netherlands (http://www.philips.com)

Table of Contents

Adaptive Retrieval

Structuring Multimedia

User Integration and Profiling

A Method for Processing the Natural Language Query in Ontology-Based Image Retrieval System

Myunggwon Hwang, Hyunjang Kong, Sunkyoung Baek, and Pankoo Kim[*]

Dept. of Computer Science
Chosun University, 375 Seosuk-dong Dong-Ku Gwangju 501-759 Korea
{mghwang,kisofire,zamilla100,pkkim}@chosun.ac.kr

Abstract. There is a large amount of image data on the web because of the development of many image acquisition devices nowadays. Hence, many researchers have been focusing on the study how to manage and retrieve these huge images efficiently. In this paper, we use two kinds of ontologies in the image retrieval system for processing the natural language query. We use the domain ontology for describing objects in images and we newly build the spatial ontology for representing the relations between these objects. And then, we suggest the method for processing the user query formatted by the natural language in the ontology-based image retrieval system. Based on our study, we got the conclusion that the natural language query processing is the very important part for improving the efficiency of the image retrieval system.

1 Introduction

Nowadays, the study on the image retrieval has been actively progressing. Until now, the basic image retrieval methodologies are the *Text-Matching, Contents-based and Concept(Ontology)-based* methods.[2][3] In these methodologies, users generally use simple keywords as the user query. The Ontology-based image retrieval system uses the ontologies to understand the meaning of the user query, but the ontologies just solve the ambiguousness between words. Hence, the user query used in ontology-based system is also simple keywords. Nowadays, huge number of images has been creating through the various image acquisition devices such as the digital camera, scanner and phone-camera. Thus, we need more intelligent image retrieval techniques for searching the images efficiently. In present day, the users tend to use a descriptive sentence to find images because they want to search for images as fast as possible, they do not want to spend long time retrieving images. Thus, the user query is getting descriptive and natural language type. As a result, the method for processing the natural language query is demanded for improving the performance of the image retrieval system. In this paper, we use two kinds of ontologies in our proposed system to handle the natural language query. One is the domain ontology, which contains many concepts and represents the relations between these concepts. The other is the spatial ontology, which contains three basic relations and many words about the relations.

---

[*] Corresponding author.

S. Marchand-Maillet et al. (Eds.): AMR 2006, LNCS 4398, pp. 1–11, 2007.
© Springer-Verlag Berlin Heidelberg 2007

We use some parts of the WordNet for building the domain ontology and we newly make the spatial ontology based on the survey paper, WordNet and OXFORD Dictionary for the purpose of processing the natural language queries. The basic idea of our study is that most user queries are including the words representing the spatial relationships. It is the significant feature of user queries for supporting our study. Therefore we use the features to design the newly proposed image retrieval system and try to process the natural language queries.

In the 2nd Section, we introduce the related works - the ontology-based image retrieval and the query processing methodologies. Then in Section 3, we explain the spatial ontology building steps and our system architecture based on the ontologies. And we describe the method for processing the natural language queries in the ontology-based system in details. We test and evaluate our system comparing with other systems in Section 4. At the end of this paper, we conclude our study and suggest the future works.

2   Related Works

2.1   Ontology-Based Image Retrieval

The traditional information retrieval systems have the mismatch problem among the terminologies. For solving the problem, many researchers have studied to apply the ontology theory to the system. Many works show that ontologies could be used not only for annotation and precise information retrieval, but also for helping the user in formulating the information need and the corresponding query. It is important especially in applications where the domain semantics are complicated and not necessarily known to the user. Furthermore, the ontology-enriched knowledge base of image metadata can be applied to construct more meaningful answers to queries than just hit-lists.

The major difficulty in the ontology-based approach is that the extra work is needed in creating the ontology and the detailed annotations.[5][6][7] We believe, however, that in many applications this price is justified due to the better accuracy obtained in information retrieval and to the new semantic browsing facilities offered to the end-user. We are trying to implement semantic techniques to avoid so much hard work with the ontology building the trade off between annotation work and quality of information retrieval can be balanced by using these less detailed ontologies and annotations. Although this approach could address the mismatch problem between the terms, it is still not suitable for image retrieval system because they did not consider the features of the image data. Therefore, we are not get the good results in the ontology-based image retrieval system.

2.2   User Query Processing

Due to the development of internet technology, infinite information is published in the web. And the volume is getting increase. So, most internet users depend on the information retrieval engines for searching information. The purpose of these information retrieval engines is efficient ranking for user who wants information in huge web documents.[9] And many ranking methods are introduced. For examples, through clever term-based scoring, link analysis, evaluation of user traces and so on. But existing retrieval systems are mostly based on just word matching between query language and words in documents. Let's suppose someone who input a query, "tiger sits in the cage". So the systems are giving the results including 'tiger' or 'cage'. These methods show much information related to the user queries, but show the information of a little relevance even without relation. In result, the user must spend much time for additional work.

3   System Architecture and Spatial Ontology Building Process

In this Section, we introduce the background studies for processing the natural language query. The core studies are building the spatial ontology and designing the image retrieval system based on constructed ontologies.

3.1   Background Studies

3.1.1   Design of Ontology-Based Image Retrieval System

Our system uses the ontologies to describe the contents of images and search images. Especially, when users use natural language query for retrieving images in our system, our system is able to process the query based on the ontologies.

Our system consists of three parts.

- *Super User Interface Part : User can describe and manage the images.*
- *End User Interface Part : User can retrieve images using the natural language queries.*
- *Ontology Part : Domain and spatial ontologies exist in this part.*

Figure 1 illustrates the architecture of our system.

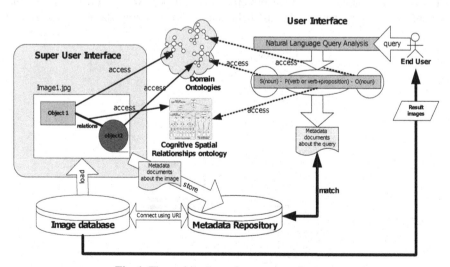

Fig. 1. The architecture of our proposed system

Our system has two significant features. First feature is to apply the spatial ontology for representing the relations between objects in images. Second feature is to apply the method for processing the natural language query. At result, we could expect the efficient image retrieval through our system. We explain two features used in our system by details in Section 3.1.2 and 3.1.3.

3.1.2 Spatial Ontology Building Steps

For processing the natural language query, the spatial ontology plays the core role in our study. So, we built the spatial ontology following as four steps. Figure 2 shows the spatial ontology building steps.

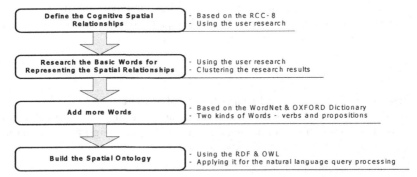

Fig. 2. The steps for building the spatial ontology

[Step 1] *Define the Cognitive Spatial Relations*

In the existing image retrieval system, if the system uses the spatial relations between objects, the system mostly use the region-based spatial relationships. In this case, the problems are either the spatial relations but not have the semantic meaning or system may define the spatial relations incorrectly. In this paper, we try to define the cognitive spatial relations newly. We used the survey for defining the cognitive spatial

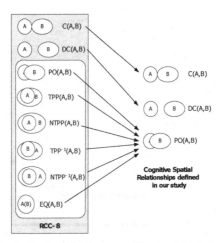

Fig. 3. The model of the cognitive spatial relations

relations. We prepare the 200 images containing the objects and spatial relations between objects. And then, we examine the spatial relations recognized by users when the users look at images. At the result of survey paper, the cognitive spatial relations are represented three basic relatons - 'connect', 'disconnect' and 'partOf'. Figure 3 illustrates the model of the cognitive spatial relations comparing with the RCC-8.[1]

[Step 2] *Examine the Root Words for Representing the Spatial Relations*
In step 1, we realized that three spatial relations are necessary for describing the contents of images in detail. In this step, for building the spatial ontology, firstly we get the terms about which words are used to describe images by the users through survey paper. And then, we build the spatial ontology based on the cognitive spatial relations with the results of survey paper. The lists showed in figure 4 are the results obtained from the process of replication concerning the representation of the spatial relations of each spatial verb.

image #3	image #33	image #40	image #55	image #59	image #141	
Research results (spatial relationships 1)connect 2)partof 3)disconnect, C_SR:cognitive spatial relationships)						
number	C_SR	Answers of the Researchers					
3	1	lying	lying	lie	lying	lying	lie	sit
33	2	swim	search	swim	swim	cross	look pretty	swim
40	1	kiss	kiss	kiss	kiss	kiss	love	play
55	3	on the left	bigger	beside	behind	left of	beside	beside
59	3	wait	in front	waiting	stand	in front	look	stand
141	2	fly	soars	fly	fly	fly	fly	fly

Fig. 4. The parts of the survey paper

Figure 4 shows the parts of survey paper. According to results of the survey, we realized that most users have similar feeling and use similar spatial verbs to describe images. After clustering the results, we select the root words from the results of survey paper for building the spatial ontology.

[Step 3] *Add Terms Related to Root Words based on WordNet and Dictionary*
In this step, we built the spatial ontology based on the cognitive spatial relations, survey paper, WordNet and OXFORD dictionary. Figure 5 shows the architecture of the spatial ontology proposed by our study.

In figure 5, the cognitive spatial relations are situated at the top level and the second level consists of the two parts – spatial verbs and spatial prepositions. The bottom level is containing many terms related to second level verbs based on the WordNet and OXFORD Dictionary. The significant fact through survey paper of the step 2 is that not only verbs but also prepositions are very important to represent the cognitive spatial relations. Therefore, we consist of the spatial verbs part based on the WordNet and the spatial postpositions part using the OXFORD Dictionary for building the more complete spatial ontology.

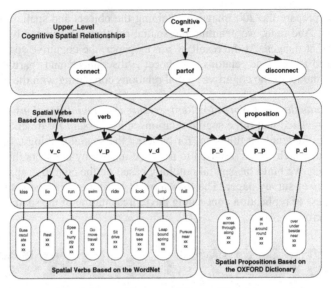

Fig. 5. The architecture of the spatial ontology

[Step 4] *Build the Spatial Ontology*
In our study, firstly we define the cognitive spatial relations from the *RCC-8*, and secondly collect and select the basic words for describing the spatial relations using survey paper. And then, we add terms related to root words for building more complete spatial ontology based on the WordNet and OXFORD dictionary. Finally, in Step 4, we write spatial ontology using the ontology language such as RDF and OWL for applying it to our proposed ontology-based image retrieval system.

3.2   The Method for Processing Natural Language Query in Our System

When users want to search images, they generally use the natural language as the query. Most users want to find images as fast as possible and they do not want to spend much time. Thus, user query is getting descriptive like as the natural language. So, the study for processing the natural language query is a very important task. For example, they use query like as *"the birds fly in the sky"* in the existing image retrieval systems. However, these systems just pick out the nouns in the query and

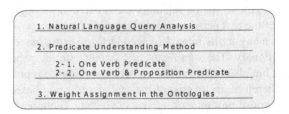

Fig. 6. Natural Language Query Processing Steps

match with the annotation about images and give the result images to users. There are some efforts to process the user query more semantically. That is the ontology-based image retrieval system. It also uses the nouns in the query and tries to understand the meaning of the nouns using ontology. However, it just uses the simple words and image annotations. It is far from the natural language query processing. In our study, we use the domain and spatial ontologies to process the natural language query. The steps of our method are like figure 6.

[Step 1] *Analysis of the Natural Language Query*
Firstly, the system analyzes the user query to the RDF-Triple format. For example, the user query *"the birds fly in the sky"* is analyzed the RDF-Triple like as *S(bird)-P(fly)-O(sky)*. As mentioned Section 3.1, most queries consist of the *Subject-Predicate-Object(RDF-Triple)* type and it is the common natural language format. Secondly, the system processes the nouns and verbs detection from the user queries and ignores the pronouns and etc. And then, the nouns are assigned the subject and object of the RDF-Triple format. However, it is not important that the nouns are assigned either subject or object.

[Step 2] *Method for Understanding the Predicate*
In this study, the second step is the core part to process the natural language query. It is to grasp the predicate from the user query. In our system, we just consider the spatial relationships in the user query based on the spatial ontology. Hence, our system can address the natural language queries that are containing the spatial verbs. About the other queries, which do not contain the spatial verbs, the accuracy of the results of our system is similar to the existing ontology-based system. However, about the queries including the spatial verbs, our system give higher accuracy than existing systems in the image retrieval.

In here, there are commonly two types of predicates in the natural language queries.

    <2-1>First Type : The predicate includes just one verb
    <2-2>Second Type : The predicate that consists of one verb and one preposition

About two types of the predicate, our system processes them as follows:

Firstly, if the system meets the <2-1>, the system accesses the spatial verbs of the spatial ontology in figure 5 and finds the same concept or instance in the spatial ontology. If there is the same term in the spatial ontology, the system grasps the spatial relations in the top level about the verb. And, if there are no classes or instances matched with the predicate in the spatial ontology, we ignore the predicate during the query processing. At that time, the accuracy of the results of the image retrieval is similar to the ontology-based image retrieval system. Second, in case of <2-2>, the system processes the preposition in the predicate first of all. If the preposition matches with the concept or instance in the spatial ontology, we use the top level spatial relations about the preposition and the verb in the predicate ignores. Or else, the preposition does not exist in the spatial ontology, the system progresses the same processing step to the case <2-1>.

[Step 3] *Weight Values Assignment*

About the *RDF Triple(s-p-o)*, the system accesses the ontologies to assign the adaptive weight and then, shows the result images in order. In here, we give the adaptive weights to each *Subject-Predicate-Object* term for more correct image retrieval. The total steps for processing the natural language query are described like figure 7.

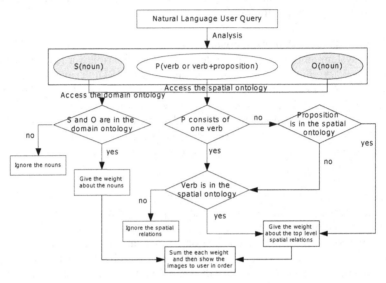

Fig. 7. The flow for processing the natural language query

Through many tests in our study, we realized that it is possible to process the natural language query in the ontology-based image retrieval system by using the spatial ontology and the natural language query processing method.

4   Experimental Results and Evaluation

We have evaluated our system formatively. We measure the accuracy of our system and compare it to the other systems. We performed three controlled experiments, in which human experts measure the accuracy of the search results using three kinds of the systems. The systems for the test are as follows:

1. *Existing text matching image retrieval system – google.com*
2. *The ontology-based image retrieval system*
3. *Our proposed image retrieval system*

For testing, we prepare the user query such as '*birds fly in the sky*' that is the natural language type. And then, we tested in each system about the query. Figure 8, 9 and 10 show the search results of three systems about the query.

Fig. 8. The results in the google.com

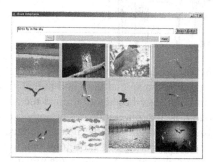 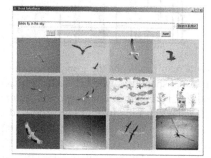

Fig. 9. The results in ontology-based system   **Fig. 10.** The results in our proposed system

In figure 8, 9 and 10, we realized that our proposed system could understand the natural language query. In figure 9, the ontology-based system could understand the meaning of nouns in the query such as 'bird' and 'sky' but it could not process the verb(fly) in the query. So, the ontology-based system is not suitable for processing the natural language query as just applying ontology. For more correct evaluating, we tested five more user queries and examined the query results in the three systems. The five user queries are listed as below :

Query 1 : Car
Query 2 : Swan and river
Query 3 : Bus moves the road
Query 4: Birds fly in the sky
Query 5: Dog plays on the grass

Table 1 shows the results of the image retrieval in the three test systems about five queries. For measuring the accuracy, we use the simple formula showing as below:

$$\text{Accuracy} = \frac{\text{Correct images matched with the query}}{\text{All images searched throughout the system}}$$

Table 1. The accuracy of result images throughout the test

	Query 1	Query 2	Query 3	Query 4	Query 5
Google.com	0.728	0.832	0.214	0.338	0.125
Ontology-based system	0.946	0.937	0.438	0.457	0.281
Our proposed system	0.946	0.937	0.743	0.697	0.775

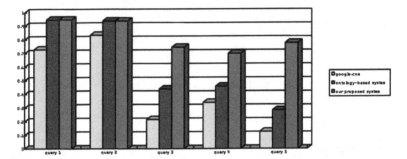

As a result, we got the conclusion that our proposed system provided the highest accuracy, especially, when the user's query contains the spatial verb and preposition. About query 1 and 2, our proposed system and ontology-based system had the same result values. It tells us that our proposed system is also one kinds of ontology-based system but we additionally use the spatial ontology to address the natural language query. It is the big different feature of our system comparing to the original ontology-based system. Throughout our system, the users can expect more semantic image retrieval about the natural language query.

6   Conclusion and Future Works

In this paper, the core study is to process the natural language query. And then, we verify the advancement of the image retrieval system based on the ontologies as we applied new methods to the system. In our system, the spatial ontology plays the core part. As a result, we can expect more efficient image retrieval throughout our system. However, we have also the limitation that our system just addresses the natural language queries that contain the spatial verbs and prepositions. We should study for processing more complicated natural language query. It remains to our future study.

Acknowledgement

This research was supported by the MIC(Ministry of Information and Communication), Korea, under the ITRC(Information Technology Research Center) support program supervised by the IITA(Institute of Information Technology Advancement)" (IITA-2006-C1090-0603-0040)

References

1. Deborah L. McGuinness, Daniele Nardi, Peter F.Patel-Schneider, "The Description Logic Handbook: Theory, implementation, and applications", Cambridge University Press, January 2003.

2. Arnold W.M. Smeulders, "Content-Base Image Retrieval at the End of the Early Years", IEEE Transactions on pattern analysis and machine intelligence, Vol. 22, No. 12, December, 2000.
3. Ching-chih Chen, and James Z. Wang, "Large-scale Emperor Digital Library and Semantics-sensitive Region-based Retrieval", Proceeding of the International Conference on Digital Library -- IT Opportunities and Challenges in the New Millennium, National Library of China, Beijing, China, pp. 454-462, July 9-11, 2002.
4. Huamin Feng, Rui Shi, Tat-Seng Chua, "A bootstrapping framework for annotating and retrieving WWW images", Proceedings of the 12th annual ACM international conference on Multimedia, October 2004.
5. Von-Wun Soo, Chen-Yu Lee, Chung-Cheng Li, Shu Lei Chen, Ching-chih Chen, "Automatic metadata creation: Automated semantic annotation and retrieval based on sharable ontology and case-based learning techniques", Proceedings of the 3rd ACM/IEEE-CS joint conference on Digital libraries, May 2003.
6. HuaMin Feng, Tat-Seng Chua, "Image retrieval: A bootstrapping approach to annotating large image collection", Proceedings of the 5th ACM SIGMM international workshop on Multimedia information retrieval, November 2003.
7. Meng Yang, Barbara M. Wildemuth, Gary Marchionini, "Technical poster session 1: multimedia analysis, processing, and retrieval: The relative effectiveness of concept-based versus content-based video retrieval", Proceedings of the 12th annual ACM international conference on Multimedia, October 2004.
8. Carmine Cesarano, Antonio d'Acierno, Antonio Picariello, "Intelligent web information access: An intelligent search agent system for semantic information retrieval on the internet", Proceedings of the 5th ACM international workshop on Web information and data management, November 2003.
9. Xiaohui Long, Torsten Suel, "Indexing and querying: Three-level caching for efficient query processing in large Web search engines", Proceedings of the 14th international conference on World Wide Web, May 2005.

SAFIRE: Towards Standardized Semantic Rich Image Annotation

Christian Hentschel, Andreas Nürnberger, Ingo Schmitt, and Sebastian Stober

Faculty of Computer Science
Otto-von-Guericke-University Magdeburg, D-39106 Magdeburg, Germany
chentsch@student.uni-magdeburg.de,
{nuernb,stober}@iws.cs.uni-magdeburg.de,
Ingo.Schmitt@iti.cs.uni-magdeburg.de

Abstract. Most of the currently existing image retrieval systems make use of either low-level features or semantic (textual) annotations. A combined usage during annotation and retrieval is rarely attempted. In this paper, we propose a standardized annotation framework that integrates semantic and feature based information about the content of images. The presented approach is based on the MPEG-7 standard with some minor extensions. The proposed annotation system SAFIRE (Semantic Annotation Framework for Image REtrieval) enables the combined use of low-level features and annotations that can be assigned to arbitrary hierarchically organized image segments. Besides the framework itself, we discuss query formalisms required for this unified retrieval approach.

1 Introduction

Due to the vast amounts of images that are digitally available today, the development of advanced techniques for storing, structuring and especially for efficiently retrieving images are required. The image retrieval process entails several specific problems, e.g. the extraction of relevant and descriptive features, the problem of computing the similarity between images or images and a user query that require flexible and adaptive similarity measures, and the problem of designing interactive user interfaces that provide besides basic query support also visualization techniques for the retrieved set of images [16,22]. Unfortunately, several aspects of this process are still insufficiently studied. This involves problems of automatically extracting descriptive features or segmenting images into descriptive regions, but also the lack of methods to appropriately analyze and process user queries. Thus image retrieval is still a very time consuming task, since usually several search steps are necessary until a desired image is found.

The vision that most research currently follows is that of a system where a user can provide a natural language query, in which the desired content is described, in order to retrieve the searched images. However, the main problem in this setting is the semantic gap between the user need on one hand and the features that we can currently extract automatically from images on the other hand: Unfortunately, it is not yet possible to extract reliably and automatically a semantic content description of an image except of one of a very restricted

S. Marchand-Maillet et al. (Eds.): AMR 2006, LNCS 4398, pp. 12–27, 2007.
© Springer-Verlag Berlin Heidelberg 2007

image collection. In order to circumvent this problem some research projects focus on the problem of extracting more descriptive features in order to allow more reliable image comparison within interactive retrieval systems. Others try to design systems that enable semantic annotation of images. Unfortunately, only a few projects try to make use of a standardized way to merge research results from both sides in order to iteratively bridge the gap between both approaches.

In this paper, we propose a standardized annotation framework that integrates semantic and feature based information about the content of images. The presented approach is based on the MPEG-7 standard with some minor extensions. Therefore, parts of the information stored can be used or maintained by a great number of tools. It enables the combined use of low-level features and annotations that can be assigned to arbitrary hierarchically organized image segments.

In the following, we first discuss briefly related work in order to motivate our approach. In Sect. 3 we provide an overview of the developed framework. In Sect. 4 we discuss the used MPEG-7 extensions and propose in Sect. 5 a refined model for semantic querying. Finally, we give in Sect. 6 a brief overview of our prototype and the annotation process.

2   Related Work

In order to narrow the semantic gap between linguistic user queries and image collections different strategies can be applied. The two orthogonal strategies are to use only (low level) features extracted from the image itself or to use only textual annotations and to ignore completely information that could be extracted from the image. The latter approaches use, e.g., if an image is stored in a web page or in an electronic document, only the surrounding text and captions (see, for example, Google Image Search). The former approaches usually make use of highly interactive and adaptive retrieval systems that require as starting point either a sample image or provide initially an overview of the available image collection [2,31]. This is done either by randomly selecting images or by structuring the collection and representing a prototypical image for each discovered cluster [25]. Starting from this overview, the user has to iteratively navigate through the collection in order to retrieve the searched images.

Meanwhile, several approaches for semantic annotation of image collections have been proposed. The main idea is to support the annotation of images with free text or keywords in order to enable structuring of the collection itself and to support a more 'semantic' retrieval of images in huge collections. Some of the proposed tools even make use of ontologies in order to enable an unambiguous keyword annotation, see e.g. [3,13]. One main problem of these tools is that text and descriptive keywords have to be assigned manually. Therefore, motivated by the success of community based portals, recently several annotation or so-called tagging platforms like Flickr and Marvel[1] have been developed that allow users to freely upload and annotate images. The idea is to make use of the self-organization process of huge communities in

---

[1] See http://www.flickr.com and http://www.research.ibm.com/marvel/

order to structure and to annotate image collections as well as to support this process – in case of Marvel – by means of machine learning techniques. We can also find approaches that try to make use of partially annotated image collections or a small set of sample queries and images. By training a classifier, unseen images can be automatically labelled (supervised or unsupervised) by propagating annotations of sample images (training samples) to the remaining or newly added ones. The probability for a single keyword belonging to a specific image is estimated based on the distances and density of the training samples in the applied model space [21,17,10].

Furthermore, much relevant work deals with the problem of modelling vagueness in the retrieval process. At the beginning of the nineties, techniques based on fuzzy logic [34] were applied to traditional database technology in order to cope with vague or uncertain information, which is especially important if we try to combine (low level) image features with textual annotation. The capability to deal with vagueness is even fundamental if we like to process natural language queries [34]. An overview of recent work in the area of databases is given in [11]. Unfortunately, the problem of query processing, which includes information aggregation, similarity measures and ranking, is still frequently underestimated, see e.g., [28,4,24]. Therefore, we discuss this problem in more detail in Sect. 5.

One problem of many approaches mentioned above is that they still consider an image as an integral entity, i.e. all annotations refer to the image as a whole and not to individual parts in it. Even though, some methods for automatic image segmentation in retrieval systems have been proposed [6,23], they still rely on low level image features.

One further problem of most approaches mentioned above is the use of very specific annotation formats. This makes the exchange of annotations and the development of benchmark collections and learning methods for automatic annotation very difficult. However, several standards for storing image metadata are available: Dublin Core[2] is a metadata scheme that can be used to describe documents or objects on the internet. The Exchangeable Image File Format (EXIF)[3] specifies standards related to digital still cameras. EXIF metadata are commonly included in JPEG images. However, both Dublin Core and EXIF provide only limited support for annotations and do not allow to specify and annotate regions within images. Standards that do provide this are FotoNotes[TM4], JPEG-2000 metadata[5] and MPEG-7[6]. All these standards are based on XML. The former two are bound to specific image formats, JPEG and JPEG-2000 respectively. Only the latter is independent from the format of the medium being described and stored separately.

3 Requirements of a Standardized Annotation Approach

A framework that enables a standardized way to create, store, and maintain semantic rich annotated images has to follow certain rules and has to provide

---

[2] The Dublin Core Metadata Initiative (DCMI), http://dublincore.org
[3] http://www.exif.org
[4] http://fotonotes.net
[5] Joint Photographic Experts Group, http://www.jpeg.org/jpeg2000/metadata.html
[6] Moving Picture Experts Group (MPEG), http://www.chiariglione.org/mpeg/

a basic set of features. It must be possible to store information about image segments together with their spatial and hierarchical relation, i.e. segments may be grouped in arbitrary hierarchies. Furthermore, it has to provide means for storing low and high level features as well as textual (semantic) annotations for each segment, group and the image itself. A further fundamental requirement is that all information – from low level features to high level semantic annotations – have to be stored in a data structure that can be easily modified, is well documented and possibly already supported by existing software tools. Therefore, we decided to make use of the MPEG-7 standard with some minor extensions we regard to be necessary. Thus, users can already use a wide variety of tools to maintain and access collections of annotated images. Since MPEG-7 was designed for describing multimedia data in general, a further advantage is, that image annotations can be easily embedded into video sequences as well.

Currently, an automatic assignment of high-level semantics to low-level features of an arbitrary image is still impossible. There exist several approaches, which lead to considerably good results – however they are restricted to a specific domain. By including domain knowledge in form of objects to be detected as well as their low-level visual features and spatial resolution, Voisine et al. [32], for example, accomplish a semantic interpretation of Formula One and Tennis video sequences. In [15] an approach is presented to prove, that again domain specific cues for segmentation can be learned from pre-clustered image sets in order to gain high classification rates. Since we did not want to be a priori restricted to a specific image domain, the annotation process we present requires user interaction to introduce the required model information. In order to support the user during the annotation task itself, an annotation system should meet the following requirements:

- provide initial automatic segmentation and user interaction mechanisms in order to minimize the required amount of user actions,
- allow to create, delete and modify semantic regions,
- allow to structure segments into more general region groups to create a region hierarchy (i.e. atomic regions as created by the user or an automated process can be grouped into semantic units which again can be grouped likewise),
- offer methods to automatically compute low and if possible higher level features for all levels of the segment hierarchy,
- provide methods for (semantic) annotations on every level of the region hierarchy,
- support methods to automatically propose (semantic) annotations based on existing annotations,
- provide capability to create different views on the same image (e.g. create different atomic regions and different region hierarchies),
- ensures a semantic unambiguous annotation, e.g. by including references to unique items of an ontology.

Providing the possibility to link ambiguous terms or phrases to unique entries in an ontology (already during the process of annotation) has several advantages: Firstly, it avoids ambiguous annotations. For example, the noun "bank" has about 10 different senses according to the WordNet ontology [20]. Among them, only one meaning is appropriate in a given context. Someone searching for an image showing a bank in the sense of a financial institution should not receive an image describing a river bank as a search result. Secondly, apart from disambiguation of annotations, the linkage to unambiguous entries (WordNet SynSets) allows for an automated extension of image annotations e.g. by synonyms. Utilizing the EuroWordNet InterLingual Index [33] even makes it possible to perform multilingual searches.

Finally, by using synonyms and homonyms as defined in an ontology for a specific image keyword, the content description of an image can be improved by providing a more universally applicable semantic annotation. This can help to augment the relevance of the retrieval results.

The image annotation system prototype presented in this paper fulfills many of the requirements mentioned above. It exploits the MPEG-7 standard for data storage and offers an intuitive user interface for semi-automatic image annotation. By providing the possibility to link textual queries and annotations to the WordNet ontology, word disambiguation becomes feasible. The underlying system architecture is presented in Fig. 1.

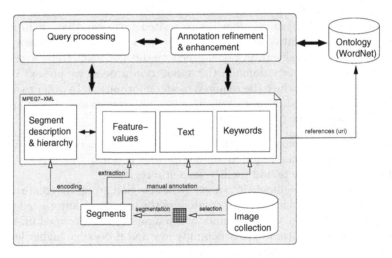

Fig. 1. Structure of the System Architecture

4   Image Description

Information about the segments of an image, their automatically extracted low level features and their manual annotations are stored in an MPEG-7 conform XML data format. MPEG-7 is based on an XML schema and provides a very flexible framework for describing audiovisual data that can be easily extended. Furthermore, the use of this common standard eases data exchange with other applications.

Regarding the storage of image segmentation information, our approach makes use of the StillRegion and StillRegionSpatialDecomposition description scheme (DS) as defined in MPEG-7.[7] The `StillRegion` DS represents an image or a part of it. Several visual descriptors for automatically extractable low level features such as shape, color or statistical texture measures of such a `StillRegion` are already defined in the MPEG-7 standard. In particular we (intend to) make use of the `DominantColor` and `ScalableColor` Description Tools and intend to exploit the Homogeneous Texture Descriptor defined by MPEG-7. Furthermore, MPEG-7 provides means to model spatial as well as semantic relations as e.g. used in [18]. The `StillRegionSpatialDecomposition` DS allows to decompose a `StillRegion` according to some criteria. Such a decomposition comprises a set of still regions (or references to still regions) which again may be decomposed thus allowing hierarchical decompositions. As the number of decompositions for each still region is unbounded, it is even possible to store any arbitrary number of hierarchical decompositions for an image by solely using `StillRegion` and `StillRegionSpatialDecomposition` DS. This method however would create an unnecessary overhead of redundant data if more than one hierarchical decomposition has to be stored because of the following reason: The preferred way to incorporate a still region that is already contained in a different hierarchical decomposition would obviously be to use a reference to the already stored data instead of creating a copy. Referencing a still region would however mean to implicitly reference all decompositions associated with this region, as well. But these associated decompositions will usually differ, thus making it necessary to store duplicates of the same still region with different decompositions but identical features that ought to be stored only once. To circumvent this data overhead, we defined the custom visual descriptor shown in Fig. 2.

An `HierarchicalSegmentationDescriptor` comprises a so called "flat decomposition" and an arbitrary number of `HierarchicalSegmentations`. A flat decomposition is a `StillRegionSpatialDecomposition` containing all still regions of all `HierarchicalSegmentations` defined subsequently. The `HierarchicalSegmentations` in turn solely contain references to the still regions of the flat decomposition or (references) to sub-segmentations. This way, it is ensured that each still region is defined only once. The flat decomposition may be associated with the still region corresponding to the whole image instead of being stored directly in the custom visual descriptor. In this case, it is referenced by `FlatSegmentationRef`. The advantage of this approach is, that information of the flat decomposition is accessible for tools that can only process pure MPEG-7 annotations and ignore the content of the custom visual descriptor. A simple example for an `HierarchicalSegmentationDescriptor` is given in Fig. 2.

For the annotation of still regions, the `Linguistic` Description Scheme [12] of the version 2 schema definition of MPEG-7[8] is used. This DS is based on the GDA tag set[9] and provides means to annotate linguistic data associated with multimedia content. Its descriptive power is much more comprehensive compared to the `TextAnnotation` datatype included in the first release of the

---

[7] ISO/IEC 15938-5:2003, available at http://www.iso.org

[8] ISO/IEC 15938-10:2005: Information technology - Multimedia content description Interface – Part 10: Schema definition, available at http://www.iso.org

[9] http://i-content.org/GDA/tagset.html

```
<complexType name="HierarchicalSegmentationDescriptorType">
  <complexContent>
    <extension base="mpeg7:VisualDType">
      <sequence>
        <choice minOccurs="1" maxOccurs="1">
          <element name="FlatSegmentation" type="mpeg7:StillRegionSpatialDecompositionType"
            minOccurs="0" maxOccurs="1"/>
          <element name="FlatSegmentationRef" type="mpeg7:ReferenceType" minOccurs="0"
            maxOccurs="1"/>
        </choice>
        <element name="HierarchicalSegmentation" type="HierarchicalSegmentationType"
          minOccurs="0" maxOccurs="unbounded"/>
      </sequence>
    </extension>
  </complexContent>
</complexType>
<complexType name="HierarchicalSegmentationType">
  <complexContent>
    <extension base="mpeg7:SpatialSegmentDecompositionType">
      <sequence>
        <element name="StillRegionRef" type="mpeg7:ReferenceType" minOccurs="0"
          maxOccurs="1"/>
        <choice minOccurs="0" maxOccurs="unbounded">
          <element name="Semantic" type="mpeg7:SemanticType"/>
          <element name="SemanticRef" type="mpeg7:ReferenceType"/>
        </choice>
        <choice minOccurs="1" maxOccurs="unbounded">
          <element name="SubStillRegionRef" type="mpeg7:ReferenceType"/>
          <element name="SubSegmentation" type="HierarchicalSegmentationType"/>
          <element name="SubSegmentationRef" type="mpeg7:ReferenceType"/>
        </choice>
      </sequence>
    </extension>
  </complexContent>
</complexType>

<!--    example:    -->
<VisualDescriptor xsi:type="HierarchicalSegmentationDescriptorType">
  <FlatSegmentationRef idref="flatDecomposition" />
  <HierarchicalSegmentation>
    <StillRegionRef idref="imageRegion" />
    <SubStillRegionRef idref="skyRegion" />
    <SubStillRegionRef idref="roadRegion" />
    <SubSegmentation>
      <StillRegionRef idref="carRegion" />
        <SubStillRegionRef idref="windscreenRegion" />
        <SubStillRegionRef idref="carDoorRegion" />
    </SubSegmentation>
    <SubSegmentation>
  </HierarchicalSegmentation>
</VisualDescriptor>
```

Fig. 2. Top: Custom description scheme modeling hierarchical decompositions. Bottom: A simple example for the **HierarchicalSegmentationDescriptor** defined above. The still region representing the whole image has 3 subregions for the sky, a road and a car. The region of the car has subregions for the windscreen and a door of the car.

MPEG-7 standard[10]. We currently only use the **Linguistic** DS to enrich image annotations with references to external resources such as ontologies. However, far more sophisticated extensions are imaginable such as those described in [12]. Using the **Linguistic** DS for image annotations, any single term or group of

---

[10] Refer to ISO/IEC 15938-5:2003 available at http://www.iso.org for specifications or [19] for an overview on MPEG-7 description tools that also cover textual annotation.

```
<Sentence xml:lang="en" id="annotation_1">
  <Phrase id="annotation_1.1">
    My
    <Phrase semantics="WordNet:SynSetID=2471824 EuroWordNet:ILISynSetID=8542395">
      brother
    </Phrase>
  </Phrase>
  at
  <Phrase id="annotation_1.2">
    the
    <Phrase semantics="WordNet:SynSetID=86786241 EuroWordNet:ILISynSetID=1332468">
      bank
    </Phrase>
    of the Thames
  </Phrase>
</Sentence>
```

Fig. 3. Image annotation "My brother at the bank of the Thames." where the terms "brother" and "bank" are linked to SynSets in WordNet and EuroWordNet InterLingual Index (ILI) [33].

terms can be linked to several external resources by specifying corresponding URIs in the `semantics` attribute of an encapsulating `LinguisticEntityType` element, e.g. `<Phrase>` or `<Sentence>`. An example annotations is shown in Fig. 3.

Annotations in turn can be assigned to still regions by using the `SemanticRef` element defined in the `StillRegion` DS. A `SemanticRef` may point to any part of the annotations contained in the `Linguistic` DS decribed above making it possible e.g. to link segments of an image to specific phrases of a sentence that describes the images as one. Recalling the example annotation in Fig. 3, the phrases "my brother" and "bank of the Thames" could be assigned to segments of the image as shown in Fig. 4.

```
<image>
  <SemanticRef idref="annotation_1" />              <!-- sentence annotating the whole image -->
  ...
  <SpatialDecomposition overlap="true" gap="true" criteria="flat decomposition of the image"
    id="flatDecomposition">
    <StillRegion id="region_1">
      <SemanticRef idref="annotation_1.1" />        <!-- annotation: my brother -->
      <SpatialLocator>...</SpatialLocator>
    </StillRegion>
    <StillRegion id="region_2">
      <SemanticRef idref="annotation_1.2" />        <!-- annotation: the bank of the Thames -->
      <SpatialLocator>...</SpatialLocator>
    </StillRegion>
  </SpatialDecomposition>
</image>
```

Fig. 4. Example for assigning annotations to still regions. The referenced annotations are shown in Fig. 3.

5   Searching for Images

Our annotation framework is designed to create and to provide a full range of data describing the content of images. That data include automatically extracted low-level features, user-defined structured data as well as annotations like keywords and textual descriptions with references to an ontology. They are assigned to image segments organized in segmentation hierarchies. Additionally, segments can stand in mutual spatial relationships.

There are various paradigms of searching images based on different types of data:

1. *text retrieval* on textual descriptions and keywords;
2. *navigation* through the image collection by means of a highly interactive user interface and clusters pre-computed from low-level features;
3. *content-based retrieval* based on query images, low-level features and an appropriate similarity measure; and
4. *database query* on spatial relationships, segment descriptions and user-defined data.

There has been a huge amount of research done on these individual search paradigms. Each of them comes with its own limitations and none of them can be seen as the best search paradigm. However, only few attention is paid to the *combination* of them into one unifying query system. Combining various search paradigms requires a sophisticated query language which enables the user to formulate queries that are possibly composed of different query conditions. The main problem is therefore, how to combine query conditions from different paradigms into one unifying formalism. Optimally, a query system is capable of processing natural language queries. In order to be as close as possible to that vision we decided to take advantage of formal logic as basic formalism.

Querying Using Logic-Based Approaches
First order logic is the main concept of database query languages like SQL and XQuery. Unfortunately, they do not adequately offer concepts needed for processing queries which combine retrieval and traditional database search conditions. For example, the keyword query `keyword = 'rock'` as a typical database query returns a set of images for which that condition holds. Contrarily, the query `image is visually similar to a given query image` is a content-based retrieval query returning a list of images sorted in descending order by their respective similarity scores. Assume, we want to conjunctively combine both queries into one query:

$$keyword = \text{`rock'} \quad AND \quad image \approx query\ image$$

What would be the result, a list or a set of images? The problem here is the illegal logical combination of an exact query providing us boolean values with an imprecise retrieval query returning similarity scores from the interval $[0, 1]$. There are two prominent approaches to circumvent that conflict:

Boolean Query: The idea realized in most logic-based query systems like in commercial database systems is to transform the retrieval query into a boolean one. This is achieved by applying a threshold value. That is, every similarity score greater than the threshold is considered true otherwise false. This approach has several drawbacks. First, finding a suitable threshold value is not an easy task.

Second, as result, we lose the information of what degree the similarity condition holds. Thus, we cannot discriminate among images from the result set w.r.t. their similarity to the query image. Especially in queries composed of several conditions we need that lost semantics.

Retrieval Query: The idea here is to transform the database query into a kind of retrieval query. That is, logic values from the database query evaluation are mapped to the score values 1 for `true` and 0 otherwise. These scores can then be arithmetically combined with the scores from a retrieval query, e.g. by a simple weighted sum. However, it is not clear at all which combination formula should be applied for a specific query. There is a plethora of possible aggregation formulas for that scenario. Furthermore, there is no logic framework (conjunction, disjunction, negation) supporting the formulation of complex queries. That is, we cannot utilize the rich theory of database querying.

Summarizing, the first approach lacks support for similarity scores whereas the second one fails with respect to an available logic for query formulation and processing.

A straightforward solution to the problem is to take advantage of fuzzy logic [9] as proposed, for example, in [34]. In fuzzy logic, similarity scores as well as boolean truth values are interpreted as fuzzy set membership values which can be combined via logical junctors to construct complex queries. Scoring functions t-norm and t-conorm behave like the logical conjunction and disjunction, respectively. Examples of query languages based on fuzzy logic are the `same` algebra [8], WS-QBE, $\mathcal{SDC}$, and $\mathcal{SA}$ as proposed in [27,28]. Fagin's weighting schema [9] is used in those languages in order to equip search conditions with different weights of importance. For example, matching a keyword condition should be of more weight than a visual similarity condition. Bellmann and Giertz [1] proved that fuzzy logic with t-norm `min` for conjunction and t-conorm `max` for disjunction obeys the rules of the boolean algebra. Thus, most query processing techniques known from the database theory are still valid.

Nevertheless, there are some common problems of fuzzy-based querying. First, applying the standard fuzzy norms `min/max` in our context suffers from a specific property: The minimum as well as the maximum of two certain scores returns always just one of them and ignores completely the other one. For example, assume two conjunctively combined retrieval conditions. The condition which returns smaller scores dominates completely the result semantics. Contrarily, a *nondominating* t-norm which respects both scores simultaneously would better meet our understanding of query combination. Actually, fuzzy logic comes with different non-dominating t-norms, e.g. the algebraic product. Unfortunately, none of them holds idempotence. Thus, in combination with a t-conorm, e.g. the algebraic sum, distributivity cannot be guaranteed. Furthermore, we are faced with problems of failing associativity and distributivity [29] when Fagin's weighting schema is used, even on the `min/max` pair. Table 1 summarizes the properties of the approaches discussed so far.

The problem of dominance turns out to be even more serious when we examine the way how fuzzy logic is utilized for query evaluation. As shown in Fig. 5 (left)

Table 1. Properties of different approaches to combine retrieval and database queries

approach	scores	distributivity	non-dominating
boolean query	no	yes	—
retrieval query	yes	—	—
fuzzy logic (min/max)	yes	yes	no
fuzzy logic (not min/max)	yes	no	yes
weighted fuzzy logic	yes	no	—

fuzzy logic relies on *importing* scores (here two score functions) and truth values (here from one database condition) and interpreting them as membership values. Thus, the generation of membership values is *not under control* of fuzzy logic. Therefore, there is a high risk that scores are not comparable due to possibly different score functions producing an error-prone dominance. Figure 5 (right) depicts exemplarily two fictive non-comparable score functions. If the scores from both function are combined by the min-function, the scores from function A would predominate the ones from function B. Furthermore, assume a and b are different perceived similarity values of one image based on texture and color histogram, respectively. Using non-comparable score functions can even change the order of different scores (b < a but a' < b') making the distinction between conjunction and disjunction meaningless.

Despite of the problems discussed above, we use for our framework the query language WS-QBE since (1) it provides a user-friendly QBE-interface for query formulation, (2) it is especially designed to support multimedia queries, and (3) its implementation and source code is available and can therefore be easily adapted to specific needs. However, our long-term goal is to find a formalism unifying the generation of similarity scores, classical database evaluations as well as their combination via a logic. One promising approach in that direction is the usage of quantum mechanics and quantum logics. Since their underlying model is a vector space and many retrieval problems can be formulated in vector space there is a natural mapping into quantum mechanics [26].

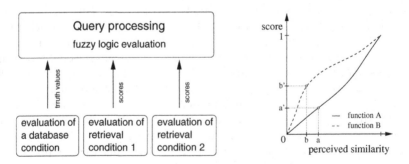

Fig. 5. Fuzzy evaluation by importing truth and score values (left) and score values from two different score functions (right)

6   An Image Annotation Prototype

Based on the requirements defined in Sect. 3 we developed a first prototype to support region based image annotation and retrieval: SAFIRE (Semantic Annotation Framework for Image REtrieval). SAFIRE implements an intuitive user interface to attach automatically extracted low-level features as well as semantic meta data to an image (see Figure 6).

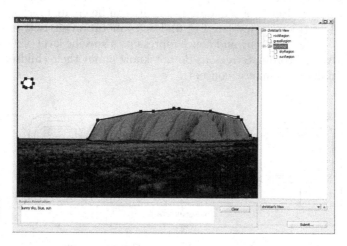

Fig. 6. Screenshot of annotation interface

As one of our main goals was to implement an approach that enables the user to annotate images on a segment level, we first of all needed to establish a way to identify regions in an image. Unfortunately, due to missing segmentation algorithms that provide appropriate segmentation of arbitrary images into meaningful regions, annotating images on a region level currently cannot exclusively rely on automated image segmentation. However, sophisticated algorithms exist, that can help to provide an adequate initial segmantation which is less tedious to be adapted than it would be when a segmentation of an image was to be created from scratch. Currently we apply here a simple k-means clustering on the pixel color data [14] which provides rather poor results. One of the very next steps in improving SAFIRE's performance will be to replace this algorithm with a more sophisticated one, such as the one used in the Blobworld system [7]. The results of this initial segmentation step are presented to the user. By using a canvas-like interface, the user can refine existing regions as well as create new and delete invalid ones. For each newly created region, the system automatically computes low level features - namely the shape, the color distribution as well as texture measures. These features are automatically stored in MPEG-7 conform documents – as described in Sect. 4 – and can be used in a query process to determine similarity between different regions of different images.

In a subsequent step, newly added or existing regions can be enriched by adding annotations describing the semantics of a region. The user can select regions through the annotation tool and attach keyword lists to each of them. As the image as a whole can be seen as a region as well, a global image annotation can be attached likewise. Typically, an image can be split into atomic regions representing the smallest semantic entities. These entities can be grouped into superordinate regions depicting a more abstract view on an image. In general, any image can be split into groups of semantic regions which likewise can be split again until the atomic level is reached. Our annotation framework supports this idea by enabling the user to group newly created regions into sematic units of higher abstraction. Hence, a semantic hierarchy can be created for every image, represented by a tree-like view (see Fig. 6). Each annotation is strictly related to a specific level in the hierarchy and hence represents a specific level of abstraction. Consequently, superordinate regions do not know about their children, as they represent a different semantic concept.

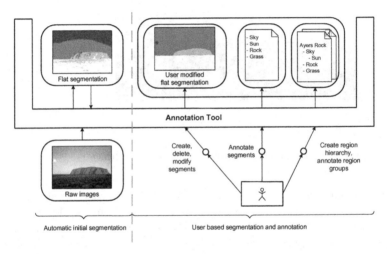

Fig. 7. Segmenting and annotating images in SAFIRE

What is identified as a semantic entity of an image is strongly related to the focus of the beholder. Two different people may examine an image from two completely different perspectives and hence come to two completely different semantic hierarchies. For example a car manufacturer would 'disassemble' a picture of a car on a street into all its visible components such as doors, windows and wheels in order to annotate them with the appropriate component identifier. On the other hand, a less technically motivated beholder of the same image would probably show no interest in the cars components but rather segment the car as a whole annotating it with more abstract keywords such as 'cabriolet, red'. Both these segmentations are valid and should be supported by the system as equally correct. SAFIRE addresses this aspect by enabling different users to create different segment group trees for a single image. The underlying atomic entities are shared among the views. How they get grouped into regions of higher abstraction, however, is an individual decision. Like atomic regions, region groups can be annotated just as well. An overall view of the framework presenting the mentioned annotation steps is given in Figure 7.

As a next step, we will integrate the image retrieval component described above. Further on, more sophisticated automatic image segmentation algorithms, see e.g. [30,5], will be analyzed and added to the framework.

7   Conclusions and Future Work

In this paper we have proposed an annotation structure based on the MPEG-7 standard that allows us to store information about image segments together with their low and higher level features. In order to retrieve images using these annotations, we presented a logic-based query method that supports combined queries on numerical features and text based annotations. Furthermore, we presented the SAFIRE system that supports a user during the annotation process. It enables the user to cluster images into semantic entities on different levels of abstraction. As different beholders of an image might have a different focus on its contents, different semantic views on one image are supported. Each level of abstraction offers the ability to attach keyword lists to explicitly store the depicted content of a region. In addition to semantic annotations, for each atomic region a number of automatically computed low-level features is stored.

Our long-term goal is to develop a data collection containing features as well as annotations freely available on the web. We hope that annotated MPEG-7 files can serve to initiate the creation of a data archive for the development of new search and learning mechanism as well as a reference data set for evaluations like the TRECVID dataset is for video annotations. Our current work is focused on the evaluation of methods using annotated image segments to infer annotations for new and unseen images. This could be done by matching semantically described segments from our database with new images.

References

1. R. Bellman and M. Giertz. On the Analytic Formalism of the Theory of Fuzzy Sets. *Information Science*, 5:149–156, 1973.
2. A. D. Bimbo. *Visual Information Retrieval*. Morgan Kaufmann, 1999.
3. S. Bloehdorn, K. Petridis, C. Saathoff, N. Simou, V. Tzouvaras, Y. Avrithis, S. Handschuh, Y. Kompatsiaris, S. Staab, and M. G. Strintzis. Semantic annotation of images and videos for multimedia analysis. In *Proc. of Second European Semantic Web Conf. (ESWC 2005)*, 2005.
4. M. Boughanem, Y. Loiseau, and H. Prade. Rank-ordering documents according to their relevance in information retrieval using refinements of ordered-weighted aggregations. In *Adaptive Multimedia Retrieval: User, Context, and Feedback, Postproc. of 3rd Int. Workshop*, pages 44–54. Springer-Verlag, 2006.
5. N. V. Boulgouris, I. Kompatsiaris, V. Mezaris, D. Simitopoulos, and M. G. Strintzis. Segmentation and content-based watermarking for color image and image region indexing and retrieval. In *EURASIP Journal on Applied Signal Processing*, pages 418–431. Hindawi Publishing Corporation, 2002.

6. C. Carson, S. Belongie, H. Greenspan, and J. Malik. Blobworld: Image segmentation using expectation-maximization and its application to image querying. *IEEE Trans. on Pattern Analysis and Machine Intelligence*, 24(8):1026–1038, 2002.
7. C. Carson, M. Thomas, S. Belongie, J. M. Hellerstein, and J. Malik. Blobworld: A system for region-based image indexing and retrieval. In *Third International Conference on Visual Information Systems*. Springer, 1999.
8. P. Ciaccia, D. Montesi, W. Penzo, and A. Trombetta. Imprecision and user preferences in multimedia queries: A generic algebraic approach. In *Proc. of FoIKS: Foundations of Information and Knowledge Systems*, pages 50–71. Springer, 2000.
9. R. Fagin. Fuzzy Queries in Multimedia Database Systems. In *Proc. of the Seventeenth ACM SIGACT-SIGMOD-SIGART Symposium on Principles of Database Systems, June 1-3, 1998, Seattle, Washington*, pages 1–10. ACM Press, 1998.
10. H. Feng and T.-S. Chua. A bootstrapping approach to annotating large image collection. In *MIR '03: Proc. of the 5th ACM SIGMM Int. Workshop on Multimedia Information Retrieval*, pages 55–62, New York, NY, USA, 2003. ACM Press.
11. J. Galindo, A. Urrutia, and M. Piattini. *Fuzzy Databases: Modeling, Design and Implementation*. Idea Group Publishing, 2005.
12. K. Hasida. The linguistic DS: Linguisitic description in MPEG-7. *The Computing Research Repository (CoRR)*, cs.CL/0307044, 2003.
13. L. Hollink, G. Schreiber, J. Wielemaker, and B. Wielinga. Semantic annotation of image collections. In *In Proc. of Workshop on Knowledge Markup and Semantic Annotation (KCAP'03)*, 2003.
14. A. K. Jain and R. C. Dubes. *Algorithms for Clustering Data*. Prentice Hall, Inc., New Jersey, 1988.
15. S. Konishi and A. Yuille. Statistical cues for domain specific image segmentation withperformance analysis. In *IEEE Conference on Computer Vision and Pattern Recognition*, volume 1, pages 125–132, 2000.
16. S. Kosinov and S. Marchand-Maillet. Overview of approaches to semantic augmentation of multimedia databases for efficient access and content retrieval. In *Adaptive Multimedia Retrieval, Postproc. of 1st Int. Workshop*, pages 19–35, 2004.
17. J. Lu, S. ping Ma, and M. Zhang. Automatic image annotation based-on model space. In *Proc. of IEEE Int. Conf. on Natural Language Processing and Knowledge Engineering*, pages 455 – 460, 2005.
18. M. Lux, J. Becker, and H. Krottmaier. Caliph & Emir: Semantic annotation and retrieval in personal digital photo libraries. In *Proc. of CAiSE 03 Forum at 15th Conf. on Advanced Information Systems Engineering*, pages 85–89, 2003.
19. J. M. Martínez. MPEG-7: Overview of MPEG-7 description tools, part 2. *IEEE MultiMedia*, 9(3):83–93, 2002.
20. G. Miller, R. Beckwith, C. Fellbaum, D. Gross, and K. Miller. Five papers on WordNet. *Int. Journal of Lexicography*, 3(4), 1990.
21. A. P. Natsev, M. R. Naphade, and J. Tesic. Learning the Semantics of Multimedia Queries and Concepts from a Small Number of Examples. In A. Press, editor, *Proc. of the 13th ACM Int. Conf. on Multimedia*, pages 598–607, 2005.
22. A. Nürnberger and M. Detyniecki. Adaptive multimedia retrieval: From data to user interaction. In *Do smart adaptive systems exist? - Best practice for selection and combination of intelligent methods*. Springer-Verlag, 2005.
23. J.-F. Omhover and M. Detyniecki. Strict: An image retrieval platform for queries based on regional content. In *Proc. of Int. Conf. on Image and Video Retrieval (CIVR 2004)*, 2004.
24. J.-F. Omhover, M. Rifqi, and M. Detyniecki. Ranking invariance based on similarity measures in document retrieval. In *Adaptive Multimedia Retrieval: User, Context, and Feedback, Postproc. of 3rd Int. Workshop*, pages 55–64. Springer, 2006.

25. S. Rüger. Putting the user in the loop: Visual resource discovery. In *Adaptive Multimedia Retrieval: User, Context, and Feedback, Postproc. of 3rd Int. Workshop*, pages 1–18. Springer-Verlag, 2006.
26. I. Schmitt. Basic Concepts for Unifying Queries of Database and Retrieval Systems. Technical Report 7, Fakultät für Informatik, Univ. Magdeburg, 2005.
27. I. Schmitt and N. Schulz. Similarity Relational Calculus and its Reduction to a Similarity Algebra. In *Proc. of 3rd Intern. Symposium on Foundations of Information and Knowledge Systems (FoIKS'04)*, pages 252–272. Springer-Verlag, 2004.
28. I. Schmitt, N. Schulz, and T. Herstel. WS-QBE: A QBE-like Query Language for Complex Multimedia Queries. In *Proc. of the 11th Int. Multimedia Modelling Conf. (MMM'05)*, pages 222–229. IEEE CS Press, 2005.
29. N. Schulz and I. Schmitt. A Survey of Weighted Scoring Rules in Multimedia Database Systems. Preprint 7, Fakultät für Informatik, Univ. Magdeburg, 2002.
30. C. Stauffer and W. E. L. Grimson. Adaptive background mixture models for real-time tracking. In *Proc. IEEE Conf. on Computer Vision and Pattern Recognition*, pages 246–252, 1999.
31. R. C. Veltkamp and M. Tanase. Content-based image retrieval systems: A survey. Technical Report UU-CS-2000-34, CS Dept., Utrecht University, 2000.
32. N. Voisine, S. Dasiopoulou, F. Precioso, V. Mezaris, I. Kompatsiaris, and M. Strintzis. A genetic algorithm-based approach to knowledge-assisted video analysis. In *IEEE International Conference on Image Processing*, 2005.
33. P. Vossen. EuroWordNet general document version 3, final, July 19 1999.
34. L. A. Zadeh. Fuzzy Logic. *IEEE Computer*, 21(4):83–93, Apr. 1988.

Ontology-Supported Video Modeling and Retrieval

Yakup Yildirim and Adnan Yazici

Dept. of Computer Engineering, Middle East Technical University, Ankara, Turkey
yy@alumni.bilkent.edu.tr, yazici@ceng.metu.edu.tr

Abstract. Current solutions are still far from reaching the ultimate goal, namely to enable users to retrieve the desired video clip among massive amounts of visual data in a semantically meaningful manner. With this study we propose a video database model that provides nearly automatic object, event and concept extraction. It provides a reasonable approach to bridging the gap between low-level representative features and high-level semantic contents from a human point of view. By using training sets and expert opinions, low-level feature values for objects and relations between objects are determined. At the top level we have an ontology of objects, events and concepts. Objects and/or events use all these information to generate events and concepts. The system has a reliable video data model, which gives the user the ability to make ontology-supported fuzzy querying. Queries containing objects, events, spatio-temporal clauses, concepts and low-level features can be handled.

1 Introduction

As a large amount of video data becomes publicly available, the need to model and query such data efficiently becomes significantly important. There are basically three ways of retrieving previously stored video data:

- Free browsing
- Text-based retrieval
- Content-based retrieval

In order to overcome the inefficiencies and limitations of the first two methods, many researchers started to investigate possible ways of retrieving video clips based solely on its contents. Many research groups are actively working in the area and a fairly large number of prototypes and commercial products are already available. Some of the currently available CBIR (content-based information retrieval) systems are:

- QBIC [9] (developed at the IBM Almaden Research Center, can be used for both static and dynamic image retrieval. QBIC supports queries based on example images, user-constructed sketches, and selected colors and texture patterns.)

S. Marchand-Maillet et al. (Eds.): AMR 2006, LNCS 4398, pp. 28–41, 2007.

- BilVideo [6] (provides full support for spatio-temporal queries that contain any combination of spatial, temporal, object-appearance, external-predicate, trajectory-projection and similarity-based object-trajectory conditions by a rule-based system built on a knowledge-base.)
- Extended-AVIS [12] (supports modeling the semantic content of video data including the spatial properties of objects. Spatio-temporal queries on the video, including querying spatial relationships between objects in the video and querying moving objects in the video is possible. Fuzziness in spatial and spatio-temporal queries, therefore fuzzy querying is possible.)
- COBRA [17]
- MultiView [8], ClassView [7] (provides approaches to bridging the gap between low-level representative features and high-level semantic. Also they propose clustering mechanisms to support more efficient multilevel video representation, summarization, indexing, and access techniques.)
- VideoQ [4] (supports video querying by examples, visual sketches, and keywords.)
- Netra-V [5] (uses color, shape, texture, and spatial location information in the segmented image regions to search and retrieve similar images from the database.)

Video content has been mostly analyzed either at the feature or at the semantic level in literature. Features characterize low-level visual content such as color, texture, shapes, and possibly other features. Objects and events describe semantic content. Feature-based models use automatically extracted features, which represent the content of a video, but they hardly provide semantics that describe high-level video concepts. Therefore, low-level features alone are not sufficient to fulfill the users need alone. Because it is very difficult to explore semantic content from the raw video data, semantic models usually use free text/attribute/keywords annotation to represent high-level concepts of the video data which results in many drawbacks.

For large video databases, manual object extraction appears as another major problem. Nearly all of the studies in literature use manual techniques for object extraction. Also because of human faults, insensitive extraction results can be resulted.

Under this purpose we propose an ontology-supported video database model which provides a reasonable approach to bridging the gap between low-level representative features and high-level semantic contents from a human point of view. Our model offers nearly-automatic mapping from low-level features to high-level contents. Only definitions of objects, events and concepts in terms of attributes and components and a fuzzy ontology must be well defined by the users/experts for the domain to be modeled. With the video data model that we introduce here, we relate and combine features and semantic content to generate high-level concepts. Fuzziness in the semantic content and in low-level features of video is also considered in our model. Thus, the system supports fuzzy querying over the extracted semantic components and low-level features (attributes) of these components.

The rest of the paper is organized as follows: In Section 2, the main modeling components are described. Section 3 discusses the ontology concept that we used in this study. The design and architecture of our model are introduced in Section 4. An example domain used as a case study in this paper is described in Section 5, before we draw the conclusions in Section 6.

2   Modeling Components

A video data model is different from a traditional data model and should include the elements that represent the video content. It should also be able to capture and represent various types of information about video objects along with their structures, operations and properties, as well as relationships among objects.

Users want to query the content instead of the raw video data and expecting tools that manipulate the video content in the same structured way as a traditional database manages numeric and textual data.

We must make distinction between two important things that should be modeled: the structure and the content of video. Partitioning video into small manageable units derives structural elements of a video by segmenting video. The segmentation results in some syntactical, semantical, and temporal segments.

The content of a video also need be modeled. Modeling the video content can be done in three dimensions; feature-based modeling, semantic-based modeling, feature and semantic modeling. Audio, free text/keywords, features, objects, events, temporality, motion, spatial relations can be partially or fully used to form a video model [16].

Structure of a video is generally analyzed in terms of objects and events. We introduce concept (complex event series) as the new modeling component. Low-level features and spatial/spatio-temporal relationships between objects and events constitute the concept layer (Fig. 1). Temporal knowledge like ordering operations and spatio-temporal relations between objects are used to define events and concepts.

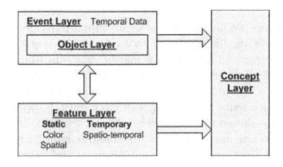

Fig. 1. Component Layers of Video Sources

Objects, events, concepts, low-level features, spatio-temporal knowledge and fuzziness are the main and auxiliary modeling components of this video model.

2.1 Objects

Detecting the objects that human beings use for judging visual similarity semantically is very important to support content-based video retrieval. Automatic object extraction for supporting content-based video indexing and retrieval is very challenging. Fortunately, not all the objects in video need to be extracted and used for characterizing the semantic visual concepts because users may decide visual similarity semantically based on specific types of objects [14]. Since objects for content-based video indexing applications are not necessarily the semantic objects from the human point of view [18], they can be specific types of objects, which are meaningful for detecting and characterizing relevant semantic visual concepts.

We use a semi-automatic object identification algorithm to identify objects. Either by experts or by using a training set, the properties of objects and relations between objects are determined. For instance, if an object has a color distribution of %70 red, places left of object Y or top of object Z, does not move for a period of M units then this object is object X.Object classification is done by:

- Low-level feature values like color distribution, shape, texture.
- Spatial knowledge.
- Spatio-temporal change. (A set of consecutive key frames must be searched to gain knowledge for this property)

Extraction phase starts when we have enough knowledge to separate one object from others. For each video, object extraction is done at first. For each separated region, descriptor vectors are calculated. By comparing the values gained from experts/training set and the calculated values, the most appropriate object is signed and stored. Each entity has a set of frame sequences attached to it. These are the frames in which the entity appears in the video. The collected information about entities is indexed with some special index structures.

2.2 Events

Event is the other major component of video sequences. Temporal information between events like before, after, meets, during, starts is used. The time intervals of events are stored for each event. Relations between objects and events like:

- Occurs
- Spatial relations between objects
- Object trajectory knowledge
- Event-Event Initiates, Finishes, Covers, Overlaps are used to define events.

2.3 Concepts

Concepts can be:

- Continuous similar event sequences. (i.e., dense press in a football match is defined as for a period of time game is played in one of the teams site.)
- Related event sequences. (Relation can be between events or objects within the events.)
- Object trajectory knowledge
- Event-Event Initiates, Finishes, Covers, Overlaps are used to define events.

To derive concepts, we use the extracted objects and generated events. All the derived concepts are stored with their frame intervals.

3 Ontology

Ontology is a collection of concepts (is a class of items that together share essential properties that define that class) and their interrelationships, which provide an abstract view of an application domain. Simply ontology is an explicit specification of conceptualization. Ontology differs from conceptual models by having declarative data in its model. We use this feature in both object extraction and query phase for video databases. For each domain, the generic video ontology differs at the lower level with the domain specific data.

In our video model we use an object, event and concept ontology for the upper layer of the data model which concerns fuzziness. For each domain there must be a defined ontology for objects, events and concepts. With this knowledge we derive events. By the same way concepts are generated by the object-event definitions in the ontology.

Using ontology in modeling and retrieval of multimedia data is a hot study area. Studies like Semantic Retrieval of Multimedia Data [11] focuses on the reasoning issue with an ontology definition to search multimedia data.

In the literature there exist some studies/researches on ontology-based modeling. Some of them are published in [10], [3] and [19].

4 Video Model

In our model the main building block is objects. Events are collection of objects and object relations. Event generation is done automatically after event definitions are done in terms of objects. Also concepts are defined in terms of objects and events. Object properties, relations between objects and events and the domain ontology construct a bridge between objects, events and concepts.

For the starting point, key frames of videos must be segmented into regions. After region segmentation, features (color, shape, color distribution etc.) are extracted for each region. If some regions have similar properties for a period of time (consecutive keyframes), it seems to be a possible object [13]. By using similarity functions, objects identified from regions are assigned to their actual names by using information gained from the training set/experts. For each object, a vector of descriptor values is used to represent a related object. Low-level features of objects are stored in a video database and used for querying. At the top level we also have ontology of objects, events and concepts. We use this ontology and relations between components to generate events and concepts. At last we have a set of objects, events and concepts with their related frame lists for each video in the database.

The query processing in multimedia environment is quite different from the query process in traditional database management systems. In a multimedia environment, browsing has additional importance and queries can be based not only on an exact matching but also on approximate matching, using degrees of similarity.

Our system has a reliable data model and ontology-supported structure, which give the ability to user to make an ontology-supported querying capability. Queries containing objects, events, spatio-temporal clauses, trajectory clauses, and low-level features of objects are answered. The architecture of the model is shown in Fig. 2.

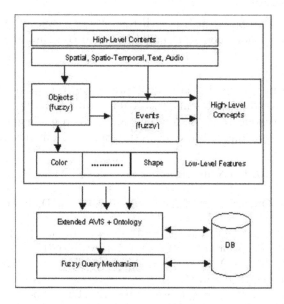

Fig. 2. The Architecture of the Video Model

Making queries directly through the basic data structures gives us some flexibility. For compound queries we do not need to match each phrase exactly. We also use the given ontology in the query phase. If a query statement has a component that was not extracted, we answer that query by using the ontology. For example; in a defined ontology the object horse but not the object animal exists. We can extract all horses from related videos. When we modify our ontology and add animal and establish a relation between horse and animal, we can directly reach frames those contain possible animals. For compound queries we search through the related data structures for each component (object, event, and concept) and take the intersection of intervals.

In our model, we use ontology to extract components of the model (Ontology → Data). Also by using the training set we prepare the initial version of the object ontology (Data → Ontology). Experts can modify and add components (events, concepts) to the ontology at any time.

We think that another important property to be handled in multimedia domain is fuzziness. We consider fuzziness in object features, relations between components, ontology and the query mechanism. So the user can make more flexible query formulations and get more accurate query results.

4.1   Semantic Video Analysis Algorithm

Below the whole process from object extraction to query phase for a video database of a specific domain is given as an algorithm in Fig. 3.

4.2   Detail Design

We use the model proposed in [12] with the ontology concept. We adapt that model to generate a new model presented here and combine it with an (fuzzy) ontology.

Data Structures. All of the data structures have frame sequences (a set of contiguous frames) containing semantically important data, like an object or an event. So we have enough information to generate the frame segment tree (FST) to be used for the indexing purpose. Data structures used in our model are listed below:

- **VideoData** {ID, FileName, Domain (Category), Name, Description, Year, Length}
- **Object** {ID, ObjectName, VideoID, FeatureVectorID, IntervalList (IntervalID)}
- **Event** {ID, EventName, VideoID, IntervalList (IntervalID)}
- **Concept** {ID, ConceptName, VideoID, IntervalList (IntervalID)}
- **Interval** {ID, VideoID, IntervalName, IntervalType, StartTime, EndTime, FeatureVectorID, RegionList}
- **Region** {ID, VideoID, Origin, StartTime, EndTime, LocationID}
- **Location** {ID, VideoID, X1, Y1, X2, Y2}
- **IntervalNode** {ID, VideoID, ObjectList, EventList, ConceptList, ParentID, LeftChild, RightChild}

Making queries directly through the basic data structures gives us some flexibility. For compound queries we do not need to match each phrase exactly.

For spatial knowledge we use the minimum bounding rectangles (MBR) for two-dimensional coordinate system. To lower the calculation cost, motion vectors, as a temporal feature, are stored. All of the data structures described in this section is shown as Fig. 4.

Input: a video database
Output: semantically analyzed videos ready for querying
Begin
for each video in the training set **do**
       Manually select objects of that domain
       Store low-level features of the objects to be used in the learning phase
       if there are spatial relations between objects **then**
          Store spatial relations between objects
       end if
       if there are spatio-temporal behaviors **then**
          Store spatio-temporal behaviors
       end if
end for
Domain experts define relations between objects and events for the domain
Domain experts define a fuzzy ontology of the domain.
for each video in the database **do**
    Make sequence detection
    Make scene detection
    Identify keyframes
    Make frame segmentation
    Make object extraction (The descriptors from the training phase are used)
    for each extracted object **do**
    Calculate a vector of descriptor values.
    end for
    Automatically extract events, concepts and their attributes
    Store all information about objects, events, concepts
end for
Get and Parse the query statement
if there is a fuzzy concept **then**
    Use similarity functions
    Use fuzzy ontology
end if
Retrieve related scenes of videos from the database.
end

Fig. 3. Semantic Video Analysis Algorithm

Properties and Relations. Objects have properties. These properties represent low-level features. Objects, events and concepts have different types of relations between each other. These relations can be spatial, temporal or spatio-temporal. Also in the domain ontology relation types to represent relationships between components are used. Below types of relations and properties used are given:

- **Property:** Color, shape, texture, spatial info, frame identifier. (fuzziness)
- **Relations:**
  - Ordering operations: before, after, during, covers, overlaps, contains
  - Topological:left, right, top, bottom
  - Directional: moves toward, passes, moves west, moves north-west

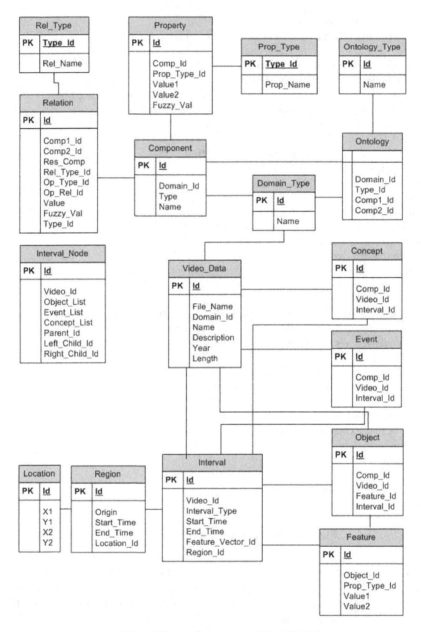

Fig. 4. Data Structures of the Model

- Distance between objects: places near, places away
- Causal: starts, initiates, finishes
- Interval ordering functions: first, last, nth
- Numerical: greater, less
- **Domain ontology:** is-a, contains, kind-of, part-of, instance-of, ...

To lower the calculation cost, motion vectors, as a temporal feature, are stored. Local and static features like color, shape and spatial data makes our model more valid. Another reason to use low-level features is to answer query clauses containing low-level features.

5 Case Study (Football Videos)

Areas those need (uncertain) information and retrieval capability about concepts as well as objects and events can be a target domain for this model. We choose football videos as the case study. Below some model component examples of this domain is given:

- Objects: Goal post, goalkeeper, defense player, middle-field player, referee, coach, audience, corner line, ball.
- Events: Free kick, corner, assist, goal, penalty, foul, swagger, volley, offside, injury, running.
- Concepts: Dense press, good play, win, lose.

These components have values for low-level attributes like:

- Goal post has a color of white.
- Ball has a circular shape.
- Game field has a color of green.

Relations with other components that are used to generate relationship structure and ontology can be like:

- Defense player is a player.
- Goalkeeper stays near to goal post.
- Injury happens after a foul and defined with a stationary player on the game field.
- Foul happens especially with 2 players of different team near to each other.
- Free kick is an event that is formed by ball object, player object and running event. Each component has special properties to form that event. (Running event must be towards to the ball).
- Penalty kick is defined with a goalkeeper staying on the goal line, a stationary ball, a player moving towards to the ball and all other players staying back of the penalty area.
- Goal event occurs after an assist event or a number of swagger events or a free kick or a corner kick. It has relations with players, ball, defense players and the goal post. Ball must follow a trajectory from one site of the goal line to other site.
- Win concept occurs if number of goals scored is more than number of goals given away.
- Dense press occurs when number of corners exceeds a threshold value or ball occurs near to one teams penalty area for a long time.

Ontology_Type

Id	Name
1	is_a
2	capture
3	kind_of
4	part_of
5	instance_of

Domain_Type

Id	Name
1	Football
2	Documentary
3	News

Prop_Type

Type_Id	Prop_Name
1	Col. Dist.
2	Shape
3	Texture

Property / **Explanation**

Id	Comp_Id	Prop_Type	Value1	Value2	Fuzzy V.	Explanation
1	1	1	232		0.2	Goal post has a color of white
2	1	2	circle			Ball has a circular shape
3	29	1	453		0.1	Game field has a color of green.

Rel_Type

Type_Id	Rel_Name
1	before
2	after
3	during
4	starts
5	initiates
6	meets
7	finishes
8	covers
9	overlaps
10	left
11	right
12	moves-toward
13	moves-away
14	passes
15	places near
16	greater
17	less
18	contain
19	stationary
20	on
21	different
22	same
23	top
24	bottom
25	moves_west
26	moves_south
27	first
28	last

Componet

Domain	Id	Type	Name
1	1	O	ball
1	2	O	player
1	3	O	goal poast
1	4	O	goal keeper
1	5	O	referee
1	6	O	coach
1	7	O	audience
1	8	O	corner line
1	9	E	Free Kick
1	10	E	Corner
1	11	E	Assist
1	12	E	Goal
1	13	E	Penalty
1	14	E	Foul
1	15	E	Swagger
1	16	E	Volley
1	17	E	Offside
1	18	E	Injury
1	19	E	Running
1	20	C	Dense Press
1	21	C	Good Play
1	22	C	Win
1	23	C	Lose
1	24	O	defense_player
1	25	O	mid_field player
1	26	O	forward
1	27	O	Alex Fergusson
1	28	O	Ronaldo

Object_List

Id	Comp_Id	Video_Id	Interval_Id	Feature_Id
1	1	1	1	3
2	1	1	14	8
3	2	1	23	56

Event_List

Id	Comp_Id	Video_Id	Interval_Id
1	9	1	34

Concept_List

Id	Comp_Id	Video_Id	Interval_Id
1	22	1	0

Ontology

Domain	Type_Id	Comp1_Id	Comp2_Id
1	1	24	2
2	1	25	2
3	1	26	2
4	1	3	2
5	3	10	9
6	5	27	6
7	5	28	4

Fig. 5. Data Structures with Sample Values

Data structures with sample values for football domain are given in Fig. 5. The ontology definition for Football is represented with a tree-like structure as Fig. 6.

By defining the values for low-level features and relations between the components of the domain, we use the algorithm defined in Section 4.1 to extract objects, events and concepts from videos and store their attributes and relations in the data structures defined in section 4.2.1. Query statements are parsed and related frames are determined by searching through the calculated values in the data structures.

Until now we mentioned about the visual content of videos. For the football domain, we plan to add multimodality to our study. Football videos contain an extra content to be used both in object/event extraction and ontology-based querying. The announcer continuously gives information about the objects and events about the match. By using tools those convert speech to text and those extract subjects (objects) and verbs (events), we can make object/event

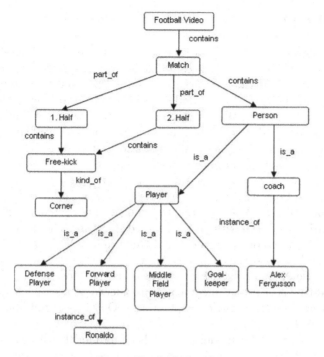

Fig. 6. Football Ontology

extraction directly. For domains such as football where its really hard to identify objects, this knowledge strengthens this model. The extracted information will be stored as XMLs with their related frames. Also we can improve the domain ontology with the information gained from speech-text. Because any event can be expressed by more than one word during speech, all possible words can be expressed in the ontology to relate them with each other. For instance, the announcer can say kick the ball or hit the ball as the starter event of the free-kick event where we can figure out both means the same event from the ontology.

Lets consider the query statement Retrieve all frames where a free-kick goal happens. given to our model. The event definitions free-kick and goal will be searched through extracted data of videos. The definitions of these events are given with relations or/and in the ontology of that domain. Pointers to the related frames for these events are found.

Related frames from different videos are returned as query results. Below we give some other query examples of this domain:

- Retrieve number of goals made by Team A.
- Retrieve all penalty kicks resulting with a goal.
- Retrieve all frames where player X runs from right to left with ball.
- Retrieve number of corner kicks used from the right corner flag.
- Retrieve all videos where Team B wins.
- Retrieve number of long passes made by Team A.
- Retrieve all fouls made by players wearing blue form.

6 Conclusion

With this study we proposed a nearly-automatic object, event, concept identification and query facility over these components. We use predefined relations between objects/events in video frames and a given fuzzy ontology to make automatic extraction of objects, events and concepts of videos to be used for answering semantic video queries. We make an ontology-supported video modeling and retrieval. Fuzziness used in component declarations, ontology and in the querying phase improves the modeling/query success ratio. Our study also handles semantic relation declarations between components (initiates, covers, places left).

For region segmentation we adapt a region segmentation tool like Columbias Automatic Video Region Segmentation Software or Automatic video object segmentation for MPEG-4 [20]. All the components are stored in the database (Berkeley XML DBMS [1]) with an XML-based structure. There are other XML-based studies for video object and event representation. VERL/VEML is an example study, which also uses ontology for video event representation [15]. For retrieval, we use XQuery [2], which currently is the most recent XML query language and the most powerful compared to older languages, such as XQL and XML-QL. (from object, event, concept tables). Ontology definitions are represented with OWL.

We plan to extend this model to a multimode model, which also captures audio and text information in videos. In order to this we will use a structural and event based multimodal video data model.

References

1. Berkeley db xml web site. www.sleepycat.com.
2. Xquery web site. www.w3.org/XML/Query.
3. Jie Bao, Yu Cao, Wallapak Tavanapong, and Vasant Honavar. Integration of domain-specific and domain-independent ontologies for colonoscopy video database annotation. In *International Conference on Information and Knowledge Engineering (IKE 04)*, 2004.
4. Shih-Fu Chang, William Chen, Horace Jianhao Meng, Hari Sundaram, and Di Zhong. A fully automated content-based video search engine supporting spatio-temporal queries. *IEEE Transactions on Circuits and Systems for Video Technology (CSVT)*, 8(5):602–615, September 1998.
5. Yining Deng, Debargha Mukherjee, and B. S. Manjunath. Netra-v: Toward an object-based video representation. In *Storage and Retrieval for Image and Video Databases (SPIE)*, pages 202–215, 1998.
6. M. E. Donderler. *Data Modeling and Querying for Video Databases*. PhD thesis, Bilkent University, Turkey, 2002.
7. J. Fan, X.Zhu, and J.Xiao. Content-based video indexing and retrieval. In *SPIE Proceed. V.*, volume 4315, 2002.
8. Jianping Fan, Walid G. Aref, Ahmed K. Elmagarmid, Mohand-Said Hacid, Mirette S. Marzouk, and Xingquan Zhu. Multiview: Multilevel video content representation and retrieval. *Journal of Electronic Imaging*, 10(4):895–908, 2001.

9. Myron Flickner, Harpreet Sawhney, Wayne Niblack, Jonathan Ashley, Qian Huang, Byron Dom, Monika Gorkani, Jim Hafner, Denis Lee, Dragutin Petkovic, David Steele, and Peter Yanker. Query by image and video content: The qbic system. *Computer*, 28(9):23–32, 1995.

10. H. M. Haav. A survey of concept-based information retrieval tools on the web. In *Advances in Databases and Information Systems: proc. Of 5th East-Europen Conference ADBIS 2001*, volume 2, pages 29–41, 2001.

11. Samira Hammiche, Salima Benbernou, Mohand-Sacid Hacid, and Athena Vakali. Semantic retrieval of multimedia data. In *MMDB '04: Proceedings of the 2nd ACM international workshop on Multimedia databases*, pages 36–44, New York, NY, USA, 2004. ACM Press.

12. Mesru Koprulu, Nihan Kesim Cicekli, and Adnan Yazici. Spatio-temporal querying in video databases. In *FQAS*, pages 251–262, 2002.

13. JeongKyu Lee, Jung-Hwan Oh, and Sae Hwang. Strg-index: Spatio-temporal region graph indexing for large video databases. In *SIGMOD Conference*, pages 718–729, 2005.

14. Jiebo Luo and S. P. Etz. A physical model-based approach to detecting sky in photographic images. *Image Processing, IEEE Transactions on*, 11(3):201–212, 2002.

15. Ram Nevatia, Jerry Hobbs, and Bob Bolles. An ontology for video event representation. In *CVPRW '04: Proceedings of the 2004 Conference on Computer Vision and Pattern Recognition Workshop (CVPRW'04) Volume 7*, page 119, Washington, DC, USA, 2004. IEEE Computer Society.

16. M. Petkovic and W. Jonker. An overview of data models and query languages for con-tent-based video retrieval. In *International Conference on Advances in Infrastructure for Electronic Business, Science, and Education on the Internet, l'Aquila, Italy*, 2000.

17. M. Petkovic and W. Jonker. Content-based retrieval of spatio-temporal video events. In *Proceedings International Conference Managing Information Technology in a Global Economy*, 2001.

18. Arnold W. M. Smeulders, Marcel Worring, Simone Santini, Amarnath Gupta, and Ramesh Jain. Content-based image retrieval at the end of the early years. *IEEE Trans. Pattern Anal. Mach. Intell.*, 22(12):1349–1380, 2000.

19. Peter Spyns, Robert Meersman, and Mustafa Jarrar. Data modelling versus ontology engineering. *SIGMOD Rec.*, 31(4):12–17, 2002.

20. Wei Wei and King Ngi Ngan. Automatic video object segmentation for mpeg-4. In *VCIP*, pages 9–19, 2003.

Learning to Retrieve Images from Text Queries with a Discriminative Model

David Grangier[1,2], Florent Monay[1,2], and Samy Bengio[1]

[1] IDIAP Research Institute, Martigny, Switzerland
firstname.lastname@idiap.ch
[2] Ecole Polytechnique Fédérale de Lausanne (EPFL), Switzerland

Abstract. This work presents a discriminative model for the retrieval of pictures from text queries. The core idea of this approach is to minimize a loss directly related to the retrieval performance of the model. For that purpose, we rely on a ranking loss which has recently been successfully applied to text retrieval problems. The experiments performed over the *Corel* dataset show that our approach compares favorably with generative models that constitute the state-of-the-art (e.g. our model reaches 21.6% mean average precision with Blob and SIFT features, compared to 16.7% for PLSA, the best alternative).

1 Introduction

Several application domains, such as stock photography providers or web search engines, need tools to search large collections of pictures from text queries. In most commercial applications, these tools generally rely on some manually-produced text associated with each picture and then apply text retrieval techniques over such texts. Although effective, this approach has a major drawback: its human annotation step is a costly process, moreover it often results in incomplete and subjective annotations. In order to circumvent this limitation, several automatic annotation techniques have recently been proposed, e.g. [1,2,3,4,5]. Automatic image annotation is generally performed relying on a generative model that aims at estimating the distribution of words given any picture from a training set of annotated images. Such models include, for instance, Cross-Media Relevance Models (CMRM) [3], Latent Dirichlet Allocation (LDA) [5] or Probabilistic Latent Semantic Analysis (PLSA) [6].

In this paper, we introduce an alternative to these approaches. The proposed model, Passive-Aggressive Model for Image Retrieval (PAMIR), relies on discriminative learning. This means that the model parameters are not selected to maximize the likelihood of some annotated training data; they are instead selected to maximize the retrieval performance of the model over a set of training queries. This has several advantages when compared to generative approaches: from a theoretical point of view, it is attractive to solve the targeted problem directly instead of solving the more complex problem of data generation [7]. From a practical point of view, discriminative methods have been highly successful

S. Marchand-Maillet et al. (Eds.): AMR 2006, LNCS 4398, pp. 42–56, 2007.

in several domains and our experiments also confirm this advantage (for single word queries, PAMIR attains 30.7% mean average precision with Blob+SIFT features compared to 24.5% for the second best model, PLSA).

The remainder of this paper is organized as follows: Section 2 introduces our approach, Section 3 presents the features used to represent text queries and images, Section 4 briefly describes previous related research. Section 5 reports the experiments and results. Finally, Section 6 draws some conclusions.

2 Passive-Aggressive Model for Image Retrieval

In this section, we first define the ideal goal that an image retrieval model F is targeting, which allows us to define a training loss L related to this objective. Then, we introduce the parameterization of our model F_w and we explain the optimization procedure adopted to select the parameters w^* that minimize L over a given training set D_{train}.

2.1 Ranking Loss

Before introducing the ranking loss, we should first recall the ideal goal of an image retrieval system. Given a set of pictures P and a query q, such a system should rank the pictures of P such that the pictures relevant to q appear above the non-relevant ones. In order to address such a problem, a scoring function F that assigns a real value $F(q, p)$ to any query/picture pair (q, p) is generally introduced [8]. Given a query q, a retrieval system then simply computes the scores $\{F(q, p), \forall p \in P\}$ and ranks the pictures of P by decreasing scores. The effectiveness of such a system is hence mainly determined by the choice of an appropriate function F. In fact, optimal retrieval performance would be achieved if F satisfies

$$\forall q, \forall p^+ \in R(q), \forall p^- \notin R(q), F(q, p^+) > F(q, p^-), \tag{1}$$

where $R(q)$ refers to the pictures of P which are relevant to q. In other words, if F satisfies (1), the retrieval system will always rank the relevant pictures above the non-relevant ones.

Hence, our learning problem is to identify a function F which is likely to satisfy (1) for any unseen queries and pictures, given only a limited amount of training data D_{train}. For that purpose, we need a loss function L such that the selection of a function F minimizing $F \rightarrow L(F; D_{train})$ ensures that F also yield good retrieval performance over unseen data. In fact, such a loss has recently been introduced in the text retrieval literature [9,10] and we propose to apply it to our image retrieval problem. This loss, referred to as the *ranking loss* in the following, assumes that we are given a set of training triplets,

$$D_{train} = ((q_1, p_1^+, p_1^-), \ldots, (q_n, p_n^+, p_n^-),$$

where, for all k, p_k^+ is a picture relevant to query q_k and p_k^- is a picture non-relevant to query q_k, and is defined as follows:

$$L(F; D_{train}) = \sum_{k=1}^{n} l(F; q_k, p_k^+, p_k^-)$$

$$= \sum_{k=1}^{n} \max(0, 1 - F(q_k, p_k^+) + F(q_k, p_k^-)).$$

This means that minimizing L favors the selection of functions F such that, for all k, the score $F(q_k, p_k^+)$ is greater than $F(q_k, p_k^-)$ by at least a *margin* of 1 (the choice of 1 is arbitrary here and any positive constant would lead to the same optimization problem). This notion of *margin* is a key aspect of this criterion and has shown to yield good generalization performance when applied over different text retrieval tasks [9,10].

2.2   Model Parameterization

In this section, we describe a family of parameterized functions F_w that are suitable for our task. This parameterization is inspired from text retrieval, i.e. the retrieval of *text* documents from *text* queries. In this case, documents and queries are generally represented with *bag-of-words* vectors, i.e. each text item t is assigned a vocabulary-sized vector in which the ith component is a weight related to the presence or absence of term i in t (see Section 3 for a detailed description). Each query/document pair (q, d) is then assigned a score corresponding to the inner product of their vector representation [8], i.e.

$$F^{text}(q, d) = q \cdot d = \sum_{i=1}^{T} q_i \cdot d_i,$$

where T is the vocabulary size.

In our case, we adopt a similar approach and we compute the score of a picture/query pair (q, p) according to:

$$F_w(q, p) = F^{text}(q, f_w(p)) \tag{2}$$

where f_w is a linear mapping from the picture space $\mathcal{P}$ to the text space $\mathcal{T} = \mathbb{R}^T$. In other words, f_w is defined as,

$$\forall p \in \mathcal{P}, f_w(p) = (w_1 \cdot p, \dots, w_T \cdot p)$$

where $w = (w_1, \dots, w_T) \in \mathcal{P}^T$.

2.3   Passive-Aggressive Loss Minimization

As mentioned above, our goal is to identify the parameters w^* that minimizes $w \rightarrow L(F_w; D_{train})$. For that purpose, we rely on the *Passive-Aggressive* minimization algorithm[1] [11]. This algorithm iteratively constructs a sequence of weights $w^0, \ldots, w^m$ according to the following procedure: the first vector is set to be zero ($w^0 = 0$) and, at any iteration $i > 0$, we select the weight w^i as a trade-off between remaining close from the previous weight w^{i-1} and satisfying the ith training constraint,

$$w^i = \arg\min_w \|w - w^{i-1}\|^2 + C \cdot l(F_w; q_i, p_i^+, p_i^-). \qquad (3)$$

where C is the *aggressiveness* hyperparameter that controls this trade-off. This problem (3) can then be solved analytically [11], leading to:

$$w^i = w^{i-1} + \tau_i v_i, \quad \text{where} \quad \tau_i = \min\left\{ C, \frac{l(w^{i-1}; (q_i, p_i^+, p_i^-))}{\|v_i\|^2} \right\}$$
$$\text{and} \quad v_i = (q_1(p_k^+ - p_k^-), \ldots, q_T(p_k^+ - p_k^-)).$$

After the last training iteration m, the best weight w^* is selected among $w^0, \ldots, w^m$ according to some validation data D_{valid}: $w^* = \arg\min_{w \in \{w^0, \ldots, w^m\}} L(F_w; D_{valid})$. The two hyperparameters, i.e. the aggressiveness C and the number of iterations m, are selected by cross-validation.

3   Text and Visual Features

This section describes the features used to represent text queries and pictures.

3.1   Text Features

The queries are represented with *bag-of-words* vectors, i.e. each query q is represented with a vocabulary sized vector,

$$q = (q_1, \ldots, q_T),$$

where q_i is the weight of term i in q and T is the vocabulary size. Each term weight q_i is assigned according to the *normalized tf idf* weighting, i.e.

$$q_i = \frac{tf_{i,q} \cdot idf_i}{\sqrt{\sum_{j=1}^{T}(tf_{j,q} \cdot idf_j)^2}}$$

where $tf_{i,q}$ refers to the number of occurrences of i in q and $idf_i = -log(r_i)$, r_i being the fraction of training captions in which i occurs.

3.2   Visual Features

Similarly to previous work, e.g. [1,6], we adopt a *bag-of-visterms* representation for pictures. In this framework, the representation of a picture p is assigned

---

[1] The proof that the *Passive-Aggressive* algorithm actually minimizes the loss $L(F_w; D_{train})$ is not reported here due to space limitation but can be easily infered from [11].

according to a 4-step process. In a first step, salient regions of p are detected. Then, each region is described with a feature vector. Each of these feature vectors is then mapped to a single discrete value according to a codebook (in general, this codebook is built through k-means clustering of the set of feature vectors extracted from all training images). The picture p is then represented as an histogram over the codebook, i.e.

$$p = (vtf_{p,1}, \ldots, vtf_{p,V}), \tag{4}$$

where V is the codebook size and $vtf_{p,i}$ is the number of regions in p whose vector is mapped to the ith codebook value.

In our case, we use two alternative types of visterm representation, i.e. Blob and Scale Invariant Feature Transform:

Blobs are based on the visual properties of large color-uniform regions. In this case, the salient regions are detected through a normalized cut algorithm, each region is then described by a 36-dimensional vector describing colors (18), texture (12) and shape/location (6). Region quantization is then performed according to the k-means clustering of the training regions. More details about these features can be found in [1].

SIFTs are based on the distribution of edges in regions located around salient points of the image. In this case, the salient regions are detected with a Difference-of-Gaussians detector, and each region is then described according to a 128-bin edge histogram. Like for Blobs, region quantization is also performed according to the k-means clustering of training regions. More details about these features can be found in [12].

SIFTs and Blobs have also been used jointly in our experiments. In this case, a single histogram per picture is obtained by concatenating the Blob and SIFT histograms.

Like for text representation, we do not use the vtf vector (4) directly, we instead use a representation similar to the *normalized tf idf* weighting[2], i.e.

$$p_i = \frac{vtf_{i,p} \cdot vidf_i}{\sqrt{\sum_{j=1}^{V}(vtf_{j,q} \cdot vidf_j)^2}},$$

where $vidf_i = -log(vr_i)$, vr_i referring to the fraction of training regions mapped to the ith codebook vector.

4   Related Work

Most of the previous work in image retrieval from text queries focussed on an intermediate step, image auto-captioning, the underlying idea being to apply

---

[2] Due to space limitation, we do not report the preliminary experiments over validation data highlighting the advantage of this weighting strategy over standard vtf histograms.

text retrieval techniques over the automatically inferred captions. The goal of such approaches is hence not to optimize directly a criterion related to retrieval performance but to find the most probable caption given a picture. In this context, several models have been introduced in the last decade and the following describes three of them: we present Cross-Media Relevance Model (CMRM) [3], Cross-Media Translation Table (CMTT) [4] and Probabilistic Latent Semantic Analysis (PLSA) [6]. Other models, such as Latent Dirichlet Analysis [5] or Hierarchical Mixture Model [2], could also have been present in this section. However, due to space constraints, we decided to focus on the models that have shown to be the most effective over the benchmark *Corel* dataset [1].

4.1 Cross-Media Relevance Model

The core idea of CMRM [3] is to estimate the joint probability of a term t and a test picture p^{test} as its expectation over the training pictures,

$$P(t, p^{test}) = \sum_{p^{train} \in D_{train}} P(p^{train}) \cdot P(t, p^{test}|p^{train}).$$

The image p^{test} is considered as a set of discrete features or visterms (see Section 3), i.e. $p^{test} = \{v_1, \ldots, v_m\}$, which means that:

$$P(t, p^{test}) = \sum_{p^{train} \in D_{train}} P(p^{train}) \cdot P(t, v_1, \ldots, v_m|p^{train}).$$

Terms and visterms are then assumed to be independent given a training image, leading to:

$$P(t, p^{test}) = \sum_{p^{train} \in D_{train}} P(p^{train}) \cdot P(t|p^{train}) \prod_{i=1}^{m} P(v_i|p^{train}) \quad (5)$$

The probability $P(p^{train})$ is then assumed to be uniform over D_{train}, while $P(t|p^{train})$ and $P(v_i|p^{train})$ are estimated through maximum likelihood with Jelinek-Mercer smoothing [3]. The probability $p(t|p^{test})$ is then simply inferred from (5) using Bayes rule. Although simple, this method has shown to yield good performance over the standard *Corel* dataset [3].

4.2 Cross-Media Translation Table

The CMTT approach is inspired from cross-lingual retrieval techniques [4]. Given a term t and a picture p^{test}, CMTT estimates $p(t|p^{test})$ according to a translation table, containing the similarities $sim(t, v)$ between any textual term t and any visterm v:

$$p(t|p^{test}) = \frac{w_{t,p_{test}}}{\sum_{i=1}^{T} w_{i,p_{test}}}, \quad \text{where } w_{t,p_{test}} = \sum_{i=1}^{m} sim(t, v_i),$$

$v_1, \ldots, v_m$ being the visterms of p^{test}. The translation table is built from the training set D_{train} according to the following methodology: in a first step, each term t and each visterm v is represented by a $|D_{train}|$ dimensional vector in which each component i is the $tf \cdot idf$ weight of term t (or visterm v) in the ith training example. The vectors of all terms and visterms are then represented as a matrix, $M = [t_1, \ldots, t_T, v_1, \ldots, v_k]$, and Singular Value Decomposition (SVD) is then applied over this matrix as a noise removal step, yielding $M' = [t'_1, \ldots, t'_T, v'_1, \ldots, v'_k]$. The similarities between a visterm v and a term t are then computed according to:

$$\forall i, j, \; sim(t_i, v_j) = \frac{cos(t'_i, v'_j)}{\sum_{k=1}^{V} cos(t'_i, v'_k)}.$$

CMTT has been successfully applied to the Corel data. In particular, the application of SVD has shown to improve noise robustness. However, cosine similarity only allows to model simple term/visterm relationships. This limitation has been circumvented with the introduction of more complex models, like PLSA.

4.3   Probabilistic Latent Semantic Analysis

PLSA, initially introduced for text retrieval [13], has recently been applied to image retrieval problems [6]. This model assumes that the observation of a picture p and a term t are independent conditionally to a discrete latent variable $z_k = \{z_1, \ldots, z_K\}$,

$$P(p, t) = P(p) \sum_{k=1}^{K} P(z_k|p) P(t|z_k),$$

where K is a hyperparameter of the model. A similar conditional independence assumption is also made for visterms,

$$P(p, v) = P(p) \sum_{k=1}^{K} P(z_k|p) P(v|z_k).$$

In this framework, the different parameters of the model, i.e. $P(z_k|p), P(t|z_k), P(v|z_k)$ are trained through the Expectation Maximization (EM) algorithm. In fact, a modified version of EM is applied such that the latent space is constrained toward the text modality. This yields a latent space that better models the semantic relationships between pictures, which has shown to be more effective empirically [6].

5   Experiments and Results

In this section, we first present the experimental setup and then discuss the results.

Table 1. Picture Set Statistics

	P_{train}	P_{valid}	P_{test}
Number of pictures	4,000	500	500
Number of Blob clusters		500	
Avg. # of Blobs per pic.	9.43	9.33	9.37
Number of SIFT clusters		1,000	
Avg. # of SIFTs per pic.	232.8	226.3	229.5

Table 2. Query Set Statistics

	Q_{train}	Q_{valid}	Q_{test}
Number of queries	7,221	1,962	2,241
Avg. # of rel. pic. per q.	5.33	2.44	2.37
Vocabulary size		179	
Avg. # of words per query	2.78	2.51	2.51

5.1 Experimental Setup

The experiments presented in this section have been performed over the *Corel* dataset, following the setup introduced in [1]. This dataset consists of $5,000$ captioned images which are split into $4,500$ development images and 500 test images. The image captions are manual annotations, based on a vocabulary of 179 words.

As a feature extraction step, we extracted Blob and SIFT visterms relying on a codebook built through k-means clustering of the development pictures (see Section 3). For PAMIR training, we split the development set into a $4,000$ image train set ($L(F_w, D_{train})$ is minimized over this set, see Section 2) and a 500 image validation set (the number of iterations m and the aggressiveness parameter C are selected relying on this set). Since no retrieval queries were available as such for this *Corel* data, we used as queries all subsets of the 179 words which have at least one relevant image according to the following rule: "a picture p is considered as relevant to a query q if and only if the caption of p contains all the words in q". Such queries have already been used in previous work, e.g. [3,14]. Table 1 and Table 2 summarize image and query set statistics.

In order to assess PAMIR effectiveness, we used mean average precision(mAP), the standard evaluation measure in Information Retrieval benchmarks [8]. For any query, average precision is defined as the average of the precision (i.e. the percentage of relevant pictures) measured at each ranking position where a relevant picture appears and mAP corresponds to the mean of average precision over the Q_{test} set. For the sake of comparison, we also report the performance of CMRM, CMTT and PLSA that we trained and evaluated according to the same setup.

5.2 Overall Performance

Table 3 reports the mean average precision for the CMRM, CMTT, PLSA and PAMIR models when Blobs, SIFTs and their combined representation are

Table 3. Mean average precision (%) for test queries

	CMRM	CMTT	PLSA	PAMIR
Blobs	10.4	11.8	9.7	11.9
SIFTs	10.8	9.1	12.3	**16.0**
Blobs + SIFTs	14.7	11.5	16.7	**21.6**

used. The PAMIR model achieves the best retrieval performance for the three image representations, with a significant improvement according to the Wilcoxon signed-rank test at 95% confidence over the three other models for SIFTs and Blobs+SIFTs (this outcome is indicated by bold values in the tables). Although it does not contain any color information, the SIFT representation leads to a more accurate ranking of the test images for the PLSA and PAMIR models than the Blob representation (27% and 34% relative improvement respectively). This might be explained considering the difference between the two representations, which not only relies in the region descriptors, but also in the number, and the size of the considered regions (see Section 3). While the Blobs representation only consists of a maximum of ten regions, the average number of regions sampled per image with the Difference of Gaussians point detector is around 230 in our dataset. The SIFT representation therefore presents richer statistics than the Blob representation, and these statistics seems better exploited by PLSA and PAMIR.

The two representations are complementary, and their combination interestingly achieves a higher score than the Blob or SIFT representation individually for the CMRM, PLSA, and PAMIR models. The relative improvement of Blobs+SIFTs over SIFTs is 41% for the CMRM model, 36% for the PLSA model, and 35% for the PAMIR model. Only CMTT fails to take advantage of the combination, and achieves a similar performance with the Blobs+SIFTs and Blobs. The poor performance of CMTT model over SIFTs might explain the difference. The PAMIR model does take the best benefit of the combined representation, and outperforms the second best model, PLSA, with a 29% relative improvement. These results justify the combination of a small set of large, color-based regions (Blobs) with a larger set of small, texture-based regions (SIFTs) to represent an image.

A majority of studies [1,6,4,2] evaluates the retrieval performance based on single-word queries. We therefore compare the four models using the three image representations for the subset of single-word queries in Table 4. On this set of single-word queries, the CMTT model achieves the best performance when the Blob representation is used, and the PAMIR model performs the best image ranking for the SIFT and Blob+SIFT representation. The relative increase in performance with respect to PLSA, the second best model, is 39% and 25% for SIFTs and Blobs+SIFTs respectively.

Comparing Tables 3 and 4, one should remark that the performance is higher for single-word queries. This result can be explained by the number of relevant pictures per query. The subset of 179 single-word queries has a higher average number of relevant images (9.4) than the set of all 2, 241 queries (2.4). This means

Table 4. Mean average precision (%) over single-word test queries

	CMRM	CMTT	PLSA	PAMIR
Blobs	14.2	**17.2**	15.5	16.6
SIFTs	14.2	15.1	17.1	**23.8**
Blobs + SIFTs	19.2	19.1	24.5	**30.7**

that these queries correspond to an easier retrieval problem [8], that naturally results in higher mean average precision values. Moreover, the words appearing in queries with many relevant pictures occur more frequently in the training data, allowing the model to achieve better generalization performance. The influence of the number of relevant images on PAMIR results is shown in Table 5. The single-word queries are divided into three sets, defined by the number of relevant images per query. The mean of the average precision of the queries within each range indicates that the average precision is higher for queries with more relevant documents, which confirms the above explanation.

We showed that the PAMIR model takes the best advantage of the Blobs+SIFTs combination, outperforming the PLSA-based generative model and other approaches significantly. The good performance of the PAMIR model justifies the use of a ranking-based criterion for retrieval applications.

5.3   Per-query Performance

The mean average precision measure summarizes the overall retrieval performance of a model in a single number, but does not indicate the per-query performance. To have a more complete evaluation, we compare the average precision of each single-word query obtained with the PAMIR model over the different types of image representation. We also propose to compare the results of PAMIR and PLSA, the second best model, on a per-query basis.

Figure 1 shows the relative increase in performance between SIFT and Blob representations. The histogram shows five ranges of relative improvement, with the corresponding queries on the right. In this figure, we consider only the queries that correspond to a minimum of 10% of average precision for one of the two representations in order to avoid unreliable measurements of relative improvement. Among the 124 resulting single-word queries, 65 are improved by more than 30% when SIFTs instead of Blobs are used. For instance, for queries like *house*, *town*, *street*, *city*, *arch*, *buildings*, *window*, and *bridge*, images are ranked with a higher

Table 5. Mean average precision (mAP) in percent obtained with PAMIR for Blobs+SIFTs for three sets of single-word queries defined by the number of relevant images

query range	# queries	mAP (%)
$0 < \#rel.pic. \leq 2$	47	15.5
$2 < \#rel.pic. \leq 7$	69	26.7
$7 < \#rel.pic.$	63	46.5

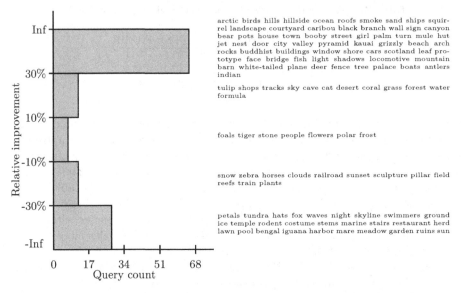

Fig. 1. Histogram of the relative increase of the average precision of single-word queries between the SIFTs and Blobs representations. The words corresponding to each bin are shown on the right.

average precision when represented with SIFTs instead of Blobs features. As these concepts naturally correspond to local edge structures, it seems consistent that SIFTs better capture the corresponding image content. It is more surprising that the average precision of single-word queries like *ocean* or *black* is improved by more than 30% when SIFTs instead of Blobs features are used. The opposite trend is also observed with other queries, for which the PAMIR model achieves a higher score with the Blob representation. For 28 queries, the relative gain obtained by using Blobs instead of SIFTs is over 30%. The ranking of color-based concepts like *sun*, *ice*, *night*, and *garden* is learned with a higher accuracy by the PAMIR model when images are depicted with Blobs rather than SIFT features, which seems consistent. The fact that the queries *temple* and *restaurant* are improved when Blobs instead of SIFTs are used is less intuitive.

As shown in Tables 3 and 4, the combination of the two representations improves the retrieval performance of the PAMIR model for all queries on average. To have an indication of the difference in performance at query level, Figure 2 shows the histogram of the relative improvement in average precision obtained with the Blobs+SIFTs over the best average precision obtained between Blobs and SIFTs individually. Note that this second performance is only theoretical, given that the *best* representation is chosen on the test data for each query. As for Table 1, only single-word queries resulting in a 10% minimum average precision with one of the two representations are considered. While 42 out of the 129 considered queries do not significantly benefit from the combined representation, with a relative difference between 10% and −10%, the average precision of 66

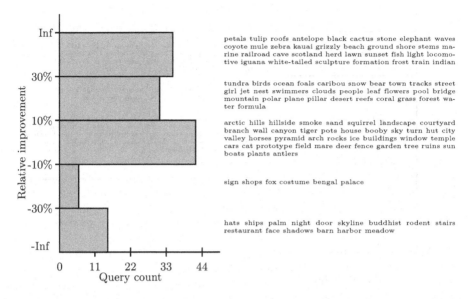

Fig. 2. Histogram of the relative increase of the average precision of single-word queries obtained with the Blobs+SIFTs representation and the best average precision achieved with the Blobs and SIFTs representations. The words corresponding to each bin are shown on the right.

words is improved by more than 10% when Blobs+SIFTs is used. Moreover, the increase is over 30% for 35 single-word queries. The words *ocean* and *black*, that were surprisingly better represented by SIFT instead of Blob features (see Table 1), achieve a higher average precision when the SIFTs representation is completed with the Blobs features. This confirms the intuition that these specific queries should benefit from some color-based visual information. Although the best representation between SIFTs and Blobs has been selected a-posteriori for this evaluation, only 21 queries suffer a performance loss greater than 10% when using the combination instead of this unrealistic individual feature setup. This result hence highlights the complementarity of Blob and SIFT representation.

Keeping this combined feature setup, we propose to compare the performance of PAMIR with the best alternative, PLSA, on a per-query basis to have a deeper understanding of the difference between both models. Figure 3 shows the relative improvement in average precision for single-word queries between the PAMIR and the PLSA models, for the Blobs+SIFTs representation. Like for the above histograms, only the queries with a minimum average precision of 10% for one of the two models are considered to prevent unreliable measurements of relative improvement. This leads to 127 queries. Out of these, the ranking of 70 queries is improved by more than 10% when PAMIR instead of PLSA is used, while 26 queries only are better ranked by PLSA by more than 10%. The PAMIR model improves the ranking of 53 queries by more than 30% relative improvement. This further confirms the result of the Wilcoxon signed-rank test which concluded that

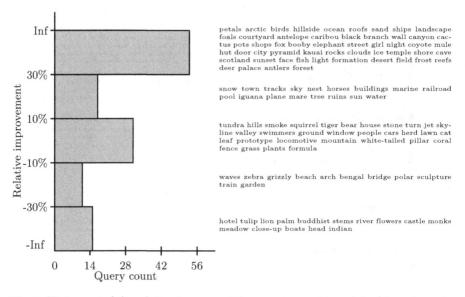

Fig. 3. Histogram of the relative increase of the average precision of single-word queries between the PAMIR and the PLSA model, using the Blobs+SIFTs representation.The words corresponding to each bin are shown on the right.

PAMIR advantage is consistent over the query set. An illustration of the rankings obtained by PLSA and PAMIR is shown in Figure 4 for the queries *pillar* and *landscape*, which are respectively improved by more than 10% and 30% by the PAMIR model. Note that only the first five top-ranked images are shown, which does not necessarily reflect the whole ranking performance measured by the average precision measure. For the *pillar* query, both models retrieve relevant images in the top-five, except for the last image retrieved by PLSA. The second query shows the case where the ranking obtained by the PAMIR model is clearly better for the top-five images. The first two and the fourth images retrieved by PLSA are not related to the *landscape* concept, while only the fourth image retrieved by the PAMIR model is not a *landscape* image. These examples confirm the advantage of PAMIR over PLSA, showing the practical benefit of using a learning procedure appropriate to the image retrieval problem.

6   Conclusions

In this work, a discriminative model for the retrieval of pictures from text queries has been proposed. This model relies on the recently proposed Passive-Aggressive algorithm for training [11] and its parameters are selected to minimize a loss related to the ranking performance over a set of training queries. The choice of such a loss is motivated by recent work in the context of text retrieval [9,10]. The experiments performed over the *Corel* dataset show that the advantage of discriminative approaches observed for text data translates to image retrieval:

Fig. 4. First five images retrieved with the PLSA and the PAMIR models for the queries *pillar* and *landscape*

the proposed model PAMIR is reported to yield significantly better results than generative models that consistitute the state-of-the-art (e.g. PAMIR mean average precision is 21.6% when Blob and SIFT features are used, compared to 16.7% for PLSA, the second best model).

These results are promising and this work yield several possible future research directions. For instance, other parameterization could be investigated: as any passive-aggressive algorithm [11], the PAMIR model could rely on non-linear kernels, allowing the application of kernels which avoid the feature quantification step, such as [15]. Another extension of this work would be to modify PAMIR such that it could be applied over much larger datasets, where the application of any learning procedure, generative or discriminative, is challenging.

Acknowledgments

This work has been performed with the support of the Swiss NSF through the NCCR–IM2 project. It was also supported by the PASCAL European Network of Excellence, funded by the Swiss OFES.

References

1. Duygulu, P., Barnard, K., de Freitas, N., Forsyth, D.: Object recognition as machine translation: Learning a lexicon for a fixed image vocabulary. In: European Conference on Computer Vision (ECCV). (2002) 97–112
2. Barnard, K., Duygulu, P., Forsyth, D., de Freitas, N., Blei, D.M., Jordan, M.I.: Matching words and pictures. Journal of Machine Learning Research (JMLR) **3** (2003) 1107–1135
3. Jeon, J., Lavrenko, V., Manmatha, R.: Automatic image annotation and retrieval using cross-media relevance models. In: ACM Special Interest Group on Information Retrieval (SIGIR). (2003)
4. Pan, J.Y., Yang, H.J., Duygulu, P., Faloutsos, C.: Automatic image captioning. In: International Conference on Multimedia and Expo (ICME). (2004) 1987–1990
5. Blei, D., Ng, A., Jordan, M.: Latent dirichlet allocation. Journal of Machine Learning Research **3** (2003) 993–1022
6. Monay, F., Gatica-Perez, D.: PLSA-based image auto-annotation: constraining the latent space. In: ACM Multimedia. (2004) 348–351
7. Vapnik, V.: Statistical Learning Theory. John Wiley and Sons, New York (1998)
8. Baeza-Yates, R., Ribeiro-Neto, B.: Modern Information Retrieval. Addison Wesley, Harlow, England (1999)
9. Joachims, T.: Optimizing search engines using clickthrough data. In: International Conference on Knowledge Discovery and Data Mining (KDD). (2002)
10. Grangier, D., Bengio, S.: Exploiting hyperlinks to learn a retrieval model. In: NIPS Workshop on Learning to Rank. (2005) 12–17
11. Crammer, K., Dekel, O., Shalev-Shwartz, S., Singer, Y.: Online passive-aggressive algorithms. In: Conference on Advances in Neural Information Processing Systems (NIPS). (2003)
12. Lowe, D.G.: Distinctive image features from scale-invariant keypoints. International Journal of Computer Vision (IJCV) **60**(2) (2004) 91–110
13. Hofmann, T.: Unsupervised learning by probabilistic latent semantic analysis. Machine Learning **42** (2001) 177–196
14. Lavrenko, V., Manmatha, R., Jeon, J.: A model for learning the semantics of pictures. In: Conference on Advances in Neural Information Processing Systems (NIPS). (2003)
15. Wallraven, C., Caputo, B.: Recognition with local features: the kernel recipe. In: International Conference on Computer Vision (ICCV). (2003)

A General Principled Method for Image Similarity Validation

Frédéric Cao and Patrick Bouthemy

IRISA / INRIA
Campus universitaire de Beaulieu
35042 Rennes Cedex, France
{fcao,bouthemy}@irisa.fr

Abstract. A novel and general criterion for image similarity validation is introduced using the so-called *a contrario* decision framework. It is mathematically proved that it is possible to compute a fully automatic detection criterion to decide that two images have a common cause, which can be taken as a definition of similarity. Analytical estimates of the necessary and sufficient number of sample points are also given. An implementation of this criterion is designed exploiting the comparison of grey level gradient direction at randomly sampled points. Similar images are detected *a contrario*, by rejecting an hypothesis that resemblance is due to randomness, which is far more easy to model than a realistic degradation process. The method proves very robust to noise, transparency and partial occlusion. It is also invariant to contrast change and can accomodate global geometric transformations. It does not require any feature matching step. It can be global or local, only the global version is investigated in this paper.

1 Introduction

Establishing that two images, or parts of images, are similar is a general concern in image analysis and computer vision. It is involved in a number of problems or applications, and more specifically in image or video retrieval [1,16]. In this paper, we answer the following question: can we automatically assess that two images are similar and with which degree of confidence? A second question is: can we compute "universal" thresholds to decide that two images are similar? This problem is very difficult in full generality since image similarity should be defined up to a large group of invariance, which may depend on the application: contrast change, occlusion, transparency, noise, translation, scaling, geometric deformation, etc.

In this paper, we investigate the global case. Even on complete images, this is a central issue for image retrieval: checking whether or not an image is present in a database or in a video stream. The designed solution is based on statistical arguments. It requires very simple information computed on the image intensities. It is extremely stable with respect to noise (it still works with an additive Gaussian noise with standard deviation 30 or a 50% impulse noise). The search is

S. Marchand-Maillet et al. (Eds.): AMR 2006, LNCS 4398, pp. 57–70, 2007.

totally processed online and is very efficient (10 frames/s on a 2.4GHz PC, with no optimization). The implemented version only relies on the direction of the image gradient, and is therefore contrast invariant. We have demonstrated that it is robust to occlusion and transparency. Finally, we will mention how global geometric transformations can be handled. Let us point out that the similarity measure does not require any feature matching step.

The paper is organized as follows. A brief review of related work is made in Section 2. In Section 3, the *a contrario* decision framework is introduced and used to define an automatic criterion for the similarity between two images. The method will be introduced in parallel of a more usual hypothesis testing framework, but we emphasize that decision only relies on the likelihood of one hypothesis (which is that the two compared images are not the same). The implemented test compares the image gradient direction at some random points. Similarity is detected *a contrario*, by rejecting an hypothesis that resemblance is due to randomness. In Section 4, we show that this number of sample points can be chosen to maintain a probability of detection very close to 1, when we assume white Gaussian noise. However, we insist that detection does not rely on such a Gaussian noise assumption. It will be observed that, in practice, the required number of samples is seldom above a few hundreds, even for quite important noise. Section 5 contains experimental results of image comparison and retrieval in databases of typically 10,000 images. We cope with several kinds of image perturbations as strong Gaussian and impulse noise, JPEG compression, transparency, occlusion. We also handle a prior registration before detecting similar pairs. Summary and concluding remarks are given in Section 6.

2   Related Work

The statistical arguments we introduce can be related to the work of Lisani and Morel [8]. Their approach uses the direction of the gradient of a grey level image, and they detect local changes in registered stereo pairs of satellite images. Our method is dual since, on the contrary, we use the gradient direction in both images to decide that they have much spatial information in common. Detection thresholds are computed by using an *a contrario framework*, as introduced by Desolneux, Moisan and Morel [2], and extended for spatio-temporal problems in [18]. More ancient work [17] used the same kind of ideas but detection thresholds were not computed. Other image features widely used are SIFT descriptors [9,10] which are basically local direction distributions. Nevertheless, the indexing and comparison of descriptors is achieved by a nearest-neighbor procedure. Hence, there is no decision involving an automatic threshold setting, which is precisely our main concern. On the other hand, we think that our methodology can be adapted to the comparison of SIFT features as well, instead of using the direction of the spatial intensity gradient.

Basically, our method consists in sampling random points in two images and counting the number of points such that the difference of the spatial intensity gradient direction is small enough. Using the gradient direction as image feature for image similarity detection was already proven useful (e.g., [13]). This step is embedded in a probabilistic framework which will be subsequently discussed. Let us point out that contrarily to methods as RANSAC [4], the estimation of the registration parameters is completely separated from the similarity decision step, which makes the proposed method more general. In particular, our method can consider different types of image features, independently of the image information used to perform the registration. Furthermore, it can be used to validate the performance of the registration methods themselves.

Probabilities will be computed in a model representing the absence of similarity (so-called *background model*, in the statistical meaning). Some similar idea can be found in [5] where the authors study the influence of "conspiracy of random".

3   A Contrast Invariant Image Comparison Method

In what follows, we always assume that images are grey-level valued with size $N \times N$. Let u and v be two images. To facilitate understanding, the development below is instantiated for the case where image gradient direction is the considered image feature. However, let us stress that this framework is general and other kinds of image features could be utilized as well.

For any point x, let us denote by $\theta_u(x)$ and $\theta_v(x)$ the directions of the image gradient of u and v at point x. Let us denote by $D_{u,v}(x)$ the angle difference between $\theta_u(x)$ and $\theta_v(x)$ on the unit circle $\mathbb{S}^1$. When there is no risk of ambiguity, we elude the subscript and write $D(x)$ instead. It is a real value in $[0, \pi]$. Since we want this measure to be accurate, we only consider points where both image gradients are large enough (larger than 5 in practice). Now, two images differing from a contrast change have the same gradient direction everywhere, which ensures that the method is contrast invariant.

Even though the proposed method is not a classical hypothesis testing, let us formulate it this way, to explain its principle. From the observations of the values of $D(x)$, let us consider that we aim at selecting one of the two following hypotheses: $\mathcal{H}_0$: u and v are unrelated images. $\mathcal{H}_1$: u and v have similar content. Modeling Hypothesis $\mathcal{H}_1$ is equivalent to model the type of degradation that can lead from u to v, and only very simplistic models are usually at hand. In an image retrieval application, v can belong to a database of typically 10^6 images (10 hours of video). Hence, false alarms (that is, accept $\mathcal{H}_1$ while $\mathcal{H}_0$ actually holds) have to be controlled, else the system will become impractical. Because of the large size of the database, this implies that it is necessary to ensure very small probabilities of false alarms. The proposed method is to base the decision only on $\mathcal{H}_0$, which is far more easy to model. It allows us to attain very small probabilities of false alarm. Moreover, there is no need to compare the likelihood of the two hypotheses, since we can derive automatic thresholds on the likelihood of $\mathcal{H}_0$, which allows us to reject it very surely.

Hypothesis $\mathcal{H}_0$ models the absence of similarity. Thus, the following assumption is made: for some set of points $x_1, ..., x_M$, the values $D(x_i)_{i \in \{1,...,M\}}$ are independent, identically distributed in $[0, \pi]$. This probabilistic model will be called the *a contrario* model (or background model). The principle of the detection is to compute the probability that the real observation has been generated by the *a contrario* model. When this probability is too small, the independence assumption of the two images is rejected and similarity is detected (validated).

Let $\alpha \in (0, \pi)$, and $q_\alpha = \frac{\alpha}{\pi}$ be the probability that the considered angle is less than or equal to α. For any set of distinct points $\{x_1, \ldots, x_M\}$, the probability, under $\mathcal{H}_0$, that at least k among the M values $\{D(x_1), \ldots D(x_M)\}$ are less than α is given by the tail of the binomial law

$$B(M, k, q_\alpha) = \sum_{j=k}^{M} \binom{M}{j} q_\alpha^j (1 - q_\alpha)^{M-j}.$$

Definition 1. *Let $0 \leqslant \alpha_1 \leqslant \ldots \leqslant \alpha_L \leqslant \pi$ be L values in $[0, \pi]$. Let u a real valued image, and $x_1, \ldots x_M$, M distinct points. Let us also consider a database $\mathcal{B}$ of $N_\mathcal{B}$ images. For any $v \in \mathcal{B}$, we call number of false alarms of (u, v) the quantity*

$$NFA(u, v) = N_\mathcal{B} \cdot L \cdot \min_{1 \leqslant i \leqslant L} B(M, k_i, q_{\alpha_i}), \tag{1}$$

where k_i is the cardinality of

$$\{j, \, 1 \leqslant j \leqslant M, D_{u,v}(x_j) \leqslant \alpha_i\}.$$

We say that the pair (u, v) is meaningful (more specifically, ε-meaningful), or that u and v are similar (more specifically, ε-similar) if $NFA(u, v) \leqslant \varepsilon$.

The interpretation of this definition will be made clear after stating the following proposition. Let us just mention now that the probability given by the tail of the binomial law has to be multiplied by the number of tests done, i.e., the considered number (L) of quantized values of the gradient direction and the overall number $(N_\mathcal{B})$ of tested images, to evaluate the NFA.

Proposition 1. *For a database of $N_\mathcal{B}$ images such that the gradient direction difference with a query u has been generated by the background model, the expected number of v such that (u, v) is ε-meaningful is less or equal than ε.*

Proof. For all i, let us denote by K_i the random number of points among the x_j such that $D(x_j)$ is less than α_i. For any v, (u, v) is ε-meaningful, if there is at least $1 \leqslant i \leqslant L$ such that $N_\mathcal{B} \cdot L \cdot B(M, K_i, q_{\alpha_i}) < \varepsilon$. Let us denote by $E(v, i)$ this event. Its probability $P_{\mathcal{H}_0}(E(v, i))$ satisfies

$$P_{\mathcal{H}_0}(E(v, i)) \leqslant \frac{\varepsilon}{L \cdot N_\mathcal{B}}.$$

Indeed, for any real random variable X with survival function $H(x) = P(X > x)$, it is a classical fact that $P(H(X) < x) \leqslant x$. By applying this result to K_i, we get the upper bound on $P(E(v, i))$. The event $E(v)$ defined by "(u, v) is ε-meaningful" is $E(v) = \cup_{1 \leqslant i \leqslant L} E(v, i)$. Let us denote by $\mathbb{E}_{\mathcal{H}_0}$ the mathematical expectation under the *a contrario* assumption. Then

$$\mathbb{E}_{\mathcal{H}_0}\left(\sum_{v \in \mathcal{B}} 1_{E(v)}\right) = \sum_{v \in \mathcal{B}} \mathbb{E}_{\mathcal{H}_0}(1_{E(v)})$$

$$\leqslant \sum_{\substack{v \in \mathcal{B} \\ 1 \leqslant i \leqslant L}} P_{\mathcal{H}_0}(E(v, i))$$

$$\leqslant \sum_{\substack{v \in \mathcal{B} \\ 1 \leqslant i \leqslant L}} \frac{\varepsilon}{L \cdot N_{\mathcal{B}}} = \varepsilon. \qquad \square$$

Definition 1 together with Proposition 1 mean that there is in average less than ε images v in the database $\mathcal{B}$ that could match with u by chance, that is to say, when $\mathcal{H}_0$ holds. As a matter of fact, any detection must be considered as a false alarm under hypothesis $\mathcal{H}_0$ (hence the denomination of NFA - number of false alarms -, which might be at first misleading for the reader since the NFA value is used to detect the really similar image pairs, as specified in the Algorithm summary given next page).

Thus, it is chosen to eliminate any observation (i.e., any image v, given image u) having a frequency of the order of ε (or more) in the *a contrario* model. In Section 5.1, it will be checked that Hypothesis $\mathcal{H}_0$ is sound for two unrelated images.

Even though this is theoretically simple, it may be difficult to numerically evaluate the tail of the binomial law. A sufficient and more tractable condition of meaningfulness is given by the following classical result, first proved by Hoeffding [6].

Proposition 2. *Let $H(r, p) = r \ln \frac{r}{p} + (1 - r) \ln \frac{1-r}{1-p}$, be the relative entropy of two Bernoulli laws with parameters r and p. Then, for $k \geqslant Mp$,*

$$B(M, k, p) \leqslant \exp\left(-M \cdot H\left(\frac{k}{M}, p\right)\right). \tag{2}$$

This inequality leads to the following sufficient condition of meaningfulness.

Corollary 1. *If*

$$\max_{\substack{1 \leqslant i \leqslant L \\ k_i \geqslant Mq_{\alpha_i}}} H\left(\frac{k_i}{M}, q_{\alpha_i}\right) > \frac{1}{M} \ln \frac{LN_{\mathcal{B}}}{\varepsilon}, \tag{3}$$

the pair (u, v) is ε-meaningful.

In this corollary, it appears clearly that the values of k such that (u, v) is ε-meaningful only depends on the logarithm of L, $N_{\mathcal{B}}$ and ε. In practice, we choose L about 32 which is compatible with our perceptual accuracy of directions. In other terms, the α_i must be understood as quantization steps of $(0, \pi)$. We also take $\varepsilon = 1$ since it means that we may have in average less than 1-false detection. However, as we shall see, really similar images have much smaller NFA and the choice of ε is not really important. Thus, in all experiments, we always set $\varepsilon = 1$, and we can therefore claim that the decision threshold is automatically derived.

The algorithm to be implemented is actually simple and of very low computational complexity. Indeed, it involves only a few computations as indicated below.

Algorithm

Let us fix $M > 1$, and L quantized values $(\alpha_i)_{1 \leqslant i \leqslant L}$.
For a pair of image u, v:

1. Draw M random points x_1, ..., x_M.
2. Compute the difference of the gradient direction $D(x_j)$.
3. For each i
   (a) Count the number of x_j such that $D(x_j) \leqslant \alpha_i$, denoted by k_i.
   (b) Compute $N_{\mathcal{B}} L \sum_{n=k_i}^{M} \binom{M}{n} q_{\alpha_i}^n (1 - q_{\alpha_i})^{M-n}$ (with $q_{\alpha_i} = \frac{\alpha_i}{\pi}$).
4. $NFA(u, v)$ is the minimum of these values.
5. Test if $NFA(u, v) \leqslant \varepsilon$.

In practice, we take M varies between 200 and 500 (this is discussed below), $L = 32$ (this hardly has any incidence). Let us point out that the quantity $-\log_{10} NFA$ can be considered as a confidence level, while being a more tractable number.

4 Random Sampling

4.1 Problem Statement

The *a contrario* model assumes that the values $D(x_j)$ are i.i.d. in $(0, \pi)$. This implicitly means that it is assumed that the direction $\theta_u(x_j)$ and $\theta_v(x_j)$ are independent for a given x_j, and that all the directions $\theta_u(x_j)$ are also mutually independent. (The same holds for v.) The NFA is nothing but a measure of the deviation to this hypothesis. If a few points are randomly drawn in the image, this assumption is clearly reasonable. However, since natural images contain alignments the second assumption becomes clearly false if we sample too many points. Moreover, if the two images have a casual alignment in common, this segment will induce a very strong deviation from the independence assumption, and the images could be wrongly considered as similar. We then face the following dilemma for choosing the number of samples M:

- it must be large enough to allow us to contradict the independence hypothesis and to obtain small values of the number of false alarms for two similar images.
- it must be small enough to avoid the "common alignment problem". If we draw a few hundreds points uniformly in the images, then they are aligned very unlikely.

In order to evaluate the typical magnitude of the number of sample points, let us assume that v differs from u by an additive Gaussian noise $\mathcal{N}(0, \sigma^2)$, which will be our hypothesis $\mathcal{H}_1$. We insist that we use this $\mathcal{H}_1$ to only determine the magnitude of the sufficient number of sample points, but since we cannot assert that this model is realistic, the detection eventually relies only upon the background model $\mathcal{H}_0$. By computing the gradient by a finite difference scheme, it is possible to assume that the gradient coordinates of v are also corrupted by a white Gaussian noise (with a variance depending on the numerical scheme). If the law of the gradient norm is empirically estimated, it becomes possible to compute the law of the direction variation D, $P_{\mathcal{H}_1}(D < \alpha)$.

4.2   Bounds on the Number of Sample Points

By definition, we detect the pair (u, v) as ε-meaningful, if $NFA(u, v) < \varepsilon$. If $\mathcal{H}_1$ holds, we would like to detected meaningful pairs with a high probability. Hence, we would like the value $P(NFA(u, v) < \varepsilon | \mathcal{H}_1)$ to be large whenever v is a (noisy) version of u. Let us also assume that u is an image of a query base $\mathcal{Q}$ containing $N_{\mathcal{Q}}$ images (and v is still in the database $\mathcal{B}$). If we want less than ε detection in the *a contrario* model by comparing all the pairs in $\mathcal{Q} \times \mathcal{B}$, we have to multiply the NFA definition (1) by $N_{\mathcal{Q}}$. Let

$$k_\alpha = \inf\{k, \text{ s.t. } N_{\mathcal{Q}} \cdot N_{\mathcal{B}} \cdot L \cdot B(M, k, q_\alpha) < \varepsilon\}.$$

To make things simpler, assume that we compute the NFA with only one value of angle α (so that $L = 1$). Since there is no ambiguity, we drop the subscript α. If K is the random number of points such that $D < \alpha$, the pair (u, v) is detected if and only if $K \geqslant k$. The probability of detection under $\mathcal{H}_1$ is therefore

$$P_D \equiv P(K \geqslant k | \mathcal{H}_1) = B(M, k, p). \qquad (4)$$

where

$$p = P_{\mathcal{H}_1}(D < \alpha),$$

which is known, since we have here a model of noise.

Definition 2. *We call number of misses*

$$\mathcal{M}(M, k) = N_{\mathcal{Q}} N_{\mathcal{B}}(1 - B(M, k, p)). \qquad (5)$$

As for the number of false alarms, if $\mathcal{M}(M, k) < \varepsilon$, it is clear that the expected number of misdetections under hypothesis $\mathcal{H}_1$ is less than ε.

   The noise model clearly implies that p (the probability that gradient directions are alike when both images are the same) is larger than q (probability that the directions are alike for unrelated images, i.e. the *a contrario* model) unless the images are constant of $\sigma = +\infty$, which is of little interest, and $p \to q$ when $\sigma \to +\infty$ (up to a normalization of grey level, the image tends to a white noise).

From estimates on the tail of the binomial law, we obtain the following necessary conditions on the number of samples M.

Proposition 3. *Assume that $\mathcal{M}(M, k) < \varepsilon$. Then, for some positive constant $C \simeq 0.39246$,*

$$M(p - q)^2 \geq \min(p(1 - p), q(1 - q)) \left(C + \ln \frac{N_{\mathcal{Q}} N_{\mathcal{B}}}{\varepsilon \sqrt{M}} \right). \qquad (6)$$

The proof is given in appendix.

The estimate above tells that, when the noise amount σ becomes large, M grows like $\frac{1}{(p-q)^2}$. This is not strictly exact because of the $\ln M$ term on the right side of (6). This term is unavoidable since it appears in any sharp lower bound of the tail of the binomial law. In the following Proposition 4, it will be proved that the order of magnitude $O((p - q)^{-2})$ is sufficient.

Proposition 4. *If*

$$M \geq \frac{2}{(p - q)^2} \ln \frac{N_{\mathcal{B}} N_{\mathcal{Q}}}{\varepsilon}. \qquad (7)$$

then $\mathcal{M}(M, k) < \varepsilon$.

In practice, we do not know neither that the two images are the same nor the amount of noise. However, the purpose of this result is to determine the order of magnitude of the sufficient number of sample points. Numerical evaluation shows that it is a few hundreds which is compatible with the size of usual images.

5   Numerical Applications and Experiments

5.1   Justification of the Background Model

The background model should be sound for two unrelated images. Let us make the following experiment. Let us compute the empirical distribution of the gradient direction on two images. Because of quantization and presence of strongly privileged directions, these two histograms are not uniform at all. Nevertheless, the distribution of the difference of the directions, taken at *two* random locations (that is, different points in the two images) is the circular convolution of these histograms. On many pairs of images, we indeed checked that the difference of the repartition function with a uniform distribution in $(-\pi, \pi)$ is everywhere less than 0.01.

5.2   Number of Sample Points Under Hypothesis $\mathcal{H}_1$

On Fig. 1, we discuss (see the caption) the relation between σ (the noise standard deviation), M (the number of sample points) and the detection rate as explained in subsection 4.2. By varying σ and M, we empirically retrieve the bound estimate of subsection 4.2.

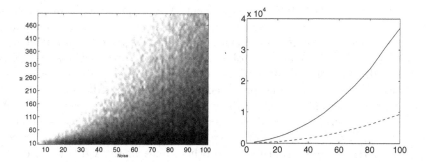

Fig. 1. We match an image with some of its corrupted versions by a white Gaussian noise, for σ varying between 5 and 100 (horizontal axis), and for a number of samples M between 10 and 500 (vertical axis). For each couple (σ, M), 50 trials are drawn, yielding $N_B = 250000$. The grey level in the left plot is the number of similarity detections (white for 50 and black for 0). The curves on the right are the sufficient and necessary values of M for controlling the number of misses, given by (6) and (7) respectively. As expected, the empirical results on the left are between these curves and bounds are not sharp.

5.3   Experiments of Image Retrieval and Image Comparison

We have tested the robustness of the method for image retrieval in a video stream with respect to the following degradations: noise (impulse, Gaussian or JPEG compression), transparency, partial occlusion. The image comparison is directly applied with no preprocessing of any type. There are actually some applications to such a detection method: for instance, to segment television video stream one may look for particular jingles or some recurrent images. Current methods work by computing local features and matching them. It thus requires to pre-compute those features, organize and store them in feature databases. The proposed method only needs the spatial image gradient on a few hundred points.

Fig. 2. The middle image is a 50% impulse noise version of the original one. In a database of 10^5 images, they still match with a NFA close to 10^{-5}. The right plot shows the confidence values $(-\log_{10}(NFA))$ for the first 50000 images of the sequence, the query being the noisy image. The peaks indeed correspond to exactly the same view of the stadium.

We first consider the following experiment. We select a single image in a sequence containing about one hour program of an athletics meeting (86096 images). This image represents a view of the stadium. To make the problem still more complex and to evaluate the robustness to noise, a white Gaussian noise with standard deviation $\sigma = 30$ is added to this image, and the resulting image will be taken as the query. The proposed criterion is applied with $M = 500$ random sample points in the images. The true image was detected with a NFA equal to 10^{-14}. About 20 images (belonging to the same static shot) are detected around the true image, which is of course correct as well. Moreover, this very same view of the stadium appears three other times in the video (before the selected true image). All of them are detected with a very low NFA (or equivalently, with a high confidence value, as shown in Fig.2). There was a single true false alarm (unrelated image) with a NFA equal to $10^{-0.73}$, which was probably due to the presence of the logo, but this NFA is coherent with the prediction: it is close to 1. No false alarms were obtained for an impulse noise of 50%. We have also applied JPEG compression to the original images. Extreme JPEG compression (quality less than 10) may lead to false detections since gradient orientation is constrained by the blocking effect. For usual compression ratio (quality 75), this effect was not observed.

On Fig. 3, two images of a movie are compared. The scene exhibits a strong transparency effect and an important contrast change. Thus, the grey levels in those images are different. Obviously, image intensity is not a good criterion at all, since the images apparences are different although the images clearly have a common cause. The gradient direction comparison proves that these images are similar in the sense that there resemblance cannot be explained by the *a contrario* model. It was empirically checked that sample points were quite uniformly distributed in the images. This experiment demonstrates that we are able to assess that two images are similar even if they are affected by transparency effects.

Fig. 4 shows the robustness to partial occlusion. The score panel occludes the bottom part of the image in this video of tennis match. The two images are detected as very similar since their NFA is about 10^{-50}. Since an hour of

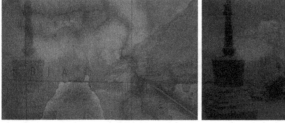

Fig. 3. Robustness to transparency. The two images are selected from a movie. The background is fixed, but the contrast changes a lot and a transparency layer is also moving. Nevertheless, with 200 sample points, the confidence value is $-\log_{10}(NFA) = 43.2$, and images are thus detected as very similar.

video contains about 10^5 images, such a NFA value asserts that the image pairing remains meaningful for any size of database. The threshold on the image gradient norm is equal to 5 in this experiment. If we take it equal to 0.2 (still with 200 sample points), the NFA increases since we select points where the gradient orientation is dominated by quantization. However, with an equal probability, we select points with larger gradients, and the gradient directions then match very well. Therefore, the NFA is still very low, and about 10^{-32}.

Fig. 4. Robustness to occlusion. Despite the partial occlusion the two images are detected as very similar with confidence value of $-\log_{10}(NFA) = 50.1$. The right plot gives the position of the 200 sample points. There are not points in constant areas (because of the gradient threshold). However, some points are selected in the non-matching area (scores), but the NFA is still very low.

As a last experiment, let us give a short insight of how geometrical invariance might be taken into account. We apply exactly the same decision scheme to pairs of consecutive images in a video sequence, but we first register the images by using the robust multiresolution motion estimation method by Odobez and Bouthemy [12], (the corresponding Motion-2D software is available on line at http://www.irisa.fr.vista/Motion2D) which computes a 2D parametric motion model that corresponds to the dominant image motion, which is usually related to the camera motion. The evolution of the NFA through time is represented on Fig. 5 (more precisely, the confidence values given by $-\log_{10}(NFA)$ are plotted). It indicates if the consecutive images of the video sequence (once registered) can be stated as similar or not. As expected, confidence is high in case of similarity since NFA are always lower than 10^{-20}, except at very precise instants that correspond to shot changes. Let us point out that an accurate registration of the two images to be compared is nevertheless required to properly exploit the proposed method for image similarity detection.

6   Conclusion and Perspectives

We have described a novel and fast method allowing us to efficiently compare two images from a random sampling of points and to decide whether they are actually similar or not. It can be used for image comparison and image retrieval in databases or in video stream. Actually, the argument is quite general and the

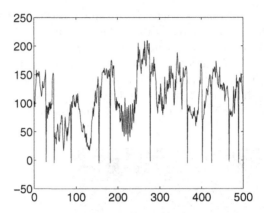

Fig. 5. Similarity evaluation between successive images of a video stream after registration. Plot of the confidence values $-\log_{10}(NFA)$) for 500 consecutive pairs in a MPEG video sequence. Most of the time, the NFA is below 10^{-20}. The sudden drops correspond to shot changes. The NFA is thus a reliable value as predicted by Proposition 1.

thresholds are rigorously proved to be robust and can be fixed once for all, for any type of images. Hence the user does not have to tune any parameter. Preliminary results have demonstrated the accuracy and the efficiency of the proposed method. Nevertheless, a more extensive experimental evaluation could be carried out. As an extension, our approach could also be applied to parts of images instead of entire images, so that the methodology could be used in many other applications of image retrieval, image matching or registration evaluation. These parts of images could be extracted from local characteristics as keypoints [11] or local frame based on stable directions [7,14]. We could then estimate the same detection bounds for system similar to [15]. This work is in progress.

A   Proofs

Proof of Prop. 3. From (4), we know that $1 - P_D = B(M, M - k, 1 - p)$. A refined Stirling inequality [3] implies that

$$\frac{\varepsilon}{N_B N_Q} > B(M, M - k, 1 - p)$$

$$\geqslant \binom{M}{M - k} (1 - p)^{M-k} p^k$$

$$\geqslant \frac{2}{\sqrt{2\pi M}} e^{-1/6} e^{-MH(1-k/M,1-p)}.$$

Thus

$$M \cdot H\left(1 - \frac{k}{M}, 1 - p\right) > C + \ln \frac{N_B N_Q}{\varepsilon \sqrt{M}},$$

with $C = \frac{1}{6} + \frac{1}{2}\ln\frac{\pi}{2} \simeq 0.39246$. Since $k > Mq$, we also have $H\left(1 - \frac{k}{M}, 1 - p\right) < H(1 - q, 1 - p)$. By convexity of H,

$$H(1 - q, 1 - p) \leqslant (p - q)\partial_x H(1 - q, 1 - p) = (p - q)\ln\left(\frac{1 - q}{q}\frac{p}{1 - p}\right).$$

Moreover

$$\ln\left(\frac{1 - q}{q}\frac{p}{1 - p}\right) = \int_q^p \frac{dx}{x(1 - x)} \leqslant (p - q)\max_{x\in[p,q]}\frac{1}{x(1 - x)}.$$

Since the function on the right hand side is convex, it attains its maximum on the boundary of the interval, and this completes the proof. □

Proof of Prop. 4. We first prove the following lemma, bounding from above the number of samples necessary to pass the test of similarity.

Lemma 1. *Let us fix $M > 0$ and $L = 1$ and let k be the minimal number of samples with similar directions such that the pair (u, v) is ε-meaningful.*

$$k \leqslant 1 + Mq + \left(\frac{M}{2}\left(\ln\frac{N_B N_Q}{\varepsilon}\right)\right)^{1/2}. \tag{8}$$

Proof. Since $k = \inf\{j \text{ s.t. } N_B N_Q \cdot B(M, k, q) < \varepsilon\}$, $B(M, k - 1, q) > \frac{\varepsilon}{N_B N_Q}$ holds, also yielding

$$H\left(\frac{k - 1}{M}, q\right) < \frac{1}{M}\ln\frac{N_B N_Q}{\varepsilon}.$$

Convexity properties of the entropy H yield $H(r, q) \geqslant 2(r - q)^2$. Setting $r = \frac{k-1}{M}$ gives the result. □

If M is large enough, we can assume that $k < Mp$ from (8). A sufficient condition to $\mathcal{M}(M, P) < \varepsilon$ is

$$H\left(1 - \frac{k}{M}, 1 - p\right) > \frac{1}{M}\ln\frac{N_B N_Q}{\varepsilon}$$

Since by convexity $H(r, p) \geqslant 2(r - p)^2$, it suffices that

$$2\left(p - \frac{k}{M}\right)^2 \geqslant \frac{1}{M}\ln\frac{N_B N_Q}{\varepsilon},$$

which is implied by

$$p - q - \left(\frac{1}{2M}\ln\frac{N_B N_Q}{\varepsilon}\right)^{1/2} > \left(\frac{1}{2M}\ln\frac{N_B N_Q}{\varepsilon}\right)^{1/2},$$

and the result directly follows. □

References

1. R. Brunelli, O. Mich and C.M. Modena. A survey on the automatic indexing of video data. *Jal of Visual Communication and Image Representation*, 10(2):78–112, 1999.
2. A. Desolneux, L. Moisan, and J.M. Morel. A grouping principle and four applications. *IEEE Trans. on Pattern Analysis and Machine Intelligence*, 25(4):508–513, April 2003.
3. W. Feller. *An Introduction to Probability Theory and its Applications*, volume I. J. Wiley, 3rd edition, 1968.
4. M.A. Fischler and R. C. Bolles. Random sample consensus: a paradigm for model fitting with applications to image analysis and automated cartography. *Communications of the ACM*, 24(6):381–395, 1981.
5. W.E.L. Grimson and D.P. Huttenlocher. On the sensitivity of the Hough transform for object recognition. *IEEE Trans. on Pattern Analysis and Machine Intelligence*, 12(3):255–274, 1990.
6. W. Hoeffding. Probability inequalities for sum of bounded random variables. *J. of the Am. Stat. Assoc.*, 58:13–30, 1963.
7. J.L. Lisani, L. Moisan, P. Monasse, and J.M. Morel. On the theory of planar shape. *SIAM Multiscale Mod. and Sim.*, 1(1):1–24, 2003.
8. J.L. Lisani and J.M. Morel. Detection of major changes in satellite images. In *IEEE Int. Conf. on Image Processing*, ICIP'03, Barcelona, Sept. 2003.
9. D. Lowe. Object recognition from local scale-invariant features. In *IEEE Int. Conf. on Computer Vision*, ICCV'99, Corfu, Sept. 1999.
10. D. Lowe. Distinctive image features from scale-invariant keypoints. *Int. Jal of Computer Vision*, 60(2):91–110, 2004.
11. K. Mikolajczyk, T. Tuytelaars, C. Schmid, A. Zisserman, J. Matas, F. Schaffalitzky, T. Kadir, and L. Van Gool. A comparison of affine region detectors. *Int. Jal of Computer Vision*, 65(1-2):43 - 72, November 2005.
12. J.M. Odobez and P. Bouthemy. Robust multiresolution estimation of parametric motion models. *Jal of Visual Communication and Image Representation*, 6(4):348–365, 1995.
13. J. Peng, B. Yu, and D. Wang Images similarity detection based on directional gradient angular histogram. *16th Int. Conf. on Pattern Recognition*, ICPR'02, Quebec, August 2002.
14. C.A. Rothwell. *Object Recognition Through Invariant Indexing*. Oxford Science Publications, 1995.
15. J. Sivic and A. Zisserman. Video Google: a text retrieval approach to object matching in videos. In *IEEE Int. Conf. on Computer Vision*, ICCV'03, Nice, Oct. 2003.
16. A.W.M. Smeulders, M. Worring, S. Santini, A. Gupta, and R. Jain. Content-based image retrieval at the end of the early years. *IEEE Transactions on Pattern Analysis and Machine Intelligence*, 22(12):1349–1380, 2000.
17. A. Venot, J.F. Lebruchec, and J.C. Roucayrol. A new class of similarity measures for robust image registration. *Computer Vision Graphics and Image Processing*, 28:176–184, 1982.
18. T. Veit, F. Cao and P. Bouthemy. Probabilistic parameter-free motion detection. In *IEEE Conf. on Computer Vision and Pattern Recognition*, CVPR'04, Washington D.C., June 2004.

Rank-Test Similarity Measure Between Video Segments for Local Descriptors

Alain Lehmann, Patrick Bouthemy, and Jian-Feng Yao

IRISA/INRIA
Campus universitaire de Beaulieu
35042 Rennes Cedex, France

Abstract. This paper presents a novel and efficient similarity measure between video segments. We consider local spatio-temporal descriptors. They are considered to be realizations of an unknown, but class-specific distribution. The similarity of two video segments is calculated by evaluating an appropriate statistical criterion issued from a rank test. It does not require any matching of the local features between the two considered video segments, and can deal with a different number of computed local features in the two segments. Furthermore, our measure is self-normalized which allows for simple cue integration, and even on-line adapted class-dependent combination of the different descriptors. Satisfactory results have been obtained on real video sequences for two motion event recognition problems.

1 Introduction

Since the amount of multimedia data is rapidly growing, automatic systems are needed to process this huge amount of data. Therefore, the development of methods which are able to recognize semantically similar things is crucial. Such methods must be applicable in the context of video databases to group similar video segments together, to satisfy queries, to browse or to summarize videos [2,3,5,7,9,10].

To perform a recognition task, one has to define the descriptors to be extracted from the video segment. Two complementary approaches can be distinguished. The fist category extracts global features from the whole video segment. They are simple to implement, but may have problems with complex scenes. An example for motion recognition using a global approach is [14] where a simple non-parametric distance measure based on histograms of spatial and temporal intensity gradients has been used. In [11], sports videos have been characterized with probabilistic motion models describing the dominant image motion (i.e. the camera motion) and the residual scene motion. These models are learnt from global occurrence statistics computed over the whole video segment and maximum likelihood (ML) criteria were used.

On the other hand, local methods extract features from spatio-temporally localized regions to alleviate the problems of the global approach. A difficulty of these local approaches is, however, that the segments are no longer represented by a single feature vector, but a set of feature vectors. As a consequence, the comparison of segments is no longer straightforward and is normally achieved by matching the local features between the processed video and videos of the database. In [8], a set of local space-time

S. Marchand-Maillet et al. (Eds.): AMR 2006, LNCS 4398, pp. 71–81, 2007.

descriptors for recognizing motion patterns are presented and evaluated. The matching of the features is done in a greedy manner, whereas different distance measures have been tested.

Our method belongs to the local approach category and aims at overcoming the remaining difficulties faced by local methods. More specifically, we have designed an original dissimilarity measure which does not need an explicit pairing of the local feature vectors of the two segments and can deal with a different number of computed feature vectors in the two segments to be compared. It is based on a simple statistical test and is easy to compute as it involves ranking operations only. The (general) assumption behind our approach is that the observed values of each local descriptor in a video segment is drawn from a given (but unknown) distribution which depends on the dynamic-content class that the video segment belongs to. The basic idea is then simply to test whether the two feature value sets extracted from the two video segments for the considered local descriptor are generated from the same class-dependent distribution or not. Furthermore, we can combine the different local descriptors in a class-dependent adaptive way. We have considered two types of local motion-related descriptors for characterizing the dynamic content of a video sequence. The first one accounts for the space-time spread of the interest points which is assumed to be related to the trajectory of the moving objects. The second one attempts to capture the intensity of the motion, and we have actually adapted the scene motion model of [11] to our local setup.

As the description of motion events is a non-trivial problem, a single descriptor is indeed not sufficient and a group of local descriptors has to be used. Boosting [4,13] has become a popular method for automatic feature selection or combination. However, the generalization to multi-class classification is not obvious, even if some investigations have been undertaken [12]. A disadvantage of the boosting algorithms is however their computationally expensive learning stage. We have defined a simple method which is able to learn the ability of the individual descriptors to discriminate a given class from the remaining ones. It is then exploited to deduce a proper weighting to combine the different local descriptors in the designed statistical test.

The remainder of this paper is organized as follows. The classification framework comprising the statistical dissimilarity measure and the cue integration technique is introduced in Section 2. In Section 3, the interest point selection stage and the considered local motion features are presented. Finally, experimental results of motion event classification are reported in Section 4. Concluding remarks are given in Section 5.

2   Classification Framework

2.1   Dissimilarity Measure Between Two Video Segments

The task of motion event recognition can be seen as the problem of classifying a given video segment according to some predefined classes $c \in C$. To achieve this task we are previously given several examples s for each class, for which we know the class membership, i.e. $C(s) \in C$. This set of examples will be further denoted as video database S. The problem of event recognition can be formulated as the search for the minimum of a dissimilarity function Φ:

$$\hat{C}(r) = \arg\min_{c \in \mathcal{C}} \Phi(r|c) \tag{1}$$

where r is the tested video segment. We now reformulate the classification problem as a retrieval problem, i.e, we try to find the most similar segment s^* in our database S and base the classification on the class of s^*.

$$\hat{C}(r) = C(s^*), \quad \text{where } s^* = \arg\min_{s \in \mathcal{S}} \Phi(r, s|C(s)) \tag{2}$$

Actually, we consider the three best segments using majority voting to increase the robustness. In case that all three segments belong to different classes, the class of the best segment is chosen. In order to find the most similar segment we have to define a dissimilarity measure for two given segments r and s which may be class dependent. This class dependency can be justified by the fact that not all given descriptors have to be characteristic for all given classes. However, we have to ensure that the different dissimilarity measures are comparable in terms of their values such that a segment which is more similar than one of another class also gets a smaller value.

Before we can define a dissimilarity measure, we have to specify how we represent a given video segment. As stated in the introduction, we use local features to characterize the segment content, that is a set of feature values. The considered local spatio-temporal descriptors will be introduced in Section 3 along with the technique to select the spatio-temporally localized regions of interest where these local descriptors are computed.

As one single descriptor is not sufficient to capture the complex notion of a motion event, we indeed consider a set of $d = 1 \ldots L$ different local descriptors. Hence, we also have to specify a way to combine the dissimilarity values of the different descriptors. We consider a weighted sum, and the dissimilarity measure between two video segments r and s is finally given by

$$\Phi(r, s|(C(s)) = \sum_{d=1}^{L} \omega_d(C(s))T_d(r, s) \tag{3}$$

where T_d is a similarity test which is now defined in the next subsection and ω_d is a family of class-dependent weights which will be explained in subsection 2.3.

2.2 Wilcoxon Rank-Sum Test

In a method using local descriptors, a video segment is represented by a *set* of m feature vectors of dimension L (the number of considered descriptors), where m is the number of selected interest points in the video segment. We are then facing the problem of comparing two sets of feature values $\mathcal{F}_r, \mathcal{F}_s$ of not necessarily equal size m_r, m_s.

Let us first consider the case where we exploit a single descriptor only ($L = 1$). Instead of establishing correspondence between the elements of the two sets, we consider the values as realizations of an unknown distribution $\mathcal{D}$. Hence, to decide whether two segments r, s are from the same class it is sufficient to decide, whether the values are drawn from the same unknown distribution or not, i.e. testing the hypothesis $\mathcal{H}_0 : \mathcal{D}_r \equiv \mathcal{D}_s$.

Accordingly, we have to deal with two sets of scalar values only in that case (i.e., the values of the local descriptor computed in the video segments r and s respectively).

The two-sample Wilcoxon rank-sum test is a well-known statistical method to test this hypothesis $\mathcal{H}_0$ for scalar values [6]. This non-parametric test has the advantage to be distribution-free and avoids the fit of any specific model. More precisely, the Wilcoxon rank-sum statistic (in a normalized form) is expressed as:

$$W_d = \left(\frac{12(m_r + m_s)}{m_r m_s}\right)^{\frac{1}{2}} \sum_{j=1}^{m_r} \left(\frac{R_j}{m_r + m_s + 1} - \frac{1}{2}\right) \tag{4}$$

where R_j is the rank of the j-th value of the first feature set in the combined feature set, i.e., the position in the ordered sequence of the union of descriptor value sets $\mathcal{F}_r$ and $\mathcal{F}_s$. The distribution of W_d will converge for $m_r, m_s \to \infty$ to the $\mathcal{N}(0,1)$-distribution if the hypothesis $\mathcal{H}_0$ is fulfilled. Otherwise, it will be far from zero.

Hence, we define $T_d = W_d^2$ as an indicator of dissimilarity for the local descriptor d (since positive values are required to establish the combined dissimilarity measure between video segments as defined in Eq.(3)). As a consequence of its non-parametric form, T_d is distribution-free. In particular, it is independent of the magnitude of the compared feature values. This property is important when we consider a class-dependent weighting as it automatically ensures the normalization of the dissimilarity value for all considered descriptors.

2.3 Feature Combination by Weighting

As the Wilcoxon rank-sum test is only defined for scalar data, we cannot apply the test directly on the descriptor tuples. Instead, we treat each local descriptor separately as an individual descriptor and we will then combine the individual evaluations T_d as defined in Eq.(3).

The simplest way to combine the dissimilarity of all individual descriptors would be to just sum them, i.e., a uniform weighting. However, not all descriptors have to be relevant for all classes and hence, a uniform weighting may arbitrarily degrade the quality of the overall dissimilarity measure. Instead, we try to learn the discriminative power of each individual descriptor d from the training data and deduce a proper weighting function ω for our overall dissimilarity measure defined in Eq.(3).

An indicator for the appropriateness of a descriptor d is the success probability $\mathcal{P}[t_c < t_f | d]$ that the test value t_c for a segment pair (i.e., the pair formed by the tested segment r and the segment s considered in the database) yielding a correct classification is smaller than the value t_f for a segment pair yielding a false one. More precisely, we consider the two cases where either both segments of the pair are of the same class c or one segment is of class c and the other one is *not* of class c, and we define the corresponding conditional probability densities of the test value:

$$\begin{aligned} p_d(t|c) &= \mathcal{P}[T_d(r,s) = t | C(r) = C(s) = c] \\ p_d(t|\bar{c}) &= \mathcal{P}[T_d(r,s) = t | C(r) = c, C(s) \neq c] \end{aligned} \tag{5}$$

Hence, the success probability of a descriptor d given a class c can be calculated as

$$\mathrm{Succ}(d|c) = \mathcal{P}(t_c < t_f | t_c \sim p_d(\cdot|c), t_f \sim p_d(\cdot|\bar{c}))$$
$$= \int_0^\infty p_d(t_c|c) \int_{t_c}^\infty p_d(t_f|\bar{c}) dt_f dt_c \tag{6}$$

The empirical histograms of the two conditional distributions (obtained from the training set) exhibit a pronounced peak at zero. We thus represent them using the specific mixture model proposed in [11] for such histograms:

$$\hat{p}_d(t|c) = \lambda_d(c)\delta_0(t) + (1 - \lambda_d(c))\frac{1}{\beta_d(c)} e^{\frac{-t}{\beta_d(c)}} \mathbb{1}_{(t>0)} \tag{7}$$

where δ_0 denotes the indicator function at 0 ($\delta_0(t) = \mathbb{1}_{(t=0)}$). Such a low-dimensional parametric probabilistic model introduces an implicit smoothing which prevents overfitting to the data. In practice, the estimate for the mixture weight λ_d is defined as the fraction of samples $t < \epsilon$ (typically, with $\epsilon = 0.1$). The estimate for $\beta_d(c)$ is simply the mean of all values $t \geq \epsilon$. The formula for $\hat{p}_d(t|\bar{c})$ is similar. The equation for the success probability can now be calculated as:

$$\mathrm{Succ}(d|c) = \lambda_d(c) + (1 - \lambda_d(c))(1 - \lambda_d(\bar{c}))\frac{\beta_d(\bar{c})}{\beta_d(c) + \beta_d(\bar{c})} \tag{8}$$

To keep the final dissimilarity measures comparable across different classes, we have to normalize these success probabilities, so that the sum over all descriptor types is one. Since the differences of these probabilities are rather small, we apply an exponential stretchting to get finally the family of weights:

$$w_d(c) = \frac{1}{Z} e^{\alpha \mathrm{Succ}(d|c)} \qquad \text{with } Z = \sum_d e^{\alpha \mathrm{Succ}(d|c)} \tag{9}$$

We empirically found $\alpha = 10$ to be convenient.

3   Local Motion Features

3.1   Selection of the Interest Points

The selection of the interest points where the set of local descriptors will be computed is based on a simple criterion to retain the regions with a high density of scene motion activity, i.e.,

$$A(p,t) = \frac{1}{|\mathcal{W}|} \sharp \{(q, \tau) \in \mathcal{W}(p,t) : |FD(q,\tau)| > \gamma\} \tag{10}$$

where $\mathcal{W}$ is a spatio-temporal neighbourhood window (e.g. $15 \times 15 \times 3$) and the FD is the temporal frame difference, $FD(p,t) = I(p, t+1) - I(p,t)$ where I is the intensity function. We can also accomodate the case of a moving camera by first compensating the dominant image motion (represented by an affine motion model) which can be usually assumed to be related to the camera motion. Then, it can be cancelled by considering the DFD (Displaced Frame Difference) values, instead of the FD values, defined by $DFD_\theta(p,t) = I(p + w_{\hat\theta_t}(p), t+1) - I(p,t)$, where θ designates the vector of six parameters involved in the affine motion model. Concerning the threshold γ, we set $\gamma = 80$ which results in a highly selective process. We could use as well a more elaborated scheme to select the space-time interest points such as the one proposed in [8], but it turned out that this simple way was sufficient for the experiments we carried out.

The actual selection of the points is achieved in a greedy fashion, where we successively select points with maximal value of criterion (10). To avoid that all points are selected from about the same positions, and hence, to ensure that they are sufficiently spread over the whole video segment, we successively mask the surrounding of every selected interest point. Accordingly, the criterion $A(p,t)$ is explicitly modified after each selection in the sense that all FD (or DFD) values in a neighbourhood $\mathcal{W}'$ of the selected interest point are set to zero. In our experiments, this mask $\mathcal{W}'$ has been chosen such that the blocks $\mathcal{B}$ which are introduced in subsection 3.3 do not overlap.

The selection process is stopped as soon as the criterion value falls below a threshold related to the initial criterion maximum, i.e., $\tau \max_{(p,t)} A(p,t)$, while we used $\tau = 0.01$ in the experiments.

3.2   Trajectory Information

The trajectory of the moving objects in the image sequence seems an appropriate descriptor to characterize motion content in video. However, the automatic detection of objects and the estimation of their trajectories in complex scenes are not that easy. Hence, we introduce a much simpler local descriptor which tries to capture the space-time spread of the interest points. Its value can be considered as a sample of the distribution accounting for the cloud shape formed by the detected interest points. Let us consider the 3D point cloud (see Fig. 1) generated by the interest points in the volume formed by the image sequence.

Since we must not consider the absolute position of the moving objects (as we do not assume the video segments to be aligned), but only their relative space-time evolution, we have to compute local measurements relatively to the center of gravity of these points.

To compactly describe the point cloud, we consider for each interest point $p_i = (x_i, y_i, t_i)$ the following measurement: $\nu(p_i) = (x_i - \bar{x})^g (y_i - \bar{y})^h (t_i - \bar{t})^l$, of order $o = g + h + l$, where $(\bar{x}, \bar{y}, \bar{t})$ is the center of gravity of all interest points. Hence, we can calculate a feature vector for each interest point p_i where the different components or descriptors correspond to different combinations of g, h and l values. In our experiments, we consider combinations with $o = 1, .., 6$.

Even though these measurements were inspired from the calculation of moments, there are some sensible differences. If we would compare video segments using moments, i.e. the sum of the actually computed quantities, we would face the problem that the range of values of moment differences for different orders are not equivalent. It would make the definition of an appropriate distance measure difficult. Anyway, such a descriptor is a global one and not a local one. A second difference is that the

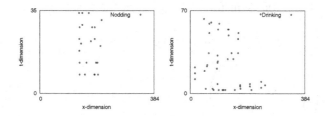

Fig. 1. Illustration of the point clouds (projection onto the xt-plane) for the classes "nodding" (left) and "drinking" (right). In case of "drinking", the subject grabs the glass of water, drinks and puts it back which results in the plotted left-right-left pattern. As "nodding" is just a rotation of the head, a different pattern is then observed.

first-order central moments are always zero by definition and do not yield any information. In contrast, the first-order measurements we consider have proven to be discriminative (by looking at the weighting factors).

3.3 Motion Intensity Information

The motion intensity (velocity) is another important source of information to characterize motion events. If we consider for example walking and running people, the trajectory descriptor could probably not be very different, whereas a velocity-related descriptor should be. We have adapted the scene motion characterization introduced by [11] to our local approach. The histogram of the considered low-level motion features is no longer computed over the whole video segment, but in a block $\mathcal{B}_i$ of size $32 \times 32 \times 5$ surrounding the interest point p_i, where the considered motion feature is the averaged normal flow magnitude

$$\bar{v}(p,t) = \frac{\sum_{q \in \mathcal{W}(p)} \|\nabla I(q,t)\|^2 \cdot |v_n(q,t)|}{\max\left(|\mathcal{W}|\eta^2, \sum_{q \in \mathcal{W}(p)} \|\nabla I(q,t)\|^2\right)} \tag{11}$$

where $\mathcal{W}$ is a 3×3 neighbourhood window, η^2 is a noise related threshold and $v_n = \frac{-\partial I/\partial t}{\|\nabla I\|}$. Again, we could accomodate camera motion, if any, by considering the residual normal flow magnitude.

As proposed in [11], the histogram of these motion quantities is modeled with a mixture distribution of a Dirac measure at 0 (corresponding to the symbolic state "no motion") and a continuous part representing the real motion values. In contrast to [11], the continuous part is modeled with a log-normal distribution instead of the zero-mean Gaussian restricted to $(0, \infty)$, since the latter was no longer suitable for the values computed in most space-time blocks. It can be explained by the fact that the blocks are placed on regions with rather high motion activity. We get for a given block $\mathcal{B}$:

$$\mathcal{P}[v|\mathcal{B}] = \lambda \delta_0(v) + \frac{1-\lambda}{v\sqrt{2\pi}\sigma} e^{-\frac{1}{2}\left(\frac{\log \frac{v}{m}}{\sigma}\right)^2} \mathbb{1}_{(v>0)} \tag{12}$$

The maximum likelihood estimation of the parameters yields:

$$\hat{\lambda} = \frac{1}{M} \sum_{v \in \mathcal{B}} \mathbb{1}_{(v \leqslant \varepsilon)}, \qquad \hat{m} = exp(\hat{\mu}) \qquad \text{with } \hat{\mu} = \frac{1}{\bar{M}} \sum_{v \in \mathcal{B}, v > \varepsilon} \log v \qquad (13)$$

$$\hat{\sigma}^2 = \left(\frac{1}{\bar{M}} \sum_{v \in \mathcal{B}, v > \varepsilon} \log^2 v \right) - \hat{\mu}^2 \qquad (14)$$

where M is the total number of samples in the block $\mathcal{B}$ and $\bar{M}$ is the number of samples with $v > \varepsilon = 0.1$.

4   Motion Event Classification

The performance of our method has been evaluated on two different video databases for two event recognition problems. As the camera is fixed in both cases, we do not have to compensate for camera motion. For the evaluation we used a leave-one-out validation strategy. Every video segment has been classified based on the remaining ones. The group of local descriptors includes for each interest point (or block) the local trajectory-related descriptors up to order 6 and the three local motion intensity descriptors λ, m, σ (or part of them according to the experiments carried out).

4.1   Gesture Video Database

The first considered database consists of human gestures (see Fig. 2). There are six different classes, i.e., "shaking one's head", "nodding", "clapping hands", "answering the phone" and "drinking water". All these gestures have been carried out several times by seven different subjects. The total size of the database is 211 video segments (which correspond here to the acquired clips). Furthermore, it has to be noted that videos are all recorded from the same viewpoint and the subject are centered in the screen.

As all the gesture of the same class of an individual subject resembled each other very much, the validation has further been constrained, so that we not only exclude the current test segment, but all video segments of the same subject. This makes the evaluation still more rigorous.

First, we tested our method using only the trajectory descriptors. The obtained results are reported in Figure 3. To show the influence of our class-dependent weighting scheme, the results using just uniform weighting are shown in the top row. It can be seen, that there is a rather large confusion between the classes "shaking" and "nodding" and also between "clapping" and "waving hands". The first confusion is rather evident as the moving object in both gestures, i.e. the head, stays at the same position and hence, the point cloud is rather compact and shows no significant spatio-temporal evolution. The later one may be explained by the fact that the main motion of both gestures is horizontal. Furthermore, our simple descriptor cannot reveal whether there is one or several moving objects, i.e. both hands in case of "clapping" or one hand in case of "waving".

The results using class-dependent weighting are shown in the bottom row of Figure 3. As for the classes "clapping" and "waving hands", the confusion has been mostly

Fig. 2. Example for each class of the "Gesture" database

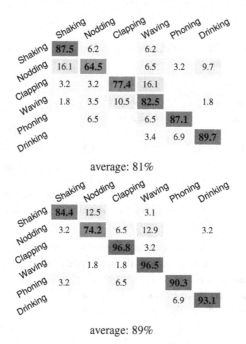

Fig. 3. Confusion matrices for the "Gesture" video database with (top) uniform and (bottom) class-dependent weighting

resolved. Due to the similarity of the two first gesture types (explained before), it still remains a slight confusion between them. Looking at the overall performance, this class-dependent weighting significantly increased the classification rate by 8% to 89%.

The results with the addition of the descriptors of motion intensity are left out as they did not yield any significative further improvements. The fact that all gestures are carried out at more or less the same velocity may explain why these additional descriptors are not capable to increase the performance in this experiment.

4.2 Basketball Video Database

The "Basketball" database (see Fig. 4) consists of 228 video clips of different length. Three event classes are considered: "shot on the basket", "lay-up" and "one-on-one". In contrast to the "Gesture" videos, the videos are taken from a variety of view points; hence, there is no implicit alignment anymore. The camera remains stationary for each shot. The difficulty of these videos is that the intra-class variability is rather high as the movements (especially in case of "one-on-one") are not as clearly defined as for example for "clapping hands".

Fig. 4. Example for each of the three classes of the "Basketball" database: Shot on the basket (left), lay-up (middle) and one-on-one (right)

Fig. 5. Confusion matrices for the "Basketball" video database. Uniform weighting (left), class-dependent weighting (middle) and class-dependent weighting with all descriptors (right).

Again, we considered the classification performance with uniform and class-dependent weighting (see Fig. 5) to show the influence of the later one. We get a rather poor classification rate in case of class "one-on-one" using the uniform weighting. It may be due to the fact that there is always a shot on the basket at the end of the "one-on-one" video segments. As in the first test, the class-dependent weighting is able to correct a lot of misclassifications (while introducing just a very few ones). The overall classification performance is again increased by about 8%.

In contrast to the gesture sequences, the basketball video classes involve a large variability in terms of motion intensity (e.g., sudden movement in case of a dribbling) which can be exploited by the descriptors which characterize the intensity of the movement. The left column in Fig. 5 contains the results which we obtained including the motion intensity descriptors. As expected, the additional descriptors are capable to improve the classification rate further to 90%.

5 Summary and Conclusions

We have proposed a novel dissimilarity measure between video segments for local descriptors based on the Wilcoxon rank-sum test. This measure can be computed very efficiently, and it does not require any pairing of the features of the compared video segments and can straightforwardly handle a different number of feature values (i.e., interest points) per video segment. Accordingly, the video segments can be of different length and no prior alignment between video segments is required. Another appealing property is the easiness to combine several descriptors while taking into account their discriminative power w.r.t. the considered video contents. The proposed framework has been tested on two motion classification problems and quite satisfactory results have been obtained using simple local motion features related to object trajectory and scene motion intensity observed in the image sequence. Comparable results might be reached by some other methods, but the key point here, beyond the very good classification rate obtained considering the difficulty of the motion event recognition problem, is that our method is very general, fast and flexible. The proposed video segment similarity criterion can be applied as well to any kind of features for video comparison, video classification or video retrieval.

Acknowledgements. This work was partly supported by the IST European project Lava.

References

1. R. Brunelli, O. Mich and C.M. Modena. A survey on the automatic indexing of video data. *Jal of Visual Communication and Image Representation*, 10(2):78–112, 1999.
2. D. DeMenthon and D. Doerman. Video retrieval using spatio-temporal descriptors. In *ACM Multimedia'03*, Berkeley, Nov. 2003.
3. N. Dimitrova, H.-J. Zhang, B. Shahraray, I. Sezan, T. Huang and A. Zakhor. Applications of video-content analysis and retrieval. *IEEE Multimedia*, 9(3):42–55, July-September 2002.
4. Y. Freund and R. E. Schapire. A decision-theoretic generalization of on-line learning and an application to boosting. *J. Comput. Syst. Sci.*, 55(1):119–139, 1997.
5. S. Haidar, P. Joly and B. Chebaro. Style similarity measure for video documents comparison. In *Conf. on Image and Video Retrieval*, CIVR'05, Singapore, July 2005.
6. J. Hájek and Z. Šidák. *Theory of rank tests*. Academic Press, New York, 1967.
7. A. Kokaram, N. Rea, R. Dahyot, A.M. Tekalp, P. Bouthemy, P. Gros and I. Sezan. Browsing sports video. *IEEE Signal Processing Magazine*, 23(2):47-58, March 2006.
8. I. Laptev and T. Lindeberg. Local descriptors for spatio-temporal recognition. In *SCVMA'04, Int. Workshop on Spatial Coherence for Visual Motion Analysis*, Prague, May 2004.
9. Y.-F. Ma and H.-J. Zhang. Motion pattern-based video classification and retrieval. EURASIP Journal on Applied Signal Processing, 2:199–208, 2003.
10. N. Moënne-Loccoz, E. Bruno and S.Marchand-Maillet. Video content representation as salient regions of activity. In *Conference on Image and Video Retrieval*, CIVR'04, Dublin, July 2004.
11. G. Piriou, P. Bouthemy, and J-F. Yao. Extraction of semantic dynamic content from videos with probabilistic motion models. In *European Conf. on Computer Vision, ECCV'04*, Prague, May 2004, Vol. LNCS 3023, Springer.
12. R.E. Schapire. Using output codes to boost multiclass learning problems. In *ICML '97, Proc. of the Int. Conf. on Machine Learning*, 1997.
13. P. Viola, M. J. Jones and D. Snow. Detecting pedestrians using patterns of motion and appearance. *Int. Journal of Computer Vision*, 63(2):153–161, July 2005.
14. L. Zelnik-Manor and M. Irani. Event-based video analysis. In *Proc. Int. Conf. on Computer Vision and Pattern Recognition*, Kauai, Hawaii, volume 2, pages 123–130, December 2001.

Can Humans Benefit
from Music Information Retrieval?

Frans Wiering

Department of Information and Computing Sciences, Utrecht University,
PO Box 80 089, NL-3508 TB Utrecht, Netherlands
frans.wiering@cs.uu.nl

Abstract. In the area of Music Information Retrieval (MIR), great technical progress has been made since this discipline started to mature in the late 1990s. Yet, despite the almost universal interest in music, MIR technology is not that widely used. There seems to be a mismatch between the assumptions researchers make about the users' music information needs, and the actual behaviour of a public that to begin with may not even treat music as information. Therefore, the emphasis of MIR research should be more on the emotional, social and aesthetic meaning of music to regular, untrained people. MIR applications could greatly benefit from using the results of recent research into the spontaneously-developed musical competence of untrained listeners.

Keywords: music information retrieval, musical similarity, musical content, music psychology, user interfaces.

1 Introduction

Music Information Retrieval (MIR) has been defined by Stephen Downie as 'a multidisciplinary research endeavor that strives to develop innovative content-based searching schemes, novel interfaces, and evolving networked delivery mechanisms in an effort to make the world's vast store of music accessible to all' [6]. Among the contributing disciplines are computer sciences, information retrieval, audio engineering, digital sound processing, musicology and music theory (the latter two are generally separated in the US, but not in Europe), library science, cognitive science, psychology, philosophy and law [8]. Many researchers are motivated by their personal interest in music and therefore tend to use their own audio collection as a testbed. They often do not have advanced musical knowledge, for which they usually turn to the music professionals in the community, generally scholars and librarians.

The professional viewpoint of music is also much in evidence in an important tradition of computer-supported musicology that already emerged early in the history of computing. Indeed, this is where the expression 'Musical Information Retrieval' was first used around 1965 [15]. As a discipline, MIR has been maturing since the late 1990s. Since 2000, the yearly ISMIR conference has played a key role in this development by providing a platform where the representatives of different disciplines meet. Virtually all ISMIR papers are available online at http://www.ismir.net/all-papers.html. The most recent single-publication overview of MIR is [19].

S. Marchand-Maillet et al. (Eds.): AMR 2006, LNCS 4398, pp. 82–94, 2007.
© Springer-Verlag Berlin Heidelberg 2007

After briefly introducing some central notions in MIR (section 2), I will discuss some interrelated issues in section 3 that I consider relevant for the future development of MIR. They all relate to treating music first of all as information, which I believe unnecessarily narrows the scope of the discipline. In order to prevent any misunderstandings, I would like to emphasise that I do not wish to underestimate the importance of the research that has been done so far, and especially not the part of it that is technically oriented. On the contrary, the amount and quality of this research make it possible to examine the consequences of assumptions that have guided MIR research so far, and to discover where new challenges for MIR research can be found. My focus will be on those challenges that I hope the Adaptive Multimedia Retrieval community—which is not listed in [8]—is interested in helping to explore.

2 Central Notions in MIR

Rather than attempting an overview of MIR, I will discuss in this section some central notions in MIR: the representation of musical content, musical similarity, retrieval methods and MIR systems. User related issues will be mentioned in passing, but I will treat these more fully in section 3.

2.1 Metadata-Based and Content-Based Approaches

Two main approaches to MIR can be discerned: metadata-based and content-based. In the former, the issue is mainly to find useful categories for describing music, distinguishing for example between different recordings of the same composition, or between artist-as-creator and artist-as-performer, or to organise the myriad of genre descriptions that exist for music. These categories are expressed in text. Hence, existing text-based retrieval methods can be used to search those descriptions, and can also be applied to another important feature of the musical content: the texts of vocal music.

The more challenging approaches in MIR are thus the ones that deal with the actual musical content, e.g. pitch, melody and rhythm. The first problem one encounters is that musical content comes in two formats: sound and notation. It would seem that the most natural one to select is sound. Humans in general have well-developed abilities to extract features from a musical signal: they can distinguish pitches, melodies and harmonies, rhythms and beat patterns, they can identify instruments, and at times they are strongly moved by the emotions these features evoke. Extracting these features from audio and using them to let people retrieve the music they like seems the obvious thing to do. This however has proved to be very difficult. Only monophonic transcription, the detection of 'pitch events' in a single melody, is now considered a solved problem, even though engineering problems remain. Transcription of polyphony, music in which several pitch events may occur at the same time, is still very much an unsolved issue. Interesting recent methods that do not depend on precise pitch detection are harmonic matching [22] and chroma-based matching [3].

Many researchers, especially those from the professional domain, have opted for the second approach, notation, using 'symbolic' representations of music. These involve encodings of musical scores in one of the many available encoding systems [4, 23]. Even though mainly meant for performers, music notation can be said to model music perception and cognition to a certain extent. For example, one or more notes usually correspond to one perceived pitch event. However, the 'chunking' of melodies that takes place in early perception and that is very important for the mental representation of music [24] is generally not made explicit in notation. Also, the output of audio transcription is often in a format that shares a number of features with notation. Therefore, methods developed for searching music notation are likely to be relevant to audio as well.

2.2 Musical Similarity

In Information Retrieval, we want to find documents that are relevant to a user's information need, as expressed in a query. In content-based MIR, this aim is usually described as finding music that is similar to a set of features or an example. Note that by equating user need to similarity, some imaginable needs are ruled out, notably surprise. Musical similarity is thus a central issue in MIR, but it is not a simple concept. There are several reasons for this.

First, many interrelating features are involved in the perception of musical similarity. I have already mentioned melody, rhythm, harmony and instruments as features. Similarity in one such feature does not necessarily lead to perception of overall similarity. For example: if the pitches of two melodies are the same but the rhythm is very different, listeners may not consider these melodies as similar.

Second, there are many different types of musical similarity. Similarity can for example be said to exist between:

- two different performances played from the same notation, for example Beethoven's Fifth Symphony;
- varied repetitions of the melody in a strophic song, for example Frank Sinatra's *My Way*;
- different performances of the same pop song, for example Frank Sinatra's and Sid Vicious's performances of *My Way*;
- works created by the same artist;
- works in a similar style, so using a related musical idiom;
- music that sounds like a given work because it uses similar 'materials,' for example bits of melody or chord progressions;
- music that has certain features that relate to its function, for example tempo, metre and rhythm in dance music;
- music belonging to the same genre, for example Jazz or Gregorian chant;
- music originating from same culture: for example Western, Indian, or medieval music;
- music that contributes to one's social identity, for example Hip hop or Death Metal;
- music that displays the same atmosphere (romantic) or emotion (love).

Most listeners deal with these types of similarity as a matter of course. In addition, there are forms of similarity that belong to other kinds of users, notably music industry and music professionals [25, 27]. Music industry may be interested in music that plagiarizes other music, or in music that can be sold to an audience with a known musical taste. Music professionals may be interested in finding music of similar difficulty, ensemble composition, style, or where similarity is an indication of 'musical influence.' Examples of the last type include quotation, allusion, recomposition, parody and the use of certain compositional techniques. Advanced listeners may be interested in such forms of similarity as well.

It is possible to adequately deal with some of the above-listed types of similarity by means of metadata such as titles or composer's names. Classifying music by genre is known to be problematic because of the ambiguity of terminology and the fact that much music 'plays' with genre. Verbally describing techniques or melodic characteristics in a consistent way is considered to be harder yet. But even if we could agree on descriptors for these, there is simply too much music to make manual description by humans feasible. This makes the research into content-based methods for retrieving music such an important task.

2.3 Retrieval Methods

In response to the just-described multiplicity of music similarity, many different computational methods for measuring it have been devised (surveyed in [25] and [27]). The most generic forms of similarity are generally best served by audio-based methods such as self-organising maps of music [20]. Very specific matching is also possible in the audio domain: in audio fingerprinting different, possibly degraded, broadcasts of the same recording can be identified [12]. Chroma-based matching [3] is able to trace similarity in musical content between closely-related compositions.

Similarity measures that act on symbolic representation are generally based on string matching, set comparison, or probabilistic methods. These are generally suitable for very specific tasks such as finding different instances of the same work, melodic variation and music based on same harmonic sequence. Methods that address the middle level of similarity (musical style, specific genre) are still very weakly developed. The reason why this area is so hard to address is probably that such forms of similarity involve quite a number of musical characteristics. Automatic detectors for these characteristics are still immature, and how these interrelate to create a sense of style or genre is not sufficiently understood yet.

2.4 MIR Systems

Many MIR systems are described in [25]; however, few of these can be described as mature, functional, end-user oriented systems. No doubt the most popular one is Pandora (http://www.pandora.com), which however relies on matching human feature annotations. Systems like Themefinder (http://www.themefinder.org) and Musipedia (http://www.musipedia.org) are notation-based engines that use string-matching techniques. These systems provide access to relatively large collections of melodies and seem to have a well-defined audience. At Utrecht University, Rainer Typke built the Orpheus engine (http://give-lab.cs.uu.nl/orpheus), which is first of all a research prototype for testing weight flow distances such as the Earth Mover's Distance as similarity measures for music [26]. Orpheus is able to search large collections efficiently and with good results. It is currently being developed into a user-centred framework called Muugle (http://give-lab.cs.uu.nl/muugle) [2]. Designing, building and evaluating *usable* music information retrieval systems, especially for untrained listeners, is what I consider to be one of the most important goals for MIR research in the next few years.

3 Some Problems in MIR

For the sake of argument, I would like to present here a deliberately simplistic view of mainstream MIR, which is based on elements presented in the above account. Obviously, it does not do justice to the subtlety and originality of much research being done in the area, but it will help to clarify some issues that I believe to be crucial to the future of the discipline. This view of MIR is as follows.

In designing and realising MIR systems, it is assumed that music is represented by its information content, that users generally have the goal to search for musical information and that their information need can be expressed as a musical query. The system matches this query to the collection and returns a subset of this collection to the user, who finally picks the item that best satisfies his needs. If, as often happens, users do not succeed in finding the music they are looking for, then it is assumed to be because they do not have sufficient musical abilities to express their information need.

My criticism on this view is first of all that it considers music primarily as information. It assumes untrained users think of music as information, and furthermore underestimates the importance of other user needs besides information (such as mood, emotion, exploration and surprise). Second, it does not sufficiently take spontaneously-developed musical skills of listeners into account. Paying more attention to these factors may result in design of new retrieval methods and new forms of interaction, and the integration of MIR techniques in more general applications. In the following sections I will examine these issues one by one.

3.1 Is Music Information?

In the context of Information Retrieval, the word 'information' does not mean simply 'interpreted data' but rather 'structured data that is suited to enhance a person's knowledge of the world'. Information in this sense is best exemplified by functional prose that has 'aboutness'. Scholarly papers, newspaper articles, computer manuals and travel guides clearly fall in this category: they are about some aspect of the world. Outside the domain of textual documents, diagrams, news broadcasts and documentary films can be said to be about something. On the other hand, the aboutness of literary writing, poetry for example, is problematic, because the factual subject matter is usually not the most important reason why one is interested in the work in question. Therefore one cannot separate the content of the work from the way it is expressed without losing some of its essence. By extension this lack of aboutness applies to other art forms as well, including music.

Yet considering music, and specifically music notation, as information [17] makes much sense as a professional view of music. Music notation is then a sort of two-dimensional text, in which music symbols are organised both horizontally and vertically. Digitally encoded music notation can be queried for such things as recurrent melodies or chords, or processed to make statements about its structure or authorship. In this way it can surely contribute to one's knowledge of the musical world. However, it is hard to imagine how musical content and expression could be separated. It is for example unclear how one could embed the information from one piece in another other than by quotation. In addition, musical information tells us very little about the world outside music that is not subjective. Music possesses only a weak aboutness [17], and is thus rather 'pseudo-information'. Generally, meaning in music is a very problematic concept; it does however merit further exploration, as it is at the same time very clear that music is very meaningful to so many people.

Music has often been compared to language, most recently by Fitch [7]. As a starting point he takes Hockett's thirteen design principles of language [14]. Most of these, such as *rapid fading* and *cultural transmission*, apply to music as well. But music lacks precisely those features that in language support referentiality—the fact that it can refer to objects and events—such as *displacement* (language can refer to things that are not present) and *arbitrariness* (no fixed relation between sounds and things). The feature of *interchangeability* (one can say anything one can understand) is shared by music only to a limited extent in that most people are able to pick up certain basic skills, for example to sing simple melodies, without formal training. Yet music is more than speech without meaning. It has an obvious affective and aesthetic power that makes it 'a-referentially expressive,' one of the nine design principle that Fitch distinguishes for music.

Fig. 1. Three different continuations of the same chord sequence. In each example, the first three chords are identical. These create a harmonic tension that is fully resolved in (a) by a normal ending on the 'tonic' triad: the piece could end here. In (b) another, related, consonant triad is substituted: we expect the piece to be continued. A dissonant though related chord is introduced in (c): there is a strong implication of continuation towards a resolution of this dissonance. Most untrained listeners are capable of intuitively appreciating these differences.

How does this power of music work? One common explanation goes as follows. Basic musical features can often be subdivided in ones that create tension and ones that create relaxation. For example, dissonance is experienced as a tension that is resolved by the consonance that (usually) follows it. Narmour [18] refines this notion by describing music as patterns of implication and realisation. Such patterns can be manipulated by creating an expectation that is not (completely) fulfilled, for example by using a consonance other than the expected one or even by following the first dissonance with another dissonance. For an example see Fig. 1. Such patterns work at many levels and create in the listener's mind a sequence of responses that (if the composer has done his job properly) only comes to a complete relaxation at the end of the piece. These responses are probably triggered by processes such as endorphin production that also play an important role in the sensation of emotion [21]. As musical patterns are very complex and diverse, one's emotional response to music can be very rich and meaningful. Finally, such a-referential meaning is easily connected to that of language or images that coincide with the music, as in song and film. This connection is strong enough to recreate, by means of music only, the referential meaning that originally resided in the other medium.

A-referential meaning can also be said to be present in the social functions of music, such as mother-infant bonding [7]; synchronising movement, most notably in dance; supporting activities, for example rituals, work, sports and shopping; and finally creating group coherence and identity. One evolutionary explanation of music is precisely that it makes humans function better as social animals.

If, then, the meaning of music is fundamentally a-referential, this has important consequences for MIR. The reason why most people will search for music is probably not that they want to enhance their knowledge of music by finding specific musical information, but that they search for a meaningful musical experience that satisfies their emotional or social needs. MIR systems that treat music first of all as information may not be very helpful in this scenario. One may even wonder whether a discipline named 'Music Information Retrieval' implies already in its name a perspective that is useful for professionals but marginalises other, far more numerous uses.

A Case Study: Query By Humming. The viewpoint of music as information even emerges in a particular MIR strategy, Query By Humming (QBH) that has been widely researched since it was first described in [9] with the aim of providing a 'natural way of querying.' The procedure for QBH is generally as follows: a user hums (or whistles or sings) a melodic query. The system matches the query against the musical items in a database and returns a ranked list of matching melodies. Figs 2. and 3 show an example QBH interface.

Implementation issues aside, there seem to be three problems that hamper the success of such systems (and in general, systems that require a concrete, musical query):

1. Users have considerable difficulties in generating a satisfactory query. It is often observed that they 'cannot sing in tune' or even 'cannot remember music correctly.' In fact, the task is not at all natural to them: not only must they perform music, but they must perform it exactly correct. In other words, QBH considers music as 'interchangeable,' while it is not. To give an analogy: we are all good at face recognition, but generally not at drawing them.
2. Only one type of query is possible: melody. Research into 'ecological' query formulation has shown that users wish to be able to use all sorts of sound production, including tapping, lyrics etc. [16]. Even then, many factors remain unavailable for querying, most notably harmony and instrumentation, though people certainly have a mental representation of these.
3. Does QBH satisfy a widely-felt user need? There are situations in which it does, for example if one wishes to identify and maybe acquire a song one remembers. Often, however, people will have an 'experience need,' composed of taste, expertise, mood/emotion, and/or situation/context. The need is then generally satisfied by a set of pieces that meet the requirements, not a list in ranked order or one specific item.

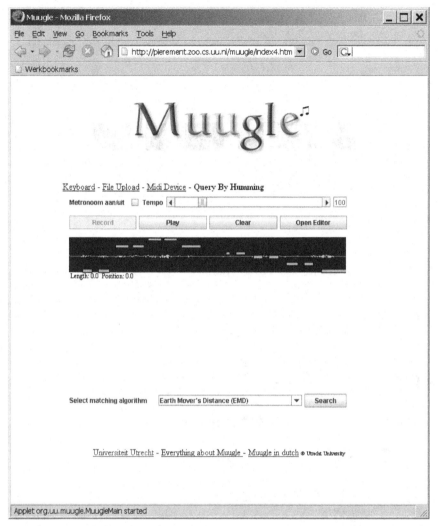

Fig. 2. Muugle's QBH interface (http://give-lab.cs.uu.nl/muugle): query interface with audio signal and transcription

All three problems relate to the fact that, despite its claim of naturalness, QBH is a task that treats music as information, so from a professional viewpoint. This task assumes that users need musical information that can be expressed in one particular musical dimension, melody, and that they possess the active musical competence to express this need. It seems to be no coincidence that QBH applications are rather unsuccessful in attracting large user communities, whereas a service like Pandora—which assumes a less specific, more common user need and does not require active musical skills—is far more successful in this respect. However, Pandora relies exclusively on manual annotation of songs, not on content-based retrieval. As

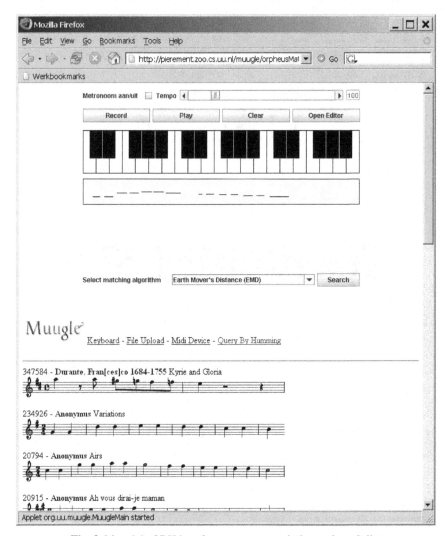

Fig. 3. Muugle's QBH interface: query transcription and result list

explained above, there are limitations to what annotation can do. Therefore I believe that finding techniques for extracting a-referential meaning from musical data and exploring its potential for users in similar services is a major research challenge for the future.

3.2   How Musical Are Humans?

One reason why MIR may concentrate on professional approaches to music is that historically the focus of attention in both musicology and music psychology used to be on the production of music by composers and performers. (Another is that working with professionals makes the evaluation of retrieval methods much easier.) Only recently the study of listeners' 'passive' competence has begun to receive similar attention. Peretz [21] gives an interesting overview of passive musical competence and the problems of testing it without presupposing professional skills. In her view, 'the ordinary adult listener is a musical expert, although s/he may be unaware of it.' Most people acquire this expertise by being exposed to music, but a surprising percentage of the population (around 50% in the UK and USA) have received some musical instruction as well. Genuine amusicality (tone-deafness, the inability to distinguish between pitches) is genetically determined and occurs in about 4% of the population. It is not the result of lack of motivation or training. Non-trained listeners generally possess the following musical abilities, among other things:

- they are able to distinguish subtle stylistic differences;
- they are equally good at learning songs as professionals;
- they can identify out-of-key notes;
- they recognize patterns of implication and realisation [1];
- they are able move to music (as in tapping the beat of music).

3.3 Interaction with MIR Applications

Non-trained listeners thus possess considerable passive musical competence, which most likely enables them to have very concrete ideas about music that satisfies their musical needs. This, and the fact that they generally have only limited active abilities, may lead to different requirements for interaction with MIR applications. Three of these are examined here briefly and in some respects speculatively.

Emotion Retrieval. Emotional meaning is an important drive for people to listen and probably to search for music. A problem is the subjectivity of the emotional response to music. However, recent research by Lesaffre et al. indicates that affective/emotive and structural descriptors are correlated [16]. The authors could demonstrate among other things a very strong correlation between the appraisal descriptor tender-aggressive and the structural descriptor loudness (soft-hard). Such correlations were used for retrieving music on the basis of affective value in an application that users were satisfied with.

In [16], descriptors are assigned to complete pieces. My vision of the (very distant) future is that these descriptors will be created by content-based techniques for short fragments of music—maybe from implication-realisation patterns—and will be combined in a sort of path through emotion space. These paths can then be compared, so that pieces with a similar 'emotional development' can be retrieved. Such methods were already announced for video retrieval [13]. How one can query for music with a certain 'emotional development' other than by example remains to be investigated.

Output Presentation. The problem with MIR output is that numerous items may be retrieved, but that in the auditory domain, one can inspect these only one at a time. This is time-consuming and also a hard task for musical memory. The obvious answer is mapping the items to the visual domain. The standard solution is to put the items in a list consisting of metadata and/or snippets of music notation (see for example Themefinder and Muugle). There are a number of interesting and more intuitive (but less informative) alternatives, presenting a 2D or even 3D music space, for example Pampalk's Islands of music [20], Van Gulik's dynamic playlists [11], and Goto's Musicream [10]. The latter two assume a collection that is already ordered by similarity. Musicream features three taps, from which streams of similar musical items emerge. The user can pick items from the streams, listen to these, and organise them.

What is still unsatisfactory about these solutions is that items are usually represented as points, disks, or by means of text labels. Can they be given some more meaningful representation? Untested ideas that recently emerged in a brainstorm include representing music as objects with a certain shape, colour, texture or movement. Users would define their own associations between visual and musical features, and musical objects would be adapted accordingly. Another option would be to present music (or at least a musical query) as a face. Faces are very individual, and in addition capable of expressing a wide range of emotions. Naturally it remains to be seen if such ideas are viable at all.

Retrieval in Context. Experiencing music is more than finding and then playing the right piece of music. I therefore expect a limited use of music search engines as separate applications. It seems more likely that they will be integrated in environments that allow different ways of exploring music and be partly or completely hidden to the end user. For example: a digital archive of some repertory (e.g. folksongs, piano music) would facilitate metadata queries, following of links between works, and the creation of new relations between them by means of retrieval tools.

Such an application may involve ways of accessing a wider context, involving for example textual documents, musical instruments, performance locations, and social functions. Music could also be part of integrated virtual cultural experience. The role of a music retrieval engine in such an environment may range from choosing appropriate background music, to supplying the right items to reconstructed events (plays, ceremonies) in which music played a role. Finally, music tends to be stereotyped if it acts in a supportive role, and it might be possible to use those stereotypes to retrieve corresponding events. For example, retrieving emotional scenes from mainstream Hollywood films might be quite feasible using the accompanying music.

4 Conclusion

The title of this paper asks whether humans can benefit from Music Information Retrieval. The problem lies in the word 'information,' not just because information in general is known to be a problematic concept, but specifically because of the 'human-oriented' meaning that it has in textual Information Retrieval and that MIR has inherited. I have tried to argue that considering music as information represents a limited view of music. Such a view is certainly appropriate for professionals (and industry—but I have barely touched upon their interests), who can gain a lot from these technologies. However, considering other humans I believe it is better not only to drop the I-word—and henceforth use the term 'Music Retrieval'—but also to rethink the area from a non-trained user's perspective. This may help researchers to concentrate on needs that better correspond to the 'experience of music'; on finding important new tasks for which techniques are still underdeveloped; to take the personal profile and especially the 'listening competence' of non-trained users as a starting point for designing novel search and interaction methods; and finally to design interesting applications in which Music Retrieval plays an invisible but essential role in letting people experience the richness of 'the world's vast store of music' [6].

Acknowledgments. I thank Stéphane Marchand-Maillet for inviting me to present this paper as a keynote at the 4th International Workshop on Adaptive Multimedia Retrieval in Geneva, 2006. Hermi Schijf did a great job in correcting my English and identifying passages that needed further clarification. Jörg Garbers's much appreciated critical comments have resulted in a number of important modifications in my text. In general, I would like to thank my colleagues and students at the Department of Information and Computing Sciences of Utrecht University for the stimulating discussions from which many ideas for this paper have emerged.

References

1. Bigand, E., Poulin-Charronnat, B.: Are We "Experienced Listeners"? A Review of the Musical Capacities That Do Not Depend on Formal Musical Training. Cognition 100 (2006) 100–130
2. Bosma, M., Veltkamp, R.C., Wiering, F.: Muugle: A Music Retrieval Experimentation Framework. In: Proceedings of the Ninth International Conference on Music Perception and Cognition, Bologna 2006, 1297–1303
3. Casey, M.: Audio Tools for Music Discovery. [online] http://www.methodsnetwork.ac.uk/ redist/pdf/casey.pdf [accessed 30 November 2006]
4. Castan, C. Music Notation Formats. [online] http://www.music-notation.info [accessed 30 November 2006]
5. Downie, J.S.: Music Information Retrieval. Annual Review of Information Science and Technology 37 (2003) 295–340
6. Downie, J.S.: The Scientific Evaluation of Music Information Retrieval Systems: Foundations and Future. Computer Music Journal 28:2 (2004) 12–23
7. Fitch, W.T.: The Biology and Evolution of Music: A Comparative Perspective. Cognition 100 (2006) 173–215
8. Futrelle, J., Downie, J.S.: Interdisciplinary Communities and Research Issues in Music Information Retrieval. In: Proceedings ISMIR 2002, 215–221
9. Ghias A., Logan, J., Chamberlin, D., Smith, B.C.: Query by Humming: Musical Information Retrieval in an Audio Database. In: Proceedings of the ACM International Multimedia Conference and Exhibition 1995, 231–236
10. Goto, M., Goto, T.: Musicream: Music Playback Interface for Streaming, Sticking, Sorting, and Recalling Musical Pieces. In: Proceedings ISMIR 2005, 404–411
11. Gulik, R. van, Vignoli, F., Wetering, H. van de: Mapping Music in the Palm of Your Hand: Explore and Discover Your Collection. In: Proceedings ISMIR 2004, 409–414
12. Haitsma, J., Kalker, T.: A Highly Robust Audio Fingerprinting System. Proceedings ISMIR 2002, 107–115

13. Hanjalic, A: Paradigm Shifts in Video Content Analysis Needed: The Why's and How's of Generic VCA Solutions. Dagstuhl Seminar on Content-Based Retrieval, April 2006
14. Hockett, C.F.: Logical Considerations in the Study of Animal Communication. In: W.E. Lanyon & W.N. Tavolga (Eds.), Animal Sounds and Communication. Washington, DC: American Institute of Biological Sciences, 1960. Cited after [E]
15. Kassler, M.: Toward Musical Information Retrieval. Perspectives of New Music 4:2 (1966) 59–67
16. Lesaffre, M., Leman, M., De Voogdt, L., De Baets, B., De Meyer, H., Martens, J.-P.: A User-Dependent Approach to the Perception of High-Level Semantics of Music. In: Proceedings of the Ninth International Conference on Music Perception and Cognition, Bologna 2006, 1003–1008
17. McLane, A.: Music as Information. Annual Review of Information Science and Technology 31 (1996) 225–262
18. Narmour, E.: The Analysis and Cognition of Basic Melodic Structures: The Implication-Realization Model. University of Chicago Press, 1990.
19. Orio, N. Music Retrieval: A Tutorial and Review. Foundations and Trends in Information Retrieval 1 (2006) 1–90
20. Pampalk, E., Dixon, S., Widmer, G.: Exploring Music Collections by Browsing Different Views. Proceedings ISMIR 2003, 201–208
21. Peretz, I.: The Nature of Music from a Biological Perspective. Cognition 100 (2006) 1–32
22. Pickens, J., Bello, J.P., Monti, G., Sandler, M., Crawford, T., Dovey, M., Byrd, D.: Polyphonic Score Retrieval Using Polyphonic Audio Queries: A Harmonic Modeling Approach. Journal of New Music Research 32 (2003) 223–236
23. Selfridge-Field, E. (Ed.): Beyond MIDI: The Handbook of Musical Codes. MIT Press, 1997
24. Snyder, B.: Music and Memory: An Introduction. MIT Press, 2001
25. Typke, R., Wiering, F., Veltkamp, R.C.: A Survey of Music Information Retrieval Systems. In: Proceedings ISMIR 2002, 153–160
26. Typke R., Wiering F., Veltkamp R.C.: Transportation Distances and Human Perception of Melodic Similarity. Musicae Scientiae 10 (2006), forthcoming
27. Veltkamp, R.C., Wiering, F., Typke, R: Content Based Music Retrieval. In: B. Furht (Ed.), Encyclopedia of Multimedia, Springer 2006, 96–105

A New Approach to Probabilistic Image Modeling with Multidimensional Hidden Markov Models

Bernard Merialdo, Joakim Jiten, Eric Galmar, and Benoit Huet

Multimedia Communications Department
Institut EURECOM
BP 193, 06904 Sophia-Antipolis, France
{merialdo,jiten,galmar,huet}@eurecom.fr

Abstract. This paper presents a novel multi-dimensional hidden Markov model approach to tackle the complex issue of image modeling. We propose a set of efficient algorithms that avoids the exponential complexity of regular multi-dimensional HMMs for the most frequent algorithms (Baum-Welch and Viterbi) due to the use of a random dependency tree (DT-HMM). We provide the theoretical basis for these algorithms, and we show that their complexity remains as small as in the uni-dimensional case. A number of possible applications are given to illustrate the genericity of the approach. Experimental results are also presented in order to demonstrate the potential of the proposed DT-HMM for common image analysis tasks such as object segmentation, and tracking.

1 Introduction

In image modeling there is a fairly wide-spread agreement that objects should be presented as collections of features which appear in a given mutual position or shape (e.g. sun in the sky, sky above landscape or boat in the water etc) [2,4]. This is also relevant on a lower level; consider analyzing local features in a small region; it is sometimes difficult even for a human to tell what the image is about.

The HMM considers observations (e.g. feature vectors representing pixels) statistically dependent on neighboring observations through transitions probabilities organized in a Markov mesh [1], giving a dependency in two dimensions. The state process defined by this mesh is a special case of the Markov random field.

Hidden Markov models (HMM) have earlier become a key technology for many applications such as speech recognition [8] and language modeling. Their success is largely due to the discovery of an efficient training algorithm, the Baum-Welch algorithm [10], which allows estimating the numeric values of the model parameters from training data. HMMs have been used in such diverse applications as acoustic modeling, language modeling, language analysis, spelling correction etc. Most of the current applications involve uni-dimensional data. In theory, HMMs can be applied as well to multi-dimensional data. However, the complexity of the algorithms grows

S. Marchand-Maillet et al. (Eds.): AMR 2006, LNCS 4398, pp. 95–107, 2007.
© Springer-Verlag Berlin Heidelberg 2007

tremendously in higher dimensions, even in two dimensions, so that the usage of plain HMM becomes prohibitive in practice [18].

In this paper, we propose a new type of multi-dimensional hidden Markov model; the dependency-tree hidden Markov model (DT-HMM). We show that for this model, most of the common algorithms keep the same linear complexity as in one dimension. We explain these algorithms and illustrate the various possible usages of the DT-HMM through a set of examples. Our contribution is mostly theoretical, to show the richness and potential of this formalism. Further research will be needed to benchmark it with existing techniques. The remainder of this paper is organized as follows: section 3 provides the theoretical basis for DT-HMM, and sections 4-6 presents the different applications and experimental results. Finally in sections 7 we give the conclusions and suggest future work.

2 Related Work

Many approaches have been proposed to overcome the complexity of 2D-HMMs [11]. Among the first ones is [5] which uses a 1D HMM to model horizontal bands of face images. A more elaborate idea is to extract 1D features out of the image or video, and model these features with one or more 1D models [15]. Another approach is to use a two-level model, called Embedded HMM or Hierarchical HMM, where a first high level model contains super-states associated to a low level HMM, which models the lines of the observed image [16]. The main disadvantage of these approaches is that they greatly reduce the vertical dependencies between states, as it is only achieved through a single super-state. Finally several attempts have been done to heuristically reduce the complexity of the HMM algorithms by making simplifying assumptions which approximate the real algorithms:

- select a subset of state configurations only [17],
- ignore correlation of distant states [6],
- approximate probabilities by turbo-decoding [9].

The main disadvantage of these approaches is that they only provide approximate computations, so that the probabilistic model is no longer theoretically sound.

3 Dependency-Tree HMM

In this section, we briefly recall the basics of 2D HMM and describe our proposed DT-HMM [7].

3.1 2D-HMM

The reader is expected to be familiar with 1D-HMM. We denote by $O=\{o_{ij}, i=1,...m, j=1,...,n\}$ the observation, for example each o_{ij} may be the feature vector of a block (i,j) in the image. We denote by $S = \{s_{ij}, i=1,...m, j=1,...,n\}$ the state assignment of the HMM, where the HMM is assumed to be in state s_{ij} at position (i,j) and produce the observation vector o_{ij}. If we denote by λ the parameters of the HMM, then, under the Markov assumptions, the joint likelihood of O and S given λ can be computed as:

$$P(O, S|\lambda) = P(O|S, \lambda)P(S|\lambda)$$
$$= \prod_{ij} p\left(o_{ij}\middle|s_{ij}, \lambda\right)p\left(s_{ij}\middle|s_{i-1,j}, s_{i,j-1}, \lambda\right) \tag{1}$$

If the set of states of the HMM is $\{s_1, \ldots s_N\}$, then the parameters λ are:

- the output probability distributions $p(o | s_i)$
- the transition probability distributions $p(s_i | s_j, s_k)$.

Depending on the type of output (discrete or continuous) the output probability distribution are discrete or continuous (typically a mixture of Gaussian distribution).

We would like to point out that there are two ways of modeling the spatial dependences between the near neighbor state variables; by a causal or non-causal Markov random field (MRF). The former is referred to as Markov mesh and has the advantage that it reduces the complexity of likelihood functions for image classification [1]. The causality also enables the derivation of an analytic iterative algorithm to estimate states with the maximum a posteriori probability, due to that the total observation is progressively built from smaller parts. The state process of DT-HMM is defined by the Markov mesh.

3.2 DT-HMM

The problem with 2D-HMM is the double dependency of $s_{i,j}$ on its two neighbors, $s_{i-1,j}$ and $s_{i,j-1}$., which does not allow the factorization of computation as in 1D, and makes the computations practically intractable.

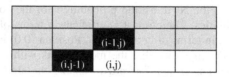

Fig. 1. 2D Neighbors

Our idea is to assume that $s_{i,j}$ depends on one neighbor at a time only. But this neighbor may be the horizontal or the vertical one, depending on a random variable $t(i,j)$. More precisely, $t(i,j)$ is a random variable with two possible values:

$$t(i, j) = \begin{cases} (i-1, j) & \text{with prob } 0.5 \\ (i, j-1) & \text{with prob } 0.5 \end{cases} \tag{2}$$

For the position on the first row or the first column, $t(i,j)$ has only one value, the one which leads to a valid position inside the domain. $t(0,0)$ is not defined.
So, our model assumes the following simplification:

$$p(s_{i,j}|s_{i-1,j}, s_{i,j-1}, t) = \begin{cases} p_V(s_{i,j}|s_{i-1,j}) & \text{if } t(i, j) = (i-1, j) \\ p_H(s_{i,j}|s_{i,j-1}) & \text{if } t(i, j) = (i, j-1) \end{cases} \tag{3}$$

If we further define a "direction" function:

$$D(t) = \begin{cases} V & \text{if } t = (i-1, j) \\ H & \text{if } t = (i, j-1) \end{cases} \tag{4}$$

then we have the simpler formulation:

$$p(s_{i,j}|s_{i-1,j}, s_{i,j-1}, t) = p_{D(t(i,j))}(s_{i,j}|s_{t(i,j)}) \tag{5}$$

Note that the vector **t** of the values t(i,j) for all (i,j) defines a tree structure over all positions, with (0,0) as the root. Figure 2 shows an example of random Dependency Tree.

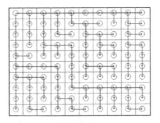

Fig. 2. Example of Random Dependency Tree

The DT-HMM replaces the N^3 transition probabilities of the complete 2D-HMM by $2N^2$ transition probabilities. Therefore it is efficient in terms of storage. We will see that it is also efficient in terms of computation. Position (0,0) has no ancestor. In this paper, we assume for simplicity that the model starts with a predefined initial state s_I in position (0,0). It is straightforward to extend the algorithms to the case where the model starts with an initial probability distribution over all states.

3.3 Fundamental Problems

As stated in [8], three fundamental problems should be solved for using HMMs:

   P1: Estimate the parameters of the model from a set of training examples,
   P2: Estimate the probability of an observation to be produced by the model,
   P3: Find the best state sequence in the emission of an observation.

A great advantage of HMM is that the same formalization can be used for a variety of tasks, many of which are relevant to Multimedia analysis:

- build a model from examples,
- classify an item,
- detect an object in a stream,
- analyze an object of known type, etc...

In the following sections, we will propose algorithms for the fundamental problems in the case of DT-HMM. We will show that these algorithms exhibit only moderate computation complexity, and we will provide illustrative examples of their usage in the context of Multimedia analysis.

4 Application to Image Segmentation

4.1 Viterbi Algorithm

The Viterbi algorithm is a solution for problem P3, it finds the most probable sequence of states which generates a given observation O:

$$\hat{Q} = \underset{Q}{\text{Argmax}} \; P(O, Q|t) \tag{6}$$

Let us define $T(i,j)$ as the sub-tree with root (i,j), and define $\beta_{i,j}(s)$ as the maximum probability that the part of the observation covered by $T(i,j)$ is generated starting from state s in position (i,j). We can compute the values of $\beta_{i,j}(s)$ recursively by enumerating the positions in the opposite of the raster order, in a backward manner:

- if (i,j) is a leaf in $T(i,j)$:

$$\beta_{i,j}(s) = p(o_{i,j}|s) \tag{7}$$

- if (i,j) has only an horizontal successor:

$$\beta_{i,j}(s) = p(o_{i,j}|s) \max_{s'} p_H(s'|s)\beta_{i,j+1}(s') \tag{8}$$

- if (i,j) has only a vertical successor:

$$\beta_{i,j}(s) = p(o_{i,j}|s) \max_{s'} p_V(s'|s)\beta_{i+1,j}(s') \tag{9}$$

- if (i,j) has both an horizontal and a vertical successor:

$$\beta_{i,j}(s) = p(o_{i,j}|s) \left(\max_{s'} p_H(s'|s)\beta_{i,j+1}(s') \right) \left(\max_{s'} p_V(s'|s)\beta_{i+1,j}(s') \right) \tag{10}$$

Then the probability of the best state sequence for the whole image is $\beta_{0,0}(s_I)$. Note that this value may also serve as an approximation for solving problem P2.

The best state labeling is obtained by assigning $s_{0,0} = s_I$ and selecting recursively the neighbor states which accomplish the maxima in the previous formulas. Note that the complexity of the algorithm is only linear in the number of positions.

4.2 Relative Frequency Estimation

Assume that we have a labeled observation, for example an image where each output block has been assigned a state of the model. (this labeled observation might have been created manually or automatically). Then, it is straightforward to estimate the transition probabilities by their relative frequency, for example:

$$p_H(s'|s, t) = \frac{N_{H,t}(s, s')}{N(s)} \qquad (11)$$

where $N_{H,t}(s, s')$ is the number of times that state s' appears as a right horizontal neighbor of state s in the dependency tree t, and $N(s)$ the number of times that state s appears in the labeling. (This probability may be smoothed, for example using Lagrange smoothing).

The output probabilities may be also estimated by relative frequency in the discrete case, or using standard Multi-Gaussian estimation in the continuous case. This provides a solution for problem P1 in the case where a labeling is available, and is called Viterbi training. Each observation is assumed (with weight 1) to have resulted from the single most likely state sequence that might have caused it i.e. in the Viterbi training the state sequence with the maximum a posteriori probability P(S|O) is assumed to be the real state sequence.

4.3 Model Training

We now show the use of the previous two algorithms to train iteratively a DT-HMM on a set of images comprised of 130 consistent images depicting *beach* (see examples in Figure 3).

Fig. 3. Example of training images

During training each image is split into blocks of 16x16 pixels, and the observation vector for each block is computed as the average and variance of the LUV (CIE LUV color space) coding $\{L_\mu, U_\mu, V_\mu, L_\sigma, U_\sigma, V_\sigma\}$ combined with six quantified DCT coefficients (Discrete Cosine Transform). Thus each block is represented by a 12 dimensional vector. Every feature vector is annotated with a sub-class as described below.

4.4 States with Semantic Labels

In order to perform semantic segmentation we enforce semantic meaning to the states by uniquely assigning a state to one sub-class. Table 1 lists the number of states assigned to each sub-class.

Table 1. The number of states for each sub-class

Sub Class	No. states
Unknown	3
Sky	7
Sea	5
Sand	6
Mountain	3
Vegetation	3
Person	4
Building	3
Boat	2
8 sub-classes	36 states

Annotations was done in practice by first segmenting the training images into arbitrary shaped regions using the algorithm proposed in [20] and then manually label each region with one of the sub classes by using an application with a graphical user interface as shown in Figure. 4.

Fig. 4. Annotating an image segment as "sky"

To make an initial model for the output probabilities a GMM (Gaussian Mixture Model) is trained with observations corresponding to each sub-class. We dedicate three GMM components for every state, which gives us for instance that "sky" has 21 components and vegetation has 9 (see Table 1). Then we group the components into clusters by k-means. The number of clusters corresponds to the number of states we have dedicated to the actual sub-class. Finally each state is assigned to a cluster, which we have scaled up by a factor of two (multiplying its component weight by 2). The transition probabilities are initialized uniformly. Then, during training we iterate the following steps:

- With (11) estimate the output and transition probabilities by counting the relative frequencies (emission of an observation by a state, horizontal and vertical successors of a state) with Lagrange smoothing.
- Generate a random dependency tree and perform a Viterbi alignment to generate a new labeling of the image. The Viterbi training procedure is adapted to select the range of states that correspond to the annotated sub-class at each position, thus constraining the possible states for the observations.

4.5 Experiment Results

During training, we can observe the state assignments at each iteration as an indication of how the model fits the training data. For example, the first ten iterations on the training image to the left in figure 4 above provide the following assignments:

Fig. 5. State segmentation after 0, 2, 6 and 10 iterations

The sequence in figure 5 shows that the model has rapidly adapted each sub class to a particular set of observations. As such, the Viterbi labeling provides a relevant segmentation of the image. The graph below shows the evolution of likelihood of the training data during the training iterations. We can see that the likelihood for the model given the data has an asymptotic behavior after 10 iterations.

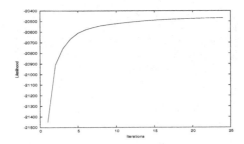

Fig. 6. Likelihood of the training data

Once the model is trained, we can apply it on new images. Below is an example of the state assignment for an image in the test set after 15 iterations, 70% of the blocks is correctly classified.

Fig. 7. State segmentation on test image

It should be emphasized that this is not just a simple segmentation of the images, but that each region is also assigned one of the 36 states (which represents one of the sub classes) of the model, and that the definition of those states has been done taking into account all training data simultaneously. We can observe that those area types are labeled with the same states during training.

5 Application to Object Tracking

In this section, we present how DT-HMMs can be applied to track an object in a video sequence. We consider a model with two types of states, object states (s^o) and background states (s^b). The general idea is to train the model on an initial image where the object has been delimited, then to use the Viterbi algorithm to find the location of the object in subsequent frames. We use a model with 6 states:

- background states: $s^b=\{s_1, s_6\}$,
- object states: $s^o=\{s_2, s_3, s_4, s_5\}$.

Assuming that a bounding box has been drawn around the object on the initial frame, we set the states on the initial frame according to the pattern in figure 8.

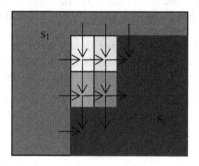

Fig. 8. Object and Background states for Object Tracking

- s_1 is the initial state of the model,
- s_6 is the final state of the model,
- The 4 object states are arranged inside a regular 2x2 grid within the bounding box.

In order to reinforce spatial constraints, we do not smooth transition probabilities, so that transitions which do not exist in the initial frame will keep a probability of zero and will remain forbidden in the subsequent frames. The output probabilities are smoothed as the color of the object may change from frame to frame.
We compared several variations of the tracking procedure:

- (b) train the model on the first frame, and use it to Viterbi align the other frames,
- (c) train a first model on the first frame, use it to Viterbi align the second frame, train a second model on this alignment, use it to Viterbi align the third frame, etc...
- (d) same as before, but train on all frames since the beginning, rather than just the current frame.

Figure 9 shows the compared results of these procedures. We can observe that, because the initial bounding box also contains background pixels, all methods have a

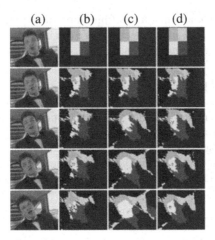

Fig. 9. Alignments at frames 70, 71, 75, 80 and 85

tendency to spread outside the actual shape of the object. This is especially true for method (c), which updates the model at every frame. Method (d) improves a little, but it still not perfect.

In order to cope with this problem, we should try to penalize background pixels which are within the object bounding box. For this purpose, we propose to modify the output probabilities of the object states with the following formula:

$$P'(o|s) \propto w_{os} * P(o|s)$$

$$w_{os} = \frac{E(s \to o)}{E(s \to o) + \sum_{s' \in s^b} E(s' \to o)} \quad (12)$$

This formula will reduce the output probability of colors which are highly probable in the background states, therefore enhancing the true object pixels only.

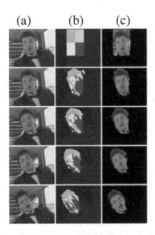

Fig. 10. Object tracking with weighted output probabilities

Figure 10 shows the result of tracking the object with method (c) using object probability weighting. It is clear that probability weighting has greatly improved the quality of object tracking.

6 Future Extensions

The DT-HMM formalism is open to a great variety of extensions and tracks. For example the algorithms that we have proposed remain valid for other ancestor functions and multidimensional Markov models.

6.1 Ancestor Dependencies

As before mentioned the state process is based on the dependencies defined by the Markov mesh, which is a special case of the Markov random field [1]. The Markov mesh defines spatial dependencies that are called "causal" because the dependent states are "past"; above and to the left of the current node. We can for example consider the following causal dependencies of a 3d and 4th order Markov mesh:

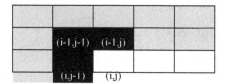 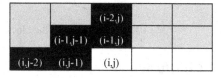

Fig. 11. Example of extended neighborhood

This only increases linearly (not exponentially) the number of transition probabilities, and therefore the complexity of the model and the algorithm.

6.2 Trees and Duals

One may notice that the value of P(O| t) depends on the specific dependency tree t that has been used in the computation. It may happen that, by chance, a given image get a more or less convenient dependency tree, and therefore a different score. The true score for an image should be:

$$P(O) = \sum_t P(O|t)P(t) \tag{13}$$

All dependency trees are supposed to be equally likely, so that P(t) is uniform. While this sum cannot be computed easily, it may be estimated by generating several trees and averaging the conditional likelihood of the output. Of particular interest is the estimation:

$$P(O) \approx \frac{1}{2}\big(P(O|t) + P(O|\bar{t})\big) \tag{14}$$

where $\bar{t}$ is the dual tree of t, defined by replacing horizontal by vertical dependencies (and vice versa), except for boundary constraints. This formulation introduces both horizontal and vertical dependencies for all neighbor pairs in the observation. In an investigation of different estimations for (13), we demonstrated that the dual approximation is more accurate than sampling with a unique random tree [19].

6.3 Multidimensional Model

The framework can also be extended to several dimensions, for example in the case of a video. Video can be regarded as images indexed with time. Considering the continuity of consecutive frames, it is often reasonable to assume local dependencies between pixels among frames. If a position is (i,j,t), it could depend on the neighbors (i-1,j,t), (i,j-1,t), (i,j,t-1) or more.

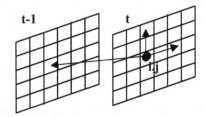

Fig. 12. Extending the block dependencies to three-dimensions

7 Conclusion

In this paper, we have presented a new type of hidden Markov models based on dependency trees. We have shown that this presentation leads to very efficient algorithms for 2D observations, and we have presented two examples to show the richness of the potential application of these models.

Our research on these models is only beginning, so that the results should not be compared now with the results from more advanced techniques. More time is needed to understand how to exploit best DT-HMM. In particular, it seems obvious that efficient models should contain a large number of states (in speech, acoustic models often have several hundred states), but these states have to be constructed in a coherent manner which has yet to be defined.

Our contribution is mostly theoretical. Examples have been used to show that the DT-HMM has a great potential for applications. We have identified several issues which are potential tracks for future research. We plan to explore the properties of this model further in the future, and are confident that this type of model will be helpful for a large panel of applications.

Acknowledgments

The research leading to this paper was supported by the Institut Eurecom and by the European Commission under contract FP6-027026, Knowledge Space of semantic inference for automatic annotation and retrieval of multimedia content - K-Space.

References

1. Kanal, L.N.: Markov mesh models in Image Modeling. New York: Academic, 1980, pp. 239-243
2. Lim, J.H., Jin, J.S.: Semantics Discovery for Image Indexing. ECCV (1) 2004: 270-281
3. Piriou, G., Bouthemy, P., Jian-Feng Yao: Extraction of Semantic Dynamic Content from Videos with Probabilistic Motion Models. ECCV (3) 2004: 145-157
4. Moreels, P., Maire M., Perona, P.: Recognition by Probabilistic Hypothesis Construction. ECCV (1) 2004: 55-68
5. Ferdinando, S., Fallside, F.: Face Identification and Feature Extraction Using Hidden Markov Models, Image Processing: Theory and Applications, Elsevier, 1993, pp 295-298
6. Merialdo, B., Marchand-Maillet, S.; Huet, B.: Approximate Viterbi decoding for 2D-hidden Markov models, IEEE International Conference on , Acoustics, Speech, and Signal Processing, Volume 6, 5-9 June 2000 Page(s):2147 - 2150 vol.4
7. Merialdo, B: Dependency Tree Hidden Markov Models, Research Report RR-05-128, Institut Eurecom, Jan 2005
8. Rabiner, L.R.: A tutorial on hidden Markov models and selected applications in speech recognition Proceedings of the IEEE, Volume 77, Issue 2, Feb. 1989 Page(s):257 – 286
9. Perronnin, F., Dugelay, J.-L.; Rose, K.: Deformable face mapping for person identification, International Conference on Image Processing, Volume 1, 14-17 Sept. 2003
10. Baum, LE.,Petrie T.: Statistical Inference for Probabilistic Functions of Finite State Markov Chains, Annual Math., Stat., 1966, Vol.37, pp. 1554-1563
11. Mohamed, M. A., Gader P.: Generalized Hidden Markov Models-Part I: Theoretical Frameworks, IEEE Transaction on Fuzzy Systems, February, 2000, Vol.8, No.1, pp. 67-81
12. Baker, J.K.:Trainable grammars for speech recognition. In Jared J.Wolf and Dennis H. Klatt, editors, Speech communication papers presented at the 97th Meeting of the Acoustical Society of America, MIT, Cambridge, MA, June 1979
13. Jelinek F., Lafferty, F. and R. L. Mercer: Basic methods of probabilistic context free grammars Technical Report RC 16374 (72684), IBM, Yorktown Heights, New York 10598. 1990
14. Jelinek, F.: Statistical Methods for Speech Recognition Cambridge, MA: MIT Press, 1997.
15. Brand, M., Oliver, N. and Pentland, A.:. Coupled hidden Markov models for complex action recognition. In Proceedings, CVPR, pages 994--999. IEEE Press, 1997
16. Fine S., Singer Y., Tishby, N.: The hierarchical hidden Markov model: Analysis and applications," Machine Learning 32(1998)
17. Li, J., Najmi, A. and Gray, R. M.: Image classification by a two-dimensional hidden markov model, IEEE Trans. Signal Processing, vol. 48, no. 2, pp. 517–533, 2000
18. Levin, E.; Pieraccini, R.: Dynamic planar warping for optical character recognition, IEEE International Conference on Acoustics, Speech, and Signal Processing, , Volume 3, 23-26 March 1992 Page(s):149 – 152
19. Jiten, J., Merialdo, B.: Probabilistic Image Modeling With Dependency-Tree Hidden Markov Models, WIAMIS 2006 : 19-21 April 2006, 7th International Workshop on Image Analysis for Multimedia Interactive Services, Hyatt Regency, Korea
20. P. F. Felzenszwalb , D. P. Huttenlocher, Image Segmentation Using Local Variation, Proceedings of the IEEE Computer Society Conference on Computer Vision and Pattern Recognition, p.98, June 23-25, 1998

3D Face Recognition by Modeling the Arrangement of Concave and Convex Regions

Stefano Berretti, Alberto Del Bimbo, and Pietro Pala*

Dipartimento di Sistemi e Informatica
University of Firenze
Firenze, Italy

Abstract. In this paper, we propose an original framework for three dimensional face representation and similarity matching. Basic traits of a face are encoded by extracting convex and concave regions from the surface of a face model. A compact graph representation is then constructed from these regions through an original modeling technique capable to quantitatively measure spatial relationships between regions in a three dimensional space and to encode this information in an attributed relational graph. In this way, the structural similarity between two face models is evaluated by matching their corresponding graphs. Experimental results on a 3D face database show that the proposed solution attains high retrieval accuracy and is reasonably robust to facial expression and pose changes.

1 Introduction

Representation and matching of face models has been an active research area in the last years, with a major emphasis targeting detection and recognition of faces in still images and videos (see [1] for an updated survey). More recently, the increasing availability of three-dimensional (3D) data, has paved the way to the use of 3D face models to improve the effectiveness of face recognition systems (see [2] for a recent survey). In fact, solutions based on 3D face models, feature less sensitivity—if not invariance—to lighting conditions and pose. This is particularly relevant in real contexts of use, where face images are usually captured in non-controlled environments, without any particular cooperation by human subjects.

Generally, three main classes of approaches can be identified to distinguish the way in which 3D face models can improve face identification with respect to traditional solutions. A first class of approaches relies on a generic 3D face model to match two 2D face images. For example, in [3] a method is proposed for face recognition across variations in pose, ranging from frontal to profile views, and across a wide range of illuminations, including cast shadows and specular

---

* This work is partially supported by the Information Society Technologies (IST) Program of the European Commission as part of the DELOS Network of Excellence on Digital Libraries (Contract G038-507618).

S. Marchand-Maillet et al. (Eds.): AMR 2006, LNCS 4398, pp. 108–118, 2007.

reflections. To account for these variations, the algorithm simulates the process of image formation in 3D space, using computer graphics, and it estimates 3D shape and texture of faces from single images.

A different class of approaches relies on using multiple imaging modalities in which information extracted from 3D shapes and 2D images of the face are combined together to attain better recognition results. In [4], face recognition in videos is obtained under variations in pose and lighting by using 3D face models. In this approach, 3D database models are used to capture a set of projection images taken from different point of views. Similarity between a target image and 3D models is computed by matching the query with the projection images of the models. In [5], Gabor filter responses in the 2D domain, and "point signature" in the 3D are used to perform face recognition. Extracted 2D and 3D features are then combined together to form an augmented vector which is used to represent each facial image. PCA-based recognition experiments, performed using 3D and 2D images are reported in [6]. The multi-modal result was obtained using a weighted sum of the distances from the individual 3D and 2D face spaces. A large experimentation in terms of number of subjects, gallery and probe images, and the time lapse between gallery and probe image acquisition, is also presented in this work.

Finally, another class of methods relies on using only 3D shapes for the purpose of face recognition. Early works focused on the use of surface curvature information and the Extended Gaussian Image, which provide one-to-one mapping between curvature normals of the surface and the unit sphere. Following a similar solution, 3D face recognition is approached in [7], by first segmenting the shape based on Gaussian curvature, and then creating a feature vector from the segmented regions. This set of features is then used to represent faces in recognition experiments. However, a key limitation of such approaches is that to enable reliable extraction of curvature data, accurate 3D acquisition is required. Other solutions have used registration techniques to align 3D models or clouds of points. In [8], face recognition is performed using Iterative Closest Point (ICP) matching of face surfaces with resolution levels typical of the irregular point cloud representations provided by structured light scanning.

In this paper, we propose an original solution to retrieval by similarity of 3D faces based on description and matching of the relative position of salient anatomical facial structures. In the proposed model, these structures relate to convex and concave regions that are identified on a 3D face by means of surface curvature analysis. Facial information captured by these regions is then represented in a compact form evaluating spatial relationships between every pair of regions. To this end, we propose an original modeling technique capable to quantitatively measure the spatial relationships between three dimensional entities. The model develops on the theory of *weighted walkthroughs* (WWs), originally proposed to represent spatial relationships between two-dimensional extended entities [9]. Then, we show how to extend the model so as to capture relationships between 2D surface regions in a 3D space. Finally, mapping regions and their relationships to a graph model and defining a distance measure between 3DWWs allows for the effective comparison of face models.

The paper is organized in four Sections and a Conclusion. In Sect.2, a method is presented for extracting salient convex and concave regions from a dense triangular mesh. The theory of 3DWWs is then developed and proposed to represent spatial relationships between surface regions in a 3D space. This enables the effective representation of a face model through an attributed relational graph accounting for face regions and their relationships. Based on this model, a similarity measure between 3DWWs is defined in Sect.3, and a method for the efficient comparison of graph representations of facial models is discussed in Sect.4. Face recognition results obtained on a 3D face database are reported in Sect.5. Finally, conclusions are outlined in Sect.6.

2   Extraction and Description of Convex and Concave Face Regions

The relative position and shape of convex and concave regions of a face, capture geometric elements of a face that can be used to enable face identification. Loci of convex and concave surface have been intensively studied in connection with researches on surface mathematics, [10,11], human perception of shapes, [12], quality-control of free-form surfaces, [13], image and data analysis [14], face recognition [15] and many other applications.

In the proposed solution, identification of convex and concave surface regions is accomplished by means of curvature based segmentation of model surface. For this purpose the mean shift segmentation procedure [16], [17] is adopted, so as to avoid use of a predefined—although parameterized—model to fit the distribution of curvature values. Specifically, the mean shift procedure relies on estimation of the local density gradient. Gradient estimation is used within an iterative procedure to find local peaks of the density. All points that converge to the same peak are then considered to be members of the same segment.

Use of the mean shift procedure to segment a 3D surface requires the definition of a radially symmetric kernel to measure the distance—both spatially and in the curvature space—between mesh vertices. This kernel is used to associate with every mesh vertex v_i a mean shift vector. During the iterative stage of the mean shift procedure, the mean shift vector associated with each vertex climbs to the hilltops of the density function. At each iteration, each mean shift vector is attracted by the sample point kernels centered at nearby vertices.

For 3D surface segmentation, the feature space is composed of two independent domains: the spatial/lattice domain and the range/curvature domain. Thus, every mesh vertex is mapped into a multi-dimensional feature point characterized by the 3-dimensional spatial lattice and 1-dimensional curvature space. Due to the different nature of the two domains, the kernel is usually broken into the product of two different radially symmetric kernels ($k^s(.)$ and $k^r(.)$ are the profiles of the kernel):

$$K_{h^s\,h^r}(v_i) = \frac{c}{(h^s)^3(h^r)}\, k^s\left(\left\|\frac{x^s}{h^s}\right\|^2\right) k^r\left(\left\|\frac{x^r}{h^r}\right\|^2\right)$$

where superscript 's' refers to the spatial domain, and 'r' to the curvature range, x^s and x^r are the spatial and range parts of a feature vector, h^s and h^r are the bandwidths in the two domains and c is a normalization coefficient.

As an example, Fig.1 shows results of the detection of convex (a) and concave (b) regions on a face model.

Regions extracted from a 3D face are 2D surface portions in a 3D reference space. Information captured by these regions is represented by modeling regions and their mutual spatial relationships. To this end, we propose a theory of 3D spatial relationships between surface entities, which develops on the model of *weighted walkthroughs* (WWs) originally defined for two-dimensional extended entities [9]. Description of spatial relationships through 3DWWs is invariant to translation and scale but not to rotation. Therefore, in order to enable invariance of face matching with respect to translation, scale and rotation, face models are first normalized: models are scaled and rotated so as to fit within a sphere of unit radius centered at the nose tip and aligning the nose ridge along the Z axis.

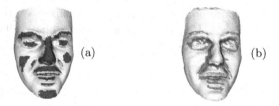

Fig. 1. Salient curvature extrema detected on a face model: triangles corresponding to convex (a) and concave (b) regions

2.1   3D Weighted Walkthroughs

In a three dimensional Cartesian reference system, with coordinate axes X, Y, Z, projections of two points, $a = \langle x_a, y_a, z_a \rangle$ and $b = \langle x_b, y_b, z_b \rangle$ on each axis, can take three different orders: *before, coincident,* or *after.* The combination of the three projections results in 27 different three-dimensional displacements (*primitive directions*), which can be encoded by a triple of indexes $\langle i, j, k \rangle$:

$$i = \begin{cases} -1 & x_b < x_a \\ 0 & x_b = x_a \\ +1 & x_b > x_a \end{cases} \quad j = \begin{cases} -1 & y_b < y_a \\ 0 & y_b = y_a \\ +1 & y_b > y_a \end{cases} \quad k = \begin{cases} -1 & z_b < z_a \\ 0 & z_b = z_a \\ +1 & z_b > z_a \end{cases}$$

In general, pairs of points in two sets A and B, can be connected through multiple different primitive directions. According to this, the triple $\langle i, j, k \rangle$, is a walkthrough from A to B if it encodes the displacement between at least one pair of points belonging to A and B, respectively. In order to account for its perceptual relevance, each walkthrough $\langle i, j, k \rangle$ is associated with a weight $w_{i,j,k}(A, B)$ measuring the number of pairs of points belonging to A and B, whose displacement is captured by the direction $\langle i, j, k \rangle$.

The weight is evaluated as an integral measure over the six-dimensional set of point pairs in A and B (see Fig.2(a)):

$$w_{ijk}(A,B) = \frac{1}{K_{ijk}(A,B)} \int_A \int_B C_i(x_b - x_a)C_j(y_b - y_a)C_k(z_b - z_a)dx_a dx_b dy_a dy_b dz_a dz_b$$

(1)

where $K_{ijk}(A,B)$ acts as dimensional normalization factor, and $C_{\pm 1}(.)$ are the characteristic functions of the positive and negative real semi-axis $(0, +\infty)$ and $(-\infty, 0)$, respectively. In particular, $C_0(\cdot) = \delta(\cdot)$ denotes the Dirac's function, and acts as a characteristic function of the singleton set $\{0\}$. Weights between A and B are organized in a $3 \times 3 \times 3$ matrix $(w(A,B))$, of indexes i, j, k (see Fig.2). As a particular case, Eq.(1) also holds if A and B are coincident (i.e., $A \equiv B$).

In Eq.(1), the weights with one, two or three null indexes (i.e., $w_{i,0,0}$, $w_{i,j,0}$, $w_{i,0,k}$, $w_{0,j,0}$, $w_{0,j,k}$, $w_{0,0,k}$ and $w_{0,0,0}$) are computed by integrating a quasi-everywhere-null function (the set of point pairs that are aligned or coincident has a null measure in the six-dimensional space of Eq.(1)). The Dirac function appearing in the expression of $C_0(\cdot)$ reduces the dimensionality of the integration domain to enable a finite non-null measure. To compensate this reduction, normalization factors $K_{i,j,k}(A,B)$ ($K_{i,j,k}$ in the following) have different dimensionality whether indexes i, j and k are equal to zero or take non-null values:

$$\begin{aligned}
K_{\pm 1,\pm 1,0} &= L_A L_B H_A H_B D_{AB} & K_{\pm 1,0,0} &= L_A L_B H_{AB} D_{AB} & K_{\pm 1,\pm 1,\pm 1} &= |A||B| \\
K_{\pm 1,0,\pm 1} &= L_A L_B H_{AB} D_A D_B & K_{0,\pm 1,0} &= L_{AB} H_A H_B D_{AB} & K_{0,0,0} &= (|A||B|)^{\frac{1}{2}} \quad (2)\\
K_{0,\pm 1,\pm 1} &= L_{AB} H_A H_B D_A D_B & K_{0,0,\pm 1} &= L_{AB} H_{AB} D_A D_B
\end{aligned}$$

where (see Fig.2(b)): $|A|$ and $|B|$ are the volumes of A, and B; L_A, H_A, D_A, L_B, H_B and D_B are the width, height and depth of the 3D minimum embedding rectangles of A and B, respectively; L_{AB}, H_{AB} and D_{AB} are the width, height and depth of the 3D minimum embedding rectangles of the union of A and B, respectively.

Developing on the properties of integrals, it can be easily proven that the twenty-seven weights of 3DWWs are reflexive (i.e., $w_{i,j,k}(A,B) = w_{-i,-j,-k}(B,A)$), and invariant with respect to shifting and scaling.

2.2   WWs Between 3D Surfaces

In that Eq.(1) accounts for the contribution of individual pairs of 3D points, computation of spatial relationships between surface entities in 3D directly descends from the general case. For 3D surfaces, Eq.(1) can be written by replacing volumetric integrals with surface integrals extended to the area of two surfaces.

In practice, the complexity in computing Eq.(1) is managed by reducing the integral to a double summation over a discrete domain obtained by uniformly partitioning the 3D space. In this way, volumetric-pixels v_{xyz} (*voxels*) of uniform size are used to approximate entities (i.e., $A = \bigcup_n A_n$, where A_n are voxels with a non-null intersection with the entity: $v_{xyz} \in \{A_n\}$ iff $v_{xyz} \cap A \neq \varnothing$). According

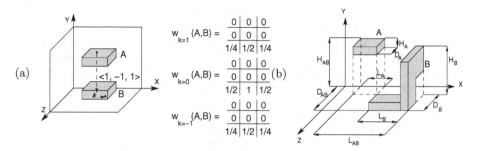

Fig. 2. (a) Walkthrough connecting a points in A with a point in B. The relationship matrix between A and B is expressed by three matrixes for $k = 1, 0, -1$, respectively. (b) Measures on A and B appearing in the normalization factors K_{ijk} of Eq.(2).

to this, 3DWWs between $A = \bigcup_n A_n$, and $B = \bigcup_m B_m$ can be derived as linear combination of the 3DWWs between individual voxel pairs $\langle A_n, B_m \rangle$:

$$w_{ijk}\left(\bigcup_n A_n, \bigcup_m B_m\right) = \frac{1}{K_{ijk}(A,B)} \sum_n \sum_m K_{ijk}(A_n, B_m) \cdot w(A_n, B_m) \qquad (3)$$

as can be easily proven by the properties of integrals. Terms $w(A_n, B_m)$, indicating 3DWWs between individual voxel pairs, are computed in closed form in that they represent the relationships occurring among elementary cubes (voxels) and only twenty-seven basic mutual-positions are possible between voxels in 3D.

3   Similarity Measure for 3DWWs

Three directional weights, taking values within 0 and 1, can be computed on the eight corner weights of the 3DWWs matrix (all terms are intended to be computed between two surface regions A and B, i.e., $w_{i,j,k} = w_{i,j,k}(A,B)$):

$$\begin{aligned}
w_H &= w_{1,1,1} + w_{1,-1,1} + w_{1,1,-1} + w_{1,-1,-1} \\
w_V &= w_{-1,1,1} + w_{1,1,1} + w_{-1,1,-1} + w_{1,1,-1} \\
w_D &= w_{1,1,1} + w_{1,-1,1} + w_{-1,1,1} + w_{-1,-1,1}
\end{aligned} \qquad (4)$$

which account for the degree by which B is on the right, up and in front of A, respectively. Similarly, seven weights account for the alignment along the three reference directions of the space:

$$\begin{aligned}
w_{H_0} &= w_{0,1,1} + w_{0,-1,1} + w_{0,1,-1} + w_{0,-1,-1} & w_{HV_0} &= w_{0,0,1} + w_{0,0,-1} \\
w_{V_0} &= w_{1,0,1} + w_{-1,0,1} + w_{-1,0,-1} + w_{1,0,-1} & w_{HD_0} &= w_{0,1,0} + w_{0,-1,0} \\
w_{D_0} &= w_{1,1,0} + w_{1,-1,0} + w_{-1,1,0} + w_{-1,-1,0} & w_{VD_0} &= w_{1,0,0} + w_{-1,0,0} \\
& & w_{HVD_0} &= w_{0,0,0}
\end{aligned} \qquad (5)$$

where $w_{H_0}, w_{V_0}, w_{D_0}$ measure alignments in which the coordinates X, Y and Z do not change, respectively; $w_{HV_0}, w_{HD_0}, w_{VD_0}$, measure alignments where coordinates XY, XZ and YZ do not change, respectively; and w_{HVD_0} accounts for overlap between points of A and B.

Based on the previous weights, similarity in the arrangement of pairs of surfaces (A, B) and (A', B') is evaluated by a distance $D(w, w')$ which combines the differences between homologous weights in the 3DWWs $w(A, B)$ and $w(A', B')$. In terms of the weights of Eqs.(4)-(5), this is expressed as:

$$\mathcal{D}(w, w') = \lambda_H |w_H - w'_H| + \lambda_V |w_V - w'_V| + \lambda_D |w_D - w'_D|$$
$$+ \lambda_{H_0} |w_{H_0} - w'_{H_0}| + \lambda_{V_0} |w_{V_0} - w'_{V_0}| + \lambda_{D_0} |w_{D_0} - w'_{D_0}|$$
$$+ \lambda_{HV_0} |w_{HV_0} - w'_{HV_0}| + \lambda_{HD_0} |w_{HD_0} - w'_{HD_0}| + \lambda_{VD_0} |w_{VD_0} - w'_{VD_0}|$$
$$+ \lambda_{HVD_0} |w_{HVD_0} - w'_{HVD_0}|$$

where λ_H, λ_V, λ_D, λ_{H_0}, λ_{V_0}, λ_{D_0}, λ_{HV_0}, λ_{HD_0}, λ_{VD_0} and λ_{HVD_0}, are non-negative numbers with sum equal to 1.

Distance $\mathcal{D}$ can be proven to exhibit the five properties that are commonly assumed as axiomatic basis of metric distances, i.e., positivity ($\mathcal{D}(w, w') \geq 0$), normality ($\forall w, w'$, $\mathcal{D}(w, w') \leq 1$), auto-similarity ($\mathcal{D}(w, w') = 0$ iff $w = w'$), symmetry ($\mathcal{D}(w, w') = \mathcal{D}(w', w)$), and triangularity ($\mathcal{D}(w, w') + \mathcal{D}(w', \hat{w}) \geq \mathcal{D}(w, \hat{w})$). Each property is proven to separately hold for each of the distance components, and it is then extended to the sum $\mathcal{D}$.

In addition, due to the integral nature of weights w_{ijk}, $\mathcal{D}$ satisfies a property of continuity which ensures that slight changes in the mutual positioning or in the distribution of points in two sets A and B result in slight changes in their 3DWWs. If the set B is modified by the addition of B_ϵ, the relationship with respect to a set A changes up to a distance which is limited by a bound tending to zero when B_ϵ becomes small with respect to B. This has a main relevance in ensuring robustness of comparison.

4   Matching Face Representations

According to the modeling technique of Sect.2, a generic face model F, is described by a set of N_F regions. In that WWs are computed for every pairs of regions (including the pair composed by a region and itself), a face is represented by a set of $N_F \cdot (N_F + 1)/2$ relationship matrixes. This model is cast to a graph representation by regarding face regions as graph nodes and their mutual spatial relationships as graph edges:

$$G \stackrel{def}{=} <N, E, \alpha, \beta>, \quad \begin{aligned} N &= set\ of\ nodes \\ E &\subseteq N \times N = set\ of\ edges \\ \gamma &: N \mapsto L_N, \ nodes\ labeling\ function \\ \delta &: E \mapsto L_E, \ edge\ labeling\ function \end{aligned}$$

where L_N and L_E are the sets of nodes and edge labels, respectively. In our framework, γ is the function that assigns to a node n_k the self-relationship matrix $w(n_k, n_k)$ computed between the region associated to the node and itself. In addition, γ associates the node with the area of the region and a type which distinguishes between nodes corresponding to concave and convex regions. The edge labeling function δ assigns to an edge $[n_j, n_k]$, connecting nodes n_j and n_k, the relationship matrix $w(n_j, n_k)$ occurring between the regions associated to the two nodes.

In order to compare graph representations, distance measures for node labels and for edge labels have been defined. Both of them, rely on the distance measure $\mathcal{D}$ between 3DWWs defined in Sect.3.

Matching a *template face graph* T, and a gallery *reference face graph* R, involves the association of the nodes in the template with a subset of the nodes in the reference. Using an additive composition, and indicating with Γ an injective function which associates nodes t_k in the template graph with a subset of the nodes $\Gamma(t_k)$ in the reference graph, this is expressed as follows:

$$\mu^{\Gamma}(T, R) \overset{def}{=} \frac{\lambda}{N_T} \cdot \sum_{k=1}^{N_T} \mathcal{D}(w(t_k, t_k), w(\Gamma(t_k), \Gamma(t_k))) + \qquad (6)$$

$$+ \frac{2(1 - \lambda)}{N_T(N_T - 1)} \cdot \sum_{k=1}^{N_T} \sum_{h=1}^{k-1} \mathcal{D}(w(t_k, t_h), w(\Gamma(t_k), \Gamma(t_h)))$$

where the first summation accounts for the average distance scored by matching nodes of the two graphs, and the second double summation evaluates the mean distance in the arrangements of pairs of nodes in the two graphs. In this equation, N_T is the number of nodes in the template graph T, and $\lambda \in [0, 1]$ balances the mutual relevance of edge and node distance.

In general, given two graphs T and R, a combinatorial number of different interpretations Γ are possible, each scoring a different value of distance. According to this, the distance μ between T and R is defined as the minimum under any possible interpretation Γ: $\mu(T, R) = \min_{\Gamma} \mu^{\Gamma}(T, R)$. In so doing, computation of the distance becomes an *optimal error-correcting (sub)graph isomorphism problem*, which is a NP-complete problem with exponential time solution algorithms. Since the proposed modeling technique results into complete graphs with a relatively large number of nodes (i.e., typical models have more than 20 regions, almost equally divided between concave and convex regions), to improve the computational efficiency, we relaxed the requirement of optimality by accepting sub-optimal matches. This is obtained by imposing that cross-matches between nodes of different type is not allowed, and renouncing to include in the distance minimization the relationships between nodes of different type. According to this, the distance $\mu(T, R)$ is computed as the sum of three separated components:

$$\mu(T, R) = \min_{\Gamma_a}[\mu^{\Gamma_a}(T_a, R_a)] + \min_{\Gamma_b}[\mu^{\Gamma_b}(T_b, R_b)] + \qquad (7)$$

$$+ (1 - \lambda) \cdot \mu_s(w(T_a, T_b), w(\Gamma_a(T_a), \Gamma_b(T_b)))$$

where T_a, R_a and T_b, R_b are the sub-graphs composed by nodes of concave and convex regions in the template and reference models, respectively (i.e., $T = T_a \cup T_b$, $R = R_a \cup R_b$). Optimal solutions $\min_{\Gamma_a}$ and $\min_{\Gamma_b}$ in matching sub-graphs are computed by using the algorithm in [18]. Finally, the third term of

Eq.(7), accounts for the relationship distance occurring between concave nodes and convex nodes in the matched sub-graphs:

$$\mu_s(w(T_a, T_b), w(\Gamma_a(T_a), \Gamma_b(T_b))) = \frac{1}{N_{T_a} \cdot N_{T_b}} \cdot \qquad (8)$$

$$\cdot \sum_{t_k \in T_a} \sum_{t_h \in T_b} \mathcal{D}(w(t_k, t_h), w(\Gamma_a(t_k), \Gamma_b(t_h)))$$

Without loss of generality, Eqs.(6)-(8) assume that the number of nodes in the template graph (N_{T_a}, N_{T_b}), are not greater than the number of nodes in the reference graph (N_{R_a}, N_{R_b}). In fact, if $N_{T_a} > N_{R_a}$ or $N_{T_b} > N_{R_b}$, graphs can be exchanged due to the reflexivity of 3DWWs, and the normality in the sum of their eight corner weights.

5   Experimental Results

The proposed approach for description and matching of faces has been experimented using models from the GavabDB database [19]. This includes three-dimensional facial surface of 61 people (45 male and 16 female). The whole set of people are Caucasian and most of them are aged between 18 and 40. For each person, 7 different models are taken—differing in terms of viewpoint or facial expression—resulting in 427 facial models. In particular, there are 2 frontal and 2 rotated models with neutral facial expression, and 3 frontal models in which the person laughs, smiles or exhibits a random gesture. All models are automatically processed, as described in the previous sections, so as to extract a graph based description of their content, encoding prominent characteristics of individual convex and concave regions as well as their relative arrangement.

In order to assess the effectiveness of the proposed solution for face identification, we performed a set of recognition experiments. In these experiments, one of the two frontal models with neutral expression provided for each person is assumed as reference (*gallery*) model for the identification. Results are given in Tab.1 as matching accuracy for different categories of test models.

It can be noted that the proposed approach provides a quite high recognition accuracy also for variations in face expression.

Table 1. Matching accuracy for different categories

Test category	Matching Accuracy
frontal - neutral gesture	94%
frontal - smile gesture	85%
frontal - laugh gesture	81%
frontal - random gesture	77%
rotated looking down - neutral gesture	80%
rotated looking up - neutral gesture	79%

In Fig.3, recognition examples are reported for four test faces of different subjects. For each case, on the left the probe face is shown, while on the right the correctly identified reference face is reported. These models also provide examples of the variability in terms of facial expression of face models included in the gallery.

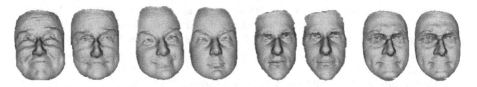

Fig. 3. Four recognition examples. For each pair, the probe (on the left) and the correctly identified model (on the right) are reported

6   Conclusions

In this paper, we have proposed an original solution to the problem of 3D face recognition. The basic idea is to compare 3D face models by using the information provided by their salient convex and concave regions. To this end, an original framework has been developed which provides two main contributions. First, 3D face models are described by regions which are extracted as zones of convex and concave curvature of 3D dense meshes through a 3D mean-shift like procedure. Then, a theory for modeling spatial relationships between surfaces in 3D has been developed, in the form of 3DWWs. Finally, we proposed a graph matching solution for the comparison between 3DWWs computed on regions extracted from a template model and those of reference models. The viability of the approach has been validated in a set of recognition experiments.

Future work will address an extended experimental validation in order to compare the proposed approach with respect to existing solutions. How issues of illumination and pose variations affect the performance of the proposed solution will be also considered.

References

1. Zhao, W., Chellappa, R., Phillips, P., Rosenfeld, A.: Face recognition: A literature survey. ACM Computing Survey **35**(4) (2003) 399–458
2. Bowyer, K., Chang, K., Flynn, P.: A survey of approaches to three dimensional face recognition. In: Proc. International Conference on Pattern Recognition, Cambridge, UK (2004) 358–361
3. Blanz, V., Vetter, T.: Face recognition based on fitting a 3d morphable model. IEEE Transactions on Pattern Analysis and Machine Intelligence **25**(9) (2003) 1063–1074
4. Park, U., Chen, H., Jain, A.: 3d model-assisted face recognition in video. In: Proc. Canadian Conference on Computer and Robot Vision. (2005) 322–329

5. Wang, Y., Chua, C., Ho, Y.: Facial feature detection and face recognition from 2d and 3d images. Pattern Recognition Letters **23**(10) (2002) 1191–1202
6. Chang, K., Bowyer, K., Flynn, P.: Face recognition using 2d and 3d facial data. In: Proc. Multimodal User Authentication Workshop. (2003) 25–32
7. Moreno, A., Sánchez, A., Vélez, J., Díaz, F.: Face recognition using 3d surface-extracted descriptor. In: Proc. Irish Machine Vision and Image Processing. (2003)
8. Cook, J., Chandran, V., Sridharan, S., Fookes, C.: Face recognition from 3d data using iterative closest point algorithm and gaussian mixture models. In: Proc. Symp. on 3D Data Processing, Visualization and Transmission. (2004) 502–509
9. Berretti, S., Del Bimbo, A., Vicario, E.: Weighted walkthroughs between extended entities for retrieval by spatial arrangement. IEEE Transactions on Multimedia **5**(1) (2003) 52–70
10. Koenderink, J.: Solid Shapes. MIT press, Boston, USA (1990)
11. Porteous, I.: Differentiation for the Intelligence of Curves and Surfaces. Cambridge University Press, Cambridge, UK (1994)
12. Hoffman, D., Richards, W.: Parts of recognition. Cognition **18** (1985) 65–96
13. Hosaka, M.: Modeling of Curves and Surfaces in CAD/CAM. Springer, Berlin (1992)
14. Eberly, D.: Ridges in Image and Data Analysis. Kluwer (1996)
15. Halliman, P., Gordon, G., Yuille, A., Giblin, P., Mumford, D.: Two- and Three-Dimensional Patterns of the Face. A.K. Peters, Natick, MA, USA (1999)
16. Comaniciu, D., Meer, P.: Mean shift: A robust approach toward feature space analysis. IEEE Transactions on Pattern Analysis and Machine Intelligence **24**(5) (2002) 603–619
17. Yamauchi, H., Lee, S., Lee, Y., Ohtake, Y., Belyaev, A., Seidel, H.P.: Feature sensitive mesh segmentation with mean shift. In: Proc. Shape Modeling International. (2005) 236–243
18. Berretti, S., Del Bimbo, A., Vicario, E.: Efficient matching and indexing of graph models in content based retrieval. IEEE Transactions on Pattern Analysis and Machine Intelligence **23**(10) (2001) 1089–1105
19. Moreno, A., Sanchez, A.: Gavabdb: A 3d face database. In: Proc. 2nd COST275 Workshop on Biometrics on the Internet, Vigo (Spain) (2004) 75–80

Fuzzy Semantic Action and Color Characterization of Animation Movies in the Video Indexing Task Context

Bogdan E. Ionescu[1,2], Didier Coquin[1], Patrick Lambert[1], and Vasile Buzuloiu[2]

[1] University of Savoie, LISTIC, BP 806, F. 74016 Annecy-Cedex, France
{Didier.Coquin,Patrick.Lambert}@univ-savoie.fr
[2] University "Politehnica" Bucharest, LAPI, 061071, Bucharest, Romania
{BIonescu,Buzuloiu}@alpha.imag.pub.ro

Abstract. This paper presents a fuzzy statistical approach for the semantic content characterization of the animation movies. The movie action content and color properties play an important role in the understanding of the movie content, being related to the artistic signature of the author. That is why the proposed approach is carried out by analyzing several statistical parameters which are computed both from the movie shot distribution and the global color distribution. The first category of parameters represents the movie mean shot change speed, the transition ratio and the action ratio while the second category represents the color properties in terms of color intensity, warmth, saturation and color relationships. The semantic content characterizations are achieved from the low-level parameters using a fuzzy representation approach. Hence, the movie content is described in terms of action, mystery, explosivity, predominant hues, color contrasts and the color harmony schemes. Several experimental tests were performed on an animation movie database. Moreover, a classification test was conducted to prove the discriminating power of the proposed semantic descriptions for their prospective use as semantic indexes in a content-based video retrieval system.

1 Introduction

During the last few years, the existing video indexing techniques have focused mainly on the semantic content annotation, as the video indexes are getting closer to the human perception. Thanks to the *"International Animated Film Festival"* [1], that has taken place, in Annecy (France), every year, since 1960, a large number of animation movies is available. Some of these movies are currently being digitized to constitute a numerical animation movie database, soon to be available on-line for general use (see Animaquid [1]). As the animation movie content understanding is highly related to the human perception and the rich artistic content is almost entirely contained in the visual information, a system which allows us to access the movie at a semantic level is then required.

S. Marchand-Maillet et al. (Eds.): AMR 2006, LNCS 4398, pp. 119–135, 2007.
© Springer-Verlag Berlin Heidelberg 2007

Animation movies are different from the conventional ones (i.e. cinema movies, conventional cartoons, etc.) in many respects: the events do not follow a natural way, objects/characters emerge and vanish without respecting any physical rules, sometimes the movements are not continuous, the predominant motion is the object motion [5], a lot of visual color effects are used, artistic concepts are used: painting concepts, theatrical concepts, and so on. Understanding the movie content is sometimes impossible, some animation experts say that more than 30% of the animation movies from [1] apparently do not have any logical meaning. However, one major characteristic is that every animation movie has its own particular **color distribution**, unlike to conventional movies which share almost all the same color distribution. Colors are selected and mixed by the artist using various color artistry concepts to express particular feelings or to induce particular sensations. At a structural level, the movie is a sequence of shots which are linked to one another by the video transitions, i.e. cuts, fades, dissolves etc. [2]. A peculiarity of the animation movies is the presence of some specific color effects, such as the "short color changes" or SCC [3].

Both, the global color distribution and the movie shot structure play an important role in the content understanding of the animation movies. They could serve as a basis for deriving semantic indexes in a content-based retrieval system. The movie color distribution provides us with detailed information on the movie's artistry content while the movie shot structure provides us with information on the movie action content.

Very little research has been done in this working field, and particularly in the animation movie domain [5]. In [6] the color artistry concepts are extracted for the indexing of artwork images. The relationships between colors are analyzed in a perceptual color space, namely LCH (intensity, chroma and hue) and several particular color techniques are used: the opponent color scheme, Itten's seven color contrasts and the color harmony schemes. However, the proposed system analyzes only the color spatial distribution applied to image indexation tasks. Understanding the movie color content requires a temporal color analysis as well. Another system, where art images and commercials are analyzed at emotional and expressional levels is proposed in [7]. Various features are used, not only the color information but also motion, video transition distribution, etc., all in order to identify a set of primary induced emotions, namely: *action, relaxation, joy and uneasiness*. The colors are analyzed at a region-based level, by considering the object's spatial relationship in the image, obtained through image segmentation.

Regarding the movie action content analysis, the existing methods are application specific and they are mainly used as feature extraction techniques for the computation of semantic movie skims or abstracts, such as movie trailers [8]. Thus, the most interesting parts of the movie or some particular events are highlighted using several statistical elements of information, as for example: the shot change ratio [21] or the edge change speed [22]. For more details see the state-of-the-art on video skimming proposed in [8].

The goal of our approach is to provide animation artists or ordinary people as well, with detailed information regarding the movie **action content** and the used **color techniques**. It continues the work presented in [4] where the movie's *global weighted color histogram* and a fuzzy representation mechanism were used to understand the meaning of the movie's color distribution. Using the same reasoning, a fuzzy symbolic characterization is performed at the movie shot level, all in order to determine the semantic meaning of the movie's action content.

The paper is organized, thus: Section 2 presents the overview of our approach. The action content characterization is described with Section 3 while the color content characterization is presented in Section 4. Several experimental results are presented and discussed with each of the two sections. The proposed content characterization methodology is used in Section 5 to classify an animation movie database from [1]. Finally, the conclusions and future work are discussed with Section 6.

2   The Proposed Approach

The proposed approach uses several analysis steps which are described with the Fig. 1.

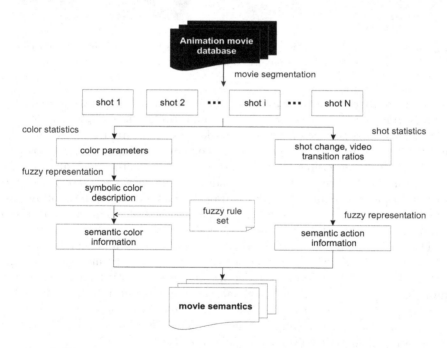

Fig. 1. The proposed semantic characterization methodology

To perform the **color** and **action** content analysis first the movie is divided into shots. Detecting the video shot boundaries, that is recovering the elementary video units, provides the basis for nearly all existing video abstraction and high-level video segmentation algorithms [2]. The sharp transitions, or cuts, are detected using a specially designed histogram-based algorithm [3] adapted to the specificity of animation movies. From the existing gradual transitions, only the fades and the dissolves are detected using a pixel-level statistical approach [11], as their occurrence is frequent in the animation movies. Moreover, using the modified camera flash detector proposed in [3] we detect an animation movie specific color effect named SCC ("short color change"). A SCC corresponds to a short time dramatic color change, such as explosions, thunders, color effects, etc. (see Fig. 2). Generally SCCs do not produce a shot change but unfortunately are, by mistake, detected as cuts. Detecting the SCCs allows us first to reduce the false positive change shots and secondly to retrieve the movies using a high amount of such effects, which are movies having a *particular action content*.

Fig. 2. SCCs examples from the movies (top) "François le Vaillant" and (bottom) "The Hill Farm" [19] (each SCC is summarized as one image)

Shots are then determined by fusing the detected video transitions and then by removing less relevant frames as they do not contain meaningful information (i.e. black frames between fades or the video transition frames). To reduce the movie temporal redundancy and thus the computational cost, a movie abstract is automatically generated. It will serve as a basis for the color analysis. As action takes most likely place in the middle of the shot, each shot is reduced to a subsequence containing $p\%$ of its frames (more detail will be captured for the longer shots as they contain more color information). The choice of the p parameter is discussed later in the Section 4.

The **action analysis** is performed by computing several low-level statistical parameters on the video transition distribution, such as the mean shot change speed, the transition ratio or the action ratio. On the other hand, the **color analysis** is performed on the movie abstract by computing the movie global weighted color histogram proposed in [10]. Several color parameters are computed from the global histogram, such as: light/dark color ratio, cold/warm color ratio, adjacent/complementary color ratio, etc.

Using a fuzzy representation approach we determine meaningful semantic color information regarding *Itten's color contrasts* [12] and the *color harmony schemes* [13], which are to be found in the animation movies from [1]. The same reasoning is used to derive meaningful symbolic information regarding the movie's action perception from the low-level video transition parameters.

3   Action Characterization

The first proposed characterization concerns the movie action content. Using the shot distribution a **video transition annotation** is automatically generated to capture the movie temporal structure. The proposed annotation describes the movie temporal evolution as a time-continuous signal interrupted by the occurrence of the video transitions. Hence, a signal is built by assigning a constant value (i.e. 1) to each movie frame. Different signal shapes are associated to each particular transition by preserving the transition length. For example, a cut is a signal 0 crossing value while a SCC is a small peak (see the red line graph in Fig. 3). This graphic annotation allows us to determine the important action parts of the movie as following.

3.1   Shot Analysis

A shot change distribution analysis is performed to highlight the movie's *action segments*. Experimental tests proved that in the animation movies from [1] the most attractive scenes are mainly related to fast repetitive shot changes. On the proposed video annotation graph these situations correspond to graph regions containing high densities of vertical lines (see the action zones in Fig. 3).

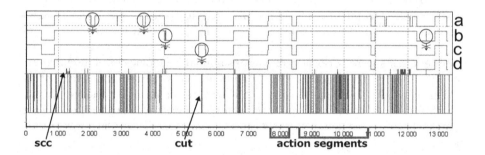

Fig. 3. Action segment computation example (movie "François le Vaillant" [19]). The video annotation graph is depicted with the red line while the action segments are depicted with the green line (*a* - *d* corresponds to the computation step).

First, we define a basic indicator, ζ_T, which is related to the time structure of the movie. It represents the relative number of shot changes, N_{sc}, within the frame interval of $T \cdot 25$ frames (as $1s = 25$ frames). Regarding ζ_T as a discrete random variable, its distribution for the entire movie could be evaluated by computing the N_{sc} values for all the overlapped time windows of size T seconds. Using ζ_T we define the mean shot change speed, $\bar{v}_T$, as:

$$\bar{v}_T = E\{\zeta_T\} = \sum_{t=1}^{T \cdot 25} t \cdot f_{N_{sc}}(t) \tag{1}$$

where $f_{N_{sc}}$ is the probability density of N_{sc}, thus:

$$f_{N_{sc}}(t) = \frac{1}{N} \sum_{i=1}^{N} \delta(N_{sc}^{i} - t) \qquad (2)$$

with N the number of the analyzed time windows of size T seconds, i the current analyzed frame interval, thus $[n_i, n_i + T \cdot 25]$ contains N_{sc}^{i} shot changes. We can also note that $N = (T_{movie} - T) \cdot 25 + 1$ and $n_{i+1} - n_i = 1$, where T_{movie} is the movie length measured in seconds. The **action segments** are further obtained with the following algorithm:

a.thresholding: all the frames within the current analyzed frame window i of size T seconds are marked as *action frames* if $\zeta_T > \bar{v}_T$. An action segment is a time continuous interval of action frames and it is represented as a binary True/False signal (see the graph **a** in Fig. 3).

b.merging: first, the SCCs are marked as action segments as they contain attractive movie information. Then, the neighbour action segments at a time distance lower than T are merged together. This step allows us to erase the small gaps as we can see in the graph **b** in Fig. 3.

c.clearing: the small action segments, thus having a length smaller than the analysis window T, are being erased. This step allows us to erase the small isolated peaks in the action segments (see the graph **c** in Fig. 3).

d.removing: all the action segments which contain only one movie shot are to be removed. It is possible to obtain false action segments due to short movie segments containing a high value of $\bar{v}_T$ (see the graph **d** in Fig. 3).

Several tests were performed on various animation movies for different values of T, $T \in \{1, ..., 10\}$ seconds. The T value is related to the granularity of the action segments. Using small values of T, will result in high densities of small length action segments (the action segments are over segmented). A good compromise between the action segment lengths and their density has proved to be taking $T = 5s$ (see Fig. 3).

3.2 Low-Level Action Parameters

Using the proposed video annotation graph and the action segment distribution we define four low-level parameters. The first one is the *mean shot change speed*, $\bar{v}_T$, defined above in equation 1, and it is related to the movie rhythm. High values of $\bar{v}_T$ correspond to a high number of shot changes, occurring within the time interval T, and thus to a fast movie rhythm.

The second parameter is the *action segment ratio*, A_{movie}, defined as the amount of action segments within the movie. Similarly, the video transition ratio, R_{trans}, is defined as the amount of fades and dissolves within the movie. Finally, the SCC ratio, R_{SCC}, is defined as the amount of the SCC color effects within the movie. The proposed parameters are defined as:

$$A_{movie} = \frac{T_{action}}{T_{movie}}, \quad R_{trans} = \frac{T_{fades} + T_{dissolves}}{T_{movie}}, \quad R_{SCC} = \frac{T_{SCC}}{T_{movie}} \qquad (3)$$

where T_{action} is the total length of the movie's action segments, T_{movie} is the movie length, T_{fades}, $T_{dissolves}$ and T_{SCC} represent the total length of the fades, dissolves and respectively SCCs. The choice of these parameters was motivated by the content descriptions proposed in the next section.

3.3   Fuzzy Symbolic Action Description

The higher-level action description is derived from the proposed low-level parameters using a **fuzzy-based representation** approach. The interest in this representation is twofold: first, it allows us to represent the low-level parameters in a human-like manner, i.e. using linguistic concepts. Secondly, it provides a normalization between 0 and 1 of the proposed parameters which facilitates the data comparing and fusion tasks.

A fuzzy symbolical description is associated to each of the four enumerated parameters. The **rhythm** concept is associated to the $\bar{v}_T$ parameter as it is related to the movie action content evolution. The degree of the representation of the rhythm concept in the movie is described with three symbols: "**low-rhythm**", "**mean-rhythm**" and "**high-rhythm**". The fuzzy meaning of each symbol is characterized by its membership function. The design of these functions is performed in a classical way using piece-wise linear functions. This definition is based on the choice of four thresholds, namely: $30, 36, 63, 69$, which were empirically determined by the manual analysis of several animation movies (see figure Fig. 4).

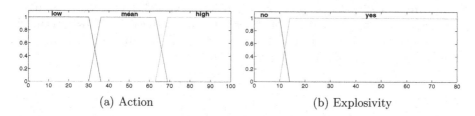

(a) Action   (b) Explosivity

Fig. 4. Example of fuzzy symbolic description: (a) the oX axis corresponds to A_{movie}, (b) the oX axis corresponds to $10 \cdot R_{SCC}$

In a similar way the **action** concept is associated to A_{movie} as containing the movie action content information, the **mystery** concept is associated to the R_{trans} parameter and finally the **explosivity** concept is associated to the R_{SCC} parameter. The action and mystery concepts are represented with three symbols as for the rhythm concept. Regarding the explosivity concept, the existing animation movies are either explosive or not, thus only two symbols will be used: "**yes**" or "**no**". An example is illustrated with Fig. 4.

The choice of the proposed descriptions and parameters was motivated by several facts. In animation movies one important feature is the movie rhythm which is related to the artistic signature of the artist. It reflects the type of action of the movie (i.e. static, dynamic, slow during the introduction and fast with the movie intrigue, etc.). Closely related is the amount of action content which defines the character of the movie (i.e. high action content, no action, etc.). If the first two descriptions are available also for the conventional movies, the mystery content is specific to animation movies. The fades and dissolves are used in the movies with specific purposes. For example, a dissolve is used to change the time of the action [2], similarly, a fade is used to change the action or, used in a fade group (a fade-out, fade-in sequence), introduces a pause before changing the action place. In animation movies, high amounts of such transitions are related somehow to the movie mystery (see the movies "Le Moine et le Poisson" 10 fades and 61 dissolves or "Coeur de Secours" 26 fades and 63 dissolves [1]). Finally the amount of the used SCC visual effects is related to the "explosive" character of the movie, as SCCs stand for explosions, thunders, dramatic color changes in the movie (see in Fig. 2).

3.4   Example of Action Content Description

The validation of our descriptions is a subjective task as a ground truth is not available. To validate the relevance of our results we have used the movie textual descriptions, known as *synopsis*, retrieved from the Animaquid research engine [1] or from the author's published documentation.

We are presenting an example of action content characterization for two representative animation movies, namely "Le Moine et le Poisson" and "Sculptures" [19]. The achieved symbolic characterizations for the movie "Le Moine et le Poisson" are: **"high-rhythm"** ($\bar{v}_{T=5s} = 2.37$), **"high-action"** ($A_{movie} = 74.51\%$), **"high-mystery"** ($R_{trans} = 4.62\%$) and **"no-explosivity"** ($R_{SCC} = 0\%$). On the other hand the movie *"Sculpture"* is characterized by **"low-rhythm"** ($\bar{v}_{T=5s} = 0.31$), **"low-action"** ($A_{movie} = 24.7\%$), **"low-mystery"** ($R_{trans} = 0.6\%$) and **"no-explosivity"** ($R_{SCC} = 0\%$).

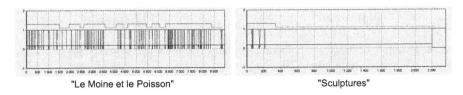

"Le Moine et le Poisson"   "Sculptures"

Fig. 5. Video transition distribution (red line) and action segments (green line). Movies from Folimage Company [19].

The two movie annotation graphs and action segment distributions are depicted with Fig. 5. The movie "Sculptures" contains only 4 video shots which indicate a slow movie rhythm and thus a reduced action content. In fact the movie's action takes place in only one scene which is characteristic for the used plasticine modeling animation technique. On the other hand, the movie "Le Moine et le Poisson" is far more dynamic containing many shot changes and thus has a high rhythm. The high mystery content comes naturally from the movie synopsis: *a monk finds a fish in a water tank near the monastery [...] He is trying repeatedly to catch it [...] The chasing becomes more and more symbolical* [1].

4 Color Characterization

The second content description is retrieved from the color distribution. In this case the color analysis is performed on the movie abstract (see Section 2). First, the frames are color reduced using the Floyd-Steinberg error diffusion filter [9] applied in the XYZ color space. The new colors are selected in the Lab color space from a predefined color palette [3]. The webmaster non-dithering 216 color palette (depicted with Fig. 6) is used due to its efficiency in terms of the availability of a color naming system and the good compromise between the total number of colors (12 elementary colors + 6 gray levels) and color richness. This palette has the colors named according to their degree of hue, saturation and intensity (i.e. "Light Hard Yellow", $R = 255$, $G = 255$ and $B = 51$). Also, an important advantage is its correspondence with Itten's color wheel [12] which is a perceptual-based color representation used in paintings to define color relationships and art concepts.

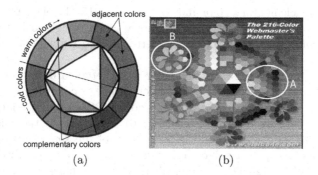

(a)   (b)

Fig. 6. (a) Itten's color wheel, (b) Webmaster non-dithering 216 color palette [14] (*zone A*: variations of an elementary color, namely Violet, and *zone B*: elementary color mixtures)

For each retained frame within the movie abstract the color histogram, $h^j_{shot_i}$ (with i the shot index and j the frame index), is computed. The movie's *global weighted color histogram* is further computed as the weighted sum of all shot mean color histograms, thus:

$$h_{movie}(c) = \sum_{i=0}^{M} \sum_{j=0}^{N_i} \frac{h^j_{shot_i}(c)}{N_i} . w_i \qquad (4)$$

where $c = 0, .., 215$ is a color index from the webmaster palette, M is the number of shots, N_i is the number of the retained frames for $shot_i$ (representing $p\%$ of its frames) and w_i is the weight of the $shot_i$. A weight of a shot is defined as $w_i = \frac{N_{shot_i}}{N_{shots}}$, where N_{shot_i} is the total number of frames for $shot_i$ and N_{shots} is the total number of the movie shot frames. The longer the shot, the more important the contribution of its color distribution to the movie's global histogram. Regarding the best choice for the $p\%$ parameter (the percentage of the retained frames for a given shot, used for the abstract computation) we found that $p \in [15\%, 25\%]$ is a good compromise between the achieved processing time and the resulting histogram quality [10].

4.1   Color Parameters

In order to extract the semantic color information, one has to analyze the human perception. One simple way is the use of the color names. Associating names with colors allows everyone to create a mental image of a given color. Using the available color naming system provided by the Webmaster color palette and the movie global weighted color histogram we are proposing an *elementary color histogram*:

$$h_{elem}(c_e) = \sum_{i=1}^{216} h_{movie}(c_i)|_{\{Name(c_e) \text{ in } Name(c_i)\}} \tag{5}$$

where c_e is an elementary color index, $c_e = 1, ..., 15$ (12 elementary colors + gray, white and black), $h_{movie}()$ is the movie global weighted histogram, c_i is the current color index from the color palette and the $Name()$ operator returns a color name.

Using $h_{elem}()$ several statistical color parameters are further computed, namely: **the color diversity** (P_{div}), the percentage of **complementary colors** (P_{compl}) and the percentage of **adjacent colors** (P_{adj}) (color relationships on Itten's color wheel are illustrated with Fig. 6). For example, the color diversity parameter, P_{div}, is computed as the proportion of the *significant* different elementary colors (occurrence percentage of more than 4%, empirically determined) from the total of 13 (12 colors + gray, where white and black are here considered as gray levels):

$$P_{div} = \frac{Card\{c_e/h_{elem}(c_e) > 4\%\}}{12 + 1} \tag{6}$$

where $Card\{\}$ returns the number of the elements of a data set, $h_{elem}()$ is the elementary color histogram and c_e is an elementary color index.

The other proposed color parameters are computed in a similar way but from the movie global weighted histogram: **the color variation** (P_{var}), the percentage of **light colors** (P_{light}), the percentage of **dark colors** (P_{dark}), the percentage of **hard colors** (P_{hard}), the percentage of **weak colors** (P_{weak}), the percentage of **warm colors** (P_{warm}) and the percentage of **cold colors** (P_{cold}) (the warm/cold colors are defined in [16], see also Fig. 6). Color hue, saturation, lightness and warmth are reflected in color names with specific words. For example the percentage of light colors, P_{light}, is computed as:

$$P_{light} = \sum_{i=1}^{216} h_{movie}(c_i)|_\wp \tag{7}$$

where $h_{movie}()$ is the movie global color histogram, c_i is a color index from the color palette with the property, $\wp$, of its name containing one of the following words: "light", "pale" or "white".

The proposed color measures were determined after the analysis of a large amount of animation movies. We found that the color intensity, saturation and warmth are important color parameters. They allow us to make the distinction between different animation movie types or genres. For example, the movies using the plasticine technique typically have dark cold color palettes (see the cluster 2.1 in Fig. 10). Moreover, each animation movie uses a particular color palette thus another discriminant parameter is the color variation/diversity (see Fig. 8). Finally, the color relationships are useful for making the distinction between movies with different color techniques such as analogous colors, complementary colors, etc. (see the cluster 2.2 in Fig. 10).

4.2 Semantic Color Description

The proposed semantic color information concerns the *color perception*, some of *Itten's color contrasts* and *color harmony schemes*, namely: the *light–dark contrast*, the *cold–warm contrast*, the *contrast of saturation* and the *adjacent–complementary contrast*. First, for each proposed low-level color parameter different symbols are associated in the same way as for the action content description in Section 3. An example is presented with Fig. 7 where the **light color** and **complementary color** concepts are associated to the P_{light} and P_{compl} parameters.

With the proposed symbols, new high-level semantic concepts are built using a fuzzy rule-based system. For example the **light-dark** information is defined with the following rules:

$$\textbf{If } (\text{"}light\ colors\text{" is "}mean\text{"}) \textbf{ and } (\text{"}dark\ colors\text{" is "}mean\text{"})$$
$$\textbf{then } there\ is\ a\ \text{"}light-dark\ contrast\text{"} \tag{8}$$
$$\textbf{If } (\text{"}light\ colors\text{" is "}low\text{"}) \textbf{ and } (\text{"}dark\ colors\text{" is "}high\text{"})$$
$$\textbf{then } the\ dark\ colors\ are\ predominant \tag{9}$$

The fuzzy descriptions for the new proposed symbols are obtained with a uniform mechanism according to the combination/projection principle using a conjunction and a disjunction operator which are the min/max operators [17].

4.3 Example of Color Content Representation

We present here an example of a fuzzy color-based semantic characterization achieved for four representative animation movies, namely: "Casa" (6min5s),

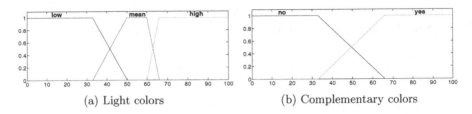

(a) Light colors   (b) Complementary colors

Fig. 7. Example of fuzzy symbolic color descriptions: (a) the oX axis corresponds to P_{light}, (b) the oX axis corresponds to P_{compl}

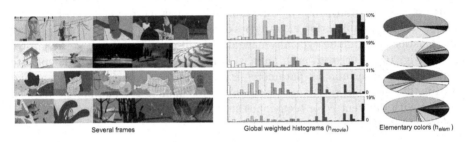

Several frames   Global weighted histograms (h_{movie})   Elementary colors (h_{elem})

Fig. 8. Color parameters, movies from top to bottom: "Casa", "Le Moine et le Poisson", "Circuit Marine" and "François le Vaillant"

"Le Moine et le Poisson" (6min), "Circuit Marine" (5min35s) and "François le Vaillant" (8min56s) [19]. The obtained global weighted color histograms and elementary color histograms are depicted with Fig. 8.

The following semantic color characterizations were obtained (the number in the brackets corresponds to the fuzzy degree, where 1 is the total affirmation):

– movie **"Casa"**: predominant colors Orange (35.4%) and Red (28.3%), moderate color diversity (1), dark-light contrast (0.9), warm colors (1), weak colors (0.8);

– movie **"Le Moine et le Poisson"**: predominant color Yellow (60.3%), moderate color diversity (1), dark-light contrast (0.9), warm colors (1), weak colors (1) and analogous colors (1);

– movie **"Circuit Marine"**: predominant colors Red (22.3%), Blue (13.3%) and Azure (10.9%), moderate color diversity (1), dark-light contrast (0.9), weak colors (0.78);

– movie **"François le Vaillant"**: predominant colors Azure (54.6%) and Cyan (24.1%), reduced color diversity (0.87), dark colors (1) and cold colors (1).

In order to validate the proposed color descriptions, in the absence of a ground truth, we have manually analyzed the movie color content. We found that the proposed color descriptions correspond to the human perception. For example, the movies "Casa" and "Le Moine et le Poisson" respectively use large amounts of Red/Orange and Yellow, therefore the colors are warm and the color diversity is moderate. Also, the use of both bright and dark colors in similar amounts leads to a light-dark contrast. On the other hand, the movie "François le Vaillant" in particular, uses high amounts of Dark Blue variations thus the color variation is high but the elementary hue diversity is low. The predominant colors are the cold dark colors.

5   Classification Tests

The proposed color-based and shot-based symbolical information (represented with the fuzzy degree of each symbol) has been used in an attempt to classify animation movies in terms of color artistry content and action content. The objective is to test the discriminating power of our attributes for a prospective use as semantic indexes in a content-based retrieval system. The tests were performed on an animation movie database from [1] containing **52 movies** (total time of 7 hours) and having a large variety of animation techniques.

5.1   The Classification Method

For the classification task we have used the k-means unsupervised clustering method due to its efficiency in terms of the reduced computational time and the good quality of its results [20]. Like many other types of numerical minimizations, the solution that k-means gives often depends on the starting points. It is possible for k-means to reach a local minimum, hence a probably wrong solution. In order to overcome that problem, the clustering is repeated several times (i.e. 10 iterations), each with a new set of initial centroids. The final solution is the one with the lowest total sum of distances, over all replicates.

Also, as the k-means clustering method is based on the nearest-neighbor approach, it is sensitive to the choice of *the distance measure*. Several distance measures have been used, namely: Euclidean, cityblock, cosine and correlation distances. Classification tests conducted using the color descriptions have proved that in our application the Euclidean distance achieves the best results in terms of cluster bounding and homogeneity. It will be further used for the classification task.

The quality of the results is evaluated by analyzing the cluster silhouettes and the achieved vector repartitions. A silhouette is defined as a graphic plot which displays a measure of how close each point in one cluster is to points in the neighbouring clusters. The measure ranges from +1 (maximum distance), through 0, to -1 (indicating points that are probably assigned to the wrong cluster) [23] (see Fig. 9).

To overcome the difficulty of visualizing and thus analyzing n-order data sets (with $n > 3$) we are using the principal component analysis or PCA [18] which decorrelates the data. The visualization of the results is performed using only the first three principal components in a 3D plot, as they account for as much of the variability in the data as possible.

Moreover, the number of the existing movie classes, N, is entirely related to the used movie database. The high diversity of the available movies makes the choice of the right number of classes difficult, thus several experiments were performed for different values of N. As the proposed characterizations are related to the human perception, the validation of the results was conducted by the manual analysis of the obtained movie clusters.

5.2   Experimental Results

Several classification tests were performed in order to classify the similar content animation movies.

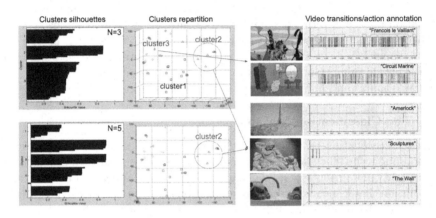

Fig. 9. Classification using the fuzzy action descriptions. The cluster repartition is displayed using the first 3 main components.

The first test was performed using **both the action and color information**. With a number of classes varying from $N = 3, ..., 7$, only two relevant movie clusters are obtained (almost unchanged with the value of N): movies with a reduced rhythm, action content and color diversity and movies with a medium color diversity, dark colors and a high/mean action content. That is due to the fact that the color content is *not related* to the action content. For example, a movie with dark-cold colors is not restricted to a low action content (see for example the movie "François le Vaillant", Section 4.3). Hence, a classification test is further carried out individually based on the color and action descriptions.

For the classification test using only **the action symbolic information** the number of classes is $N = 2...5$. Some of the results are depicted with Fig. 9. For the case of $N = 3$ classes the movies are divided into three particular clusters: $cluster_1$ - movies with high rhythm and mean action, $cluster_2$ - low rhythm and action content and $cluster_3$ - high action content, mean rhythm and high mystery. Varying the number of classes up to $N = 5$, the $cluster_2$ is unchanged. The $cluster_2$ contains mainly the movies using particular animation techniques, namely: sand, paper or plasticine modeling. It appears that the movies using these techniques are characterized by a reduced number of shots as the action mostly takes place in only one scene (see Fig. 5).

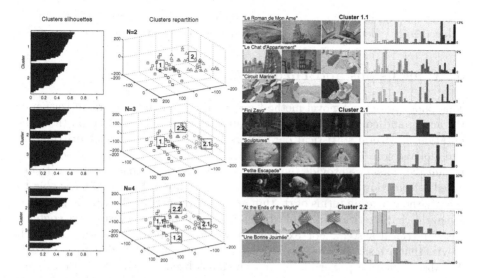

Fig. 10. Classification using the color information. The cluster repartition is displayed using the first 3 main components.

The third classification test was conducted using only the **color symbolic information** with the number of classes varying from $N = 2...4$. The obtained results are depicted with Fig. 10. For the case of $N = 2$ clusters, the movies are divided into colorful movies with predominant bright colors and high/moderate color variations ($cluster_1$ in Fig. 10), and respectively dark cold adjacent color movies with a reduced color diversity ($cluster_2$ in Fig. 10). Associating sadness with dark cold colors, the $cluster_2$ contains all the movies that could be referred to as sad. It also contains the movies using the already mentioned particular animation techniques (sand, paper or plasticine modelling) as the movies sharing these techniques are also restricted to a very reduced color palette due to the texture of the materials. For the case of $N = 3$ classes, the $cluster_2$ is divided into two clusters. The first sub-cluster, $cluster_{2.1}$, mainly contains the cold dark color movies, while the second sub-cluster, $cluster_{2.2}$, mainly contains the analogous color movies (see Fig. 10). Using $N = 4$, only the $cluster_1$ is divided into high color variation movies, $cluster_{1.1}$, and movies with no particular color characteristics, $cluster_{1.2}$.

One important result of the color-based classification is the separation of the *dark cold color movies* (that could be referred to as sad movies, $cluster_{2.1}$) and *colorful movies* from the other movies ($cluster_{1.1}$, see Fig. 10). On the other hand using the action-based classification one could retrieve the movies with a reduced number of shots (slow rhythm) and the movies with high action content (see Fig. 9). Thus the collaboration of the two classifications (for example, the classification using the action parameters of the movies from the dark cold color movie cluster) could lead to the retrieval of the particular animation techniques, namely sand and plasticine modelling, which are typically represented by a very reduced color palette, dark cold colors and a reduced rhythm and action content.

6   Conclusions and Future Work

This paper presents a novel method for the fuzzy semantic characterization of the action and color contents of the animation movies. It is based on the computation of several statistical parameters both on the movie shot distribution and global color distribution. The interest of the obtained semantic descriptions is multiple. First, we provide the animation artists, or ordinary people, with detailed information regarding the movie artistic content. Second, we are able to classify the movies in terms of rhythm and color properties. Third, the proposed semantic characterizations could be used as human-like indexes in a content-based retrieval system. For example, it would be an intuitive way to search movies that are sad (i.e. dark cold colors) or movies with a high action content. The discriminating power of our attributes has been proved by several classification tests performed on an animation movie database from [1]. Generally, the action content is not related to the color distribution, except in the case of a particular animation technique which is the plasticine modelling (having a dark cold color distribution and a low rhythm). Thus, the movie retrieval task will be more efficient performed independently using the color and respectively the action information. Future work will consist in adding the movie motion content analysis to the proposed semantic descriptions.

Acknowledgments

The authors would like to thank CICA - Centre International du Cinema d' Animation [1] and Folimage company [19] for providing us with the animation movies and for their tehnical support.

References

1. Centre International du Cimema d'Animation. "http://www.annecy.org".
2. R. Leinhart, Reliable Transition Dectection in Videos: a Survey and Practitioners Guide. International Journal of Image and Graphics. **1**(3) (2001) 469–486.
3. B. Ionescu, V. Buzuloiu, P. Lambert, D. Coquin. Improved Cut Detection for the Segmentation of Animation Movies. IEEE International Conference on Acoustic, Speech and Signal Processing, Toulouse, France, (2006).
4. B. Ionescu, P. Lambert, D. Coquin, V. Buzuloiu. Fuzzy Color-Based Semantic Characterization of Animation Movies. CGIV 3th European Conference on Colour in Graphics, Imaging, and Vision, University of Leeds, United Kingdom, (2006).
5. G. Cees, M. Snoek, M. Worring. Multimodal Video Indexing: A Review of the State of the Art. Multimedia Tools and Application. **25**(1) (2005) 5–35.
6. J.A. Lay, L. Guan. Retrieval for Color Artistry Concepts. IEEE Transaction on Image Processing. **13**(3) (2004) 125–129.

7. C. Colombo, A. Del Bimbo, P. Sala. Semantics in Visual Information Retrieval. IEEE Multimedia. **6**(3) (1999) 38–53.
8. B.T. Truong, S. Venkatesh. Video Abstraction : A Systematic Review and Classification. Accepted for ACM Transactions on Multimedia Computing, Communications and Applications. **3**(1) (2007).
9. R.W. Floyd, L. Steinberg. An Adaptative Algorithm for Spatial Gray Scale. Proc. SID Int. Symp. Digest of Technical Papers. (1975) 3637.
10. B. Ionescu, P. Lambert, D. Coquin, L. Darlea. Color-Based Semantic Characterization of Cartoons. IEEE International Symposium on Signal Circuits and Systems. **1**, Iasi, Romania, (2005) 223–226.
11. W.A.C. Fernando, C.N. Canagarajah, D.R. Bull. Fade and Dissolve Detection in Uncompressed and Compressed Video Sequence. IEEE International Conference on Image Processing. Kobe, Japan, (1999) 299–303.
12. J. Itten. The Art of Color: the Subjective Experience and Objective Rational of Color. New York: Reinhold. (1961).
13. F. Birren. Principles of color - a Review of past traditions and modern theories of color harmony. New York: Reinhold. (1969).
14. Visibone. "http://www.visibone.com/colorlab".
15. Y. Li, T. Zhang, D. Tretter. An overview of video abstraction techniques. Tech. Report, HP-2001-191, HP Laboratory, (2001).
16. J.A. Lay, L. Guan, Retrieval for Color Artistry Concepts. IEEE Transactions on Image Processing. **13**(3) (2004) 125–129.
17. L.A. Zadeh, Fuzzy sets. Information and Control. **8** (1965) 338–353.
18. J.E. Jackson, User's Guide to Principal Components. John Wiley and Sons, Inc., (1991) 1–25.
19. Folimage, "http://www.folimage.com".
20. G.A.F. Seber, Multivariate Observations, *Wiley*, New York, (1984).
21. A.G. Hauptmann, M.J. Witbrock. Story Segmentation and Detection of Commercials in Broadcast News Video. Advances in Digital Libraries. Santa Barbara, USA, (1998) 168–179.
22. R. Lienhart, C. Kuhmunch, W. Effelsberg. On the Detection and Recognition of Television Commercials. IEEE Confefence on Multimedia Computing and Systems. (1997) 509–516.
23. L. Kaufman, P.J. Rousseeuw. Finding Groups in Data: An Introduction to Cluster Analysis. Wiley, (1990).

Retrieval of Document Images Based on Page Layout Similarity

Naveen[*] and D.S. Guru

Department of Studies in Computer Science,
University of Mysore, Manasagangotri, Mysore – 570006, India
naveen_msc@yahoo.com, dsg@compusci.uni-mysore.ac.in

Abstract. In this paper, we address the problem of document image retrieval in digital libraries. As an essential element of this problem we have proposed a measure of spatial layout similarity with importance to category of components in document images. We have tested the method on MediaTeam document image database that provides diverse collection of document images.

1 Introduction

Creation of large databases of document images (books and journals) in digital libraries has been possible as the result of availability of low cost scanners and storage media. One of the main challenges for document image retrieval that aims at finding relevant document images from a corpus of digitized pages is the development of effective methods for estimating the similarity between the query and the document images in the database.

Previous works on similarity measure of document images are based on texture property of selected components [3, 8]. A few papers based on spatial layouts [10] have also been proposed for classification [1, 17]. In [7] a general framework for document image retrieval based on both global features and local features (based on image components) has been proposed. Recently a signature-based document retrieval [2] and a modified X-Y tree encoding [15] based layout similarity measure for retrieval have also been proposed. An overview of text and graphics retrieval system is presented in [13] and a survey [6] has investigated past research and future trends in document image retrieval. In reality there are chances of skew, translation and different scales (resolutions) during scanning of the documents. Most of the proposed approaches are computationally expensive, ineffectual and variant to different resolutions and geometric transformations. A similarity measure based on the concept of form signature for retrieval of form document images [11] that is invariant to geometric transformations and variations in geometrical proportions of form layout has also been proposed.

Among various features of a document image, its spatial layout structure and category of components in the layout provides significant information about its identity. In view of this, motivated by the work [11], we present in this paper, a model for retrieving document images based on their layout similarity. The proposed similarity measure is a modification to the similarity measure proposed in [11] to suit the

---

[*] Corresponding author.

S. Marchand-Maillet et al. (Eds.): AMR 2006, LNCS 4398, pp. 136–148, 2007.

document images and to provide significance to categories of components. The results of the experiments conducted on a corpus of about 292 document images have also been presented. We have also modified the proposed similarity measure to incorporate the areas of components during similarity measure and tested its effectiveness in similarity retrieval. In the following sections, the characterization of document layout followed by similarity measure, experimental results and conclusion are explained.

2 Layout Characterization

In order to characterize document images based on their layouts, we assume that a document image has been deskewed [4, 9], segmented [5, 12, 14] into components and assigned the category labels (text/non-text) for components with their minimum bounding rectangles (MBRs). To understand our layout characterization, consider the layout of a document image in fig. 1(a). We use h_i and v_i to denote a horizontal line and a vertical line of the minimum bounding rectangle of a component. We then extract horizontal and vertical lines of MBRs of all components in the layout and sort the horizontal lines in ascending order according to their y-coordinates and the vertical lines in ascending order according to their x-coordinates to define sequences H and V:

$$H = \{h_1, h_2, ..., h_i, ..., h_{n_H}\}, \quad y_i \leq y_j \quad if \quad i < j$$
$$V = \{v_1, v_2, ..., v_i, ..., v_{n_V}\}, \quad x_i \leq x_j \quad if \quad i < j \tag{1}$$

The structure, $L(H,V)$, constructed by H and V is called a layout signature. Figs. 1(b) and 1(c) show the layout signature of the document image layout shown in fig. 1(a). The sequence of h_i's having same y-coordinate (v_i's having same x-coordinate) is irrelevant as they are grouped in the next step.

The set of all the components in a document layout is denoted by $C = \{c_1, c_2, ..., c_i, ..., c_{n_C}\}$, where n_C is the number of components in the document layout and the category labels of the corresponding components are denoted by $T = \{t_1, t_2, ..., t_i, ..., t_{n_C}\}$ where t_i is one of the values {*Text, Non-text*}.

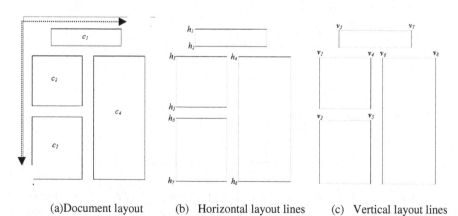

(a)Document layout   (b) Horizontal layout lines   (c) Vertical layout lines

Fig. 1. Layout signature

3 Similarity Measure

In order to define a similarity measure between two document layouts, we first introduce the concept of a grid on the document layout plane as in [11] proposed for form document images. We also perform the simple operation [11] of grouping lines in H and V as follows. Collinear horizontal lines form an H-group that is represented by the y-coordinates of the horizontal lines; collinear vertical lines form a V-group that is represented by the x-coordinates of the vertical lines. The two sequences of these groups are as follows:

$$H_G = \left\{ p_1, p_2, ..., p_i, ..., p_{n_{H_G}} \right\} \ p_i < p_j \ \ if \ i < j$$

$$V_G = \left\{ q_1, q_2, ..., q_i, ..., q_{n_{V_G}} \right\} \ q_i < q_j \ \ if \ i < j \qquad (2)$$

where n_{H_G} is the number of H-groups and n_{V_G} is the number of V-groups. Fig. 2 illustrates the H_G and V_G of the document layout in fig. 1(a).

Let A and B be contiguous subsequences of H_G and V_G respectively defined by:

$$A = \left\{ a_1, a_2, ..., a_i, ..., a_k \right\}, a_i = p_{n(i)}, \ \ n(i) < n(j) \ \ if \ \ i < j$$

$$B = \left\{ b_1, b_2, ..., b_i, ..., b_l \right\}, b_i = p_{m(i)}, \ \ m(i) < m(j) \ \ if \ \ i < j \qquad (3)$$

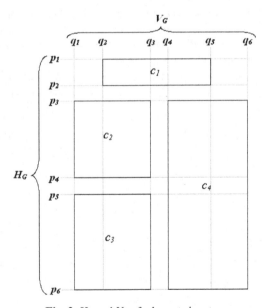

Fig. 2. H_G and V_G of a layout signature

The two contiguous subsequences A and B form a grid on the document layout plane which is denoted by $Grid(A,B)$. The mesh at row i and column j in $Grid(A,B)$ is represented by $M_{Grid(A,B)}(i,j)$. For illustration, suppose

$$A = \{a_1 = p_2, a_2 = p_3, a_3 = p_4, a_4 = p_5\} \qquad \text{and}$$

$B = \{b_1 = q_2, b_2 = q_3, b_3 = q_4, b_4 = q_5\}$ in fig. (2). The space with its top-left corner as the intersecting point (p_2, q_2) and its right-bottom corner as the intersecting point (p_5, q_5) forms the $Grid(A,B)$. The space with its top-left corner as the intersecting point (p_3, q_2) and its right-bottom corner as the intersecting point (p_4, q_3) forms a mesh denoted by $M_{Grid(A,B)}(a_2, b_2)$.

By superimposing $Grid(A,B)$ on the layout signature, the following two functions can be defined:

$$\text{Intersect}\left(c_k, M_{Grid(A,B)}(i,j)\right) = \begin{cases} 1, & \text{if } c_k \cap M_{Grid(A,B)}(i,j) \neq \varnothing \\ 0, & \text{if } c_k \cap M_{Grid(A,B)}(i,j) = \varnothing \end{cases} \tag{4}$$

$$\text{Segments}\left(c_k, Grid(A,B)\right) = \sum_{i=1}^{|A|-1} \sum_{j=1}^{|B|-1} \text{Intersect}\left(c_k, M_{Grid(A,B)}(i,j)\right) \tag{5}$$

where $|A|$ denotes the number of elements in sequence A and c_k is the kth component in the document layout. The function $\text{Intersect}\left(c_k, M_{Grid(A,B)}(i,j)\right)$ indicates that whether the component c_k overlaps with the mesh $M_{Grid(A,B)}(i,j)$ in the $Grid(A,B)$ or not. The function $\text{Segments}\left(c_k, Grid(A,B)\right)$ gives the number of segments of the component c_k, that is the number of meshes with which the component c_k overlaps.

We denote the set of all the components intersecting $Grid(A,B)$ by $C_{Grid(A,B)}$:
$C_{Grid(A,B)} = \{c_k \mid \text{Segments}\left(c_k, Grid(A,B)\right) > 0\}$. In order to reflect the number of text components in a mesh of $Grid(A,B)$, we define $N_{Grid(A,B)}^{Text}(i,j)$ as follows:

$$N_{Grid(A,B)}^{Text}(i,j) = \sum_{\substack{c_k \in C_{Grid(A,B)} \\ \text{and} \\ t_k = Text}} \left\lceil \frac{\text{Intersect}\left(c_k, M_{Grid(A,B)}(i,j)\right)}{\text{Segments}\left(c_k, Grid(A,B)\right)} \right\rceil \tag{6}$$

Similarly, the number of non-text components in a mesh of $Grid(A,B)$ is given by

$$N_{Grid(A,B)}^{Nontext}(i,j) = \sum_{\substack{c_k \in C_{Grid(A,B)} \\ \text{and} \\ t_k = Nontext}} \left\lceil \frac{\text{Intersect}\left(c_k, M_{Grid(A,B)}(i,j)\right)}{\text{Segments}\left(c_k, Grid(A,B)\right)} \right\rceil \tag{7}$$

The proposed similarity measure is based on comparing the number of text and non-text components in the corresponding meshes of two grids with the same dimension. Suppose that $L(H^u, V^u)$ is an input layout signature and $L(H^r, V^r)$ is a reference layout signature. By grouping horizontal and vertical lines of MBRs of all the components, we obtain the horizontal line group H_G^u and vertical line group V_G^u of the input document image and the horizontal line group H_G^r and vertical line group V_G^r of the reference document image. According to eqn. (2), H_G^u is described as:

$$H_G^u = \left\{p_1^u, p_2^u, \dots, p_i^u, \dots, p_{n_{HG}^u}^u\right\} \tag{8}$$

Similarly V_G^u, H_G^r and V_G^r are described accordingly. We define k_h and k_v by

$$k_h = \min\left(\left|H_G^u\right|, \left|H_G^r\right|\right)$$
$$k_v = \min\left(\left|V_G^u\right|, \left|V_G^r\right|\right) \tag{9}$$

Suppose that A^u and A^r are contiguous subsequences of lengths k_h of H_G^u and H_G^r respectively, and B^u and B^r are the contiguous subsequences of lengths k_v of V_G^u and V_G^r respectively. Then the similarity between two document layout signatures $L(H^u, V^u)$ and $L(H^r, V^r)$ is defined as follows:

$$S = 1 - \frac{w_1 S_{Text}\left(A^u, B^u, A^r, B^r\right) + w_2 S_{Nontext}\left(A^u, B^u, A^r, B^r\right)}{n_C^u + n_C^r} \tag{10}$$

where

$$S_{Text}\left(A^u, B^u, A^r, B^r\right) = \sum_{i=1}^{k_h-1} \sum_{j=1}^{k_v-1} \left| N_{Grid\left(A^u, B^u\right)}^{u^{Text}}(i, j) - N_{Grid\left(A^r, B^r\right)}^{r^{Text}}(i, j) \right|$$

$$S_{Nontext}\left(A^u, B^u, A^r, B^r\right) = \sum_{i=1}^{k_h-1} \sum_{j=1}^{k_v-1} \left| N_{Grid\left(A^u, B^u\right)}^{u^{Nontext}}(i, j) - N_{Grid\left(A^r, B^r\right)}^{r^{Nontext}}(i, j) \right| \tag{11}$$

and w_1 and w_2 are the weights. Different values of w_1 and w_2 change the significance of text/non-text components during similarity measure.

High similarity values can be obtained in some cases (a query image is a part of reference image or in the other case a query image envelops the reference image) by considering all possible contiguous subsequences of H_G^u, V_G^u, H_G^r and V_G^r. We define H_S^u the set of all contiguous subsequences of lengths of k_h of H_G^u as

$$H_S^u = \left\{A_1^u, A_2^u, \ldots, A_{n_{H_S^u}}^u\right\}, \quad \left|A_i^u\right| = k_h, \quad n_{H_S^u} = \left|H_G^u\right| - k_h + 1 \tag{12}$$

Similarly, V_S^u the set of all contiguous subsequences of lengths k_v of V_G^u, H_S^r the set of all contiguous subsequences of lengths k_h of H_G^r and V_S^r the set of all contiguous subsequences of lengths k_v of V_G^r are given by

$$V_S^u = \left\{B_1^u, B_2^u, \ldots, B_{n_{V_S^u}}^u\right\}, \quad \left|B_i^u\right| = k_v, \quad n_{V_S^u} = \left|V_G^u\right| - k_v + 1$$

$$H_S^r = \left\{A_1^r, A_2^r, \ldots, A_{n_{H_S^r}}^r\right\}, \quad \left|A_i^r\right| = k_h, \quad n_{H_S^r} = \left|H_G^r\right| - k_h + 1$$

$$V_S^r = \left\{B_1^r, B_2^r, \ldots, B_{n_{V_S^r}}^r\right\}, \quad \left|B_i^r\right| = k_v, \quad n_{V_S^r} = \left|V_G^r\right| - k_v + 1 \tag{13}$$

Now the maximum possible similarity S_M between two layout signatures $L(H^u, V^u)$ and $L(H^r, V^r)$ is defined by

$$S_M = \max\left(1 - \frac{w_1 S_{Text}\left(A_i^u, B_j^u, A_k^r, B_l^r\right) + w_2 S_{Nontext}\left(A_i^u, B_j^u, A_k^r, B_l^r\right)}{n_C^u + n_C^r}\right) \tag{14}$$

where

$$A_i^u \in H_S^u, 1 \le i \le n_{H_S^u}, \qquad B_j^u \in V_S^u, \ 1 \le j \le n_{V_S^u},$$

$$A_k^u \in H_S^r, 1 \le k \le n_{H_S^r}, \qquad B_l^r \in V_S^r, \ 1 \le l \le n_{V_S^r}.$$

and $S_{Text}\left(A_i^u, B_j^u, A_k^r, B_l^r\right)$ and $S_{Nontext}\left(A_i^u, B_j^u, A_k^r, B_l^r\right)$ are same as from eqn. (11).

As we are considering the maximum similarity value among possible contiguous subsequences, there are chances of the retrieval of visually less similar images as more similar as illustrated in experimental results. With the intension of finding the more realistic similarity measure we obtain the final true similarity S_T as defined by

$$S_T = S_M \times \frac{\min\left(\left|H_G^u\right| + \left|V_G^u\right|, \ \left|H_G^r\right| + \left|V_G^r\right|\right)}{\max\left(\left|H_G^u\right| + \left|V_G^u\right|, \ \left|H_G^r\right| + \left|V_G^r\right|\right)} \tag{15}$$

where S_M is as defined in eqn. (14).

As we are computing similarity as the number of components in the corresponding meshes in the grids of two document layouts irrespective of their geometric sizes, the similarity measure is invariant to translation, scaling and moderate variations in geometrical proportions of components in the document layout. The variations in geometrical proportions of components are said to be moderate if the varied components' boundaries when projected onto X-axis or Y-axis does not overlap with the boundaries of others. However, if the components in either query or reference database image layouts overlap, then the similarity value between them reduces. It is not necessary to consider the problems due to skew (rotation) as they are eradicated by skew correction of document images during the process of obtaining document layouts.

However, in practical situations, it may not be acceptable, the retrieved images with variations in geometrical proportions of components. To cope with such situations we incorporated the factor, areas of components by the ratios of areas of meshes to the total area of the corresponding subsequences' grid. With this incorporation the similarity between two document layouts can be computed by the similarity measure defined by eqn. (15) with the modification to eqn. (11) as described below:

$$S_{Text}\left(A^u, B^u, A^r, B^r\right) = \sum_{i=1}^{k_h-1}\sum_{j=1}^{k_v-1}\left|N_{Grid\left(A^u, B^u\right)}^{u^{Text}}(i, j) * Ar_{Grid\left(A^u, B^u\right)}(i, j) - N_{Grid\left(A^r, B^r\right)}^{r^{Text}}(i, j) * Ar_{Grid\left(A^r, B^r\right)}(i, j)\right|$$

$$S_{Nontext}\left(A^u, B^u, A^r, B^r\right) = \sum_{i=1}^{k_h-1}\sum_{j=1}^{k_v-1}\left|N_{Grid\left(A^u, B^u\right)}^{u^{Nontext}}(i, j) * Ar_{Grid\left(A^u, B^u\right)}(i, j) - N_{Grid\left(A^r, B^r\right)}^{r^{Nontext}}(i, j) * Ar_{Grid\left(A^r, B^r\right)}(i, j)\right| \tag{16}$$

where $Ar_{Grid\left(A^u, B^u\right)}(i, j) = \dfrac{\text{Area of mesh } (i,j)}{\text{Total area of the grid formed by}\left(A^u, B^u\right)}$ and

$$Ar_{Grid\left(A^r, B^r\right)}(i, j) = \frac{\text{Area of mesh } (i,j)}{\text{Total area of the grid formed by}\left(A^r, B^r\right)}$$

According to (10), (14) and (15), $S, S_M, S_T \in [0,1]$. The larger the values of S, S_M and S_T, more the two document layouts are similar to each other.

4 Experimental Results

We have considered 292 document images of different classes (Advertisement, Article and Manual) and their ground truth information of MBRs and categories of

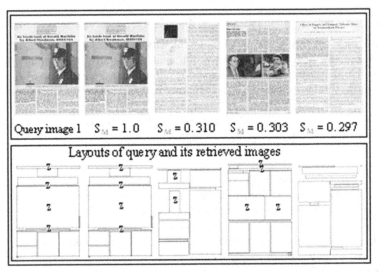

(a) Retrieval results for query image 1

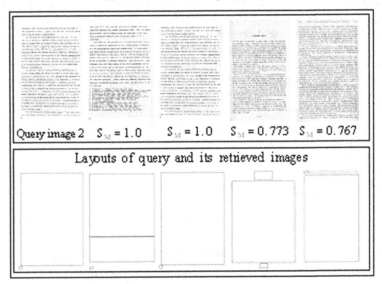

(b) Retrieval results for query image 2

Fig. 3. Query results using S_M in (14)

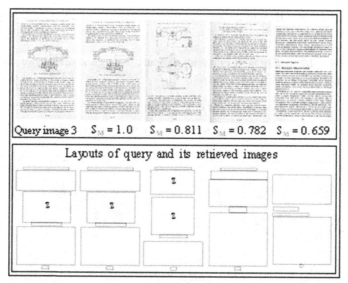

(c) Retrieval results for query image 3

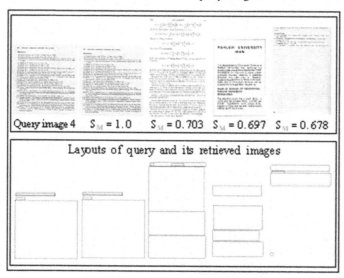

(d) Retrieval results for query image 4

Fig. 3. (*continued*)

components available in the MediaTeam document database [16] for our experimentation. First we find the layout signatures and then we compute $N^{Text}_{Grid(A,B)}$ and $N^{Nontext}_{Grid(A,B)}$ using eqns. (6) and (7) (where $A = H_G$ and $B = V_G$), for all the reference document images in the database and are stored. The retrieval procedure needs to determine only the layout signature followed by $N^{Text}_{Grid(A,B)}$ and $N^{Nontext}_{Grid(A,B)}$

of a query image and then to compute the similarity with all reference images in the database. We have taken $w_1 = w_2 = 1$ in our experiments giving equal importance to both text and non-text components.

To decrease the miss-match rate and computational complexity, we consider the reference layout signatures satisfying $\left| \left| H_G^u \right| - \left| H_G^r \right| \right| \le 2$, $\left| \left| V_G^u \right| - \left| V_G^r \right| \right| \le 2$ and $\left| n_C^u - n_C^r \right| \le 5$. Using these conditions the top four retrieved images with their layouts and similarity values corresponding to four query images using the similarity measure

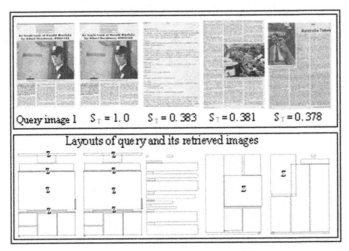

(a) Retrieval results for query image 1

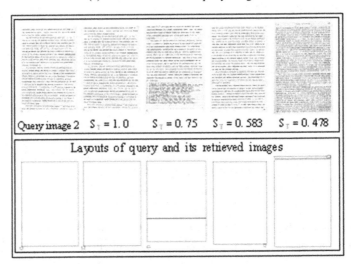

(b) Retrieval results for query image 2

Fig. 4. Query results using S_T in (15)

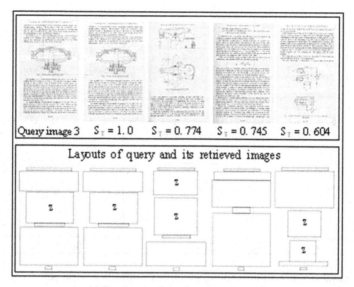

(c) Retrieval results for query image 3

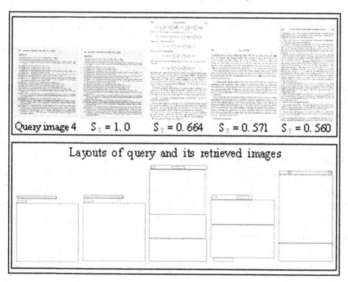

(d) Retrieval results for query image 4

Fig. 4. (*continued*)

S_M in eqn. (14) are shown in fig. 3(a-d). The symbol 'Z' on the components of layouts in figs. 3 & 4 indicates their category as non-text. The retrieved document images for the query document image containing non-text components shown in figs. 3(a), 3(c), 4(a) and 4(c) demonstrates the significance of our similarity measure to categories of components. Fig. 4(a-d) shows the retrieval results using the similarity measure S_T in eqn. (15) for the same four query images used in previous

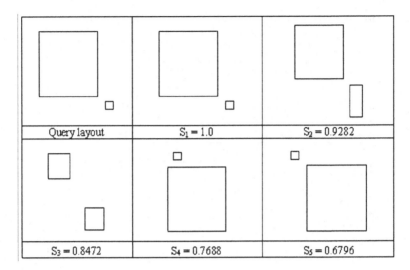

Query layout	$S_1 = 1.0$	$S_2 = 0.9282$
$S_3 = 0.8472$	$S_4 = 0.7688$	$S_5 = 0.6796$

Fig. 5. Retrieval results for the query layout using the modification in eqn. (16) in similarity measure in eqn. (15)

experimentation and without any constraint on lengths of H_G^u, V_G^u, H_G^r, V_G^r, and number of components n_C^u and n_C^r in selecting reference images in database. Notice that the first two retrievals in fig. 3(b) have the same similarity value even though their layouts are different and also notice that the retrieval results in fig. 3 using the similarity measure by eqn. (14) would be of high miss-match devoid of the constraints $\left| \left| H_G^u \right| - \left| H_G^r \right| \right| \leq 2$, $\left| \left| V_G^u \right| - \left| V_G^r \right| \right| \leq 2$ and $\left| n_C^u - n_C^r \right| \leq 5$. These miss-matches due to the best possible matching of contiguous subsequences using the similarity measure by eqn. (14) have been resolved using similarity measure by eqn. (15) as shown in fig. 4(a-d). In order to show the effectiveness of our similarity measure incorporating the factor, area as given in eqn. (16), we have tested the method on over 100 synthetic layouts, variants of 10 layouts forming 10 classes of layouts. A query and its top 5 retrieved layouts with their similarity values S_i's using the similarity measure in eqn. (15) with the modification in eqn. (16) are shown in fig. 5.

We have also tested our system by giving query images at different scales (resolutions). Even then the retrieved images are almost same with almost the same similarity values.

5   Conclusion

In this paper, we have addressed the problem of document image retrieval. As the central issue of this problem we have proposed a modified similarity measure, based on the characterization of spatial layout structures as layout signatures of document images. The main contribution of this paper is providing significance to categories (text/non-text) of components in document images in the similarity measure. The invariance to moderate variations in geometrical proportions of components confirms that the similarity measure is tolerant to minor errors caused during segmenting the document image into components. Another contribution of this paper is to provide importance to areas of components during the similarity measure which is necessary in situations of accurate similarity measure. Another essence of our similarity measure is the reduction in computational time as we considered all possible contiguous subsequences compared to the possible subsequences (not necessarily contiguous) considered in [11], which is exponential in computational time. From experiments, it is evident that the proposed similarity measure can also be applied to a heterogeneous collection of document images. Results from this initial retrieval can be used by later stages of document processing including content extraction and understanding.

Our method can be improved to precise similarity measure by considering more categories (Graphics, Halftones, Tables, Math-zones etc.,) of components and polygonal bounded components rather than MBRs in the document images. It can also be enhanced to specific application by considering logical labels (such as title, address etc.,). As further work we are concentrating on indexing for efficient retrieval.

Acknowledgement

This work is a part of the UGC sponsored major research project No. F.30-259/2004 (SR). The UGC support is highly appreciated.

References

[1] Appiani E, Cesarini F, Colla A. M, Diligenti M, Gori M, Marinai S and Soda G, (2001), "Automatic document classification and indexing in high-volume applications", *Int'l Journal on Document Analysis and Recognition,* Vol. 4, pp. 69-83.

[2] Chalechale A, Naghdy G and Mertins A, (2003), "Signature-based Document Retrieval", *Proc. of 3rd IEEE Int'l Symposium on Signal Processing and Information Technology,* pp. 597-600.

[3] Cullen J. F, Hull J. J and Hart P. E, (1997), "Document Image Database Retrieval and Browsing using Texture Analysis", *Proc. Fourth Int'l Conf. Document Analysis and Recognition,* pp. 718-721.

[4] Das A. K and Chanda B, (2001), "A fast algorithm for skew detection of document images using morphology", *Int'l Journal on Document Analysis and Recognition,* Vol. 4, pp. 109-114.

[5] Das A. K, Saha S. K and Chanda B, (2002), "An empirical measure of the performance of a document image segmentation algorithm", *Int'l Journal on Document Analysis and Recognition,* Vol. 4, pp. 183-190.

[6] Doermann D, (1997), "The Retrieval of Document Images: A Brief Survey", *Proc. Fourth Int'l Conf. Document Analysis and Recognition,* pp. 945-949.

[7] Doermann D, Sauvola J, Kauniskangas H, Shin C, Pietikainen M, and Rosenfeld A, (1996), "The development of a general framework for intelligent document image retrieval", *In Proc. of Document Analysis sytems workshop,* pp. 605-632.

[8] Eglin V and Bres S, (2003), "Document page similarity based on layout based on layout visual saliency: Application to query by example and document classification", *Proc. Seventh Int'l Conf. Document Analysis and Recognition,* pp. 1208-1212.

[9] Guru D. S, Punitha P and Mahesh S, (2004), "Skew Estimation in Digitized Documents: A Novel Approach", *Proc. Forth Indian Conf. on Computer Vision, Graphics & Image Processing,* pp. 314-319.

[10] Hu J, Kashi R and Wilfong G, (1999), "Document Image Layout Comparison and Classification", *Proc. Fifth Int'l Conf. on Document Analysis and Recognition,* pp. 285-289.

[11] Jain A. K and Liu J, (1998), "Image-Based Form Document Retrieval", *14th International Conference on Pattern Recognition,* Vol. 1, pp. 626-629.

[12] Jain A. K and Yu B, (1998), "Document Representation and Its Application to Page Decomposition", *IEEE Trans. on Pattern Analysis and Machine Intelligence,* Vol. 20, no. 3, pp. 294-308.

[13] Jaisimha M. Y, Bruce A, and Nguyen T, "Docbrowse: A system for textual and graphical querying on degraded document image data", *In DAS,* pp 581-604, 1996.

[14] Lee S-W and Ryu D-S, (2001), "Parameter-Free Geometric Document Layout Analysis", *IEEE Trans. on Pattern Analysis and Machine Intelligence,* Vol. 23, no. 11, pp. 1240-1256.

[15] Marinai S, Marino E, Cesarini F and Soda G, (2004), "A General System for the Retrieval of Document Images from Digital Libraries", *First Int'l Workshop on Document Image Analysis for Libraries(DIAL'04),* pp. 150-173.

[16] Sauvola J, and Kauniskangas H, (1999), MediaTeam Document Database II, a CD-ROM collection of document images, University of Oulu, Finland

[17] Shin C, Doermann D and Rosenfeld A, (2001), "Classification of document pages using structure-based features", *Int'l Journal on Document Analysis and Recognition,* Vol. 3, pp. 232-247.

Multimedia Content Adaptation Within the CAIN Framework Via Constraints Satisfaction and Optimization

Fernando López, José M. Martínez, and Víctor Valdés

Grupo de Tratamiento de Imágenes, Escuela Politécnica Superior
Universidad Autónoma de Madrid — E-28049 Madrid, Spain
{f.lopez, josem.martinez, victor.valdes}@uam.es

Abstract. This paper presents a constraints programming based approach to decide which of a set of available content adaptation tools and parameters should be selected in order to perform the best adaptation of a media asset targeting to enhance the final user's experience in a particular usage scenario. The work is within the scope of the Universal Multimedia Access (UMA) framework and makes use of MPEG standards for content and usage environment description. The proposed technique has been evaluated within the CAIN framework, a content adaptation engine that integrates different content adaptation tools, and that uses media and usage environment metadata to identify the best adaptation tool from the available ones. First, mandatory constraints are imposed. If there is more than one adaptation tool capable of adapting the content fulfilling every mandatory constraint, another group of desirable constraints are applied to reduce the solution space. If at this step there are still several adaptation tools or parameter values able to adapt the content fulfilling mandatory and desirable restrictions, a final optimization step chooses the best adaptation tool and parameters.

1 Introduction

The development of both, new access networks providing multimedia capabilities and a wide and growing range of terminals, makes the adaptation of content an important issue in future multimedia services. Content adaptation is the main objective of a set of technologies that can be grouped under the umbrella of Universal Multimedia Access (UMA) [1]. This means the capability of accessing to rich multimedia content through any client terminal and network. In this way content adaptation bridge content authors and content consumer in a world of increasing multimedia diversity.

In order to perform content adaptation it's necessary to have the description of the content and the description of the terminal and network conditions. To enhance the user's experience [2], not only terminals and networks parameters, but also user personalization and environmental conditions should be taken into account when adapting. This information imposes some constraints to the content coding parameters (and even others characteristics as semantic content or duration) to be delivered.

S. Marchand-Maillet et al. (Eds.): AMR 2006, LNCS 4398, pp. 149–163, 2007.

These constraints are imposed according to terminal capabilities, network conditions, user preferences and handicaps, environmental conditions, etc.

In this way, content adaptation may be performed via a content adaptation engine to provide to the user the best experience for the content requested within the available usage environment. The different available content adaptation tools may diverge in adaptation approach (e.g., transcoding, transmoding, ...), range of parameters values, supported input and output formats, performance (in terms of processing requirements, quality, etc.), ...

Several approaches have been proposed to perform content adaptation [3][4][5][6]. In [3] the authors propose a method where adaptations tools are described by inputs, outputs, preconditions and effects. In this paper we propose to describe adaptation tools using a capabilities description tool inspired in MPEG-7 MDS [7]. Constraints programming [8] is used to select the more suited content adaptation tool and parameters from the available specific content adaptation tools. It should be noted that [3] proposes to use a planning algorithm to find a chain of elementary adaptation operations that transform the media accordingly, whilst our framework considers adaptation tools that perform combined adaptations, not elementary ones. The adaptation engine selects only one adaptation tool from the available ones (we are evaluating to extend our solution to allow concatenation of adaptation tools in a future).

The paper is structured as follows. Section 2 presents an overview of CAIN, the content adaptation framework within the work presented in this paper is developed. Section 3 presents the architecture of the Decision Module (DM), which is the module in charge of taking the decision about which adaptation tool to use and with which parameters. Section 4 presents our proposal for content adaptation based on solving a Constraints Satisfaction Problem (CSP) [8]. Section 5 deals with methods to fulfil every mandatory constraint, whereas section 6 deals with the same problem when looking to impose as many desirable constraints as possible. Section 7 exposes the proposed solution to the problem of selecting the optimum adaptation tool and parameters when there are several configurations satisfying mandatory and desirable constraints. Section 8 concludes the paper and overviews current and future work.

2   Overview of CAIN

In this section we summarize CAIN [9] (Content Adaptation INtegrator), the framework within the work described in this paper is developed. CAIN is a content adaptation manager designed to provide metadata-driven content adaptation [10]. Different Content Adaptation Tools (CATs) allow integrating different content adaptation approaches [11]: transcoding, transmoding, scalable content, temporal summarization, that may be just signal driven or include semantic driven adaptation [12].

Fig. 1 summarizes the CAIN adaptation process: When CAIN is invoked; it receives the media content, an MPEG-7 MDS [7] and an MPEG-21 BSD [13] compliant content description, and an MPEG-21 DIA [13] usage environment description (user characteristics, terminal capabilities, and network characteristics). All those inputs are parsed and the extracted information is sent to the Decision

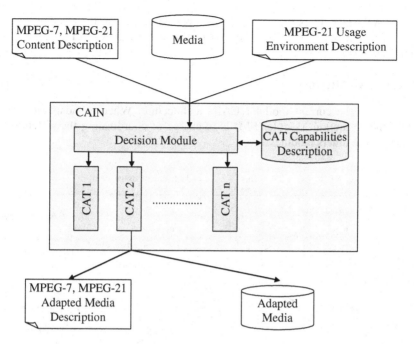

Fig. 1. CAIN adaptation process

Module (DM). The DM decides which of the available CATs must be launched to produce adapted content and metadata. The output of the system is the adapted content and the adapted media description (according to MPEG-7 and MPEG-21 (g)BSD).

2.1 Extensibility in CAIN and the DM

CAIN was proposed as an extensible content adaptation engine. Besides the CATs currently integrated in CAIN [14], there exists the need for integration of new CATs and codecs in the future.

CAIN architecture has been designed to allow the addition of new CATs. In order to allow the addition of new CATs, we have defined an API specification and a CAT Capabilities Description File with information about both the input and output formats accepted by the CATs and their adaptation capabilities. Therefore, each new CAT to be added to CAIN should implement a defined API to communicate with the DM and should provide this information in a CAT Capabilities Description File.

The CAT Capabilities Description Scheme [15] defines the adaptation capabilities, specifying in each case which kinds of adaptations the CAT is able to perform and the possible list of parameters that define the mentioned adaptation, such as input format, output format, and different features depending on which kind of adaptation is being defined: e.g., accepted input/output, frame-rate, resolution, channels, bitrate, etc...

The CAT Capabilities Description File is parsed to sign up the CAT in the CAIN Registry, which is necessary for the DM to know that a new CAT is available and which are its characteristics.

2.2 CAIN Architecture

Fig. 2 shows the current modular CAIN architecture. When an adaptation request arrives, the Execution Module (EM) is in charge of coordinating the different tasks assigned to the others modules.

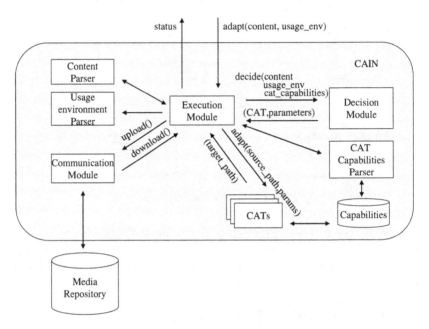

Fig. 2. The CAIN architecture

First the EM receives through the *adapt()* operation the media content identifier, and a usage environment description (according to MPEG-21 DIA [13]). Using the media content identifier, the EM requests the Communication Module (CM), through the *download()* operation, to retrieve from the Media Repository the media content and its corresponding content description (according to MPEG-7 MDS [7] and MPEG-21 DIA BSD [13]). CAIN is currently implemented in Java so these XML documents are parsed (using the Content Parser Module and the Usage Environment Parser module) and represented as Java objects. The EM is also in charge of parsing the CAT Capabilities Description File (using the CAT Capabilities Parser module).

All of this parsed information is delivered to the DM through the *decide()* operation, which has to look for the CAT that best fulfils the adaptation requirements. The selected CAT and execution parameters are sent back to the EM, which, using the Communication Module (CM), gets the content from the media repository and executes the selected CAT, through the *adapt()* operation, passing the retrieved media content and the parameters given by the DM. The CAT returns the adapted content and the adapted media description to the EM. Finally, the adapted media content as well at its description (in form of standard MPEG-7 and MPEG-21 description files) is stored (using the *upload()* operation of the CM) in the Repository. Every access to the Media Repository, for reading and writing media and media descriptions, are performed via the CM.

2.3 Supported Media

With regard to media resources, the current implementation of CATs in CAIN [14] supports mainly images and videos, as can be seen in Table 1 where the mapping between media formats and CAT categories is depicted. For images, JPEG-2000 has been selected due to its scalability features. In the case of video, MPEG video formats and the scalable video coding (SVC) format introduced in [16] has been selected.

Table 1. Relationship between media types and CAT categories

Media type	CAT category
MPEG-1/2/4 SP video, MPEG-1 audio	Transcoding
JPEG 2000, SVC	Scalable content
MPEG-1/2	Semantic driven
MPEG-1/2/4 SP video	Transmoding

2.4 Description Tools for Metadata-Driven Adaptation

The following three subsections describe the description tools used within CAIN to support metadata-driven adaptation, which are grouped in content, usage environment, and CAT capabilities description tools. A more in deep description of these metadata can be found in [9] and [15].

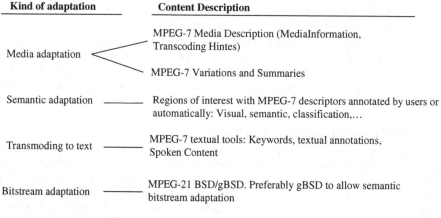

Kind of adaptation	Content Description
Media adaptation	MPEG-7 Media Description (MediaInformation, Transcoding Hintes) MPEG-7 Variations and Summaries
Semantic adaptation	Regions of interest with MPEG-7 descriptors annotated by users or automatically: Visual, semantic, classification,...
Transmoding to text	MPEG-7 textual tools: Keywords, textual annotations, Spoken Content
Bitstream adaptation	MPEG-21 BSD/gBSD. Preferably gBSD to allow semantic bitstream adaptation

Fig. 3. Content description tools for adaptation

2.4.1 Content Description Tools

The content description tools are based on MPEG-7 MDS and MPEG-21 DIA BSD. Fig 3 summarizes the adaptation tools supported by CAIN and the content description used for this adaptation. The media description metadata should provide support for the following content adaptation modalities:

- Media format adaptation: Supported by MPEG-7 media description (Media Information, transcoding hints...).
- Bitstream adaptation (truncation): Supported by MPEG-21 Bitstream Syntax Description (DIA BSD or gBSD). If the number of formats is reduced, BSD may be the best option, although it does not provide the capability of associating semantic labels (this may provide some "semantic" transcoding capabilities) as gBSD does.
- Media adaptation based on predefined variations and summaries: Supported by MPEG-7 variations and summaries descriptions.
- Semantic and knowledge-based adaptation: Supported by MPEG-7 and JPEG-2000 regions of interest with importance, MPEG-21 gBSD markers, ... annotated by users or labelled in an automatic or supervised way via analysis algorithms.
- Transmoding to text: Supported by MPEG-7 keywords, textual annotations,...

2.4.2 Usage Environment

Usage environment description tools cover the description of terminal and network resources, as well as user preferences and characteristics of the natural environment. The context description is based on a subset (in the sense of an MPEG Profile [17]) of MPEG-21 DIA Usage Environment Descriptions Tools as shown in Fig. 4. Usage environment description tools (MPEG-21 DIA) include:

- User characteristics: With user interactions (imported from MPEG-7 MDS), presentation preferences, accessibility characteristics and location characteristics.
- Terminal description: Currently its uses static terminal description, leaving the possibility of using dynamic characteristics (CPU load, available free storage space, free RAM ...) for further versions. In any case it will be required to receive from the client the current information about the terminal being used (either the complete description or a pointer to a static description).
- Network description: Currently its uses a static network description too, leaving the possibility of using dynamic characteristics (current congestion, error rate, delay time ...) for furthers versions. In any case it will be required to receive from the client the current information about the network being used (either the complete description or a pointer to a static description).

2.4.3 CAT Capabilities Description Tools

Obviously not every CAT can perform every adaptation operation (bitrate reduction, transcoding, transmoding, audio/video summarization...). In order to achieve CAIN extensibility it's necessary to annotate CATs capabilities. The selected CAT Adaptation Capabilities Description Scheme [14] (see Fig. 5) is based on the *MediaFormatD* Description Tool (from MPEG-7 Multimedia Description Schemes [7]), which describes the information related to a file format and coding parameters of the media.

Usage Environment description tools (MPEG-21 DIA)
User Description Tools
Usage Preferences
Media Format: content, bit rate, visual coding (format, frame height, frame width, frame aspect ratio and frame rate), audio coding (format, audio channels, sample rate, bits per sample).
Presentation Preferences
o   AudioPresentationPreferences: Volume, output device, balance.   o   DisplayPresentationPreferences: Colour temperature, brightness, saturation, contrast.   o   ConversionPreferences: Media type conversion preferences and priorities.   o   PresentationPriorityPreferences: Modality (audio, video...) priorities
Terminal Capabilities Tools
Codec Capabilities
Audio, video and image coding/decoding supported formats.
Display Capabilities
Supported display modes (resolution, refresh rate), screen size, colour bit depth.
Audio Output Capabilities
Supported audio modes (sampling frequency, bits per sample), low frequency, high frequency, number of channels…
Storage Characteristics
Input transfer rate, output transfer rate, size, writable.
Network Characteristics Tools
Network Capability
Maximum capacity and minimum guaranteed.

Fig. 4. Usage environment description tools for adaptation

The main adaptation capabilities description tools elements used to describe CAT capabilities are:

1. **Header.** The header allows the identification of the described CAT and includes a name and an optional textual description.
2. **Adaptation modality.** This element allows the definition of each adaptation modality with the possible media formats each adaptation modality is able to receive and to produce. It's composed by an adaptation mode (defines as an MPEG-7 Classification Scheme that allows to describe the modality in detail), and a reference to one or more media systems the CAT is able to perform. For example, for a CAT performing video summarization, there can be different modalities, like keyframe replication (which do not reduce the timeline to allow easy audio synchronization), video skimming, and image story board.
3. **Media systems.** Each instance of this element allows the definition of media formats at system level by indicating: File format name, file format extension, references to zero or more visual elementary stream, references to zero or more

audio elementary stream, and optionally a scene coding format. These elements allow the description of the media system formats each CAT adaptation modality is able to read (input), write (output), or both (common to avoid redundancies).

4. **Elementary streams.** These elements allow the description of video and audio coding parameters. Besides the type of the stream (video, audio, image) the parameters are grouped on input, output and common (in order to reduce redundancies) parameters. The set of parameters are based on MPEG-7 MDS *MediaFormatD* element, with some simplifications and extensions looking to allow the definition of adaptation capabilities. When defining a coding format, each feasible parameter will be considered by the DM as a restriction. If no restriction is imposed over a particular property of the codec, it must be considered that the codec is able to deal with any value of this property.

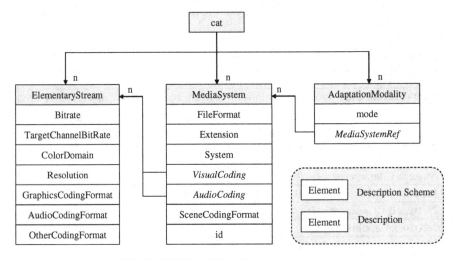

Fig. 5. CAT Capabilities Description Scheme

3   The Decision Module

The Decision Module (DM) is a software module receiving an input in form of a content description, a *mandatory usage environment description*, and a *desired usage environment description*. This module searches for the CAT that produces the best content adaptation, defined as the adaptation that matches more constraints, and therefore yielding the best experience to the user.

Terminal capabilities and network characteristics have been included in the mandatory usage description, whereas the user preferences have been included in the desirable usage environment description. Some user preferences (user's handicaps) have been included in the mandatory usage description.

Fig. 6 illustrates a hypothetical adaptation process that the DM has to look for. As input we have a content description for a video that is available in a specific format, bitrate, and colour depth (this information must be provided by the Media Repository; if this is not the case, CAIN includes a media description generation module in charge of obtaining the media description of the content); a mandatory usage environment description that describes constraints to be imposed to the adapted content (a different video format, a smaller bitrate, and smaller colour depth); and a desired usage environment that describes the user preferences for maximizing colour depth, and enough quality from the bitrate point of view.

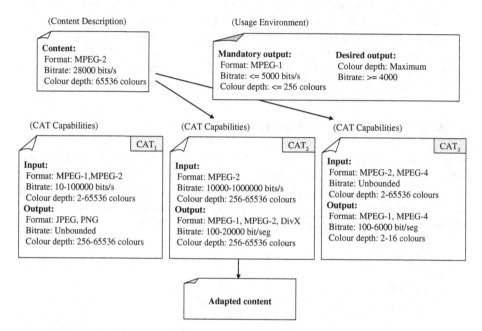

Fig. 6. Example of context where the best CAT to adapt the content must be selected

Thus, the DM searches through the CATs' capabilities descriptor and selects the CAT that produces an output that fulfils all these constraints, or at least the mandatory ones. The selection criterion is blind in the sense that one CAT that fulfils all the constraints (mandatory and desirable), at the expense of degrading excessively some parameters not mentioned by the constraints (e.g. screen size), is preferable to another that doesn't fulfils all the constraints given by the usage environment, although the latter would not alter the parameters that were not provided.

If the DM cannot find a CAT capable of fulfilling all the requirements, constraints imposed by the desirable usage environment are incrementally removed (see section 6), trying to find a CAT that at least fulfils mandatory constraints. In the case that the DM finds various CATs that satisfy all constraints, an optimization process (see section 7) is carried out in order to select the one yielding the best user's experience.

4   Content Adaptation as a Constraints Satisfaction Problem

Constraints formalize the dependencies in a physical world in terms of a logical relation among several unknowns. Methods for solving Constraint Satisfaction

Problems [8] allow efficient navigation of large search spaces to find an optimal solution that satisfies given constraints.

In our approach we propose that content description parameters determine both the variables and the domain of the variables, whereas the usage environment and the CAT capabilities descriptions must be formalized as constraints.

As exposed below, we have defined constraints between media and CAT input capabilities, as well as constraints between CAT output capabilities and the usage environment. These constraints have been defined as equalities and inequalities with only one term in each side of the constraint equations. This observation allows us to use fast (real time) resolution methods for the satisfaction problem, like Gauss-Jordan elimination, as well as fast optimization methods, like the simplex algorithm.

5   Applying Mandatory Constraints

In the example proposed in Fig. 6, based on the content description, we define the following variables: initial video format F_0, initial bitrate B_0, and initial colour depth C_0. Also based on the usage environment we define as target variables: terminal accepted format F_n, network maximum bitrate B_n, and terminal maximum accepted colour depth C_n. Thus these variables got the following domains:

$$
\begin{aligned}
&F_0 = MPEG\text{-}2 & &F_n = MPEG\text{-}1 \\
&B_0 = 28000 & &B_n \leq 5000 \\
&C_0 = 65535 & &B_n \geq 4000^* \\
& & &maximize(C_n)^* \\
& & &C_n \leq 256
\end{aligned}
\tag{1}
$$

* These constraints are desired ones.

Based on the existing CAT we define FI_j, FO_j as sets with, respectively, the available input and output format of each CAT_j in the CAIN registry. In the same way we define BI_j, BO_j as the input and output bitrate accepted range of each CAT_j, and CI_j, CO_j as the available colour depth in the input and output of each CAT_j.

For instance, in the previous example we have the following domain for each variable:

$$
\begin{aligned}
&FI_1 = \{MPEG\text{-}1,\ MPEG\text{-}2\} & &FO_1 = \{JPEG, PNG\} \\
&BI_1 = [10..100000] & &BO_1 = \text{Unbounded} \\
&CI_1 = [2..65536] & &CO_1 = [256..65536] \\[6pt]
&FI_2 = \{MPEG\text{-}2\} & &FO_2 = \{MPEG\text{-}1, MPEG\text{-}2, DivX\} \\
&BI_2 = [10000..1000000] & &BO_2 = \text{Unbounded} \\
&CI_2 = [256..65536] & &CO_2 = [256..65536] \\[6pt]
&FI_3 = \{MPEG\text{-}2,\ MPEG\text{-}4\} & &FO_3 = \{MPEG\text{-}1, MPEG\text{-}4\} \\
&BI_3 = \text{Unbounded} & &BO_3 = [100..6000] \\
&CI_3 = [2..65536] & &CO_3 = [2..16]
\end{aligned}
\tag{2}
$$

Note that some variables domains in formula (1) are constrained by equalities and other variables are constrained by inequalities. We can transform inequalities in sets as follows:

$$
\begin{array}{ll}
F_0 = MPEG\text{-}2 & F_n = MPEG\text{-}1 \\
B_0 = 28000 & B_n = [min..5000] \\
C_0 = 65535 & B_n = [4000..max]^{*} \\
& maximize(C_n)^{*} \\
& C_n = [min..256]
\end{array}
\tag{3}
$$

[*] These constraints are desired ones.

Where *min* is a constant minimum value for the parameter (usually cero), and *max* a maximum constant value for this parameter.

Based on the CAT capabilities, we can define three rules with the constraints as the premise of the rules and with the boolean variables $CAT_1,...,CAT_3$ as the consequents of the rules, which indicate where each CAT_j satisfy the constraints of the problem:

$$
\begin{array}{l}
F_0 \in FI_1 \land F_n \in FO_1 \land B_0 \in BI_1 \land B_n \cap BO_1 \land C_0 \in CI_1 \land C_n \cap CO_1 \rightarrow CAT_1 \\
F_0 \in FI_2 \land F_n \in FO_2 \land B_0 \in BI_2 \land B_n \cap BO_2 \land C_0 \in CI_2 \land C_n \cap CO_2 \rightarrow CAT_2 \\
F_0 \in FI_3 \land F_n \in FO_3 \land B_0 \in BI_3 \land B_n \cap BO_3 \land C_0 \in CI_3 \land C_n \cap CO_3 \rightarrow CAT_3
\end{array}
\tag{4}
$$

Note that whenever a parameter takes a value and the other takes a range the term appears as a belonging relation ($\in$), and when both parameters are sets we use an intersection relation ($\cap$).

Now we apply a CSP solver to each premise of the rules to determine which CATs can be applied and we reach the solution {$CAT_1=false$, $CAT_2=true$, $CAT_3=true$}, this result indicate that only CAT_2 and CAT_3 are applicable.

Note that at this point there is not a unique solution to the problem, but a set of solutions equally valid from the mandatory usage environment point of view. Concretely applying CAT_2 constraints, output variables take the following domain:

$$
\begin{array}{l}
F_n = MPEG\text{-}1 \\
B_n = [100..5000] \\
C_n = [256]
\end{array}
\tag{5}
$$

And applying CAT_3 constraints, output variables take the domain:

$$
\begin{array}{l}
F_n = MPEG\text{-}1 \\
B_n = [100..6000] \\
C_n = [2..16]
\end{array}
\tag{6}
$$

6 Applying Desirable Constraints

If there is not any CAT capable of fulfilling the mandatory constraints, the DM fails reporting that it's not possible to adapt the content with the proposed usage environment. Otherwise, if we suppose that the above mandatory constraints have been fulfilled by one or more CATs (as in the previous example), we apply the desirable constraints as we detail below.

Desirable constraints differ from mandatory constraints in three aspects: First, desirable constraints must not be completely fulfilled. Even, they could not be fulfilled at all. Second, they are ordered by a desirable constraints priority list (explained below). Third, besides equalities and inequalities constraints, desirable constraints can also have maximization and minimization functions.

The *Desirable Constraints Priority List (DCPL)* is an ordered list of constraints desirable to be fulfilled. This list is ordered from high to low relevance. The DCPL is by default system defined, so usually the user doesn't need to provide this information if he/she doesn't want. Desirable constraints are applied following this algorithm:

1. Take the first constraint of the DCPL and try to fulfil it.
2. If after applying this constraint there is not a feasible adaptation that fulfils requirements, ignore these constraints. Else keep this constraint and reduce the range of the domain of variables in formula (5) and (6) accordingly.
3. Repeat this algorithm with the rest of the DCPL.

Although currently the DCPL uses a proprietary format, the MPEG-21 DIA [13] standard has specified a set of tools (Terminal and Network Quality of Service, and Universal Constraints Descriptions Tools). These tools provide a generic mechanism for the definition of constraints, and therefore they are the best candidates for being used to describe the DCPL in the future.

In the above example there exist two desirable constraints, supposing that they are prioritized from top to bottom:

$$maximize(C_n)$$
$$B_n=[4000..max] \tag{7}$$

After applying these desired constraints, following above proposed algorithm, the output variables of the CAT_2 reach the following domain:

$$F_n=MPEG-1$$
$$B_n=[4000..5000] \tag{8}$$
$$C_n=256$$

And CAT_3 output variables are restricted to this one domain:

$$F_n=MPEG-1$$
$$B_n=[4000..6000] \tag{9}$$
$$C_n=16$$

7 Content Adaptation with Optimization

In the previous example, several (namely two) CATs reached the desired target and therefore, in order to select only one, a final optimization step is required. It should also be noted that, although in the previous example F_n and C_n are assigned to one value, B_n has a range of values that "a priory" are equally valid from the statement of the problem. We say that a *solution is defined* if all the variables have only one possible value. During this optimization step we reach two objectives: to select the preferred CAT to perform the adaptation, and to select a value for those parameters with more than one feasible value. That is, we pretend to reach one and only one defined solution. Note that this step can be considered an optimization step because we pretend to select the CAT that provides the best adaptation from those ones that fulfil all the mandatory constraints (mandatory and desired).

We define a *Content Provider Optimization Priority List (CPOPL)* as the list proposed by the media content provider to prioritize some variables over others. The CPOPL is a list composed by *optimization elements*, where each optimization element is a constraint defined in a way that only equalities, maximization, and minimization are allowed (no unequally are allowed in order to avoid more that one solution equally valid to the problem). The algorithm for this final optimization step is as follows:

1. For each optimization element of the CPOPL
   a. If this optimization element is applicable
      i.   Apply the optimization element to each solution
      ii. If there is only one solution, select this solution and abandon this loop
2. Use the rest of the CPOPL optimization elements to transform the solution in a defined solution

At this point we must observe that the finally selected CAT depends on the CPOPL. If the content provider prefers to maximize colour depth over bitrate, the CPOPL must be defined in the following order:

$$F_n=MPEG\text{-}4$$
$$maximize(C_n) \tag{10}$$
$$minimize(B_n)$$

In this case the first optimization element is ignored because there is no solution where the video output format can be *MPEG-4*. The second optimization element selects CAT_2 over CAT_3 because $C_n=256$ in CAT_2 is bigger than $C_n=16$ in CAT_3.

If, on the other hand, the content provider prefers to minimize bitrate over colour depth, the CPOPL must be in the following order:

$$F_n=MPEG\text{-}4$$
$$minimize(B_n) \tag{11}$$
$$maximize(C_n)$$

In this case, again, the first optimization element is ignored because there is no solution where the video output format can be *MPEG-4*. The second optimization element reduces values of the CAT_2 output to:

$F_n=MPEG-1$
$B_n=4000$ (12)
$C_n=256$

And of the CAT_3 output to:

$F_n=MPEG-1$
$B_n=4000$ (13)
$C_n=16$

Now, the third optimization element chooses CAT_2 over CAT_3, and this is the selected solution. Note that in this concrete optimization example the algorithm has selected CAT_2 over CAT_3 in both cases. This is due to the fact that both CAT have the same limit over the minimum bitrate of $B_n=4000$. Also note that, to ensure that every parameter of the selected CAT has a unique value, the CPOPL must be complete, that is, every parameter must appears (as an equality, maximization or minimization) in the CPOPL.

8 Conclusions

This paper presents a Constraints Satisfaction Problem (CSP) method for solving the task of finding the best available content adaptation tool (and its parameters) to adapt content, fulfilling a large group of adaptation constraints obtained from a standardized description of the usage environment. The proposed solution finds the best available adaptation tool, if an adaptation solution exists.

The proposed systems work over metadata that describes content and usage environment (using both MPEG-7 and MPEG-21 standardized specifications). In order to support the extensibility to incorporate new content adaptation tools, a specific adaptation capabilities description scheme (MPEG-7 inspired) is used.

The current DM implementation uses only a subset of all the metadata supported within CAIN, and, in order to improve adaptation, the remainder constraints over metadata will be added in the near future to the DM.

Acknowledgments

This work is partially supported by the European Commission 6th Framework Program under project FP6-001765 (aceMedia). This work is also supported by the Ministerio de Ciencia y Tecnología of the Spanish Government under project TIN2004-07860 (MEDUSA) and by the Comunidad de Madrid under project P-TIC-0223-0505 (PROMULTIDIS).

References

[1] A. Vetro, "MPEG-21 digital item adaptation: enabling universal multimedia access", IEEE Multimedia, 11(1):84 - 87, Jan-March 2004.

[2] F. Pereida, I. Burnett, "Universal Multimedia Experiences for Tomorrow", IEEE Signal Processing Magazine, 20(2):63-73, March 2003.

[3] D. Jannach, K. Leopold, C. Timmerer, H. Hellwagner, "A knowledge-based framework for multimedia adaptation", Applied Intelligence, 24(2):109-125, April 2006.

[4] Y. Wang, J. G. Kim, S.F. Chang, "Content-based utility function prediction for real-time MPEG-4 video transcoding", in Proc. of ICIP 2003, pp 189-192, September 2003.

[5] J. Magalhaes, F. Pereira, "Using MPEG standards for multimedia customization", Signal Processing: Image Communications, 19:437-456, 2004.

[6] B.L. Tseng, C.Y. Lin, J.R. Smith, "Using MPEG-7 and MPEG-21 for Personalizing Video", IEEE Multimedia, 11(1), pp. 42-53, Jan-March 2004.

[7] ISO/IEC 15938-5, Information Technology – Multimedia Content Description Interface – Part 5: Multimedia Description Schemes.

[8] K. Marriott, "Programming with constraints an introduction", The MIT Press, 1998.

[9] J.M. Martínez, V. Valdés, J. Bescós, L. Herranz, "Introducing CAIN: A Metadata-Driven content Adaptation Manager Integrating Heterogeneous Content Adaptation tools", in Proceedings of the WIAMIS'2005, Montreux, April 2005.

[10] P. van Beek, J.R. Smith, T. Ebrahimi, T. Suzuki, J. Askelof, "Metadata-driven multimedia access", IEEE Signal Processing Magazine, 20 (2):40-52, March 2003.

[11] A. Vetro, "Transcoding, Scalable Coding and Standardized Metadata", in Visual Content Processing and Representation-VLBV03, LNCS Vol. 2849, pp.15-16, Springer-Verlag 2003.

[12] J.R. Smith, "Semantic Universal Multimedia Access", in Visual Content Processing and Representation-VLBV03, LNCS Vol. 2849, pp.13-14, Springer-Verlag, 2003.

[13] ISO/IEC 21000-7, Information Technology – Multimedia Frameworks – Part 7: Digital Item Adaptation.

[14] V. Váldes, J.M. Martínez, "Content Adaptation Tools in the CAIN Framework", in VLBV05, LNCS 3893, pp 9-15, 2006.

[15] V. Valdés, J.M. Martínez, "Content Adaptation Capabilities Description Tool for Supporting Extensibility in the CAIN Framework", in Multimedia Content Representation, Classification and Security-MCRS2006, B.Günsel, A.K.Jain, A.M. Tekalp, B. Sankur (eds.), Lecture Notes in Computer Science, Vol. 4105, Springer Verlag, 2006, pp. 395-402.

[16] N. Sprljan, M. Mrak, G. C. K. Abhayaratne, E. Izquierdo, "A scalable coding framework for efficient video adaptation", in Proceedings of the WIAMIS'2005, April 2005.

[17] J.M. Martínez, V. Valdés, L. Herranz, J. Bescós, "A Simple Profile for MPEG-21 Usage Environment description tools", Doc. ISO/MPEG M11239, MPEG Palma de Mallorca Meeting, October 2004.

Aspects of Adaptivity in P2P Information Retrieval

Wolfgang Müller, Andreas Henrich, and Martin Eisenhardt

Bamberg University, Bamberg , Germany
wolfgang.mueller@wiai.uni-bamberg.de
http://www.uni-bamberg.de/wiai/minf

Abstract. Peer-to-Peer networks are comprised of multiple independently administered computers (peers) that cooperate via a common protocol in order to achieve a goal common to the peers. Helping the user find relevant information in a P2P network is the subject of the field of Peer-to-Peer IR.

In order to be successful, a P2P-IR system needs to be adaptive in several respects. It has to adapt both to the user and to its environment. Within this article we detail the motivations and challenges of P2P-IR, as well as the ways in which P2P-IR systems adapt and where improvement is needed in order to achieve adaptive multimedia retrieval.

1 Introduction

Peer-to-Peer networks consist of multiple independently administered computers (peers) that cooperate with each other serving a goal that is common to the peers. The word *peer* indicates that the participants in the P2P network have equal rights and opportunities. In true P2P networks, there are no central components.

It is common grounds that there is the need to discover the network's resources in order to make use of a P2P network. This motivates the research into retrieval in P2P networks. For a couple of years, the focus lay on exact search in P2P networks, however, there is a growing interest in similarity search, *i.e.* information retrieval (IR) in P2P networks [25,18,16].

What is the motivation of such networks? In fact, currently, there is a growing proportion of user-generated media. Services like myspace.com, blogger.com or flickr.com all offer users the opportunity to put their opinion and their feelings into media objects, upload them to the site and then serve it to the world and have the result viewed and annotated for search by friends and strangers alike. In other words, there is a growing amount of data generated by end users for the use by end users.

On the other hand, Google and competitors offer search for the mainstream and increasingly also for specialized communities. However, there are limits to the current crawler-based system: a growing number of users is reluctant to give their personal data to huge data-collecting enterprises. At the same time crawlers reach their limit in the sense that many site owners of small sites complain that too much of their traffic is due to visits of web site crawlers for search engines. This puts a limit to the freshness of data accessible via web search engines.

S. Marchand-Maillet et al. (Eds.): AMR 2006, LNCS 4398, pp. 164–178, 2007.

P2P-IR offers the promise of freshness of index data. Moreover, there is the hope that as each machine in the P2P network is responsible for comparatively few documents, there is the possibility to use sophisticated query processing methods that might be too costly for classical search engines such as Google, Yahoo or MSN search.

However, looking more closely, there are several challenges to P2P search. All of them are, in fact, linked to the need for adaptivity. We identify four main aspects of adaptation that a P2P-network has to perform. One of them is IR specific, the other three are P2P specific:

IR specific: P2P-IR inherits the adaptation problems from IR.

User query behavior: The system has to adapt to the user and his information need, or more precisely to his perception of usefulness and relevance of media objects in the given query situation.

P2P specific: These adaptation problems are common to P2P systems.

User online behavior: Experience shows [11] that users of P2P networks have strongly differing behavior with respect to how long they stay online and how much data they share.

The word *churn* describes the fact that the population of a P2P network is constantly changing. We are speaking of *the* P2P network and *its* participants, but these words do not describe a P2P network well. There is as much *the population* of a P2P network as there is *the population* of a huge railway station (think: Paris, *Gare de l'Est*): The overwhelming majority of a railway station's population will be part of this population less then a quarter of an hour. However, some very few people will work at the station all day. Similarly, many measurement studies (*e.g.* [11]) in P2P networks report that many (up to $\approx 80\%$!) peers joining a P2P network stay less than one minute in the network. Evidently a P2P network has to adapt to this churn of population.

An important insight is that the churn present in P2P networks calls for restricted goals of availability. In the context of multimedia retrieval, it might be feasible to replicate indexing data, but it will be infeasible to replicate the actual documents [2].

Peer system properties: There are peers with widely differing computing power (*e.g.* from a 200MHz portable device to a 4GHz Pentium D) and network bandwidth (*e.g.* from a mediocre 40kbit/s telephone connection to 16Mbit/s DSL lines). P2P networks need to find the right compromise between fairly balancing the load and making network participation possible for users of legacy equipment.

Attacks: Finally, participating peers can be contributors or attackers. In client/server networks there is one data provider and many data consumers. If a client tries to alter a server's data, it is easy to tell who is the attacker and who is attacked. In P2P networks, however, service consumers (*i.e.* peers) are on the same side of the fence as service providers (*also* peers), so there is no easy way to tell if a contribution is legitimate or not.

In fact, all of the adaptation challenges have to do with diversity. Adapting to users means adapting to their differences. The same, P2P systems seek to *adapt to heterogeneity* of the P2P system and its environment. As we will see in the following, in some situations one can even *make use of the heterogeneity*.

1.1   Structure of the Paper

In the following we will consider image Query by visual Example (QbvE) as an example for multimedia-retrieval, a variety of Content-Based Image Retrieval. While we are aware that QbvE is not the only way of querying multimedia data, we do assume that this way of query processing is representative and the basis for many more complex and more powerful query paradigms.

In classical QbvE, images are indexed by extracting a feature vector from each image and indexing the resulting collection of vectors for search. A query is processed by transforming the query into a feature vector q and by ranking the image in the collection by the distance $\delta(q, v)$ of each feature vector v to q. The best-ranked document is the document whose feature vector has the smallest distance to the query. Typically, only k documents are of interest.

In other words, the image query is mapped onto a ranked k-Nearest-Neighbor (k-NN) query between feature vectors.

However, there is an additional complication. Typically QbvE systems try to improve query performance by solliciting feedback from the user. In this case, the user can mark documents as relevant or irrelevant to the query. The system reacts by either modifying q, or by *modifying the distance measure* δ. Especially the latter poses challenges to the indexing structure.

There is a large number of diverse approaches to performing such k-NN queries in P2P networks. Roughly, they can be sorted into three groups, namely

1. Replication in unstructured networks,
2. Approaches based on distributed hash tables, and
3. Routing by data summaries and source selection.

In the following we will describe these approaches, and we will describe how they realize adaptivity. Please note that while we find this classification useful, many systems use combinations of these approaches. Freenet, for example, performs replication as well as summary-based routing.

2   Replication in Unstructured Networks

Despite the existence of sophisticated techniques for using unstructured P2P networks (such as [22,27]), the term *unstructured networks* typically is associated with the first generation of the Gnutella P2P protocol [6]. In a classical Gnutella network, peers are connected via TCP/IP connections. Each peer is connected with a small number of *neighbors*. Each peer steadily discovers new neighbors in case its current neighbors leave the system. When receiving a query either from a user or from other peers, the receiving peer forwards the query to all its neighbors, except for the source of the query. On receiving the results it will forward these results to the source of the query, *i.e.* either to another peer or to the querying user. The querying user then can choose documents to download.

This method is simple and robust. However, it quite quickly hit the first scalability barrier. Every node receives every query. Nodes with a slow network connection eventually end up doing nothing but forwarding queries, and they are not able to serve or to request documents any more.

2.1   Adaptation to System Diversity and to User Online Behavior

A first attempt at reducing the communication load is to limit the reach of queries via a so-called *Time To Live (TTL)*, effectively forwarding the query to just a (random) subset of the peers. However, this method still treats all peers equal and does not cater for the heterogeneity of the system.

The current method of choice is to introduce so-called *super nodes* or *super peers* [27]. These peers are more powerful and reliable than the average peer and take more responsabilities in the network: Each super peer is responsible for a set of normal peers. When a normal peer connects to a super peer, it will send a replicate of all its indexing data to the super peer. Subsequent queries will be handled by the super peer[1]. The normal peer just comes into play if it can contribute to the query result. This way, normal peers are shielded from the majority of the query traffic. To summarise: super peers act as servers for normal peers, and as classical Gnutella peers among each other.

Super peer architectures make use of the heterogeneity in P2P networks. There are peers that have more bandwidth than others, and there are peers that stay longer in the network than others. In fact, the peer online time distribution is such that it is safe to assume that a peer that has stayed an hour within the network will stay much longer in the network. So, the network elects peers as super peers that have stayed online a long time and that are willing to serve as super peers. Here heterogeneity helps making the choice.

2.2   Adaptation to the Index Data

In replication based networks, the algorithm makes sure that a query reaches all super peers. As all super peers combined contain all indexing data, each super peer just has to act like a non-P2P server: it processes the query locally and forwards a ranking to the querier.

Obviously, ranked similarity queries that can be processed in one centralized server can also be processed in P2P network with a super-peer architecture.

2.3   Adaptation to the Querying User

From the above follows that also complex relevance feedback queries can be processed using super-peer methods. In fact, this seems like an opportunity for building adaptive systems that support complex, interactive query processes.

---

[1] Some systems only ship peer data summaries instead of the full indexing data.

However, when one looks at the actual query times needed to process a query in a Gnutella network, they are in the region of tens of seconds up to several minutes. The high latency between issuing and completing a query step is the main weakness of this type of architecture and currently makes it unsuitable for interactive query processes that use relevance feedback.

3   Distributed Indexing Structures

Distributed indexing structures try to get away from query processing that involves looking at all data points. As indicated by its name, the approach is similar to the approach of non-distributed indexing structures: The network maintains a structural invariant in the presence of peers that are constantly joining and leaving. The data to be indexed is inserted at the proper position in the indexing structure. On processing a query, an algorithm finds the nodes that contain the index data needed.

The main advantage of distributed indexing structures is that they are conceptually very close to non-distributed indexing structures. Their main disadvantage in the P2P setting is that peers entering the network have to upload their index data up-front when entering the network.

Most current distributed indexing structures are based on *Distributed Hash Tables (DHTs)*. DHTs are one of the main architectural advances of current P2P research with respect to the initial Gnutella architecture.

In contrast to super-peer architectures that do not provide any guarantee of search quality, DHTs consisting of N peers are able to determine in $O(\log N)$ *hops*[2] if a data item is present in the network or not. The price for this precise knowledge is high: The large majority of DHTs does not support similarity search: The operations supported are the insertion of key/value pairs and the retrieval of a value given a key. The most prominent DHTs with these properties are Chord [24], Pastry [20] and Kademlia [14]. The latter has been successfully fielded in a large-scale consumer application: eDonkey.

Most DHTs identify each node using a long bit string without semantic meaning. In addition to identifying nodes such that they can be recognized even after a change of IP address, the identifier determines the position of the node relative to other nodes in the DHT. Media object keys in DHTs are also bit sequences of the same lengths as peer IDs. The P2P algorithm now assigns to each peer within the network a region in the space of possible bit sequences for which the peer will be responsible. When inserting a key/value pair into a DHT, a routing algorithm will find the node responsible for the key and assign the key/value pair to it.

Chord, for example has a ring topology. Each peer has two neighbors, one with a smaller (right), one with a bigger ID (left). Each peer is responsible for keys that are smaller than or equal to its ID and bigger than the ID of its right neighbor. Using this architecture one would be able to find a given key in linear

---

[2] A *hop* is a step of indirection. If A sends a message to C via B, the message is routed over two *hops*.

time. In order to achieve a speedup, each node maintains $O(\log N)$ connections across the ring, the *fingers*. Judicious use of these fingers enables each peer to look up any key in $O(\log N)$ time.

CAN DHTs (Content-addressable networks, [19]) work differently. Here the space of possible IDs are multi-dimensional real-valued vectors. Typically each vector component is limited to the interval $[0; 1)$. In CAN each peer is responsible for a rectangular region in key space. While in a classic CAN each peer is only connected to peers that are responsible for the regions neighboring its own key space, there exist modifications of CANs that build small-world networks on top of the classical CAN structure, obtaining $O(\log N)$ lookup time [8]. In contrast to Chord, CAN is able to perform efficient similarity search on vectors. However, due to the curse of dimensionality [26,1], this ability is limited to small dimensionalities.

Both Chord and CAN have been used as building blocks for the design of IR-applications. In the following we will shortly describe two applications: PRISM [21], a Chord-based system, and pLSI [25], a CAN-based system.

PRISM. Indexes each vector x by placing x on a small number of nodes in a Chord DHT. Using the resulting distributed indexing structure, it can process k-Nearest-Neighbor (k-NN queries for high-dimensional vectors).

The placement of each vector in PRISM is calculated using distances to a fixed set of *reference vectors*. When processing a query, the node issuing the query q calculates the set of nodes where q would be placed and searches for similar vectors there, sending the nodes q as the query. The main innovation of PRISM is the algorithm for finding the nodes on which to place the data vectors.

In order to index a vector x, the distance of x to a number n_r of reference vectors r_i ($i \in \{1, \ldots, n_r\}$) is calculated, yielding $\boldsymbol{\delta} := (\delta_1, \delta_2, \ldots, \delta_{n_r}) := (\delta(x, r_1), \ldots, \delta(x, r_{n_r}))$. Typically, $\boldsymbol{\delta}$ has fewer dimensions than x. Now, one straightforward way to proceed would be to index $\boldsymbol{\delta}$ via a distributed vector indexing structure. The authors of PRISM, however, go a different way. In PRISM, the r_i are *ranked* by their similarity. The result of this ranking is a list of indices $\boldsymbol{\iota} = (\iota_1, \ldots, \iota_{n_r})$ such that r_{ι_1} is the reference vector closest to x, r_{ι_2} the second closest and so on.

Then, pairs of indices are formed. The pair formation is a fitting parameter, the original PRISM paper suggests $\{\iota_1, \iota_1\}$ (*i.e.* storing the a pair consisting of twice the index of the best match) $\{\iota_1, \iota_2\}$, (the reference point index of the best match and the second best match), $\{\iota_2, \iota_3\}, \{\iota_1, \iota_3\}, \{\iota_1, \iota_4\}, \{\iota_2, \iota_5\}, \{\iota_2, \iota_4\}, \{\iota_3, \iota_4\}, \{\iota_1, \iota_5\}, \{\iota_4, \iota_5\}, \{\iota_3, \iota_5\}$ for their dataset. From each of the pairs a Chord key is calculated, and this key is used for inserting the vector x into the Chord ring.

Query processing works by finding out which peers would receive the query vector q if it was a new data item and forwarding the query vector to these peers. This involves again the calculation of index pairs, which we will call *query pairs* in the following. In order to reduce query processing cost, the query processor can choose to contact only nodes pertaining to only a subset of the query pairs. Doing this also reduces recall, one has to find a useful tradeoff.

pLSI. pLSI [25] follows another approach that is more classical. Here Latent Semantic Indexing, *i.e.* a singular value decomposition [7] is performed in order to reduce the dimensionality of the vectors to be indexed. At the same time, the SVD achieves an ordering of the dimension *by their importance.* The remaining (still) high dimensional vectors are cut into low-dimensional slices. Each slice and the ID of the document it pertains to is entered as a key/document id (*i.e.* scliec/document id) pair into into a CAN. On receiving a query from its user, a peer cuts up the query vector into slices and then queries the CAN, starting with the most important dimensions. Results for several slices of each vector will be combined. As in PRISM we can process k-NN queries using pLSI.

3.1   Adaptation System Diversity and to User Online Behavior

In terms of adaptation to system diversity and user online behavior, DHT-based systems inherit their properties from DHTs.

DHTs have the advantage of being provably efficient, and they can be tested in a data-independent manner. This property has made them a subject of extensive research. One focus of this research has been making DHTs churn resistant [23], and to introduce load balancing where the load balancing that is inherent to the DHT algorithms does not suffice [10].

DHTs perform replication of key/value pairs in order to ensure high availability. Obviously, if there is much index data (*i.e.* the values of the key/value pairs) stored in the network, the continuous replication alone will generate *much* traffic.

Example: Consider an inverted file index, in which each document of $N_{d,p} = 1000$ documents per peer is represented by $m = 1000$ vector components. Assume $r = 20$ fold replication. Consider that 5% of the peers is leaving every five minutes. In (very conservative) estimations we would count each vector component to be stored as 4*bytes*. In our hypothetic but realistic setting, $0.05 \cdot N_{d,p} \cdot m \cdot r \cdot 4 = 4Mbyte$ would have to be shipped *per peer* every five minutes just to maintain the network. In other words, a peer participating 8 hours a day would have to send 10GB/month over the network just for participating.

Load balancing can be performed by having peers that hold too many keys distribute some of their keys to their neighbors.

Adaptation to differing processing power and network latency can be performed *e.g.* by sending each query to several nodes in the DHT. Query answering in DHT is a multi-step process in which the querying peer queries its neighbors for suitable next nodes that are closer to the wanted key. By sending the query to several nodes at the same time, the querier can choose the answer of the fastest answering node for continuing the query process. By this, DHTs tend to sollicit more strongly nodes that are more performant.

3.2   Adaptation to the Index Data

In contrast to replication-based systems, DHT-based IR systems make use of the structure and distribution of the data they are indexing in order to create an efficient data structure. Our preliminary experiments (see Fig. 1) suggest that *e.g.* in PRISM the dimensionality of the features indexed matters, and that this influences the number of reference points that are to be chosen depending on the data.

Similarly, the usefulness of an LSI depends on the dimensionality of the feature set and thus on the type of data to be indexed. The outcome of an LSI is data dependent. So, before indexing a collection of vectors, a pLSI network needs to perform an LSI of the data to be indexed.

The same applies when data drift over time. From time to time, a pSearch network's administrator (or an algorithm that is not reported, yet) will have to decide to adjust network parameters in order to suit the new data distribution over the peers. Another method would be to perform such a readjustment periodically, avoiding difficult, and probably faulty decisions.

3.3   Adaptation to the User

As of yet, there is *no* research we are aware of that considers adaptation of DHT-based P2P-IR networks to user feedback.

Distributed inverted files are sufficiently similar to non-distributed inverted files to be able to support the processing of relevance feedback. However, more research is needed for evaluating if the cost of distributed processing of relevance feedback queries is within reasonable bounds. [13] suggest that naive use of inverted files in large networks is beyond reasonable communication cost even when proceeding queries with few query terms.

Distributed indexing structures for non-sparse real-valued vectors, such as PRISM and pLSI suffer from the fact that they assume one distance measure when filling the indexing structure. We would expect that the performance degrades when changing that distance measure, *e.g.* in order to respond to user feedback. Indeed experiments confirm slightly degrading performance. Please see the experimental section 5 for details.

4   Routing-Based Approaches

As distributed indexing structures, routing-based approaches seek to get away from considering all data vectors for each query. However, in contrast to distributed indexing structures, summary based approaches leave the bulk of the indexing data in the peers that hold the corresponding documents. Routing based systems seek to improve the query performance by improving the network's topology and by creating routing tables that enable *semantic routing* between peers.

Creating routing tables for semantic routing involves creation of summaries of a peer's collection and shipping the collection summary to the right place in the network.

4.1   Freenet

Freenet, described in [5] performs routing by document keys. It has been extended for the use in (text) information retrieval by Kronfol [12]. To our knowledge, there is no extension of Freenet for the use of multimedia data. However, the techniques applied in Freenet have influenced other systems.

As Gnutella, Freenet is unstructured. However, Freenet queries are not forwarded from the querying node to all its neighbors. Instead, each node contains a routing table. The routing table contains a list of peer/document identifier pairs. A peer/document identifier pair p/id is entered in the routing table, if p has provided id in the past. In each node, a query will be routed to the p whose id matches most closely the query. If there is no possibility to route the query to a suitable next node, backtracking is performed. When the searched document is found, the document found will be sent back along the path of the query. Peers on this backward path of the query can choose to cache the document, and they can choose to enter themselves as the source of the result document.

4.2   DISCOVIR

A well-published system that uses summaries and topology improvements in order to perform Content Based Image Retrieval (CBIR) is DISCOVIR [18]. DISCOVIR indexes high-dimensional feature vectors. Each peer is summarised via an average feature vector $v_{p,avg}$ and σ, the corresponding standard deviation. This summary is used in two ways:

Privileged *vs.* normal links: Each peer has two classes of links. (i) Normal links that work much like Gnutella links. (ii) *Privileged links* that build a second Gnutella-like network between peers that are similar to each other. If they are similar to each other can be determined via their summaries.

Query filter: A peer that receives a query calculates the distance between the query vector q and the average vector of the peer and tests if the distance is below a threshold that is calculated relative to the standard deviation $||q - v_{p,avg}|| < c \cdot \sigma$. If the query is too far away from the average vector, the peer will not run the query on its local data. If the query is close enough to be processed locally, the query will be forwarded via privileged links, otherwise normal links are used.

Sia *et al.* report improvements with respect to classical Gnutella. However, to our knowledge, this method has not yet been tested with a realistic large-scale data distribution over peers.

4.3   PlanetP

DISCOVIR is insatisfactory in the sense a large fraction of peers has to be contacted in order to process a query.

In fact, the curse of dimensionality that makes the creation of successful distributed indexing structures difficult is also the primary source of difficulty when trying to implement multi-hop routing strategies for performing CBIR in P2P networks. Due to the curse of dimensionality, the summaries cannot be very selective, and thus cannot claim that a routing decision based on such a summary is correct with a high probability. However, multi-hop routing requires the routing decision to be correct with a very high probability.

Example: Imagine a scheme that routes a query to the peer holding the most similar vector v_t with respect to a query q. The query would be routed over 20 hops. If we assume that the routing decision is correct 99% of the time, still this method will route $0.99^{20} = 80\%$ of all queries to the correct peer. However, if we assume routing decisions to be correct at 80% of the hops, the query will reach the node holding v_t only $\approx 1\%$ of the time!

PlanetP reacts to these considerations by employing *one-hop routing*, known in the area of distributed IR and databases as data source selection, inspired by classical methods of distributed information retrieval [9,4]. In PlanetP each peer knows summaries of *all* other peers. Summaries are replicated via so-called *rumor spreading*. Obviously this scheme is not scalable as the number of peers to keep track of grows $O(N)$. We have presented a scalable version of PlanetP, Rumorama [16] whose properties will be discussed below but whose details are out of scope here.

A PlanetP-peer receiving a query q from its user (we will call this peer the *query peer*) will rank the other *peers* with respect to the query. The peers will be ranked by the probability that they contribute one or more documents to the result set of the query. After this peer ranking has been obtained, the query peer will contact the most promising peers, sending them q. The peers contacted will process q using their local data store and then return the results to the query peer. The query peer will generate a combined ranking of peers.

PlanetP is specialized on text information retrieval. PlanetP uses Bloom filters [3] as summaries. Each summary describes which index terms are present in a given peer. Unfortunately Bloom filters are not adapted to the indexing of densely populated high-dimensional vectors.

We have presented work about peer data summaries based on *cluster histograms* for use in PlanetP-like networks. These summaries can be used for collections of images and have been tested on 166-dimensional histograms extracted from stock photos and consumer photos [17,15].

In this method, first a *global k-means clustering* is derived over all the images present in the network. As shown in [15], such a clustering can be calculated efficiently, *i.e.* without having peers transfer their data collection. The result of the clustering is a set of *cluster centers* c_i. Every peer j will now assign each of its vectors v_k^j to the closest cluster center, and it will count how many vectors are assigned to which center. Doing this, it obtains a cluster histogram h_i^j that assigns to each cluster center c_i a document frequency given the peer j.

We are currently preparing a paper that presents and evaluates diverse peer ranking methods based on cluster histograms. The simplest method is the one described in [17] and will be presented here: When processing queries, the query peer first finds which center c_i is closest to q. We call the closest center c_{i_q}. The query peer then will rank the peers j by decreasing histogram value $h_{i_q}^j$ for the cluster center c_{i_q}.

Adaptation to System Diversity and to User Online Behavior. The architectures presented here are very different in nature, and thus react very differently to user online behavior and system diversity.

The outcome of Freenet's caching scheme is that popular documents are cached at many peers in the network, and that the addresses of cached copies will be contained in many routing tables. So, after inception of the network, the network structure and query performance will adapt to the users need. Moreover, peers can choose if they want to keep long or short routing tables, if they want to enter themselves as data source, and if they want to cache documents. This enables peers to choose their load. In addition, popular documents will be cached all over the network and thus the load will be well-balanced.

While Freenet does not perform search on multidimensional vectors (neither does FASD), the interest of Freenet stems from the fact that similar techniques of gradual routing improvement are used for IR, but not for CBIR, yet.

DISCOVIR, in its pure form inherits most of the disadvantages of Gnutella. A peer that has privileged links to peers with often-queried images will tend to be queried often. DISCOVIR does not give possibilities to reduce the load, except to avoid building privileged links to other peers. In this case, the peer will be only rarely contacted.

DISCOVIR also inherits Gnutella's advantages. The peer data summaries are very small, they are shipped when discovering other peers, and thus a peer entering the network *gradually* improves its connectivity which is in contrast to DHT-based approaches in which there is no gradation between indexed and non-indexed data.

PlanetP is strongly churn-resistant (as every peer knows every other peer, it is very difficult to make the system break). However, it does not cater for system diversity. Every peer in the network ist supposed to stay informed about all the other peers in the network, *i.e.* all peers stay informed about the same number of other peers, incurring the same maintenance load. The actual query load of a peer depends on the summary that it is posting. If the summary makes the peer a probable holder of many highly demanded documents, it will be contacted more often than if it posts that it contains one single rarely demanded document.

Rumorama [16], a hierarchical variant of PlanetP enables balancing of the maintenance load. Rumorama introduces a Pastry-like [20] hierarchy on top of the PlanetP network. Peers are enabled to choose with how many *friend nodes* they want to exchange summaries. Still, a structured multicast algorithm enables considering summaries of all peers when processing the query.

4.4   Adaptation to the Index Data

As the indexing data in DHT-based approaches, summaries need to be tailored to the data types that are indexed. For some types of summaries there is also the need to recompute and redistribute the summaries depending on changes in the data collection.

4.5   Adaptation to the User

Both DISCOVIR and PlanetP are expected to suffer performance losses when the distance measure changes, as the summaries are adapted to a given distance measure. This is described in the following section.

5   Experiments

In Fig. 1 we show two experiments performed using the source selection based method described in [15] and using PRISM. By changing the distance measure at query time, we also *simulated* a relevance feedback query.

For our experiments on PRISM we re-implemented PRISM in a simulator. As we were interested rather in number of distance calculations than in the number of peers contacted[3]. We used a non-tuned simple PRISM version with randomly chosen reference vectors.

Experiments on PRISM were performed with a 1 million image `flickr.com` crawl. For our experiments on the source selection based method we also used a simulator, but with a 50'000 image `flickr.com` crawl. Data distribution over peers matters when using this method. We took the approach to model each peer's data by the data corresponding to one flickr user. This way, the 50'000 images were distributed unevenly over $\approx$2'600 peers. From all images in both collections we extracted 166-D color histograms using $18 \times 3 \times 3$ HSV color bins and 4 grey levels, as described in [15].

All curves in Fig. 1 plot the fraction of 20-NN found plotted against the amount of data points considered (*i.e.* distance calculations) per query. Curves reaching 1 more quickly correspond to better performance.

Note that in this experiment our non-tuned simple PRISM version actually performs *worse than scanning the whole collection once*. Please note that the results for PRISM measured here are much worse than the results presented in [21] using 80-D features, suggesting that dimensionality matters and that careful tuning for an application can greatly improve results. In these present experiments, the source selection method performs better than PRISM.

In order to get a first impression on the behavior of both methods when changing the distance measure used for query processing with respect to the distance measure used for indexing, we simulated a changing distance measure due to user feedback by not evaluating the distance over the complete vectors, but just the distance by projecting both query and document vector on the first 20 components. The query with the changed distance measure was evaluated on the *unchanged indexing data*. The source selection method [15] takes a severe performance hit under these conditions. Our cluster-based variant of PlanetP needed to evaluate up to three times as many distances δ with the modified

---

[3] This makes sense as the number of peers contacted in PRISM depends largely on the amount of load balancing that is performed. If there is little load balancing, few peers are contacted and PRISM rather behaves like a super peer scheme using large super peers.

distance measure with respect to the original distance measure. PRISM also takes a performance hit, but much less so. However, source selection still performs better than PRISM, and still performs better than random search.

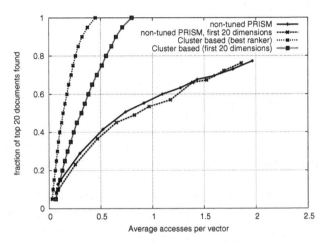

Fig. 1. Comparing PRISM and cluster-based summaries

These experiments support our intuition that both summary-based methods and distributed indexing structures will have to undergo deeper tests if they are supporting adaptive multimedia retrieval. In order to be useful, the benchmarks applied need to be application driven and need to take the data distribution over peers into account.

6 Conclusion

We have presented examples for the main types of P2P architectures for the use in Multimedia Information Retrieval. We have chosen QbvE with relevance feedback as example application. Then we have described the adaptivity properties of some example systems.

Summarizing, one can state that P2P systems have reached an impressive state of the art in terms of load balancing and adaptation to churn. P2P systems can adapt well to challenging scenarios in which users stay only shortly in the network.

There is a useful baseline: Super-peer architectures easily enable any kind of k-NN queries. Their downside is that for processing a Super-peer query, all super peers need to be contacted. Other architectures, based on DHTs or on routing approaches seek to restrict the number of peers that need to be contacted for processing a query. However, their use for relevance feedback query processing is unclear. None of the methods described here has been tested for relevance feedback queries. We feel that this is an interesting open area of research.

References

1. C. C. Aggarwal, A. Hinneburg, and D. A. Keim. On the surprising behavior of distance metrics in high dimensional spaces. In *ICDT '01: Proceedings of the 8th International Conference on Database Theory*, pages 420–434, London, UK, 2001. Springer-Verlag.
2. C. Blake and R. Rodrigues. High availability, scalable storage, dynamic peer networks: Pick two. In *Ninth Workshop on Hot Topics in Operating Systems (HotOS-IX)*, pages 1–6, Lihue, Hawaii, May 2003.
3. B. H. Bloom. Space/time trade-offs in hash coding with allowable errors. *Communications of the ACM*, 13(7), 1970.
4. J. P. Callan, Z. Lu, and W. B. Croft. Searching distributed collections with inference networks. In *Proc. 18th ACM SIGIR*, Seattle, Washington, 1995.
5. I. Clarke, O. Sandberg, B. Wiley, and T. W. Hong. Freenet: A distributed anonymous information storage and retrieval system. In *Proceedings of Designing Privacy Enhancing Technologies: Workshop on Design Issues in Anonymity and Unobservability*, pages 46–66, July 2000.
6. Clip2. The Gnutella Protocol Specification v0.4. URL: `http://www9.limewire.com/developer/gnutella_protocol_0.4.pdf`, 2000.
7. S. Deerwester, S. T. Dumais, G. W. Furnas, T. K. Landauer, and R. A. Harshman. Indexing by latent semantic analysis. *Journal of the American Society for Information Science*, 41(6):391–407, 1990.
8. P. Ganesan, B. Yang, and H. Garcia-Molina. One torus to rule them all: multidimensional queries in P2P systems. In *WebDB '04: Proceedings of the 7th International Workshop on the Web and Databases*, pages 19–24, New York, NY, USA, 2004. ACM Press.
9. L. Gravano, H. Garcia-Molina, and A. Tomasic. GlOSS: text-source discovery over the internet. *ACM Trans. Database Syst.*, 24(2):229–264, 1999.
10. D. R. Karger and M. Ruhl. Simple efficient load balancing algorithms for peer-to-peer systems. In *SPAA '04: Proceedings of the sixteenth annual ACM symposium on Parallelism in algorithms and architectures*, pages 36–43, New York, NY, USA, 2004. ACM Press.
11. A. Klemm, C. Lindemann, M. K. Vernon, and O. P. Waldhorst. Characterizing the query behavior in peer-to-peer file sharing systems. In *IMC '04: Proceedings of the 4th ACM SIGCOMM conference on Internet measurement*, pages 55–67, New York, NY, USA, 2004. ACM Press.
12. A. Z. Kronfol. FASD: A fault-tolerant, adaptive, scalable, distributed search engine, 2000.
13. J. Li, B. T. Loo, J. M. Hellerstein, M. F. Kaashoek, D. R. Karger, and R. Morris. On the Feasibility of Peer-to-Peer Web Indexing and Search. In M. F. Kaashoek and I. Stoica, editors, *IPTPS*, volume 2735 of *Lecture Notes in Computer Science*, pages 207–215. Springer, 2003.
14. P. Maymounkov and D. Mazieres. Kademlia: A peer-to-peer information system based on the xor metric, 2002.
15. W. Müller, M. Eisenhardt, and A. Henrich. Fast retrieval of high-dimensional feature vectors in P2P networks using compact peer data summaries. *Multimedia Syst.*, 10(6):464–474, 2005.
16. W. Müller, M. Eisenhardt, and A. Henrich. Scalable summary based retrieval in P2P networks. In O. Herzog, H.-J. Schek, N. Fuhr, A. Chowdhury, and W. Teiken, editors, *CIKM*, pages 586–593. ACM, 2005.

17. W. Müller and A. Henrich. Fast retrieval of high-dimensional feature vectors in P2P networks using compact peer data summaries. In N. Sebe, M. S. Lew, and C. Djeraba, editors, *Multimedia Information Retrieval*, pages 79–86. ACM, 2003.
18. C. H. Ng and K. C. Sia. Bridging the P2P and www divide with discovir - distributed content-based visual information retrieva. In *Poster Proc. of The 11th Interational World Wide Web Conf.* to be published, 2003.
19. S. Ratnasamy, P. Francis, M. Handley, R. Karp, and S. Schenker. A scalable content-addressable network. In *Proc. 2001 Conf. on applications, technologies, architectures, and protocols for computer communications*, San Diego, CA, United States, 2001.
20. A. Rowstron and P. Druschel. Pastry: Scalable, decentralized object location, and routing for large-scale peer-to-peer systems. In *Proc. 18th IFIP/ACM Intl. Conf. on Distributed Systems Platforms (Middleware)*, Heidelberg, Germany, 2001.
21. O. D. Sahin, A. Gulbeden, F. Emekci, D. Agrawal, and A. E. Abbadi. PRISM: indexing multi-dimensional data in P2P networks using reference vectors. In *MULTIMEDIA '05: Proceedings of the 13th annual ACM international conference on Multimedia*, pages 946–955, New York, NY, USA, 2005. ACM Press.
22. N. Sarshar, P. O. Boykin, and V. P. Roychowdhury. Percolation search in power law networks: making unstructured peer-to-peer networks scalable. In *Proceedings of Fourth International Conference on Peer-to-Peer Computing*, pages 2–9. IEEE, August 2004.
23. T. R. Sean Rhea, Dennis Geels and J. Kubiatowicz. Handling churn in a dht. Technical Report UCB/CSD-03-1299, EECS Department, University of California, Berkeley, 2003.
24. I. Stoica, R. Morris, D. Karger, F. Kaashoek, and H. Balakrishnan. Chord: A scalable Peer-To-Peer lookup service for internet applications. In *Proc. ACM SIGCOMM Conf.*, San Diego, CA, USA, 2001.
25. C. Tang, Z. Xu, and M. Mahalingam. pSearch: Information retrieval in structured overlays. In *First Workshop on Hot Topics in Networks (HotNets-I)*, Princeton, NJ, 2002.
26. R. Weber, H.-J. Schek, and S. Blott. A quantitative analysis and performance study for similarity-search methods in high-dimensional spaces. In *Proc. Intl. Conf. on VLDB*, New York, USA, 1998.
27. B. Yang and H. Garcia-Molina. Designing a super-peer network. In U. Dayal, K. Ramamritham, and T. M. Vijayaraman, editors, *ICDE*, pages 49–. IEEE Computer Society, 2003.

Interactive Museum Guide: Accurate Retrieval of Object Descriptions

Beat Fasel and Luc Van Gool

Computer Vision Laboratory (BIWI), ETH Zurich, Sternwartstr. 7, 8092 Zurich, Switzerland
{bfasel,vangool}@vision.ee.ethz.ch
http://vision.ee.ethz.ch

Abstract. In this paper we describe an interactive guide that is able to automatically retrieve information about objects on display in museums. A visitor can point this mobile device at exhibits and automatically retrieve descriptions about objects of interest in a non-distractive way. We investigate Gaussian image intensity attenuation and a foveation-based preprocessing approach which both allow to focus interest point extraction towards the center of an image. Furthermore, we describe a postprocessing strategy that allows to improve object recognition rates by suppressing multiple matches. The proposed interactive museum guide achieves object recognition via image matching and thus allows the use of model sets that do not need to be segmented.

1 Introduction

Many museums still present their exhibits in a rather passive and non-engaging way. The visitor has to search through a booklet in order to find descriptions about the objects on display. However, looking for information in this way is a quite tedious procedure. Moreover, the information found does not always meet the visitor's specific interests. One possibility of making exhibitions more attractive to the visitor is to improve the interaction between the visitor and the objects of interest by means of a guide. In this paper, we present an interactive museum guide that is able to automatically find and instantaneously retrieve information about the objects of interest using a standard Tablet PC. Undoubtedly, technological developments will lead to less heavy and downsized solutions in the near future. The focus of this paper is on the vision component used to recognise the objects.

1.1 Related Work

Recently, several approaches have been proposed that allow visitors to interact via an automatic museum guide. Kusunoki *et al.* [1] proposed a system for children that uses a sensing board, which can rapidly recognise type and locations of multiple objects. It creates an immersing environment by giving audiovisual feedback to the children. Other approaches include robots that guide users

S. Marchand-Maillet et al. (Eds.): AMR 2006, LNCS 4398, pp. 179–191, 2007.

through museums [2,3]. However, such robots are difficult to adapt to different environments, and they are not appropriate for individual use. An interesting approach using hand-held devices, like mobile phones, was proposed by [4], but their recognition technique seems not to be very robust to viewing angle or lighting changes.

Various object recognition methods have been investigated in the last two decades. More recently, SIFT [5] and its variants such as PCA-SIFT [6] and GLOH [7] have been successfully applied for many image matching applications. In this paper, we show that the new (Speeded Up Robust Features) algorithm [8] allows for similar recognition results when compared to SIFT while surpassing the latter with regard to speed substantially, while retaining its image description capabilities.

1.2   Interactive Museum Guide

The proposed interactive, image-based museum guide is invariant to changes in lighting, translation, scale, rotation and viewpoint variations. Our object recognition system was implemented on a Tablet PC using a conventional USB webcam for image acquisition, see Figure 1. This hand-held device allows the visitor to

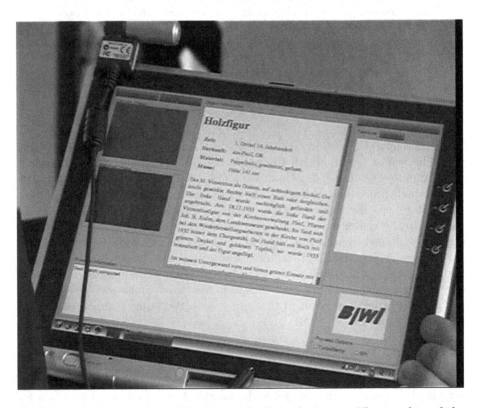

Fig. 1. Tablet PC with the USB webcam fixed on the screen. The interface of the object recognition software is operated via a touchscreen.

simply take a picture of an object of interest from any position and is provided, almost immediately, with a detailed description of the latter.

An early prototype of this museum guide was shown to the public during the 150 years anniversary celebration of the Federal Institute of Technology (ETH) in Zurich, Switzerland [9], described in more detail in a later paper [10].

The descriptions of the recognised objects of art are read to the visitors by a synthetic computer voice. This enhances the convenience of the guide as the visitors can focus on the objects of interest instead of reading the object descriptions on the screen of the guide.

In order to demonstrate the recognition capabilities of our latest implementation, we created a database with objects on display in the Swiss National Museum, Zurich, Switzerland. A sample image of each of the 20 chosen objects is shown in Figure 2.

Fig. 2. Sample images of the 20 chosen art objects from the Swiss National Museum, Zurich, Switzerland

The remainder of this paper is organised as follows. First, we introduce our object recognition system in detail (Section 2). Then, we present and discuss results obtained for a multi-class task (Section 3), and finally conclude with an overall discussion and some final remarks (Section 4).

2   Object Recognition

The proposed object recognition system encompasses several stages. First, the incoming image, taken by a user, is optionally filtered in a preprocessing stage.

The aim of the latter is to give more weight to the center of the image, where and object of interest is most likely situated. In a next step, interest points are detected and described. Finally, input images are compared to previously registered model images based on interest point correspondences between individual image pairs. This is achieved by matching their respective interest points. The model image with the highest number of matches with respect to the input image is chosen as the one which represents the object the visitor is looking for.

2.1   Image Filtering

We tested two image preprocessing approaches that allow to give more weight to the center of an input image. The first approach is known as foveation [11,12]. Hereby, the image is filtered in a non-uniform way, leading to a maximum resolution at the center (fovea) which gradually reduces towards the image borders. This can be achieved by a space-variant smoothing process, where the width of the smoothing function is small near the fovea and gradually expanding as the distance from the fovea increases. A sample foveated image is shown in the middle of Figure 3. Due to the lower resolution towards the borders of a foveated image, less interest points will be found on the background by the subsequent interest point detection algorithm. Hence, the image is described more densly in the center of the image, where the object of interest is most likely situated.

Fig. 3. On the left-hand side is shown the original, in the middle the foveated and on the right-hand side the intensity-attenuated image

Another approach is to gradually attenuate the image intensity towards the image borders. This is shown on the right-hand side of Figure 3. The gradual attenuation can be achieved easily by multiplying the image intensity of each pixel with a Gaussian centered in the middle of the image and a filter size corresponding to the size of the shortest dimension of the image to be processed.

2.2   Interest Point Detection

The SURF feature detector is based on the Hessian matrix. Given a point $\mathbf{x} = (x, y)^\top$ in an image I, the Hessian matrix $\mathcal{H}(\mathbf{x}, \sigma)$ in $\mathbf{x}$ at scale σ is defined as follows

$$\mathcal{H}(\mathbf{x}, \sigma) = \begin{bmatrix} L_{xx}(\mathbf{x}, \sigma) & L_{xy}(\mathbf{x}, \sigma) \\ L_{xy}(\mathbf{x}, \sigma) & L_{yy}(\mathbf{x}, \sigma) \end{bmatrix}, \tag{1}$$

Fig. 4. Left to right: the (discretised and cropped) Gaussian second order partial derivatives in y-direction and xy-direction, and our approximations thereof using box filters. The grey regions are equal to zero.

where $L_{xx}(\mathbf{x}, \sigma)$ is the convolution of the Gaussian second order derivative $\frac{\partial^2}{\partial x^2} g(\sigma)$ with the image I in point $\mathbf{x}$, and similarly for $L_{xy}(\mathbf{x}, \sigma)$ and $L_{yy}(\mathbf{x}, \sigma)$.

In contrast to SIFT, which approximates Laplacian of Gaussian (LoG) with Difference of Gaussians (DoG), SURF approximates second order Gaussian derivatives with box filters, see Figure 4. Image convolutions with these box filters can be computed rapidly by using integral images as defined in [13]. The entry of an integral image $I_\Sigma(\mathbf{x})$ at location $\mathbf{x} = (x, y)^\top$ represents the sum of all pixels in the base image I of a rectangular region formed by the origin and $\mathbf{x}$.

$$I_\Sigma(\mathbf{x}) = \sum_{i=0}^{i \le x} \sum_{j=0}^{j \le y} I(i, j) \tag{2}$$

Once we have computed the integral image, it is strait forward to calculate the sum of the intensities of pixels over any upright, rectangular area.

The location and scale of interest points are selected by relying on the determinant of the Hessian. Hereby, the approximation of the second order derivatives is denoted as D_{xx}, D_{yy}, and D_{xy}. By choosing the weights for the box filters adequately, we find as approximation for the Hessian's determinant

$$\det(\mathcal{H}_{\text{approx}}) = D_{xx} D_{yy} - (0.9 D_{xy})^2. \tag{3}$$

For more details, see [8]. Interest points are localised in scale and image space by applying a non-maximum suppression in a $3 \times 3 \times 3$ neighbourhood. Finally, the found maxima of the determinant of the approximated Hessian matrix are interpolated in scale and image space.

2.3 Interest Point Description

In a first step, SURF constructs a circular region around the detected interest points in order to assign a unique orientation to the former and thus gain invariance to image rotations. The orientation is computed using Haar wavelet responses in both x and y direction as shown in the middle of Figure 5. The Haar wavelets can be easily computed via integral images, similar to the Gaussian second order approximated box filters. Once the Haar wavelet responses are computed, they are weighted with a Gaussian with $\sigma = 2.5s$ centred at the interest points. In a next step the dominant orientation is estimated by summing

Fig. 5. Left: Detected interest points for a Sunflower field. This kind of scenes show clearly the nature of the features obtained from Hessian-based detectors. Middle: Haar wavelet filters used with SURF. Right: Detail of the Graffiti scene showing the size of the descriptor window at different scales.

the horizontal and vertical wavelet responses within a rotating wedge, covering an angle of $\frac{\pi}{3}$ in the wavelet response space. The resulting maximum is then chosen to describe the orientation of the interest point descriptor.

In a second step, the SURF descriptors are constructed by extracting square regions around the interest points. These are oriented in the directions assigned in the previous step. Some example windows are shown on the right hand side of Figure 5. The windows are split up in 4×4 sub-regions in order to retain some spatial information. In each sub-region, Haar wavelets are extracted at regularly spaced sample points. In order to increase robustness to geometric deformations and localisation errors, the responses of the Haar wavelets are weighted with a Gaussian, centred at the interest point. Finally, the wavelet responses in horizontal d_x and vertical directions d_y are summed up over each sub-region. Furthermore, the absolute values $|d_x|$ and $|d_y|$ are summed in order to obtain information about the polarity of the image intensity changes. Hence, the underlying intensity pattern of each sub-region is described by a vector

$$\mathbf{v} = (\sum d_x, \sum d_y, \sum |d_x|, \sum |d_y|). \tag{4}$$

The resulting descriptor vector for all 4×4 sub-regions is of length 64. See Figure 6 for an illustration of the SURF descriptor for three different image intensity patterns. Notice that the Haar wavelets are invariant to illumination bias and additional invariance to contrast is achieved by normalising the descriptor vector to unit length.

In this paper, we compare the results for SURF, referred to as SURF-64, and SIFT. The fast matching speed for SURF is achieved by a single step added to the indexing based on the sign of the Laplacian (trace of the Hessian matrix) of the interest point. The sign of the Laplacian distinguishes bright blobs on a dark background from the inverse situation. 'Bright' interest points are only matched against other 'bright' interest points and similarly for the 'dark' ones. This minimal information permits to almost double the matching speed and it

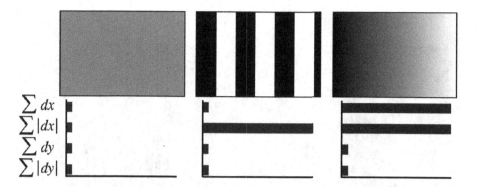

Fig. 6. The descriptor entries of a sub-region represent the nature of the underlying intensity pattern. Left: In case of a homogeneous region, all values are relatively low. Middle: In presence of frequencies in x-direction, the value of $\sum |d_x|$ is high, but all others remain low. If the intensity is gradually increasing in x-direction, both values $\sum d_x$ and $\sum |d_x|$ are high.

comes at no computational costs, as it has already been computed in the interest point detection step.

2.4 Image Matching

Traditional object recognition methods rely on model images, each representing a single object in isolation. In practice, however, the necessary segmentation is not always affordable or even possible. For our object recognition application, we use model images where the objects are not separated from the background. Thus, the background also provides features for the matching task. In any given test image, only one object or object group that belongs together is assumed. Hence, object recognition is achieved by image matching. Extracted interest points of the input image are compared to the interest points of all model images. In order to create a set of interest point correspondences M, we used the nearest neighbour ratio matching strategy [14,5,15]. This states that a matching pair is detected if its Euclidean distance in descriptor space is closer than 0.8 times the distance to the second nearest neighbour. The selected object is the one figuring in the model image with the highest recognition score S_R, corresponding to the number of total matches in M.

Traditional image matching by interest point correspondence often leads to multiple matches of the same interest point at locations with important gradient variations such as edges, see Figure 7.

Multiple matches can skew the matching process. It is therefore a good idea to suppress multiple matches, only allowing a single best match per interest point location. This is achieved by first building a table with all interest point correspondences between a test image and a model image and then removing all matches that do not have a minimal distance.

Fig. 7. On top of the image shown on the left-hand side is given a sample test image matched to an incorrect model image situated on the bottom. On the right-hand side is depicted the result for the multiple match suppression postprocessing approach, leading to the same test image associated to a correct model image.

3   Experimental Results

For each of the 20 objects of art in our database, images of size 320×240 were taken from different viewing angles. This allows for some degree of view-point independence. The database includes a total of 207 model images. These are grouped in two model sets (M1 and M2) with 106 and 101 images, respectively. The reasons for the choice for these two different model sets are the use of two different cameras and the presence of different lighting conditions. Moreover, less model images for a given object represents a more challenging situation for object recognition. Finally, we built a third model set M3 which is a fusion of the sets M1 and M2, containing 207 images.

For similar reasons, we built 3 different test sets (T1-T3) with a total of 119 images (43, 35, 41). Each set contains one or more images of all objects.

These objects of art are made of different materials, have different shapes and encompass wooden statues, paintings, metal and stone items as well as objects enclosed in glass cabinets which produce interfering reflections. The images were taken from substantially different viewpoints under arbitrary scale, rotation and varying lighting conditions.

The test image sets were evaluated on each of the model sets. The obtained recognition results are shown in the Tables 1 and 2. Listed are the results for SURF and SIFT with different preprocessing and postprocessing strategies in (Table 1) and the results with a single model set M3 encompassing both set M1 and set M2 (Table 2). It can be seen that especially the multiple match suppression postprocessing approach allows to improve recognition results.

Table 1. Image matching results for SURF (SURF-64) and SIFT for different preprocessing and postprocessing methods. **Raw** are unprocessed images, **Fov** foveated and **Att** intensity-attenuated images. **Suppressed** refers to the suppression of multiple matches.

Method	Processing	Recognition Rate						Total
		T1/M1	T2/M1	T3/M1	T1/M2	T2/M2	T3/M2	(%)
SURF	Raw	76.2	94.1	72.5	76.2	88.2	95.0	83.7
SIFT	Raw	78.6	88.2	77.5	81.0	88.2	95.0	84.8
SURF	Raw Suppressed	90.5	97.1	87.5	97.6	97.1	97.5	94.6
SIFT	Raw Suppressed	85.7	100	85.0	90.5	97.1	97.5	92.6
SURF	Fov Suppressed	83.3	97.1	92.5	95.2	100	97.5	94.3
SIFT	Fov Suppressed	88.1	97.1	90.0	92.9	94.1	95.0	92.9
SURF	Att Suppressed	90.5	97.1	90.0	88.1	91.2	97.5	92.4
SIFT	Att Suppressed	81.0	94.1	80.0	85.7	91.2	95.0	87.8

The recognition results using the unified model set M3 are better than when using the individual sets M1 and M2. However, matching time is much increased and therefore such a big model set could hardly be used on a mobile device such as a Tablet PC.

Finally, in Figure 8 to Figure 10 are shown sample input images matched to the closest model images. Shown are the results for non-preprocessed images in Figure 8, with foveation in Figure 9 and with intensity attenuation in Figure 10. Note that with the foveated and intensity-attenuated images, more features are detected that belong to the object of interest and not to the background.

Table 2. Image matching results for SURF and SIFT using a single large model set M3 consisting of the model sets M1 and M2

Method	Processing	Recognition Rate			Total
		T1/M3	T2/M3	T3/M3	(%)
SURF	Raw Suppressed	95.0	100	97.5	97.5
SIFT	Raw Suppressed	95.0	100	95.0	96.7

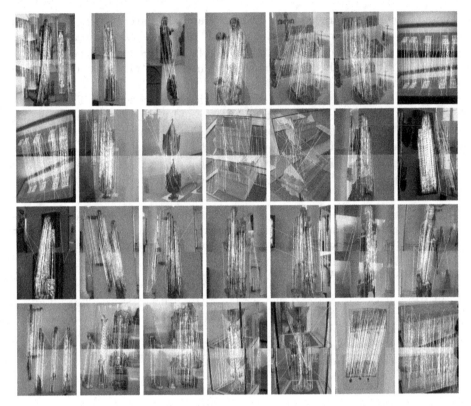

Fig. 8. Sample matching results for the raw images containing 28 objects of interest

4   Discussion and Conclusion

In this paper, we described the functionality of an interactive museum guide, which allows to robustly recognise museum exhibits under difficult environmental conditions. Our guide is robust to scale and rotation. Changes of the viewing angle are covered by the overall robustness of the descriptor up to some extent. This museum guide is running on standard low-cost hardware.

4.1   Object Recognition

With the computational efficiency of SURF, object recognition can be performed instantaneously for the 20 objects on which we tested the different schemes. The images were taken with a low-quality webcam. However, this affected the results only up to a limited extent. Note that in contrast to the approach described in [4], all the tested schemes do not use colour information for the object recognition task. This is one of the reasons for the above-mentioned recognition robustness under various lighting conditions. We experimentally verified that illumination variations, caused by artificial and natural lighting, lead to low recognition results when colour was used as the only source of information.

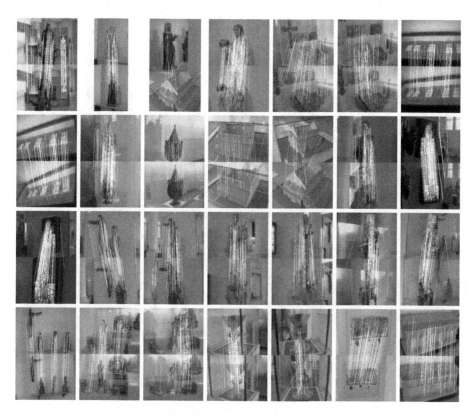

Fig. 9. Sample matching results for the foveated images containing 28 objects of interest

Background information in images can both be helpful and a hindrance when attempting object recognition by image matching. A dominating background can attract more matches than can be found on the object of interest itself and hence the recognition stability of the given object with varying view-points cannot be assumed. The proposed image preprocessing strategies allow to focus more on the center of the image, where the object of interest is most likely situated. It could be shown that both the intensity attenuation and the foveation approach are effective means that allow for a soft foreground-background segmentation.

4.2   Automatic Room Detection

With a larger number of objects to be recognised, the matching accuracy and speed decrease. Also, additional background clutter can enter the database that may generate mismatches and thus lead to false detections. However, in a typical museum the proposed interactive museum guide has to be able to cope with ten-thousands of objects with possibly similar appearance. A solution to this problem would be to determine the visitor's location by adding a Bluetooth receiver to the interactive museum guide that can pick up signals emitted from senders placed

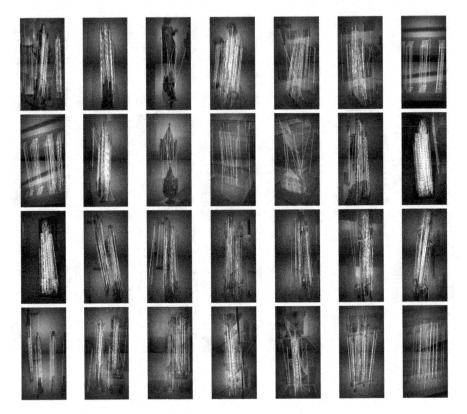

Fig. 10. Sample matching results for the intensity-attenuated images containing 28 objects of interest

in different exhibition rooms of the museum [9]. This information can then be used to reduce the search space for the extraction of relevant objects. Hence, the recognition accuracy is increased and the search time reduced. Moreover, this information can be used to indicate the user's current location in the museum.

Acknowledgements

The authors would like to acknowledge the support by the Swiss National Museum in Zurich, Switzerland. Thanks go also to the NCCR project IM2, supported by the Swiss National Science Foundation (SNF) and the Network of Excellence EPOCH, funded by the European Commission (IST programme).

References

1. Kusunoki, F., Sugimoto, M., Hashizume, H.: Toward an interactive museum guide with sensing and wireless network technologies. In: WMTE2002, Vaxjo, Sweden. (2002) 99–102

2. Burgard, W., Cremers, A., Fox, D., Hähnel, D., Lakemeyer, G., Schulz, D., Steiner, W., Thrun, S.: The interactive museum tour-guide robot. In: Fifteenth National Conference on Artificial Intelligence (AAAI-98). (1998)
3. Thrun, S., Beetz, M., Bennewitz, M., Burgard, W., Cremers, A., Dellaert, F., Fox, D., Hähnel, D., Rosenberg, C., Roy, N., Schulte, J., Schulz, D.: Probabilistic algorithms and the interactive museum tour-guide robot minerva. International Journal of Robotics Research 19(11) (2000) 972–999
4. Föckler, P., Zeidler, T., Bimber, O.: Phoneguide: Museum guidance supported by on-device object recognition on mobile phones. Research Report 54.74 54.72, Bauhaus-University Weimar, Media Faculty, Dept. Augmented Reality (2005)
5. Lowe, D.G.: Distinctive image features from scale-invariant keypoints, cascade filtering approach. International Journal of Computer Vision 60(2) (January 2004) 91–110
6. Ke, Y., Sukthankar, R.: PCA-SIFT: A more distinctive representation for local image descriptors. In: Proceedings of IEEE Conference on Computer Vision and Pattern Recognition. (2004) 506–513
7. Mikolajczyk, K., Schmid, C.: A performance evaluation of local descriptors. PAMI 27(10) (2005) 1615–1630
8. Bay, H., Tuytelaars, T., Van Gool, L.: SURF: Speeded up robust features. In: ECCV. (2006)
9. Bay, H., Fasel, B., Van Gool, L.: Interactive museum guide. In: The Seventh International Conference on Ubiquitous Computing UBICOMP, Workshop on Smart Environments and Their Applications to Cultural Heritage. (September 2005)
10. Bay, H., Fasel, B., Van Gool, L.: Interactive museum guide: Fast and robust recognition of museum objects. In: Proceedings of the first international workshop on mobile vision. (May 2006)
11. Kortum, P., Geisler, W.: Implementation of a foveated image coding system for image bandwidth reduction. 2657 (1996) 350–360
12. Chang, E.: Foveation techniques and scheduling issues in thinwire visualization (1998)
13. Viola, P., Jones, M.: Rapid object detection using a boosted cascade of simple features. In: Computer Vision and Pattern Recognition. (2001)
14. Baumberg, A.: Reliable feature matching across widely separated views. In: Computer Vision and Pattern Recognition. (2000) 774–781
15. Mikolajczyk, K., Schmid, C.: A performance evaluation of local descriptors. In: Computer Vision and Pattern Recognition. Volume 2. (June 2003) 257–263

Semantic Image Retrieval Using Region-Based Relevance Feedback

José Manuel Torres[1], David Hutchison[2], and Luís Paulo Reis[3]

[1] University Fernando Pessoa / INESC – Porto, Portugal
jtorres@ufp.pt
[2] Lancaster University, UK
dh@comp.lancs.ac.uk
[3] FEUP/LIACC – Faculty of Engineering of the University of Porto, Portugal
lpreis@fe.up.pt

Abstract. A structured vocabulary of terms, such as a textual thesaurus, provides a way to conceptually describe visual information. The retrieval model described in this paper combines a conceptual and a visual layer as a first step towards the integration of ontologies and content-based image retrieval. Terms are related with image regions through a weighted association. This model allows the execution of concept-level queries, fulfilling user expectations and reducing the so-called semantic gap. Region-based relevance feedback is used to improve the quality of results in each query session and to help in the discovery of associations between text and image. The learning mechanism, whose function is to discover existing term-region associations, is based on a clustering algorithm applied over the features space and on propagation functions, which acts in each cluster where new information is available from user interaction. This approach is validated with the presentation of promising results obtained using the VOIR - Visual Object Information Retrieval system.

1 Introduction

The increasing size of existing digital image collections means that manual annotation of images is becoming more and more an infeasible process. Content-based image retrieval (CBIR) systems attempt to solve this problem by automating the process of image indexing. Nevertheless, users want to search images at a conceptual level, and not only in terms of colour, texture or shape. Semantic modelling is thus one of the biggest challenges in image retrieval.

A key requirement for developing future image retrieval systems is to explore the synergy between humans and computers. Relevance Feedback (RF) and region-based representations are two effective ways to improve early CBIR systems. Relevance feedback is a technique that engages the user and the retrieval system in a process of symbiosis. Following the formulation of the initial query, for subsequent iterations of query refinement, the system presents a set of results and the user evaluates the results in order to refine the set of images retrieved to his or her satisfaction [7]. As pointed by several authors [2], [15], [20], [22], the adoption of a region-based representation in a concept-based image retrieval presents obvious advantages since typically, each image normally contains several distinct *visual concepts* or objects. If, additionally,

S. Marchand-Maillet et al. (Eds.): AMR 2006, LNCS 4398, pp. 192–206, 2007.
© Springer-Verlag Berlin Heidelberg 2007

the system presents the possibility of result refinement through relevance feedback techniques, then, the relevance feedback at the region-level of granularity allows a much better interaction paradigm increasing the accuracy of the information flowed from the user to the system.

This paper proposes an integrated solution of region-based image retrieval (RBIR) using RF that, as result of the interaction between users and system during the retrieval sessions, learns associations between regions and high-level concepts. The rich interaction history provided by systems that implement, simultaneously, relevance feedback and RBIR opens a possibility to allow the system to gradually learns how to be more effective along the time.

The task of visual information description is to transform user needs into a suitable form to support searching in visual collections. Moreover, the selected image indexing attributes should be sufficiently discriminatory to allow images to be retrieved in an effective and efficient way. Ideally, the descriptive information that is associated with the images, in an image retrieval system, should be closely related with the way that end users, i.e., humans, interpret images.

One of the facts deduced from several user studies in image retrieval is, as stated by Eakins [5], that most image queries are at logical level, identifying meaningful semantic objects in images as, for example, chairs or fruits. Although low-level features such as colour, texture or shape of an image, sometimes are implicit in the user queries, rarely those features are used directly in the query formulation.

Panofsky, a well-known art historian which was interested in the analysis of visual fine art pieces, identifies three levels of image analysis [16]:

- Pre-iconographic: deals with the description of image motifs such as objects and events. Essentially refers to factual and expressional facets of the image;
- Iconographic: expressing secondary subject matters such as image interpretations. Presumes that the agent describing the image is familiar with specific themes as transmitted by literary sources;
- Iconology: captures intrinsic meaning of the image and involves association with symbolic values or trends of the human mind.

Another elucidative study is the one by Roland Barthes a social and literary critic with well-known published work about the study of signs and signification. Using advertising images as examples, Barthes [1] established a semiological theory that extends also to other pictorial forms of expression. In his theory, he distinguishes two different levels of image analyses: *denotation* and *connotation*. Denotation may be viewed as a neutral expression of the visual signs, although these are the result of the meaning assigned by a given system or language within a culture. The connotative level is related with feelings, associations and aesthetics considerations.

Both, Panofsky and Barthes, agree that the analysis of a particular image gives origin to a part of the description that is objective/factual and another that depends on the interpreter agent, subjective in nature. This theory is important for the definition of the descriptive information that one generic image retrieval system should support.

There are several disadvantages in using manual textual annotations to describe images, such as the human effort required to annotate large amounts of visual information, the subjectivity of the operation and the inconsistency in the textual term assignment. Nevertheless, some of these drawbacks can be significantly reduced if:

- The type of annotation is restricted to the Panofskys pre-iconographical level or the Barthes denotative level. This factual and expressional description made at the visual object level tends to be much more objective and unambiguous than one more high level such as the iconographical or iconological ones referred by Panofsky;
- A textual thesaurus is used, the inconsistency in the term assignment is also reduced since it establishes a structure and suggests preferred terms during the process of annotation.

The proposed approach presented in this paper, adopts a textual thesaurus as the privileged knowledge representation structure to capture high-level or semantic information. Each term of the thesaurus represents a concept. Each concept can be associated with visual regions from the collection of images.

The rest of this paper is organised as follows. Section 2 reviews the background and some related work. In section 3 the semantic image retrieval framework, focusing on the two-layer model, is explained. In section 4 details of the Visual Object Information Retrieval (VOIR) system [19] are presented. Section 5 reports some experimental results obtained using the VOIR system. The final section gives concluding remarks and a brief discussion of future work.

2   Related Work

Most CBIR systems perform retrieval operations based on a whole image comparison. These systems extract global, low-level features, from each image and, during the query, return overall similar images. More recently, a new CBIR system's class appeared which adopts a region-based approach: the RBIR systems.

The MARS image retrieval system [18] is one of the most cited in the literature belonging to the CBIR class that uses global image features. At each iteration the system tries to calculate a new ideal query point. This calculation is based on the user's evaluation of the results of the previous iteration. Two methods are used to implement this technique: query point movement and query features re-weighting. These kinds of systems embody the assumption that user expectations or target images are directly mapped onto the adopted feature space. As well as estimating the ideal parameters or weights for each axis of the hyper-ellipsoid, such systems also adopt a query point calculation method that attempts to compute the ideal single point in the feature space in order to retrieve the nearest images to it.

$$Q_{k+1} = \alpha.Q_k + \beta.\sum_{i=1}^{n_1} \frac{R_i}{n_1} - \gamma.\sum_{i=1}^{n_2} \frac{S_i}{n_2} \qquad (1)$$

However, this approach is limited, since in a semantic query the user may want results associated with several visual representations and consequently several query points in the feature space should be considered.

The Falcon system for query by multiple examples [21] proposes one parametrical "aggregate dissimilarity" function that attempts to reduce the problem of using single point queries, taking into account distances between the candidate point x and the multiple good objects g_i. Experiments have supported the intuition that best results are achieved when the function mimics a fuzzy OR.

The *iFind* system [11] features a scheme to associate user-entered keywords from an uncontrolled vocabulary with corresponding images. Each of these associations has a corresponding weight that is heuristically updated during subsequent use of the system. In parallel to this, the system uses a low-level feature based relevance feedback scheme based on the work described by [17].

In [23] a method that learns relations between images based on the user feedback is presented. These relations are stored in one undirected graph that constitutes the "Semantic Layer". A further undirected graph that constitutes the "Visual Layer" is used to store pairs of images that have a (low-level) visual similarity above a certain threshold. The retrieval is performed using a process of link analysis of the graphs.

The method proposed in [9] also uses relevance feedback to split and merge image clusters that are formed in the low level feature space. Relations between the clusters are expressed using a correlation matrix. The existing clusters as well as the correlation matrix are updated during iterative use of the system.

Two of the most popular RBIR systems, are Blobworld [2] and Netra [12]. These systems introduce the notion of query by region or "blob", where each region is associated with low-level descriptors of colour, texture and shape.

The IRM technique [10], considers an overall measure of similarity between two segmented images, based on a region-matching scheme between the regions sets from the two images. A probabilistic framework to the problem of similarity matching between images represented by sets of regions is proposed in [20].

The approach described by Jing [7] combines region-based image retrieval with user relevance feedback. The implemented relevance feedback mechanism is inspired in the query point movement.

Recently, much work has been done in integrating RF into RBIR systems. Nevertheless, the possibility of formulating semantic queries using the denotative level described by Barthes or the equivalent pre-iconographic level from Panofsky is still not totally explored. Also, typically, those systems don't use the information gathered from relevance feedback interaction to improve their high-level knowledge across multiple query sessions.

3   A Semantic Image Retrieval Framework

The proposed framework, which served as the basis to the semantic image retrieval system VOIR, is depicted in figure 1. It assumes that the target images of the user are fundamentally associated with simple concepts, such as, cars, chairs or airplanes. Each concept is represented by a textual term from a textual thesaurus, i.e., a hierarchic controlled vocabulary. The use of a textual thesaurus reduces inconsistency in term assignment and provides a knowledge structure that can be explored during the searching process

A region-based approach is used for representation, query and retrieval of images. It is assumed that the images were already segmented into regions before being indexed. During the indexing operation, each region is uniquely associated with a feature vector, f, representing low-level features such as colour, texture and shape.

Low-level features and conventional distance functions, usually, are not sufficient to support the correct discrimination of *conceptual* similarity between distinct visual regions. Consequently, the framework implements a two-layer model separating conceptual categories at the upper layer from the lower layer or the visual layer composed by the low-level feature points, f. The visual layer is partitioned into visual categories, V_j. Each conceptual category, C_i, can be related with several visual categories. Each visual category is composed of several regions. Theoretically, regions sharing the same visual category are conceptually and visually similar. However, the implemented solution, described in this paper, implements a many-to-many relation between features points f and conceptual categories C, allowing regions to be associated with more than one concept.

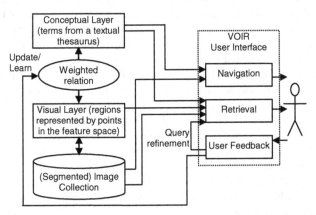

Fig. 1. Overview of the framework for semantic image retrieval

During query formulation, the user chooses textual terms from the thesaurus representing the desired concepts, and then selects, for each term, one of the visual regions already associated with the term to be used as the example during the content-based query.

4 The VOIR Semantic Image Retrieval System

VOIR prototype has been developed for testing the validity of the proposed semantic image retrieval framework [19]. The development and experiment stages were done in standalone mode with a computer running MS-Windows XP. The prototype was written in JAVA and used MySQL as the database. The generic architecture of VOIR is presented in figure 2. The system uses two distinct models of similarity assessment between image regions: (i) Relevance feedback. (ii) Learning term-region associations. Although the second directly depends on information gathered from the first, in a sense they are independent and are carried out in parallel.

The initial query session is composed by one or more visual regions. The regions are disposed spatially as a "visual template query". In the example shown in figure 3 the query being composed has two regions. The results are displayed showing segments of each result image that are the basis to the process of relevance feedback.

Definition. A *visual object*, or *group*, represents one or more neighbouring regions of the same image. It can be associated with one or more terms from the thesaurus.

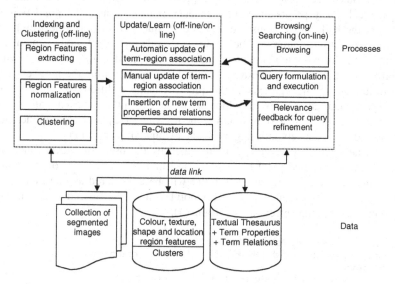

Fig. 2. VOIR system's generic architecture

VOIR allows users to manually create *groups* and to associate those groups with terms. It is possible to select *groups* from images as being relevant or irrelevant during the relevance feedback process. Each *group* is represented by a feature vector in the visual layer.

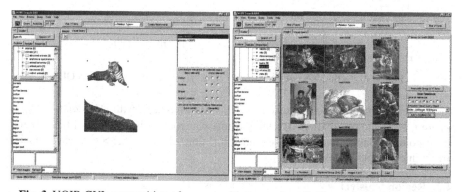

Fig. 3. VOIR GUI: composition of a query with two regions (left); result displaying (right)

4.1 Region-Based Relevance Feedback

The user, during the relevance feedback process, first selects the query region being evaluated, represented by the feature point f_q, and then selects groups (regions) from the result set and classifies them according to a five-scale score: highly-relevant,

relevant, no-opinion (default), irrelevant or highly-irrelevant. The points classified as relevant or highly-relevant, constitute the set f_r.

The relevance feedback mechanism implemented, attempts to recalculate one or multiple ideal query points, moving the query points towards the good points and away from the bad points. It also reweighs each query to increase the weight of the most discriminating features. These two methods are well documented in the literature [18]. The implemented RF mechanism extends those methods with the possibility of querying using multiple points. Instead of limiting the number of query points to just one, VOIR can expand the query by using additional query points in the feature space, marked as relevant, which are related with the same semantic category. The model is based in the assumption that the relevant groups selected by the end user belong to the same conceptual category as the evaluated query point.

When a new relevant example f_r is indicated by the user, a *boolean* function will indicate if the designated point belongs to the same visual category of the evaluated visual item f_q or not. If true, the new point will be considered as one more positive point of the evaluated item. If false, this point will be considered as another query point to be added to the current query (figure 4).

```
function isNewPointToAddToQuery(Cr, Cq, FK)
Returns Boolean: expand/keep the number of query points
parameters
    Cr: category of relevant feature point fr
    Cq: category of evaluated feature point fq
    FK: set containing all feature points whose category Ck is
    different from category Cq
static
    THR: pre-defined numeric threshold
newQueryPoint ← false
if (Cr ≠ Cq) and (Cr ≠ null) then newQueryPoint ← true
else
    Drq ← distance(fr, fq)
    for each fk in FK do
        Drk ← distance(fr, fk)
        if (Drq / Drk) > THR then newQueryPoint ← true
return newQueryPoint
```

Fig. 4. Algorithm isNewPointToAddToQuery() for query expansion VOIR

The algorithm compares the distance $D_{rq} = distance(f_r, f_q)$ with $D_{rk} = distance(f_r, f_k)$ where $f_k \in F_K$ the set of all visual items whose category C_k is different of the category C_q of point f_q. Basically the query expansion is done if $(D_{rq} / D_{rk}) > thr$, where thr is a pre-defined threshold level.

4.2 Region Clustering

The clustering algorithm is essential to implement the partition of the feature points from visual layer into distinct visual categories. The clustering algorithm adopted is the k-means algorithm [6]. The K-means is a popular partitional algorithm that starts with a random initial partition having k clusters and iteratively reassigns the feature points to clusters based on the similarity between each feature point and cluster's centre until a convergence criterion is met.

The process of partition of the feature space is obtained as the outcome of the off-line clustering procedure. This process is executed during initialization and then, the course of VOIR usage, after the addition of new groups having more than one region.

4.3 Process of Learning Term-Region Associations

The association between terms and regions is characterized by having a normalized degree of confidence d_conf where the attribute $d\_conf \in$ [0, 100]. This association is of fundamental importance since it constitutes the outcome of the process of concept learning. It can be done manually or automatically. In the first case d_conf is set to its maximum value (100), and constitutes the learning examples. In the second case it will be updated algorithmically using an exponentially decreasing function.

The process of update of the association between terms and regions as the outcome of the relevance feedback process is done off-line after some period of usage of the system. In each query session, some information is stored in the database such as: the regions used in the query, the regions that were selected as relevant/irrelevant during the query refinement process, the relevance level of each.

Suppose that one query is executed using region r_q as the query region having the associated term $term_q$ with d_conf value d_conf_q. Suppose that during the query refinement the user had selected regions $R_U = \{ru_1, ru_2, ..., ru_k\}$ as the relevant/irrelevant examples in order to refine the query having relevance/irrelevance scores $S_C = \{sc_1, sc_2, ..., sc_k\}$, selected by the user.

The propagation or update of the d_conf values is done in two steps. If the region query r_q is associated with more than one term, then the two-step algorithm described below is applied to each term associated with r_q.

- Firstly all the d_conf values of the pairs (ru_i, $term_q$) where $ru_i \in R_U$ are updated using function (2). Parameter d_conf_old represents the weight of the association before the update;

$$updateD\_conf\_1(d\_conf\_old, d\_conf_q, sc_i) = d\_conf\_old + \left(\frac{d\_conf_q}{100}\right) \times (\alpha_2 \times sc_i) \quad (2)$$

- Secondly for each $ru_i \in R_U$, all the regions r_j within the same cluster as ru_i are updated for the d_conf attribute of the pair (r_j, $term_q$) using function (3). Within the cluster containing ru_i there is one point r_{j_MAX} whose distance to ru_i is maximum. That distance is represented by the parameter $max\_distance$. represents

$$updateD\_conf\_2(max\_distance, delta_i, d_j, d\_conf\_old) =$$

$$d\_conf\_old + \left(\frac{delta_i}{100}\right) \times \alpha_3 \times \left(1 - \frac{d_j}{max\_distance}\right)^3 \quad (3)$$

The constant value $\alpha_2 = 10$ was empirically chosen. With this value, and considering that $d\_conf_q = 100$, i.e., the query object has the maximum possible d_conf value. The variation $delta_i$ for the d_conf value of ru_i as function of the user selected score relevance sc_i given to ru_i considers $delta_i = 10* sc_i$, with $sc_i \in \{3$ (highly-relevant), 1(relevant), 0 (no opinion), -1 (irrelevant), -10 (highly-irrelevant)$\}$.

The constant value $\alpha_3 = 30$ was empirically chosen. Again, consider that the variation in *d_conf* is the difference between the new value and old value: *d_conf variation = new_d_conf – d_conf_old*. The rationale behind formula (3) is that the influence of the changed region over the other regions from the same cluster decreases exponentially with the distance, being zero for the farthest point within that cluster.

The critical evaluation of the image results by the user during query sessions is used to create or update the existing associations. The outcome of this is that the system gradually learns associations between visual regions and labels from the textual thesaurus. The more the system learns, the more accurate and faster are the subsequent query sessions. In the implementation used to carry out the experiments, the visual categories, used in the concept learning process, were defined off-line using a clustering algorithm that took low-level features extracted from each region as its input data. The automatic updating of the associations between term and visual item is done periodically after the query sessions or following new manually added associations. The updating process affects all the visual items that belong to the same visual category as the visual item whose situation was changed either because was explicitly associated with a keyword or because was evaluated during a query iteration.

4.4 Semantic Layer

Besides the relations considered by a typical textual thesaurus (broad-narrow term; preferred-use term; and related term), an extension model was included to permit the implementation of additional relations between terms. Those additional relations provide semantic information, which can be useful in the context of visual information retrieval. These user relations are characterized by a relation type picked from a set of pre-existing types. Examples of some relations are, for example: "typically_together" that may be applied to pairs of terms such as (chairs, desks), (snow, mountains) or (boats, water), or "typically_above" that may be applied to pairs like (roofs, floors) or (vase, table).

These relations can be used in a visual retrieval scenario. For instance, given the example relation between the terms *chairs* and *desks*, if one user is searching for *chairs* and if in one image there is one *desk* visual object, then according to the defined relation, the likelihood of existing a chair in that image is greater than the likelihood of existing a chair in another image.

The relation type given is a fuzzy one, i.e., it doesn't assure that given a chair in one image implies that there is a desk in the same image, but it can give some decisive information to the image search engine.

Another extension to the typical thesaurus that has been considered and that can also be useful to the task of image retrieval is the possibility to associate properties with the terms or concepts that are considered in the thesaurus term list. In terms of model, it was considered a class of property types and to each type was associated a set of possible property values. The process of associate some property to a specific term from the thesaurus presupposes choosing the thesaurus term, property type and one of the values associated to the selected property type and then commit to the association. Examples of some properties are "typical_colour", associating, for example pairs like (trees, green), (sky, blue) or "typical_actions", associating pairs like (boats, sailing), (bird, flying).

The feature vector used to compute high-level similarity is composed solely by the query term *qterm* associated with each region or group used in the query formulation. Using this *qterm*, several rankings can be obtained for diverse similarity measures explored. Those rankings explore the existing semantic relations between the concepts (terms) considered by the thesaurus. Three types of semantic relations are explored: (A) Hierarchy of the used APT thesaurus; (B) User-defined relationships between the terms of the APT thesaurus; (C) User-defined properties associated with terms of the APT thesaurus.

For A), the following rankings are computed:

- Regions or groups that are also associated with the query term *qterm* having a confidence degree above a threshold *th_conf_degree*;
- Regions or groups, which are associated with terms that, in the APT thesaurus hierarchy are broader/narrower than the query term *qterm*. The ranking is established according to the confidence degree and again, only the regions/groups with confidence degree above *th_conf_degree* are considered.

For B), theoretically, for each relationship type defined, a distinct procedure to calculate similarity between visual items should be implemented. As a demonstrative example, only two types of user-defined relationships were implemented: "typically_together" and "typically_above). For both a ranking is computed, calculating the regions or groups, which are associated with terms that, in the APT thesaurus hierarchy, are related with the query term *qterm* according to one of the two properties mentioned. The ranking is established according to the confidence degree and only confidence degrees above *th_conf_degree* are considered.

Also for C), each property type defined should correspond to a distinct procedure to calculate similarity between visual items, where the property value should be faced as the argument for the function. Again, as a demonstrative example, only two types of user-defined property-types were implemented: "typical_colour" and "typical_action" with distinct ranking procedures.

4.5 Query Engine

The query engine is responsible for ranking the result images in descending order of relevance with respect to a given query. Each query is composed by k query regions, $R_Q = \{rq_1, rq_2, ..., rq_k\}$. For each query region $rq_i \in R_Q$, the ranking algorithm computes a ranking Rnq_i with the list of regions that best matches that region according to the parameters that were set to the region during the composition of the query. To each region that belongs to list Rnq_i a score is assigned.

Finally, the image ranking, *RnkImg*, will determine the order of the images in the result set displayed to the user. The score of each image in *RnkImg* is defined as the score of the region with greatest score among all regions from that image and among all rankings of regions $RNQ = \{Rnq_1, Rnq_2, ..., Rnq_k\}$. The query evaluation can, consequently, be divided in two steps: first the computation of RNQ; second the computation of the final image ranking, *RnkImg*, based on the best-scored region within each image. The computation of each region ranking $Rnq_i \in RNQ$, from the region query $rq_i \in R_Q$, is done independently. Each ranking Rnq_i is obtained as a linear fusion of L rankings according to Borda's "positional" method described in Dwork et al. [4].

For each query region $rq_i \in R_Q$ a set of L region ranks $RNQ_i = \{Rnq_{i,1}, Rnq_{i,2}, ..., Rnq_{i,l}\}$, will be generated. The L=7 region rankings currently used by the query engine implemented by VOIR are: (1) Relevance feedback low-level features: colour, texture and shape; (2) Spatial Location feature: coordinates of the region centre of mass normalized by the image dimensions; (3) Same-term textual feature; (4) Broader-terms textual feature; (5) Narrower-terms textual feature; (6) User-defined relationships terms textual feature; (7) User-defined properties textual feature.

The ranking *RnkImg* is still subject to a final processing operation; it is trimmed to consider just the first NR images. Also, to avoid some "biased behaviours" that could lead to an erroneously stabilization of the ranking presented, a proportion P_RAND of images of the total number of NR images is selected randomly from the image collection.

The value of P_RAND was set to 0.1, which means that if, for instance, the value of NR was 30, then the first 27 ranked images would be obtained using the algorithm described previously and the remaining 3 images would be selected randomly from the rest of the image collection. This technique, to include random items into the returned list, is used in several systems [11], [9].

5 Experiments

Although there are actually diverse image datasets annotated in electronic format, virtually all are "per image", i.e., the annotated words are associated with the whole image and the images in the collection are not segmented. This is easily explained by the large manual effort required to the task of annotate the regions on a large segmented image collection [3].

The collection used was a database containing "ground-truth", human-authored image segmentations made available for research use [14]. It is composed of 300 images from the Corel dataset all labelled according to diverse categories such as animals, plants, people or landscape earth features. The total number of image segments is around 3100 representing an average of approximately 10 regions per image. The number of different keywords used in the categorisation was 327, and each image has 4 or 5 different keywords associated.

The experiments were conducted using the VOIR system using, as textual thesaurus, the Australian Pictorial Thesaurus [8]. From each segmented region, during the indexing process, are automatically extracted a collection of numerical properties.

The low-level descriptors and correspondent similarity measures used for the relevance feedback process were:

- L*a*b* Color Histogram (180-bin); histogram intersection.
- Edge Histogram descriptor adapted from the correspondent MPEG-7 descriptor [13] (80-bin); histogram absolute difference.
- Shape descriptors vector composed by: proportion of image covered by the region, circularity, principal axis, six first invariants of the region central moments (9-dimension vector); euclidean distance.

To perform the clustering of existing regions, used in the process of learning term-region associations, a feature vector of dimension 13 is used. For each region the following features are computed:

- RGB color space: mean and std deviation of each component (6 values);
- L*a*b* color space: mean and std deviation of each component (6 values);
- Size: region or group relative size (1 value).

For the clustering algorithm, the value pre-selected for parameter k was 400, i.e. the number of obtained clusters is pre-defined as being 400. This value was chosen according to the image collection used in the tests. The total number of textual terms from the test collection was 327 and most of those terms were associated with just one region. The supported relation (term, region) is of type many-to-many, since it is possible for one term to be associated with several regions and, conversely, is also possible for a region to be associated with several thesaurus terms.

5.1 Experimental Procedure

The frequency of the textual terms in the collection is diverse and, for instance, while the term *water* appears in 65 images (TF=65), about 240 terms occur in just one image. Due to this fact, the 37 most frequent single terms were grouped in five intervals (T1_I1 to T1_I5 from Table 1) having distinct frequencies. The same approach was applied to pairs and triplets of terms (Table 2). This has given origin to three classes of queries: queries with one (CL1), two (CL2) and three (CL3) terms.

Table 1. The 37 most frequent terms divided in 5 intervals

Interval	Terms	Images (N)
T1_I1 (people, sky, water, trees, grasses, rocks)	6	$N \geq 30$
T1_I2 (birds, clouds, buildings, landscapes, snow)	5	$30 > N \geq 15$
T1_I3 (cats, mountains, boats)	3	$15 > N \geq 12$
T1_I4 (horses, flowers, bears, roads, mammals, women)	6	$12 > N \geq 9$
T1_I5 (pyramids, tigers, churches, fish, …)	17	$9 > N \geq 6$

For query class CL1, two distinct terms from each of the intervals T1_I1 to T1_I5 were selected. For each of the 10 terms selected, one region was randomly chosen as the query region. In the query experiments for the class CL2 was considered one pair from each of the first five intervals T23_I1 to T23_I5. For the class CL3 were considered three triplets from the interval T23_I5.

Table 2. Frequency distribution for pairs and triplets of terms

Interval	Pairs of terms	Triplets of terms	Images (N)
T23_I1	4	-	$18 \geq N \geq 15$
T23_I2	3	-	$15 > N \geq 12$
T23_I3	2	-	$12 > N \geq 9$
T23_I4	17	-	$9 > N \geq 6$
T23_I5	66	12	$6 > N \geq 3$

The kind of experiments carried out intent to measure fundamentally the following three aspects: the performance of the image retrieval system during a specific interaction session with one user (A1); the impact of the relevance feedback into the quality of the results presented during a specific interaction session with one user (A2); and the accuracy of the learned term-region association (A3).

An automatic evaluation system has been designed to simulate a real user willing to cooperate with the system, i.e., giving to the system the maximum amount possible of positive feedback with respect to the first NR=30 image results delivered by VOIR in each iteration. Given the queries selected to perform the experiments, the evaluation framework, for each query iteration and the returned result set, selects the relevant regions within that result set and feeds that information back to the VOIR system. The process is done automatically after the first formulation of the query. A similar technique has been reported in [9].

5.2 Results Obtained

Table 3 summarizes the precision and recall results for the query class CL1. From Table 3, it is observed that the values for precision and recall increase monotonically along the iterations, having greater increases during the earliest iterations.

Table 3. Precision (Pr)/Recall (Rc) for queries with one term (CL1)

Term(TF)	Iteration											
	0	1	2	3	4	5	6	7	8	9	10	
Water(65)	0.16	0.43	0.56	0.6	0.6	0.63	0.66	0.76	0.8	0.8	0.8	Pr
	0.07	0.2	0.26	0.27	0.27	0.29	0.3	0.35	0.36	0.36	0.36	Rc
Trees(56)	0.23	0.33	0.33	0.33	0.36	0.36	0.4	0.4	0.43	0.46	0.53	Pr
	0.12	0.17	0.17	0.17	0.19	0.19	0.21	0.21	0.23	0.25	0.28	Rc
Clouds(17)	0.16	0.23	0.23	0.23	0.23	0.23	0.23	0.23	0.23	0.23	0.23	Pr
	0.29	0.41	0.41	0.41	0.41	0.41	0.41	0.41	0.41	0.41	0.41	Rc
Birds(21)	0.13	0.23	0.23	0.23	0.23	0.26	0.3	0.33	0.33	0.36	0.36	Pr
	0.19	0.33	0.33	0.33	0.33	0.38	0.42	0.47	0.47	0.52	0.52	Rc
Flowers(11)	0.16	0.16	0.2	0.2	0.2	0.2	0.23	0.23	0.23	0.23	0.23	Pr
	0.45	0.45	0.54	0.54	0.54	0.54	0.63	0.63	0.63	0.63	0.63	Rc
Boats(12)	0.13	0.13	0.13	0.13	0.13	0.13	0.13	0.13	0.13	0.13	0.13	Pr
	0.33	0.33	0.33	0.33	0.33	0.33	0.33	0.33	0.33	0.33	0.33	Rc
Horses(10)	0.16	0.2	0.2	0.2	0.2	0.2	0.2	0.2	0.2	0.2	0.2	Pr
	0.5	0.6	0.6	0.6	0.6	0.6	0.6	0.6	0.6	0.6	0.6	Rc
Bears(9)	0.1	0.13	0.13	0.13	0.13	0.13	0.13	0.13	0.13	0.13	0.13	Pr
	0.33	0.44	0.44	0.44	0.44	0.44	0.44	0.44	0.44	0.44	0.44	Rc
Pyramids(7)	0.1	0.1	0.1	0.1	0.1	0.1	0.1	0.1	0.1	0.1	0.1	Pr
	0.42	0.42	0.42	0.42	0.42	0.42	0.42	0.42	0.42	0.42	0.42	Rc
Tigers(6)	0.06	0.2	0.2	0.2	0.2	0.2	0.2	0.2	0.2	0.2	0.2	Pr
	0.33	1	1	1	1	1	1	1	1	1	1	Rc

To evaluate aspect A3, all the queries in the query classes were executed in sequence (the several instants from the x-axis in figure 5) and the association between terms and regions was gradually improved. For the compilation of results, an association between a term and a region was considered only if attribute $d\_conf >= 30$ (threshold 30). The three terms mostly used in this query sequence were: *water*, used six times, *trees*, used five times, and *people* used four times. Figure 5 shows the evolution of relative true positive, i.e., true positive divided by occurrences, for those three terms.

For these three terms, the number of false positives in the prediction was nearly negligible: 0 in 92 for water; 1 in 83 for trees and 1 in 154 for people. It is also demonstrated a sustainable growing in the correct predictions, which represents a very promising result.

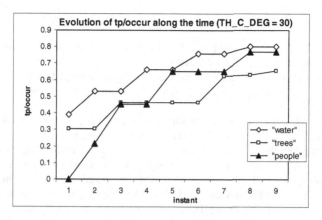

Fig. 5. Evolution of tp/occur for three terms in the experiment

6 Conclusions

The approach presented for relevance feedback in image retrieval was based on a dependency between the short-term result refinement process and the long-term concept learning process. Clearly, at the first stage of usage of the system, the influence of the first is predominant while, with time, the influence of the learned concepts is increased. The results achieved, clearly show the potential of this approach for image retrieval systems, demonstrating that the developed prototype could be implemented in a real application scenario. One of the main aspects that deserve to be highlighted is the accuracy of the term-region associations predicted having a confidence degree equal or greater than the threshold value. Also, the evaluation method adopted avoids the negative effects of automatic segmentation methods such as incorrect segmentation or over segmentation.

Other characteristics already incorporated in the VOIR prototype are being tested and evaluated as an extension of the discussed approach. These include the use of spatial relationships and of automatic image segmentation methods in larger image databases as well as its effect on the behaviour of the proposed solution.

References

1. Barthes, R., "Rhetoric of the Image," in Barthes, R. (ed.) *Image, music, text / trans. by Stephen Heath* London: Fontana, 1977, pp. 32-51
2. Carson, C., Belongie, S., Greenspan, H., and Malik, J., "Blobworld: Image segmentation using Expectation-Maximization and its application to image querying," *IEEE Transactions on Pattern Analysis and Machine Intelligence*, vol. 24, no. 8, pp. 1026-1038, 2002
3. Duygulu, P., "Translating images to words : A novel approach for object recognition." PhD Middle East Technical University, Dept. of Computer Engineering, 2003
4. Dwork, C., Kumar, R., Naor, M., and Sivakumar, D.: Rank aggregation methods for the Web. Proc. of tenth international conference on World Wide Web. 613-622. (2001). Hong Kong.

5. Eakins, J. P., "Towards intelligent image retrieval," *Pattern Recognition*, vol. 35 pp. 3-14, 2002

6. Jain, A. K., Murty, M. N., and Flynn, P. J., "Data Clustering: A Review," *ACM Computing Surveys*, vol. 31, no. 3, pp. 264-323, 1999

7. Jing, F., Li, M., Zhang, H. J., and Zhang, B., "Relevance Feedback in Region-Based Image Retrieval," *IEEE Transactions on Circuits and Systems for Video Technology*, vol. 14, no. 5, pp. 672-681, 2004

8. Kingscote, A.: The Australian Pictorial Thesaurus 2 years on. DC-ANZ Metadata Conference. (2003). Australian National University, Canberra.

9. Lee, C. S., Ma, W. Y., and Zhang, H. J.: Information Embedding Based on User's Relevance Feedback for Image Retrieval. SPIE Photonic East. (1999). Boston, USA.

10. Li, J., Wang, J., and Wiederhold, G.: IRM: Integrated Region Matching for Image Retrieval. Proc. ACM Multimedia 2000. 147-156. (2000). Los Angeles CA, USA.

11. Lu, Y., Hu, C., Zhu, X., Zhang, H. J., and Yang, Q.: A unified framework for semantics and feature based relevance feedback in image retrieval systems. Proc. of ACM Multimedia 2000. 31-38. (2000). Los Angeles, USA.

12. Ma, W. Y. and Manjunath, B. S., "NeTra: A toolbox for navigating large image databases," *Multimedia Systems*, vol. 7, no. 3, pp. 184-198, 1999

13. Manjunath, B. S., Salembier, P., and Sikora, T., *Introduction to MPEG-7, Multimedia Content Description Interface* John Wiley & Sons Ltd., 2002,

14. Martin, D., Fowlkes, C., Tal, D., and Malik, J.: A database of human segmented natural images and its applications to evaluating segmentation algorithms and measuring ecological statistics. Proc. IEEE 8th Int. Conf. Computer Vision. 416-423. (2001). Vancouver, Canada.

15. Mezaris, V., Kompatsiaris, I., and Strintzis, M. G., "Region-based Image Retrieval using an Object Ontology and Relevance Feedback," *EURASIP Journal on Applied Signal Processing*, vol. 2004, no. 6, pp. 886-901, 2004

16. Panofsky, E., "Iconography and Iconology: An Introduction to the Study of Renaissance Art," *Meaning in the visual arts* Penguin Books, 1970, pp. 26-54

17. Rui, Y. and Huang, T. S.: A Novel Relevance Feedback Technique in Image Retrieval. Proc.of ACM Multimedia. 67-70. (1999).

18. Rui, Y., Huang, T. S., Ortega, M., and Mehrotra, S., "Relevance Feedback: A Power Tool for Interactive Content-Based Image Retrieval," *IEEE Transactions on Circuits and Systems for Video Technology*, vol. 8, no. 5, pp. 644-655, 1998

19. Torres, J., Parkes, A., and Corte-Real, L.: Region-Based Relevance Feedback in Concept-Based Image Retrieval. Proc. of the 5th International Workshop on Image Analysis for Multimedia Interactive Services. (2004). Lisboa, Portugal.

20. Wang, T., Rui, Y., and Sun, J.-G., "Constraint Based Region Matching for Image Retrieval," *International Journal of Computer Vision*, vol. 56, no. 1/2, pp. 37-45, 2004

21. Wu, L., Faloutsos, C., Sycara, K., and Payne, T. R.: FALCON Feedback Adaptive Loop for Content-Based Retrieval. VLDB 2000. (2000).

22. Zhang, R. and Zhang, Z.: Hidden Semantic Concept Discovery in Region Based Image Retrieval. Proc. of the 2004 IEEE Conf. on Computer Vision and Pattern Recognition. 2, II-996-II-1001. (2004).

23. Zhuang, Y., Yang, J., and Li, Q.: A Graphic-Theoretic Model for Incremental Relevance Feedback in Image Retrieval. Proc. IEEE Int. Conf. on Image Processing 2002. (2002). New York, USA.

Image Retrieval with Segmentation-Based Query

Andrew Chupikov, Dmitry Kinoshenko, Vladimir Mashtalir, and
Konstantin Shcherbinin

Kharkov National University of Radio Electronics, Computer Science faculty,
Lenin Ave., 14, Kharkov, 61166, Ukraine
{Kinoshenko, Mashtalir}@kture.kharkov.ua

Abstract. Interest in digital images content has increased enormously over the last few years. Segmentation algorithms are used to extract region-based descriptions of an image and provide an input to higher level image processing, e.g. for content-based image retrieval (CBIR). Frequently it is difficult even for a user to single out representative regions or its combinations. Partitions and coverings of an image and range of gray levels (colors) are ones of principal constructive objects for an analysis. Their processing creates the necessary prerequisites to synthesize new features for CBIR and to consider redundancy and deficiency of information as well as its multiple meaning for totally correct and complete segmentation of complex scenes. The paper is dedicated to theoretical and experimental exploration of coverings and partitions produced by multi-thresholding segmentation.

1 Introduction

There has been a tremendous significance growth of the image content analysis in the recent years. This interest has been motivated mainly by the rapid expansion of imaging on the World-Wide Web, the availability of digital image libraries, increasing of multimedia applications in commerce, biometrics, science, entertainments etc. Visual contents of an image such as color, shape, texture, and region relations play dominating role in propagation of feature selection, indexing, user query and interaction, database management techniques. Many systems combine visual features and metadata analysis to solve the semantic gap between low-level visual features and high-level human concept, i.e. there arises a great need mainly in self-acting content-based image retrieval (CBIR) task-level systems [1,2].

To search images in an image database traditionally queries 'ad exemplum' are used. In this connection essential efforts have been devoted to synthesis and analysis of image content descriptors, namely color moments, histograms, coherence vectors, correlograms, invariant color features [3,4]; texture statistical and structural properties, determining by methods based on Fourier power spectra, Markov random fields, Gabor and wavelet transforms, fractal models, principal component analysis [5-8]; region-based and boundary-based features of shape, salient points in images [9-11]; syntax and semantic representations [12,13]. However, a user's semantic understanding of an image is of a higher level than the features representation. Low-level features with mental concepts and semantic labels are the groundwork of intelligent databases creation.

S. Marchand-Maillet et al. (Eds.): AMR 2006, LNCS 4398, pp. 207–221, 2007.
© Springer-Verlag Berlin Heidelberg 2007

Content of an image may be often summarized by a set of homogeneous regions in appropriate feature space. Therefore, there is a great need for automatic tools which should to classify and retrieve image content on the base of segmentation what is usually used to extract region-based descriptions of an image. Difficulties are given rise by not only different content entailing different segmentation of the same image but different levels of details of the image representations, e.g. at varying level of resolution [1, 14,15].

Edge-based and region-based segmentations or applications of global and composed approaches and uppermost superpositions of results obtained by distinct manners produce gray levels (or colors range) and field of view partitions and coverings. Therefore, formal analysis of all sorts of partitions and coverings dependency makes a considerable endowment for various fields of application. These problems are not adequately explored up to date and thus they need further consideration. Our contribution consists in theoretical ground of partitions and coverings (as segmentation results) analysis in order to get novel features for content-based image retrieval. The paper is organized as follows. Section 2 presents required aspects of formalization and properties of tolerance relations induced by segmentation algorithms. Section 3 describes partitions and coverings interdependence. Section 4 presents a new metric for partitions matching and discussion of extensive experiments with proposed relations.

In order to have a complete understanding of the paper a special consideration must be given to potentialities of operations with partitions and coverings to reasonably give a proper weight of redundancy and deficiency of information as well as its multiple meaning for totally correct and complete segmentation of complex scenes.

2 Formalization of Segmentation Results by Coverings

We will consider only digital images with carriers as a plane rectangular finite area $A \subset \mathbb{Z}^2$ with dimensions $N \times M$ and gray levels function $B(A) \subset \mathbb{Z}^+$ having only integer values at mesh points. For simplicity of notations, taking into account line scanning, there is no loss of generality in assuming that an image carrier is a set $A = \{1, 2, ..., n\}$ where $n = NM$ and an image $B(A)$ under arbitrary quantization with m levels is defined by a set $C = Im\, B(A) = \{n+1, n+2, ..., n+m\}$.

Generally, segmentation algorithms and most often partial segmentation results manipulations produce covering $\mathcal{P}_C$ of gray levels viz $\mathcal{P}_C = \{\mathcal{P}_1^C, \mathcal{P}_2^C, ..., \mathcal{P}_s^C\}$ where

$$C = \bigcup_{i=1}^{s} \mathcal{P}_i^C, \ \mathcal{P}_i^C \subset C, \ \mathcal{P}_i^C \neq \mathcal{P}_j^C, \ i \neq j, \ i, j = \overline{1, s}.$$

It is obvious that function B and covering $\mathcal{P}_C$ induce on A a binary relation

$$\mathcal{R}(a', a'') = \begin{cases} 1, if\ \exists \mathcal{P}_i^C \subset \mathcal{P}_C : B(a'), B(a'') \in \mathcal{P}_i^C; \\ 0, otherwise \end{cases} \tag{1}$$

where $a', a'' \in A, \mathcal{P}_i^C \subset C, i \in \{1, 2, ..., s\}$, $Dom\, \mathcal{R} = A \times A$. Relation (1) is reflexive $(\forall a \in A \Rightarrow \mathcal{R}(a, a) = 1)$ and symmetric $(\forall a', a'' \in A \Rightarrow \mathcal{R}(a', a'') = \mathcal{R}(a'', a'))$, i.e. $\mathcal{R}(a', a'')$ is a tolerance relation.

It should be noted that here left and right residue classes $\mathcal{R}_a = \{x \in A : \mathcal{R}(a, x) = 1\}$ and $\mathcal{R}_a^{-1} = \{x \in A : \mathcal{R}(x, a) = 1\}$ pro tanto coincide by virtue of symmetry. Indeed, $\forall a \in \mathcal{R}_a \Rightarrow \mathcal{R}(a, x) = 1 \Rightarrow \mathcal{R}(x, a) = 1 \Rightarrow x \in \mathcal{R}_a^{-1}$. This sequence of implications holds also in inverse order then $\mathcal{R}_a \subset \mathcal{R}_a^{-1}$ and $\mathcal{R}_a^{-1} \subset \mathcal{R}_a$, i.e. $\mathcal{R}_a^{-1} = \mathcal{R}_a$.

System of these classes generates covering $\mathcal{P}_A = \{\mathcal{P}_1^A, \mathcal{P}_2^A, ..., \mathcal{P}_q^A\}$ due to arbitrary element $a \in A$ also belongs to $\mathcal{R}_a$ by reflexivity $\mathcal{R}(a, a) = 1$. It is known that any tolerance relation induces so-called pre-classes and classes of tolerance. Let us study their dependence on given coverings in more details.

Let us remind that a set $E \subset A$ is called a pre-class of tolerance if any two elements x and y are tolerant, i.e. $\mathcal{R}(x, y) = 1$. In particular, for any element a from A a single-element set $E = \{a\}$ is pre-class of tolerance because reflexivity exists. Then a set $\mathcal{H} \subset A$ is said to be a class of tolerance if $\mathcal{H}$ is a maximal pre-class in such meaning that for any element $z \in A$, which is not contained in $\mathcal{H}$, not tolerant to z element $x \in \mathcal{H}$ exists, i.e. $\mathcal{R}(x, z) = 0$.

Note, if A is a finite set then each pre-class belongs at least to one class of tolerance. Indeed, let E be a pre-class of tolerance but not a class of tolerance. Consequently, it is not maximal, i.e. element $z \in A \backslash E$ exists and it is tolerant to every element from E. We append it to set E and analyze set $E_1 = E \cup \{z\}$. It is clear that $E_1 \subset E$ and E_1 is the pre-class of tolerance as before. If the set E_1 has not been transformed into a class of tolerance yet then the process may be continued till obtaining a class of tolerance. Because $card$ $A < \infty$, for finite steps number we will build a class of tolerance containing initial pre-class, which was required to prove. It follows that any element $a \in A$ exists in some class of tolerance because a single-element subset A is a pre-class of tolerance, but any system of tolerance classes generates covering of set A, which we shall denote by $\mathcal{H}_A = \{\mathcal{H}_1^A, \mathcal{H}_2^A, ..., \mathcal{H}_r^A\}$.

Definition 1. Arbitrary covering P we call regular if and only if for two elements $\mathcal{P}'$ and $\mathcal{P}''$ inequalities $\mathcal{P}' \backslash \mathcal{P}'' \neq \varnothing$ and $\mathcal{P}'' \backslash \mathcal{P}' \neq \varnothing$ hold.

Otherwise, if arbitrary element of covering belongs to another covering element, we shall call such covering irregular.

Proposition 1. Classes of tolerance generate regular coverings of a set A.

Proof. We have to show that there is no pair of elements, one of which is the proper subset of another. Indeed, if for tolerance classes $\mathcal{H}', \mathcal{H}'' \subset A$ the condition $\mathcal{H}' \subset \mathcal{H}''$ $\forall \mathcal{P}_i \in \mathcal{P}_C$ is valid then $\mathcal{H}'$ does not satisfy the properties of maximality, i.e. set $\mathcal{H}'$ is a pre-class but is not the class of tolerance, which contradicts the assertion.

Definition 2. Arbitrary covering $\mathcal{P}_C$ of finite set C is named orderly connective if there exists an indexation with only efficiently indexed (without omission) elements in any covering component

$$\forall P_i \in \mathcal{P}_C \ \ P_i = \{c_i, c_{i+1}, \dots, c_{i+k}\}, \ \ c_i, c_{i+1}, \dots, c_{i+k} \in C, \ \ card \ P_i = k+1.$$

Consider example of not orderly connective set. Let C consist of three elements, i.e. $C = \{1, 2, 3\}$ and $\mathcal{P}_C = \{\{1, 2\}, \{2, 3\}, \{1, 3\}\}$. Then during any reindexing (permutation of 1,2,3) not connective elements of covering with indexes 1 and 3 (with missed index 2) will definitely be presented.

Definition 3. Arbitrary triplet $T = \langle c', c'', c''' \rangle$ of different C elements with given covering $\mathcal{P}_C$ we shall call a transitive triplet if any pair of points lies at least in one covering element.

Example described above is a transitive triplet. We will denote a nontransitive triplet by $\tilde{T} = \langle c', c'', c''' \rangle$.

Generally, by analogy with (1) any pair $\langle C, \mathcal{P}_C \rangle$ induces a tolerance relation viz

$$\mathcal{O}_{P_C}(c', c'') = \begin{cases} 1, if \ \exists P_i^C : c', c'' \in P_i^C \in \mathcal{P}_C; \\ 0, otherwise. \end{cases} \tag{2}$$

Then supplement of any transitive regarding to this relation element c''' generates a transitive triplet. During this tolerance $\mathcal{O}_{P_C}$ is converted to trivial equivalence on transitive triplet, because $\mathcal{O}_{P_C}(c_i, c_j) \equiv 1$ for any $c_i, c_j \in \{c', c'', c'''\}$.

Now let us study properties of regular and orderly connective coverings.

Property 1. For any pair of elements of orderly connective and regular coverings at least one, which belongs to their union, nontransitive triplet $\tilde{T} = \langle c', c'', c''' \rangle$ exists and its two elements do not belong to one element of covering, i.e.

$$\forall P', P'' \in \mathcal{P}_C \ \exists \tilde{T} \in C : \{c', c'', c'''\} \in P' \cup P'', \ \exists c* \in P' \backslash P'', \ \exists c** \in P'' \backslash P', \ c*, c** \in \tilde{T}.$$

Proof. If P' and P'' are single-element sets, then we have a singular case when the set $P' \cup P''$ consists of only two elements thus a transitive triplet does not exist. Hence, without loss of generality it can be assumed that $card \{P' \cup P''\} \geq 3$.

There arise two cases: $P' \cap P'' = \varnothing$ or $P' \cap P'' \neq \varnothing$. As covering is orderly connective we can suppose that

$$P' = \{c_{i'}, c_{i'+1}, \dots, c_{i'+k'}\}, \ \ P'' = \{c_{i''}, c_{i''+1}, \dots, c_{i''+k''}\} \tag{3}$$

where $c_{i'}, c_{i'+1}, \dots, c_{i'+k'}, c_{i''}, c_{i''+1}, \dots, c_{i''+k''} \in C$.

Indexes in (3) satisfy condition

$$\begin{cases} P' \cap P'' = \varnothing \Rightarrow i' + k' < i''; \\ P' \cap P'' = \varnothing \Rightarrow \exists s : s \leq k', i' + s = i''. \end{cases}$$

Taking into consideration that $c_{i'+s} = c_{i''}, c_{i'+s+1} = c_{i''+1}, \dots, c_{i'+k'} = c_{i''+l-1}$ are common elements of sets P' and P'', in any case two elements $c_{i'}$ and $c_{i''+k''}$ from C

can not be tolerant respectively to relation $\mathcal{O}_{P_C}$. Indeed, otherwise (namely, if $\mathcal{O}_{P_C}(c_{i'}, c_{i''+k''}) = 1$) covering element $\mathcal{P}'''$ containing all of them will appear, i.e. $c_{i'}, c_{i''+k''} \in \mathcal{P}'''$. But in this case $\mathcal{P}'''$ would also contain all intermediate by indexes elements of C due to the connectivity condition. It follows that $\mathcal{P}' \cup \mathcal{P}'' \subseteq \mathcal{P}'''$, but this contradicts condition that $\mathcal{P}_C$ is a regular covering. Adding to these two elements arbitrary element from set $\mathcal{P}' \cup \mathcal{P}'' / \{c_{i'}, c_{i''+k''}\} \neq \varnothing$, we shall get a nontransitive triplet belonging to the union of two arbitrary elements of covering $\mathcal{P}_C$, for which the inclusions $c_{i'} \in \mathcal{P}' \backslash \mathcal{P}''$, $c_{i''+k''} \in \mathcal{P}'' \backslash \mathcal{P}'$ are fulfilled, which was required to prove.

Property 2. If for any element pair $\mathcal{P}', \mathcal{P}''$ of arbitrary covering $\mathcal{P}_C$ nontransitive triplet $\tilde{T} = \langle c', c'', c''' \rangle$ belonging to their union exists then this covering is regular.

Proof. Let us suppose contrary, i.e. existence of not regular element $\mathcal{P}'$ of covering $\mathcal{P}_C$. It means, that it is a proper subset of another element of covering $\mathcal{P}''$, i.e. $\mathcal{P}', \mathcal{P}'' \in \mathcal{P}_C$ and $\mathcal{P}' \subseteq \mathcal{P}''$. Then $\mathcal{P}' \cup \mathcal{P}'' = \mathcal{P}''$ and any three elements c', c'', c''' of the set C come into one element of covering, i.e. according to definition 3 these elements generate a transitive triplet, which contradicts our assumption and proves the property.

Property 3. Arbitrary partition of a finite set C is an orderly connective covering.

Proof. It is possible to prove the property by induction with regard to the cardinality of C. Obviously that induction base exists. If the set C consists of one or two elements then partitions consist of one or two elements also, being connective with any indexing.

Let us suppose now that for all sets of power less than or equal to n indicated property is fulfilled. Consider now a set C, for which $card\, C = n+1$. Let $c*$ be an element, which discriminates a set and a proper subset C* of power n. First, during transition to C the partition changes over the partition which covers the set $C* = C \backslash \{c*\}$. Suppose that $c* \in \mathcal{P}'$ ($\mathcal{P}'$ is an element of the initial partition $\mathcal{P}_C$). We change $\mathcal{P}'$ excluding $c*$ then according to inductive assumption new partition covers C* as $card\, C* = n$, and furthermore, it is orderly connective. It means that indexing of set C* exists such that $C \backslash \{c*\}$ is connective, i.e. $C \backslash \{c*\} = \{c_i, c_{i+1}, ..., c_{i+s}\}$. Let us assign index $i+s+1$ to the element $c*$ and increment indexation for all elements with numbers after $i+s$ by 1. Thus, connectivity of any partition element is not changed but it already covers the set C, which power is $n+1$, i.e. inductive inference is true. The proof is complete.

Definition 4. Arbitrary relation $\mathcal{F}_P$ on a set A is to be said functional relation if for given covering $\mathcal{P}$ on C and function $f : A \rightarrow C$ relationship $\mathcal{F}_P(a', a'') = 1$ is valid iff $\exists \mathcal{P}' \in \mathcal{P} : f(a'), f(a'') \in \mathcal{P}'$ where $a', a'' \in A$, $f(a'), f(a'') \in C$.

From the definition immediately follows that any functional relation is tolerance relation through reflexivity and symmetry hold. Therefore (1) is a functional relation.

Proposition 2. Functional relation will not be changed if all irregular elements will be removed from inducing covering.

Proof. Let us consider arbitrary irregular element $\mathcal{P}'$ of covering $\mathcal{P}$. If it exists (otherwise the assertion is true) then at least one element $\mathcal{P}'' \in \mathcal{P}$ will be found for which inclusion $\mathcal{P}' \subset \mathcal{P}''$ is fulfilled. Assume that for any pair a', a'' the elimination of $\mathcal{P}'$ from covering $\mathcal{P}$ would change relation $\mathcal{F}$, i.e. $\mathcal{F}_\mathcal{P}(a', a'') \neq \mathcal{F}_{\mathcal{P} \backslash \mathcal{P}'}(a', a'')$. The replacement $0 \to 1$ is not possible since initially values $f(a'), f(a'') \in C$ belong to the different elements of covering $\mathcal{P}$ and after elimination of any element from covering (it may be $\mathcal{P}'$ also) nothing can be changed. The replacement $1 \to 0$ can take place only after inclusion of element which contains $f(a')$ and $f(a'')$. Thus, change may happen only with tolerant element of the relation $\mathcal{F}_\mathcal{P}$. It means that element $\mathcal{P}''' \in \mathcal{P}$ exists and $f(a'), f(a'') \in \mathcal{P}'''$. If $\mathcal{P}' \cap \mathcal{P}''' = \varnothing$ then elimination of $\mathcal{P}'$ changes nothing because $f(a'), f(a'') \notin \mathcal{P}'$. But if $\mathcal{P}' \cap \mathcal{P}''' \neq \varnothing$ then changing can occur only if at least one of the elements $f(a'), f(a'') \in C$ comes into intersection $\mathcal{P}' \cap \mathcal{P}'''$. Due to symmetry of a tolerance relation this brings to three possible situations which are shown in fig. 1: case a) corresponds to following location of covering elements $f(a'), f(a'') \in \mathcal{P}' \cap \mathcal{P}'' \cap \mathcal{P}'''$, case b) to $f(a'), f(a'') \in \mathcal{P}'' \cap \mathcal{P}'''$, $f(a') \in \mathcal{P}' \cap \mathcal{P}'' \cap \mathcal{P}'''$ and case c) to $f(a'), f(a'') \in \mathcal{P}''$, $f(a') \in \mathcal{P}' \cap \mathcal{P}'' \cap \mathcal{P}'''$.

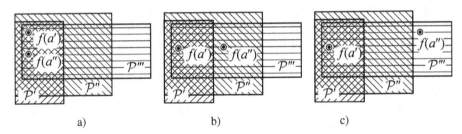

a)   b)   c)

Fig. 1. To the explanation of Proposition 2 proof

It is easily seen that the elimination of element $\mathcal{P}'$ from covering $\mathcal{P}$, as before, saves element $\mathcal{P}'''$ containing $f(a')$ and $f(a'')$. Thus we get $\mathcal{F}_{\mathcal{P} \backslash \mathcal{P}'}(a', a'') = 1$, i.e. the replacement $1 \to 0$ is also impossible, which proves assertion.

Results obtained above are the base to examine problems of relationships between gray levels coverings and partitions producing by segmentations.

3   Models of Multilevel Image Representations

We emphasize that as a rule left and right residue classes do not coincide with classes of tolerance. Consider example demonstrating this suggestion. Without restriction of generality we will choose sets A and C as sets of natural numbers $A = \{1, 2, 3, 4, 5, 6\}$, $C = \{7, 8, 9, 10, 11\}$. Define the image (the function f) $B : A \to C$ as $B(1) = 7, B(2) = 8, B(3) = 9, B(4) = 10, B(5) = B(6) = 11$. Specify gray levels coverings as $\mathcal{P}_C = \{\mathcal{P}_1^C, \mathcal{P}_2^C, \mathcal{P}_3^C\}$ where $\mathcal{P}_1^C = \{7,8\}$, $\mathcal{P}_2^C = \{8,9,10\}$, $\mathcal{P}_3^C = \{9,10,11\}$. Note that we use only a regular covering, because from proposition 2 follows that any covering can be represented as a regular one. Function $B : A \to C$ and covering $\mathcal{P}_C$ induce functional relation (2), which has matrix form

$$\mathcal{M}(\mathcal{R}_{\mathcal{P}_C}) = \begin{pmatrix} 1 & 1 & 0 & 0 & 0 & 0 \\ 1 & 1 & 1 & 1 & 0 & 0 \\ 0 & 1 & 1 & 1 & 1 & 1 \\ 0 & 1 & 1 & 1 & 1 & 1 \\ 0 & 0 & 1 & 1 & 1 & 1 \\ 0 & 0 & 1 & 1 & 1 & 1 \end{pmatrix}$$

where for arbitrary relation $\mathcal{M}(\mathcal{R})$ is $n \times n$ matrix ($n = card$ A) and

$$\mathcal{M}(\mathcal{R}) = (\delta_{ij})_{i, j=\overline{1n}}, \ \delta_{ij} = 1 \Leftrightarrow \mathcal{R}(a_i, a_j) = 1, \ a_i, a_j \in A. \tag{4}$$

Indicate left and right residue classes $\mathcal{R}_{\mathcal{P}_{C1}} = \mathcal{R}_{\mathcal{P}_{C1}}^{-1} = \{1,2\}$, $\mathcal{R}_{\mathcal{P}_{C2}} = \mathcal{R}_{\mathcal{P}_{C2}}^{-1} = \{1,2,3,4\}$, $\mathcal{R}_{\mathcal{P}_{C3}} = \mathcal{R}_{\mathcal{P}_{C3}}^{-1} = \{2,3,4,5,6\}$, $\mathcal{R}_{\mathcal{P}_{C4}} = \mathcal{R}_{\mathcal{P}_{C4}}^{-1} = \{2,3,4,5,6\}$, $\mathcal{R}_{\mathcal{P}_{C5}} = \mathcal{R}_{\mathcal{P}_{C5}}^{-1} = \{3,4,5,6\}$, $\mathcal{R}_{\mathcal{P}_{C6}} = \mathcal{R}_{\mathcal{P}_{C6}}^{-1} = \{3,4,5,6\}$ and also tolerance classes $\mathcal{H}_1 = \{1,2\}, \mathcal{H}_2 = \{2,3,4\}, \mathcal{H}_3 = \{3,4,5,6\}$. Comparing those classes we observe partial accordance. Thus a question appears: when residue classes and classes of tolerance are the same? For functional relations (1) the answer gives

Proposition 3. Let $\mathcal{F}_{\mathcal{P}_C}$ be a relation induced by function $B : A \to C$ and an orderly connective covering $\mathcal{P}_C$ then left and right residue classes of $\mathcal{F}_{\mathcal{P}_C}$ are classes of tolerance if and only if $\mathcal{P}_C$ is a partition.

Proof. Consider sufficiency. Let covering $\mathcal{P}_C$ be a partition. Examine a class from right residue classes $\mathcal{F}_{\mathcal{P}_{C}a}$ of any element $a \in A$ and its two elements $a', a'' \in \mathcal{F}_{\mathcal{P}_{C}a}$. Then $\mathcal{F}_{\mathcal{P}_C}(a, a') = \mathcal{F}_{\mathcal{P}_C}(a, a'') = 1$. From this and functionality of relation $\mathcal{F}_{\mathcal{P}_C}$ it follows that there exist two elements (suppose they are $\mathcal{P}_i^C$ and $\mathcal{P}_j^C$) of covering $\mathcal{P}_C$ such that

$$B(a), B(a') \in \mathcal{P}_i^C, \ B(a), B(a') \in \mathcal{P}_j^C. \tag{5}$$

Taking into account that B is a function completely defined on A, from (5) follows: $B(a)$ belongs to set $\mathcal{P}_i^C \cap \mathcal{P}_j^C$. On the other hand two elements of partition intersect iff they are equal, i.e. $\mathcal{P}_i^C = \mathcal{P}_j^C$, but then $B(a'), B(a'') \in \mathcal{P}_i^C$. Membership to one element of covering is evident for tolerant a' and a'' or, that is the same, $\mathcal{F}_{\mathcal{P}_{C}a}$ is a pre-class of tolerance. It is obvious that this pre-class is maximal since residue class $\mathcal{F}_{\mathcal{P}_{C}a}$ contains all tolerant to a elements. In other words, any set, which contains it, has at least one element not tolerant to a, i.e. it is not a pre-class. So, arbitrary right residue class is a class of tolerance. Sufficiency is proved.

Necessity we prove by contradiction. Let class $\mathcal{F}_{PCa}$ be a class of tolerance for arbitrary element $a \in A$ then we have to make sure that $\mathcal{P}_C$ is a partition. Suppose that this is not the case. Thus, there exist two incongruous elements $\mathcal{P}_i^C$ and $\mathcal{P}_j^C$ of covering $\mathcal{P}_C$ for which $\mathcal{P}_i^C \cap \mathcal{P}_j^C \neq \varnothing$, i.e. an element $c^* \in C$ exists such that $c^* \in \mathcal{P}_i^C \cap \mathcal{P}_j^C$. But from another hand, B is completely defined on A function, i.e. an element $a \in A$ such that $B(a) = c^*$ exists whence validity of $B(a) \in \mathcal{P}_i^C \cap \mathcal{P}_j^C$ follows.

Taking into account that $\mathcal{P}_i^C \neq \mathcal{P}_j^C$ and covering $\mathcal{P}_C$ is regular and orderly connective, from property 1 it follows that nontransitive triplet $\tilde{T} = \langle c', c'', c''' \rangle$ is in existence for elements of covering $\mathcal{P}_i^C$ and $\mathcal{P}_j^C$. Under suitable indexing ($c^* = c'$) properties of $\tilde{T}$ are the following. One element lies in intersection of covering elements but two others are in different elements, i.e.

$$c' \in \mathcal{P}_i^C \cap \mathcal{P}_j^C, \ c', c'' \in \mathcal{P}_i^C, \ c', c''' \in \mathcal{P}_j^C. \tag{6}$$

Let $a'', a''' \in A$ be pre-images of elements $c'', c''' \in C$ of not transitive triplet, i.e. $B(a'') = c''$, $B(a''') = c'''$. Then from (6) we get $\mathcal{F}_{PC}(a'', a') = \mathcal{F}_{PC}(a''', a') = 1$ and $\mathcal{F}_{PC}(a'', a''') = 0$ but this is impossible since $\mathcal{F}_{PCa}$ is left residue class containing a'' and a''' and this class is a tolerance one what means that $\mathcal{F}_{PCa}(a'', a''') = 1$. Thus, we get the contradiction, i.e. necessity is proved and the proof is completed.

Interpretation of proposition 2 is quite simple viz rational gray levels partition ensures that we can get 'regions of similarity' on an image carrier with normal understanding of tolerance classes as objects.

The proposition has obvious.

Corollary. For any functional relation $\mathcal{F}_{PC}$ coverings $\mathcal{P}_C$ (from residue classes) and $\mathcal{H}_C$ (from tolerance classes) are congruent iff they are induced by a partition.

Relationship between tolerance classes and residue classes determine following.

Proposition 4. Each residue class of any tolerant relation contains subset (class of tolerance) to which producing this residue class element belongs.

Proof. Indeed, let us fix arbitrary element $a \in A$ and examine corresponding residue class $\mathcal{R}_a$. Assume, this element belongs to the class of tolerance $\mathcal{H}_i^A$ and its arbitrary element is $a' \in \mathcal{H}_i^A$. Then $\mathcal{R}(a, a') = 1$ since these elements belong to the same class of tolerance. On the other hand $a' \in \mathcal{H}_i^A$ as it is one of image of element a. Finally, arbitrary element $a' \in \mathcal{H}_i^A$ belongs to $\mathcal{R}_a$, i.e. $\mathcal{H}_i^A \subseteq \mathcal{R}_a$, which was required to prove.

Let us analyze general form of (4) for a tolerance relation. First, $\mathcal{M}$ is $(n \times n)$ symmetric matrix with unity elements on main diagonal ($n = card$ A). Moreover, $r = card\ \mathcal{P}_C$ square blocks with unity elements are located along the main diagonal. Each ith block has dimension $s_i \times s_i$ with corresponding set $\mathcal{H}_i^A = \{a_{i_1}, \ldots, a_{s_i}\} \subset A$, which generates ith covering element of the set A. Every element of covering is a class of tolerance what is equal to possibility of blocks intersection. If not, we have a partition and equivalence classes represent the most suitable (but probably not the most adequate) object from the segmentation interpretation point of view. Finally, the general matrix form of tolerances can be written as

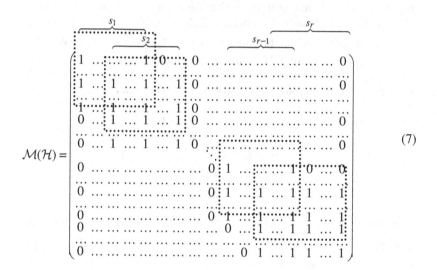

$$(7)$$

Following proposition is fulfilled.

Proposition 5. If the matrix of a tolerant relation has a block form then coverings $\mathcal{P}_A$ and $\mathcal{H}_A$ are orderly connective. Here $\mathcal{H}_A$ is a regular covering but $\mathcal{P}_A$ is also regular one if and only if residue classes or classes of tolerance for elements which have different images do not intersect.

Proof. Property of ordered connectivity directly follows from the form of matrix $\mathcal{M}(\mathcal{H})$ (7). Indeed, there exists an indexing of set A elements such that matrix is converted to the block form but then classes of tolerance $\mathcal{H}_i^A$ are blocks of the matrix $\mathcal{M}(\mathcal{H})$ which are orderly connective. Here $\mathcal{P}_i^A$ are rows or columns of matrix $\mathcal{M}(\mathcal{H})$ and are also orderly connective.

Examine now regularness of coverings. Classes of tolerance always generate regular coverings what follows from the Proposition 1. In regard to residue classes it is obvious that for elements of block matrix $\mathcal{M}(\mathcal{H})$ coinciding rows (columns) exist, i.e. covering $\mathcal{P}_A$ is not a regular one. Moreover, if we consider different rows (columns)and suppose any two elements a' and a'' belong to one block $\mathcal{H}_i^A$ intersecting with the block $\mathcal{H}_j^A$ and at the same time they are located in the following way $a' \in \mathcal{H}_i^A \setminus \mathcal{H}_j^A$, $a'' \in \mathcal{H}_i^A \cap \mathcal{H}_j^A$. Then covering by residue classes is not a regular one because $\mathcal{H}_{a'} \subset \mathcal{H}_{a''}$. Thus, a covering becomes regular if and only if blocks do not intersect and this covering contains different elements. Hence row (column) coincides with the block to which it belongs and different residue classes coincide with classes of tolerance. The proof is complete.

It is necessary to note that if all residue classes are orderly connective then the matrix $\mathcal{M}(\mathcal{H})$ has a block form. Otherwise, i.e. the situation when unity element appears in (7) in 'zero zone' leads to the correspondence of element a to the row, for which $\mathcal{P}_A$ is not orderly connective. It should be emphasized that the ordered connectivity of covering is of the essence for residue classes but not for classes of tolerance. The validity of this hypothesis is illustrated by following example

$$\mathcal{M}(\mathcal{H}) = \begin{pmatrix} 1 & 1 & 0 & 0 & 0 & 1 \\ 1 & 1 & 1 & 1 & 0 & 0 \\ 0 & 1 & 1 & 1 & 1 & 1 \\ 0 & 1 & 1 & 1 & 1 & 1 \\ 0 & 0 & 1 & 1 & 1 & 1 \\ 1 & 0 & 1 & 1 & 1 & 1 \end{pmatrix},$$

from which it follows that classes $\mathcal{H}_i^A$ of relation $\mathcal{H}$ on set $A = \{a_1, a_2, a_3, a_4, a_5, a_6\}$ generate orderly connective covering $\mathcal{H}_A = \{\{a_1, a_2\}, \{a_2, a_3, a_4\}, \{a_3, a_4, a_5, a_6\}\}$ but the matrix $\mathcal{M}(\mathcal{H})$ does not have a block form.

It is necessary to note that every functional tolerance induced by a map (a digital image) $f : A \to C$ places in correspondence to each element of covering $\mathcal{P}_C$ binary relations on set A

$$\mathcal{E}_i(a, a') = \begin{cases} 1, & \text{if } f(a), f(a') \in \mathcal{P}_i^C, \\ 0, & \text{otherwise} \end{cases} \tag{8}$$

where $i = \overline{1, q}$, $a, a' \in A$, $\mathcal{P}_i^C \in \mathcal{P}_C$, $\mathcal{P}_i^C \subseteq C$. Relation (8) is an equivalence relation producing partition elements $A_i \subseteq A$

$$a', a'' \in A_i \Leftrightarrow f(a'), f^{-1}(a'') \in \mathcal{P}_i^C. \tag{9}$$

Emphasize that classes A_i are pre-classes of tolerance as they include pairs of tolerant elements.

Answer the question: when system of pre-classes $\{A_1, A_2, ..., A_q\}$ induced by equivalencies $\mathcal{E}_i$ (rather by (9)) will be a basis (in a general sense) in space $\langle A, \mathcal{H} \rangle$ of functional tolerance?

Definition 5. Arbitrary covering $\mathcal{P}$ of any set A is named a basis if excluding of any element $\mathcal{P}_\alpha \in \mathcal{P}$ leads to appearing at least one of $a_\beta, a_\gamma, \ldots \in$ A outside of $\mathcal{P}$.

Place high emphasis on case when basis covering is orderly connective then not a single element of covering can be a proper subset of any element or union of another elements. In this regard there exists an indexing of elements of covering $\mathcal{P}_A$ when without loss of generality we may express elements of covering by formulas

$$
\begin{cases}
\mathcal{P}_1^A = \{a_1, a_2, \ldots, a_{q_1}\}, \\
\mathcal{P}_2^A = \{a_{q_1-s_1+1}, a_{q_1-s_1+2}, \ldots, a_{q_1-s_1+q_2}\}, \\
\mathcal{P}_3^A = \{a_{q_1-s_1+q_2-s_2+1}, a_{q_1-s_1+q_2-s_2+2}, \ldots, a_{q_1-s_1+q_2-s_2+q_3}\}, \\
\cdots\cdots\cdots\cdots\cdots\cdots\cdots\cdots\cdots\cdots\cdots\cdots\cdots\cdots \\
\mathcal{P}_i^A = \{a_{\sum_{k=1}^{i-1}(q_k-s_k)+1}, \ldots, a_{\sum_{k=1}^{i-1}(q_k-s_k)+q_i}\}, \\
\cdots\cdots\cdots\cdots\cdots\cdots\cdots\cdots\cdots\cdots\cdots\cdots\cdots\cdots \\
\mathcal{P}_r^A = \{a_{\sum_{k=1}^{n-1}(q_k-s_k)+1}, \ldots, a_{\sum_{k=1}^{n-1}(q_k-s_k)+q_n}\}
\end{cases}
\tag{10}
$$

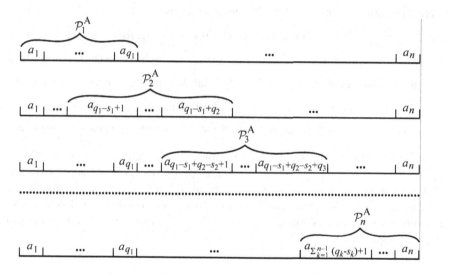

Fig. 2. An example of basis covering

where $s_0 = 0$, $0 \le s_i \le q_i - s_{i-1}$, $i = \overline{1, n-1}$, $q_i = card\,\mathcal{P}_i^A$, $s_i = card\,\{\mathcal{P}_i^A \cap \mathcal{P}_{i+1}^A\}$ $\sum_{k=1}^r q_k = n = card\,A$, $r \le n$. Covering (see fig. 2) contains 'adhering' or 'joined' elements and it does not overlap intermediate element, i.e. $\mathcal{P}_i^A \backslash (\mathcal{P}_{i-1}^A \cup \mathcal{P}_{i+1}^A) \ne \varnothing$, $\mathcal{P}_{i-1}^A \cap \mathcal{P}_{i+1}^A = \varnothing$.

The validity of this supposition can be proved by induction. Indeed, if $r = 1$ or $r = 2$ then it is possible to cover the set only as shown in fig.2. Assume now that the assertion is correct for each covering which contains $r-1$ elements. Then if we supplement r th element to covering then its $r-1$ elements cover a certain part of set A accordingly to (10). But then the r th element of covering should occupy elements of set A with last indexes but it also may occupy several last indexes covered elements of the set A so as $\mathcal{P}_i^A \cap \mathcal{P}_r^A = \varnothing$ where $i = \overline{1, r-2}$ and $\mathcal{P}_r^A \cap \mathcal{P}_{r-1}^A \neq \varnothing$ and we get $\mathcal{P}_{r-1}^A \setminus \mathcal{P}_r^A \neq \varnothing$ or $\mathcal{P}_r^A \cap \mathcal{P}_{r-1}^A = \varnothing$. Otherwise the covering would not be a basis or the ordered connectivity property would be violated.

Proposition 6. Let $\mathcal{H}$ be a functional tolerance on a finite set A then a covering $\mathcal{P}_A = \{\mathcal{P}_1^A, \mathcal{P}_2^A, ..., \mathcal{P}_p^A\}$ from full pre-images $f^{-1}(\mathcal{P}^C)$ is a basis in space of tolerance $\langle A, \mathcal{H} \rangle$ if $\mathcal{P}_C = \{\mathcal{P}_1^C, \mathcal{P}_2^C, ..., \mathcal{P}_s^C\}$ is orderly connective and it covers basis.

Proof. Through $\mathcal{P}_C$ is orderly connective and is a basis it can be represented in form (10). Then all elements $f^{-1}(\mathcal{P}_i^C)$ generate a class and not only a pre-class of tolerance. Indeed, if $a \notin f^{-1}(\mathcal{P}_i^C)$ then $f(a) \notin \mathcal{P}_i^C$ and from statement (10) it follows that there exists an element $a' \in f^{-1}(\mathcal{P}_i^C)$ which has value $f(a')$, i.e. $\mathcal{H}(a, a') = 0$. So, the pre-class $f^{-1}(\mathcal{P}_i^C)$ is a tolerance class. Prove now that the set of classes is a basis in space of tolerance. Exclude from examination the i-th element $f^{-1}(\mathcal{P}_i^C)$. In this case there exists an element $a' \in f^{-1}(\mathcal{P}_i^C)$ that does not belong to any another class $f^{-1}(\mathcal{P}_j^C)$ $(i \neq j)$, as the covering $\mathcal{P}_i^C$ is a basis. Thus, $\mathcal{H}(a, a') = 0$, i.e. the element $f(a')$ stays not covered, which contradicts the assumption. The proof is complete.

Note, all obtained results are intended for use as region-based descriptions of an image to provide an input to higher level image processing. Various superpositions of partitions and coverings, which are outcome of different segmentation algorithms at varying levels of resolution, are data-in to eliminate redundancy and deficiency of information as well as its multiple meaning for totally correct and complete segmentation of complex scenes.

4 Results and Outlook

To the utmost theoretical results presented above are in accordance with the simplest segmentation processes namely single global and adaptive thresholding, multithresholding and band-thresholding. In fig. 3 one can see the examples of partitions and coverings appearances. Obviously, for practical use of obtained theoretical ground, first of all, we have to know how different partitions or coverings could be matched.

Consider two partitions $\tilde{P}^A = \{\tilde{P}_1^A, \tilde{P}_2^A, ..., \tilde{P}_n^A\}$ and $\overline{P}^A = \{\overline{P}_1^A, \overline{P}_2^A, ..., \overline{P}_m^A\}$ of arbitrary set A (in fact a segmented image). With due regard of A finitude we may use a cardinality as a measure. We prove rigorously that the functional

Fig. 3. Examples of partitions and coverings

$$\rho(\tilde{\mathcal{P}}^A, \overline{\mathcal{P}}^A) = \sum_{k=1}^{n} \sum_{l=1}^{m} [card\{\tilde{\mathcal{P}}_k^A \vartriangle \overline{\mathcal{P}}_l^A\} card\{\tilde{\mathcal{P}}_k^A \cap \overline{\mathcal{P}}_l^A\}] \qquad (11)$$

(here $\tilde{\mathcal{P}}_k^A \vartriangle \overline{\mathcal{P}}_l^A = (\tilde{\mathcal{P}}_k^A \setminus \overline{\mathcal{P}}_l^A) \cup (\overline{\mathcal{P}}_l^A \setminus \tilde{\mathcal{P}}_k^A)$ denotes a symmetrical difference) constitutes a metric, i.e. axioms of reflexivity, symmetry and triangular inequality hold true. With regard to invariance of image carrier functional (11) is sufficiently suitable measure of images similarity with the use of partitions.

Fig. 4 illustrates representations of images in database via different partitions. As query partitions eventual segmentation results are shown in fig. 5.

Fig. 4. Images from a database and corresponding partitions (top-down)

Fig. 5. Examples of a query in form of partition for CBIR

The analysis of experimental results has shown that the application of partitions as features provides a sufficient relevance at access to an image in database with queries 'ad exemplum'. However, the direct use of partitions or coverings can reduce the reliability at selected metrics (11) search. First of all, it is explained by dependence on positioning partitions in a field of view, namely small changes of mutual position of an object and sensor may essentially garble the measure of the images similarity. Thus, the reliability, on the one hand, can be increased by preliminary normalization of geometrical transformations. On the other hand, the intellectual processing (relations analysis between elements of region-based models) not only compensates the indicated disadvantage but also provides necessary conditions for entirely correct and complete segmentation.

References

1. Chen, Y., Wang, J.Z.: Image categorization by learning and reasoning with regions. Journal of Machine Learning Research, Vol. 5 (2004) 913-939
2. Müller, H., Müller, W., Squire, D.McG., Marchand-Maillet, S., Pun, T.: Performance Evaluation in Content-Based Image Retrieval: Overview and Proposals. Pattern Recognition Letters, Vol. 22 (2001) 593-601
3. Yanai, K., Shindo, M., Noshita, K.: A Fast Image-Gathering System from the World-Wide Web Using a PC Cluster. Image and Vision Computing, Vol. 22 (2004) 59-71
4. Bauckhage, C., Braun, E., Sagerer, G.: From Image Features to Symbols and Vice Versa – Using Graphs to Loop Data – and Model-Driven Processing in Visual Assembly Recognition. International Journal of Pattern Recognition and Artificial Intelligence, Vol.18 (2004) 497-517
5. Manjunath, B.S., Ma, W.Y.: Texture Features for Browsing and Retrieval of Large Image Data. IEEE Transactions on Pattern Analysis and Machine Intelligence, Vol. 18 (1996) 837-842
6. Celebi, E., Alpkocak, A.: Clustering of Texture Features for Content Based Image Retrieval. Lecture Notes in Computer Science, Springer-Verlag, Heidelberg, Vol. 1909 (2000) 216-225.
7. Peng, J., Bhanu, B., Qing, S.: Probabilistic Feature Relevance Learning for Content-Based Image Retrieval. Computer Vision and Image Understanding, Vol. 75, (1999) 150-164
8. Cox, I.J., Miller, M.L., Minka, T.P., Papathomas, T., Yianilos, P.N.: The Bayesian Image Retrieval System, PicHunter: Theory, Implementation, and Psychophysical Experiments. IEEE Transactions on Image Processing, Vol. 9 (2000) 20-37
9. 10.Carson, C., Belongie, S., Greenspan, H., Malik, J.: Region-Based Image Querying. In: Proceedings of the IEEE Workshop on Content-Based Access of Image and Video Libraries (CVPR' 97) (1997) 42-49
10. 11.Tian, Q., Sebe, N., Lew, M.S., Loupias, E., Huang, T.S.: Image Retrieval Using Wavelet-Based Salient Points. Journal of Electronic Imaging, Vol. 10 (2001) 835-849
11. 12.Cinque., L., De Rosa, F., Lecca, F., Levialdi, S.: Image Retrieval Using Resegmentation Driven by Query Rectangles. Image and Vision Computing, Vol. 22 (2004) 15-22
12. 13.Santini, S., Gupta, A., Jain, R.: Emergent Semantics through Interaction in Image Databases. Knowledge and Data Engineering, Vol. 13 (2001) 337-351
13. 14. Sheikholeslami, G., Chang, W., Zhang, A.: SemQuery: Semantic Clustering and Querying on Heterogeneous Features for Visual Data. IEEE Transactions on Knowledge and Data Engineering, Vol. 14 (2002) 988-1002
14. 15.Greenspan, H., Dvir., G., Rubner, Y.: Context-Dependent Segmentation and Matching in Image Database. Computer Vision and Image understanding, Vol. 93, (2004) 86-109
15. 16.Ko, B.Y., Peng, J., Byun, H.: Regions-based Image Retrieval Using Probabilistic Feature Relevance Learning. Pattern Analysis & Applications, Vol. 4 (2001) 174-184

Fast Structuring of Large Television Streams Using Program Guides

Xavier Naturel, Guillaume Gravier, and Patrick Gros

IRISA - INRIA Rennes
Campus Universitaire de Beaulieu
35042 Rennes, France

Abstract. An original task of structuring and labeling large television streams is tackled in this paper. Emphasis is put on simple and efficient methods to detect precise boundaries of programs. These programs are further analysed and labeled with information coming from a standard television program guide using an improved Dynamic Time Warping algorithm (DTW) and a manually labeled reference video dataset. It is shown that the labeling process yields a very high accuracy and opens the way to many applications. We eventually indicate how the dependency to a manually labeled video dataset can be removed by providing an algorithm for a dynamic update of the reference video dataset.

1   Introduction

Television is designed to be watched live. Accessing archived television streams is problematic because no metadata describing the structure of the stream exists. It is therefore difficult to extract information from unlabeled TV archives. Television program guides provide the kind of interesting information for retrieving programs (title, genre, date, abstract) but they are far from accurate. Schedules are not respected, some programs are missing while some are inserted, and of course commercials are not indicated. Program guides still carry important information that would be very difficult to extract from the stream, like program title, genre and an approximate time of broadcast.

Our goal is to synchronize the video stream with the program guide, removing errors and adding information when posible, thus building a more accurate post-diffusion program guide which enables easy browsing and retrieval from large television archives.

This can perhaps be seen as a trivial problem, since such a synchronization could be easily done by channels, such as in the European Standard PDC [1]. However, this system cannot be used for archives, and even for live streams it is not satisfactory. Most channels are reluctant to use such a system because of its commercial skip capability, and even for the channels that use it, not every program has a PDC signal. Finally, audiovisual regulation authorities[1] cannot

---

[1] Such as the CSA (Conseil Supérieur de l'Audiovisuel) in France, which monitors the number and duration of commercial breaks, subjected to legal regulations.

S. Marchand-Maillet et al. (Eds.): AMR 2006, LNCS 4398, pp. 222–231, 2007.

rely on a channel-provided signal if they are to monitor the stream to detect frauds.

The method is divided into two parts: segmentation and labeling. Section 2 first gives a short overview of the method. Section 3 explains the segmentation process and shows that a combination of standard methods and detection of duplicates leads to an effective segmentation of large television streams into programs. Section 4 is dedicated to the assignement of labels coming from the program guide to the stream segments. In section 4.3 labeling results on three days of TV show that the method can handle large amounts of video. A final section acknowledges the need for a dynamic update of the reference video dataset and proposes an algorithm to solve this problem.

2   Overview of the Method

The general flow of the method is given in Figure 1. The first step is to segment the stream to find boundaries of programs. This gives a segmentation into programs/non-programs. A first labeling is then done using duplicate detection, i.e. detecting segments that have already been broadcasted and which have been then labeled and stored in a database (see section 3.2). This labeling is very precise since it is done at the shot level, but it labels only a very small part of the stream, mainly non-program segments. The most important part of the algorithm is the LDTW (Landmarked Dynamic Time warping) algorithm which finds the best alignment between the automatic segmentation and the EPG (Electronic Program Guide) segmentation, while taking into account labels given by duplicate detection.

The post-processing step is present to resolve ambiguity between possibly different labeling (coming from LDTW and duplicate detection).

3   Stream Segmentation into Programs

A lot of work has been devoted to find commercials in a video stream. One of the most used and effective technic is to take advantage of the rule that black frames are inserted between commercials [2,3]. While true for most of the channels and countries this method leads to a very high rate of false alarms and must be used together with another feature to provide acceptable results. Sadlier et al. [3] used silence detection, and popular features are shot frequency, motion activity [2], or text presence [4]. Another efficient method is to recognize previously known commercials [2,5]. However the drawback of the constant need to update the database of commercials used for recognition is not addressed.

Detecting program boundaries is however not equivalent to detecting commercials. Most previous works have regrettably been elusive about what is included in the term commercial, and few methods are tested over large and heterogeneous datasets. Some recent publications have not these limitations however [6,7]. In this paper, non-program segments are defined as segments that can be composed

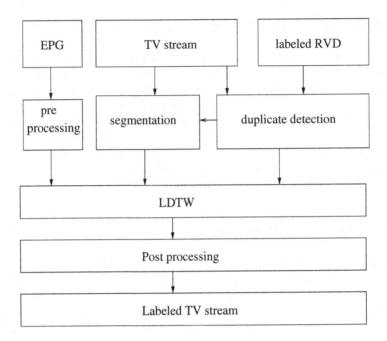

Fig. 1. Overview of the algorithm for labeling TV streams

of commercials, trailers/teasers, sponsorship or channel jingles. As its name indicates, a non-program segment is everything which is not a regular program, i.e. news, talk-show, soap opera, weather broadcast...

The proposed method for segmenting a TV stream uses two kind of independant information. The first is the classical monochromatic frame and silence indicator, explained in section 3.1. The second kind of information comes from a duplicate detection process. Non-programs are recognize as such because they have already been broadcasted and are present in a labeled reference video dataset. section 3.2 explains the process.

3.1   First Step: Using Silence and Monochromatic Frames

Silence detection emerged as a very reliable indicator of presence of commercials, at least on French television. Figure 2 shows the log-energy of the audio signals over a 1-hour duration and actually shows that energy is null between two commercials. Considering Figure 2, a simple thresholding of the log energy achieves almost flawless results. Note that the threshold does not change when considering different channels. From the image point of view, commercials are separated by black but also white or blue frames. A simple monochrome frame detector is constructed using the entropy of the luminance histogram. It unfortunately produces a very high rate of false alarms (see Table 1) since monochrome frames may appear anywhere in the stream, not only at commercials boundaries.

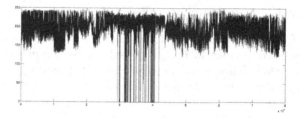

Fig. 2. Log-energy of the audio signal on a 1-hour television stream

Combining results from multiple media is usually not straightforward. Since the audio feature is far more reliable than the image one, we use a successive analysis approach, by first detecting the silence segments, then performing monochrome image detection in an enlarged window around these silence segments. The main problem is that while this method works quite well for detecting commercial breaks, it is not suited to detect others non-program segments because these are not flagged by monochrome frames and silence.

Table 1. Commercial break detection on a three hours videoset

Modality	Precision	Recall
Audio	82	90
Image	41	89
Fusion	100	90

3.2 Second Step: Improving Segmentation with Detection of Duplicates

An effective way to detect non-program segments is to look for duplicate sequences. By duplicate we mean that the content is the same, minus transmission noise and very small edition effect (modifications due to progressive transitions or small insertions). Because non-program segments are very repetitive, duplicate detections really helps to segment the stream into program/non-program segments. It is proposed in [8] to compute on each image a signature which is the concatenation of binarized low-frequency DCT coefficients. This signature is sufficiently robust to noise to be queried by exact matching, thus allowing the use of a fast retrieval structure like a hash table. The retrieved shots are further analyzed by computing a similarity function defined as the average Hamming distance between the signatures of the retrieved and query shots. More details can be found in [8].

In order for this method to be interesting, it has to have a (manually) labeled Reference Video Dataset (RVD). The RVD is a set of labeled shots. A detection of a duplicate between the query and the RVD thus results in labeling the query shot by the label of the found shot. For all our tests, 24 hours of continuous TV were labeled, indicating program names and distinguishing non-programs segments between commercials, trailers, sponsorship or other.

3.3 Information Fusion and Results

The results of the detection of duplicates and the monochromatic/silence detector are expressed as a set of images considered as non-program. Let X_1 be the set of images for silence/monochromatic detection and X_2 the set for duplicate detection, with S the entire set of images from the input stream. A pre-segmentation is then computed by $Y = S \setminus (X_1 \cup X_2)$. The resulting set Y can be seen as a set of segments, which are then classified according to their length, a small segment being a non-program segment while a large one is considered as a program segment. The threshold is set to 60 seconds. Despite this very crude definition of a program segment, results given in Table 2 are satisfactory. This table shows the results using only silence and monochromatic frames (Method 3.1) and the method using both silence/monochromatic and duplicate detection (Method 3.3).

Table 2. Program/non-program detection on three days of TV

Method	Program		Non-program	
	Precision	Recall	Precision	Recall
Method 3.1	97.9	99.7	97.2	82.8
Method 3.3	99.5	99.8	98	95.8

4 Automatic Labeling

As a pre-processing step, the EPG can be modified to become more realistic. Domain knowledge about the channel can be included in this pre-processing step. However only one simple rule is used here. It simply states that long programs (more than 1h30) should be cut into at least two parts (because they will usually be cut by commercials).

The next step is to match the stream segmentation with the program guide. A well-known method for aligning two sequences is the dynamic time warping algorithm (DTW) [9]. The DTW between 2 sequences X and Y is the minimum weight for transforming X into Y by a set of weighted edit operations. These operations are most of the time defined as substitution, insertion and deletion. The path used to reach this minimum weight provides the best alignment between X and Y, with respect to the edit operations. DTW can be efficiently computed by dynamic programming.

Given a segmentation of the stream $X_i = \{x_0 \ldots x_i\}$ and the associated program guide $P_j = \{p_0 \ldots p_j\}$ the DTW is given by:

$$D(X_i, P_j) = Min \begin{cases} D(X_{i-1}, P_{j-1}) + C_{sub}(x_i, p_j) \\ D(X_i, P_{j-1}) + C_{del}(p_j, i) \\ D(X_{i-1}, P_j) + C_{ins}(x_i, j) \end{cases}$$

Each element of X and P are a couple of values indicating the start and end of the program $x_i = (x_i^s, x_i^e)$. $C_{sub}, C_{del}, C_{ins}$ are respectively the costs of substitution, deletion and insertion and are application dependant. A classical definition is:

$$C_{sub}(x_i, p_j) = \gamma d(x_i, p_j)$$
$$C_{del}(p_j, i) = d(x_i, p_j)$$
$$C_{ins}(x_i, j) = d(x_i, p_j)$$

$1 < \gamma < 2$ to favor a substitution over a deletion+insertion; $d(x_i, p_j)$ is the local distance between the vectors coordinates of X_i and P_i and is defined as:

$$d(x_i, p_j) = \alpha |p_j^e - p_j^s - (x_i^e - x_i^s)| + \beta \left[|p_j^s - x_i^s| + |p_j^e - x_i^e| \right]$$

This local distance is designed so as to measure the similarity of length of x_i and p_j (first part, weighted by α) as well as the closeness of their broadcast time (second part, weighted by β). It has been experimentally observed that the two terms contribute in a somewhat equivalent way to the alignement, so that we have in fact $\alpha = \beta = 1$.

The DTW with this local distance is robust but it is unfortunately not error-free (see Table 4.3). Two improvements are proposed in the next sections.

4.1   Adding Landmarks in the DTW

In building the alignment method, we overlooked an important source of information: the labels attached to some program segments. These labels come from the detection of duplicates of section 3.2. While programs rarely get repeated entirely, lead-in, lead-out or special sequences specific to a program are frequently repeated. Suppose that such a detection is found in the middle of an unlabeled program segment x_i (prior to DTW). Attached to this detection is a label, indicating its type and title. If this title is found nearby in the EPG, yielding a program p_j, then one would like to force the DTW to go through the landmark (i, j).

The idea is to prune all paths that do not go through (i, j) by filling the cost matrix before computing any costs with:

$$\begin{cases} d(x_i, p_j) = 0 \\ d(x_l, p_k) = \infty \end{cases}$$

$\forall (k, l)$ such as $(k < j\ ,\ l > i)$ et $(k > j\ ,\ l < i)$.

Figure 3 shows this method for landmark (i, j). The same process is applied for every duplicate that match with an EPG label. The cost matrix is then computed by the (almost) standard DTW algorithm. This modified algorithm is called Landmarked DTW (LDTW).

4.2   Choosing Best Labels

The last improvement we introduce is a post-processing method, which therefore takes place after the DTW. The problem is the following. If duplicates have been

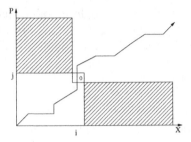

Fig. 3. Forcing local alignement in the DTW cost matrix

detected inside a program segment, it may happen that the duplicates have a different label from the one attached to the segment by the DTW. This problem arises especially when information is lacking in the EPG. Consequently the label given to the segment by the DTW cannot be right.

Two hypothesis are defined: H_0, the correct label comes from the detection of duplicates; H_1, the correct label comes from DTW. Given an observation O, the decision is made via a Bayesian hypothesis test:

$$\frac{P(O|H_1)}{P(O|H_0)} > \frac{P_0}{P_1} \text{ then } H_1 \text{ else } H_0$$

where P_i is the prior probability of hypothesis H_i. To estimate $P(O|H_i)$, the observation O is considered to be made of elementary independant observations o_k. These are then easy to estimate using a training corpus. We have:

$$P(O|H_i) = \prod_k p(o_k|H_i)$$

Three elementary observations are defined. o_1 is the length of the segment, and is considered to be gaussian. o_2 and o_3 are binary observations, which are true when a duplicate exists respectively at the beginning and at the end of the program segment. o_2 and o_3 are defined to take into account that program lead-in and lead-out are often well detected and are more likely to yield the correct label than the DTW.

4.3   Results

Evaluation of the correct labeling of program segments is not straightforward. To have a clear view of the performance of the labeling process two statistics are given in table 3: correct labeling on a frame-by-frame basis (*Image*), and correct labeling on a program basis (*Program*). The former takes into account the precision of the segmentation while the latter reflect only the quality of labeling. All methods include the pre-processing step. Only LDTW2 includes the post-processing step. As a reference, the scores obtained by the EPG are also given. Since there is no miss in the EPG, only false labeling, the recall score is always 100%.

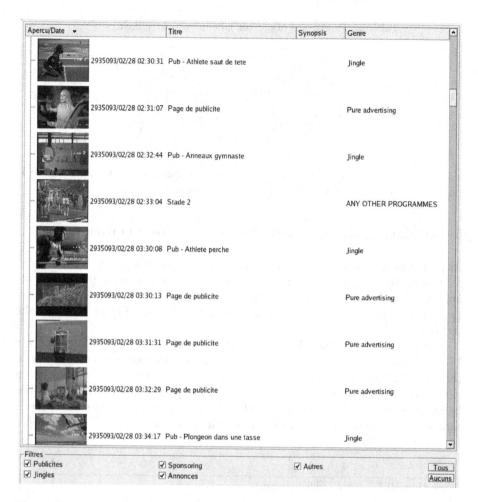

Fig. 4. Example of TV stream labeling. Program labels, e.g. 'Stade2' on this figure, usually comes from the EPG while labels for commercials, trailers and sponsorship comes from the database.

The difference between the *image* and *program* score may be surprising. It is explained by the fact that a lot of small programs are wrongly labeled. This does not really impact the *image* score, while it dramatically affects the *program* one. Most of these errors are due to a lack of information: labels are available neither from the program guide nor from the labels of the detection of duplicates. Future works include the possibility of using text detection to retrieve the correct program label directly from the stream. Figure 4 shows an exemple of labeling on 1 hour of french television.

The labeling process only takes a few seconds once the features have been computed. The feature extraction, which includes shot segmentation, silence/

Table 3. Percentage of correct labeling on three days of TV

	Image		Program	
	Precision	Recall	Precision	Recall
EPG	77.3	100	48.4	100
DTW	88	99.9	55.6	83.5
LDTW	91.6	99.9	62.1	84.9
LDTW2	92.8	99.9	78.7	88.1

monochrome frame detection and detection of duplicates, is very fast since it runs at a frame rate of 115 frames/s on a standard 3Ghz PC.

5   Updating the Labeled Reference Video Dataset

As stated in the introduction, the major drawback of using a manually labeled reference video dataset is the need to update it as new non-program segments appear. This problem can be overcome by iterating successively duplicate detection and the proposed segmentation/labeling process. Figure 5 details the procedure.

The idea is to feed the RVD with new non-program segments found by the LDTW algorithm. The updated RVD is then used to improve the accuracy of the initial segmentation which in turn might affect the labeling. This algorithm is thus used both to update the RVD and to improve the accuracy of the labeling process by using a recently updated RVD. The convergence condition is satisfied when no new labels are found, i.e. the labeling is stable. This algorithm is currently under test.

```
Function(RVD, query : video stream)
do
list_duplicates = find_duplicates(RVD,query);
update_segmentation(list_duplicates, segmentation);
Labeling = LDTW(list_duplicates, segmentation);
update_RVD(RVD, Labeling);
until (convergence)
```

Fig. 5. RVD update algorithm

6   Conclusion

A complete method for indexing large TV streams has been presented. It builds on traditionnal commercial detection technics a more elaborate process which yields much more precise and useful information, paving the way for exact and enriched EPG. Simple and efficient methods leads to a very fast process, more than 4 times faster than real-time, and is shown to be effective on three days of digital TV. Applications are numerous, from TV archives management to intelligent digital VCR and TV monitoring. Future works include improving the dynamic update of the reference video dataset and extensive testing on three weeks of TV.

References

1. EBU: Ets 300 231, television systems; specification of the domestic video programme delivery control system (pdc) (1993)
2. Lienhart, R., Kuhmunch, C., Effelsberg, W.: On the detection and recognition of television commercials. In: International Conference on Multimedia Computing and Systems. (1997) 509–516
3. Sadlier, D., Marlow, S., OConnor, N., Murphy, N.: Automatic tv advertisement detection from mpeg bitstream. Journal of the Patt. Rec. Society **35** (2002) 2–15
4. McGee, T., Dimitrova, N.: Parsing tv program structures for identification and removal of non-story segments. In: in SPIE Conf. on Storage and Retrieval for Image and Video Databases. (1999)
5. Duygulu, P., yu Chen, M., Hauptmann, A.: Comparison and combination of two novel commercial detection methods. ICME (2004)
6. Covell, M., Baluja, S., Fink, M.: Advertisement detection and replacement using acoustic and visual repetition. In: MMSP'06, IEEE 8th workshop on Multimedia Signal Procesing. (2006)
7. Liang, L., Lu, H., Xue, X., Tan, Y.P.: Program segmentation for tv videos. In: ISCAS, IEEE International Symposium on Circuits and Systems. Volume 2. (2005) 1549–1552
8. Naturel, X., Gros, P.: A fast shot matching strategy for detecting duplicate sequences in a television stream. In: CVDB'05, Baltimore (2005)
9. Sakoe, H., Chiba, S.: Dynamic programming algorithm optimization for spoken word recognition. IEEE Transactions on Acoustics, Speech and Signal Processing **26** (1978) 43–49

Variation of Relevance Assessments for Medical Image Retrieval

Henning Müller[1], Paul Clough[2], Bill Hersh[3], and Antoine Geissbühler[1]

[1] University and Hospitals of Geneva, Medical Informatics, Geneva, Switzerland
henning.mueller@sim.hcuge.ch
[2] Department of Information Studies, Sheffield University, Sheffield, UK
p.d.clough@sheffield.ac.uk
[3] Biomedical Informatics, Oregon Health and Science University, Portland, OR, USA
hersh@ohsu.edu

Abstract. Evaluation is crucial for the success of most research domains, and image retrieval is no exception to this. Recently, several benchmarks have been developed for visual information retrieval such as TRECVID, ImageCLEF, and ImagEval to create frameworks for evaluating image retrieval research. An important part of evaluation is the creation of a ground truth or gold standard to evaluate systems against. Much experience has been gained on creating ground truths for textual information retrieval, but for image retrieval these issues require further research. This article will present the process of generating relevance judgements for the medical image retrieval task of ImageCLEF. Many of the problems encountered can be generalised to other image retrieval tasks as well, so the outcome is not limited to the medical domain. Part of the images analysed for relevance were judged by two assessors, and these are analysed with respect to their consistency and potential problems. Our goal is to obtain more information on the ambiguity of the topics developed and generally to keep the variation amongst relevance assessors low. This might partially reduce the subjectivity of system-oriented evaluation, although the evaluation shows that the differences in relevance judgements only have a limited influence on comparative system ranking. A number of outcomes are presented with a goal in mind to create less ambiguous topics for future evaluation campaigns.

1 Introduction

Visual information retrieval has been an extremely active research domain for more than 20 years [1]. It includes several diverse research areas such as information retrieval, computer vision, image analysis, and pattern recognition. Despite the enormous research effort spent on analysing and retrieving images, still many questions remain and visual retrieval has still not become part of consumer or industrial applications in the same way that text retrieval has. Of all similar research domains, text retrieval is probably the one with the most realistic benchmarks and evaluation scenarios. Since the 1960s, standardised testing and comparisons between research systems and methods has been common [2], and

S. Marchand-Maillet et al. (Eds.): AMR 2006, LNCS 4398, pp. 232–246, 2007.

TREC[1] (TExt Retrieval Conference) has become the standard 'model' for large–scale evaluation of different aspects of information access [3]. Besides running several benchmarks in an annual cycle of data release, topic release, submissions, ground truthing, evaluation and workshop, TREC has also managed to analyse many TREC submissions from participating systems. In addition, analysis of the relevance judgements (or ground truth) have been undertaken by researchers to obtain a better idea of the statistical properties required to accurately and reliably compare systems [4]. Subjectivity in judgements was shown to exist but also to have only a very limited influence on comparative system rankings.

In image retrieval evaluation was neglected for a long time, although a few proposals and initiatives did exist [5,6,7], such as the Benchathlon[2]. Over the past few years, several visual information retrieval benchmarks have shown that a strong need exists to evaluate visual information retrieval in a standardised manner. TRECVID, for example started as a task in TREC but has since become an independent workshop on the evaluation of video retrieval systems [8]. The strong participation has also made this benchmark important for image retrieval where evaluation can be performed on extracted video key frames. Another initiative is ImagEval[3], financed by the French research foundation and with participants mainly from the French research community. INEX[4] (INiative for the Evaluation of XML retrieval) has also started a multimedia retrieval task in 2006. A fourth benchmarking event is ImageCLEF [9,10]. This event is part of the Cross–Language Evaluation Forum (CLEF) campaign to evaluate and compare multilingual information retrieval systems [11]. ImageCLEF concentrates on the retrieval of images from multilingual repositories and combining both visual and textual features for multimodal retrieval. A strong participation in ImageCLEF over the past two years has shown the need for standardised system comparison and the importance of creating an infrastructure to support the comparisons in this way. This can dramatically reduce the effort required by researchers to compare their approaches: able to concentrate on developing novel methods rather than issues associated with evaluation.

This article will first present an overview of ImageCLEF, its collections, topics, participants, and results. Following this, a closer look at the relevance judgements is undertaken, and in particular at the judgements for the topics assessed by two judges. The conclusions summarise our findings and provide ideas for future development of information needs (or topics).

2   ImageCLEFmed 2005

This section describes the main components of the medical ImageCLEF benchmark in 2005: ImageCLEFmed.

---

[1] http://trec.nist.gov/

[2] http://www.benchathlon.net/

[3] http://www.imageval.org/

[4] http://inex.is.informatik.uni-duisburg.de/2006/

2.1   Collections Used

A total of four collections were used for ImageCLEFmed 2005, all with separate annotations in a wide variety of XML formats containing a large variety of images. The Casimage[5] dataset [12] contains almost 9'000 images (all modalities, photographs, illustrations, etc.) of 2'000 cases with annotations mainly in French, but also in part in English. Each case can contain one to several different images of the same patient (or condition). The PEIR[6] (Pathology Education Instructional Resource) database uses annotations based on the HEAL[7] project (Health Education Assets Library, mainly Pathology images [13]). This dataset contains over 33'000 images (extremely varied but a majority of pathology images) with English annotations. Each image has an associated annotation rather than per case as in the Casimage collection. The nuclear medicine database of MIR, the Mallinkrodt Institute of Radiology[8] [14], was also made available to us. This dataset contains over 2'000 images mainly from nuclear medicine with annotations in English per case. Finally, the PathoPic[9] collection (Pathology microscopic images [15]) was part of our benchmark's dataset. It contains 9'000 images, each with extensive annotations in German (and parts translated into English).

This provided a heterogeneous database of more than 50'000 images in total, with annotations in three different languages (although the majority in English). Through an agreement with the copyright holders, we were able to distribute these images to participating research groups of ImageCLEF free of charge. Challenges of the data with respect to text include: different structures and formats, incomplete or partial annotations with a large number of empty cases, domain-specific (i.e. medical) vocabulary and images, unusual abbreviations and spelling errors. Even with a consistent XML structure, not all fields were filled in correctly with many of the fields containing free–text. Visual challenges include the large variety of data sources and sorts of images used and a considerable variation of images of the same modality or anatomic region as the images were taken and processed by a large number of different programs and machines. Image size and quality vary also strongly. Another challenge is of course the combination of visual and textual data as input for a query.

2.2   Topics

The image topics were based on a small survey administered to clinicians, researchers, educators, students, and librarians at Oregon Health & Science University (OHSU)[16]. Based on this survey, topics for ImageCLEFmed were developed along one or more of the following axes:

- Anatomic region shown in the image;
- Image modality (x–ray, CT, MRI, gross pathology, ...);

---

[5] http://www.casimage.com/
[6] http://peir.path.uab.edu/
[7] http://www.healcentral.com/
[8] http://gamma.wustl.edu/home.html
[9] http://alf3.urz.unibas.ch/pathopic/intro.htm

- Pathology or disease shown in the image;
- abnormal visual observation (eg. enlarged heart).

The goal of topic development was also to create a mix of topics to test different aspects of visual and textual retrieval. To this end, three topic groups were created: visual topics, mixed topics and purely semantic topics. The grouping of topics into these categories was performed manually based upon the assumption that visual topics would perform well with visual–only retrieval, mixed topics would require semantic text analysis together with visual information, and the semantic topics were expected not to profit at all from visual analysis of the images. The topics were generated by the ImageCLEF organisers and not by the relevance judges. A total of 25 topics (11 visual, 11 mixed and 3 semantic) were distributed to the participants. All topics were in three languages: English, French, German. Each topic was accompanied by one to three example images of the concept and one topic also contained a negative example image. In this context topics means a specific information need of a possible user that is described by multimodal means. It was verified through tests with a visual and a textual retrieval system that all topics had at least three relevant images.

2.3 Participants Submissions

In 2004 the medical retrieval task was entirely visual and 12 participating groups submitted results. In 2005, as a mixture of visual and non-visual retrieval, 13 groups submitted results. This was far less than the number of registered participants (28). We send a mail to all registered groups that did not submit results to ask for their reasons. Their non–submission was partly due to the short time span between delivery of the images and the deadline for submitting results. Another reason was that several groups registered very late, as they did not have information about ImageCLEF beforehand. They were mainly interested in the datasets and future participation in ImageCLEF. All groups that did not submit results said that the datasets and topics were a valuable resource for their research. In total, 134 ranked lists from different systems (runs) were submitted from the twelve research groups, among them 128 automatic runs that had no manual adaptation or feedback and only very few (6) manual runs that could include relevance feedback, query reformulation, or manual optimisations of feature weights based on the collection.

2.4 Pooling and Constraints for the Judgement Process

Relevance assessments were performed by graduate students who were also physicians in the OHSU biomedical informatics program. A simple interface was used from previous ImageCLEF relevance assessments. Nine judges, eight medical doctors and one image processing specialist with medical knowledge, performed the relevance judgements. Half of the images for most topics were judged in duplicate to enable the analysis of assessor–subjectivity in the judgement process.

In large collections, it is impossible to judge all documents to establish their relevance to an information need or search topic. Therefore, a method called pooling where assessors judge "pools" of documents rather than all documents in a collection [17]. In our case the unity for judgement was the image and not the case, also to make the task harder for pure text retrieval. To obtain these pools the first 40 images from the top of each submitted run were collected and used to create pools resulting in an average pool size of 892 images. The largest pool size was 1'167 and the smallest 470. We aimed to have less than 1'000 images to judge per topic to reduce effort. Even so, it was estimated to take on average three hours to judge all images in a pool for a single topic. Compared to the purely visual topics from 2004 (around one hour of judgement per topic with each pool containing an average of 950 images), the judgement process was found to take almost three times as long. This is likely due to the use of "semantic" topics requiring the judges to view the associated annotations to verify relevance, and/or the judges needing to view an enlarged version of the image. The longer assessment time may have also been due to the fact that in 2004 all images were pre–marked as irrelevant, and only relevant images required a change. In 2005, we did not have images pre–marked. Still, this process was generally faster than the time required to judge documents in previous text retrieval [18], and irrelevant images could be established very quickly. In text retrieval, however, checking documents for irrelevance takes longer and requires more cognitive effort.

2.5   Outcome of the Evaluation

The results of the benchmark showed a few clear trends. Very few groups submitted runs involving manual relevance feedback, most likely due to the requirement of more resources to do this. Still, relevance feedback has shown to be extremely useful in many retrieval tasks and its evaluation is extremely important. The ImageCLEF interactive retrieval task suffered from similar problems with a small number of participants. Surprisingly, in the submitted runs relevance feedback did not appear to offer much improvement compared to the automatic runs. In the 2004 tasks, runs with relevance feedback were often significantly better than without feedback.

The results also showed that purely textual systems (best run: Mean Average Precision (MAP)=0.2084) had better overall performance than purely visual systems (best run: MAP=0.1455). For the visual topics, the visual and textual or mixed systems gave comparable performance. By far the best results were obtained when combining visual and textual features (MAP=0.2821) [19]. The best system actually separated the topics into their main axes (anatomy, modality, pathology) and performed a query along these axes with the supplied negative feedback concepts (if an MRI is searched for, all other modalities can be fed back negatively).

3 Analysis of the Relevance Judgements and Their Variations

This section analyses our relevance judgement process of 2005 with the goal to find clues for reducing the subjectivity among relevance judges in future tasks.

3.1 The Relevance Judgement Process

In 2005, we used the same relevance judgement tool as in 2004. We used a ternary judgement scheme that allows assessors to mark images as relevant, partially relevant and non–relevant. The judges received a detailed explanation on the judgement process including the fact that partially relevant was only to be used if it cannot be outruled that the image might correspond to the concept. If only a part of the concept was fulfilled (i.e. an x–ray with emphysema when the search was for a CT with emphysema) the image had to be regarded as non–relevant. Judges had the possibility to read the text that came with the images and they also had the possibility to enlarge the images on screen to see more detail. This relevance definition is somewhat different from the relevance definition used in TREC, where a document is regarded as relevant even if only a small part of it is relevant. Much more on relevance can be found in [20,21]. The judges were given a description of relevance but no explicit description with respect to where the limits of relevance were. They could ask questions when they were unsure, which happened several times.

As the judgement tool (see Figure 1) was web–based, the judges were able to perform relevance judgements at will. In total, three weeks were foreseen for the judgement process and topics were distributed among the 8 judges, with each person responsible for three topics (and one person doing four). The image processing judge did a single topic, only. No time constraint was given on judging topics or that they had to finish judgements for one topic in one go. This was to allow for breaks in between finishing topics. Participating judges told us that a judgement took an average of three hours, but no further details were asked about the process. This is slightly more than in 2004, where visual topics took an average of one hour per topic with a slightly larger number of images per topic. After the single judgements were finished we asked judges to judge the first half of the images of three more topics. Some judges did not have the time for the double judgements and so only part of the topics are double–judged. Only the first topic was entirely judged by two judges. For the other topics the first half of the images was double–judged to have a maximum of relevant images double–judged. Indeed, as the images to be judged were ordered by the numbers of runs that they were included in, the first half contains many more relevant images than the second have resulting in most relevant images being judged twice in this process.

The images were shown on screen starting with those images that most runs had in their 1'000 submitted results. The goal of this was to have a concentration of relevant documents at the beginning when the judge is (hopefully) more

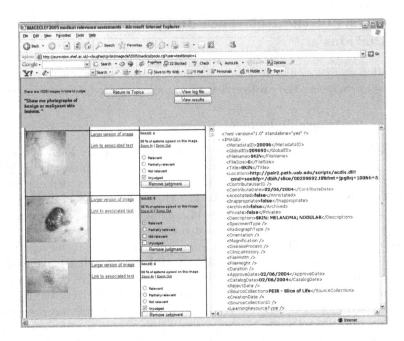

Fig. 1. A screen shot of the tool for acquiring the relevance judgements

attentive and less likely to be suffering from fatigue. However, this could lead to later images being judged less carefully as there are less relevant items.

3.2 Selection of Judges and Problems Encountered

One important point of a domain-specific benchmark is that the judges need to have a sufficient knowledge of the domain to judge topics correctly. On the other hand, this also limits the depth of the topics that can be constructed even if the judges are knowledgeable. We choose students from the OHSU graduate student program in medical informatics. All of the eight chosen students are also physicians and can thus be regarded as domain experts for the medical topics constructed in a rather general medical context. No knowledge on specific diseases was necessary as the text of the images was regarded as sufficient.

Several problems were encountered in the process. One of the problems was with respect to the relevance judgement tool itself. As it showed all images on a single screen it took fairly long to build the page in the browser (containing around 1'000 images). Another problem was that the tool required to specifically modify the settings of the browser to enable JavaScript and disable all caching so the changes were stored directly in the database. As many different browsers under Linux, Mac OS X and Windows were used, some problems with browsers occurred that lead to a loss of some judgements that afterwards had to be repeated. Unfortunately, browser-based environments still seem to suffer from differences from one environment to another.

Table 1. Differences encountered in the topics judged twice

Topic	#	same	different	+/+	0/0	-/-	+/0	-/0	+/-
1	1018	916	102 (10.02%)	193	3	720	19	50	33
2	440	372	68 (15.45%)	49	8	315	30	23	15
3	441	361	80 (18.14%)	75	1	285	8	41	31
4	383	356	27 (7.05%)	59	8	289	9	16	2
8	491	471	20 (4.07%)	14	1	456	14	5	1
9	550	517	33 (6.00%)	79	33	405	23	10	0
10	235	226	9 (3.83%)	6	0	220	1	0	8
11	492	487	5 (1.02%)	23	0	464	1	2	2
12	326	281	45 (13.80%)	10	2	269	5	22	18
13	484	338	146 (30.17%)	214	7	117	49	34	63
14	567	529	38 (6.70%)	51	0	478	22	1	15
15	445	438	7 (1.57%)	29	0	409	3	0	4
16	467	460	7 (1.50%)	1	0	459	0	1	6
17	298	224	74 (24.83%)	15	2	207	11	27	36
18	403	394	9 (2.23%)	1	0	393	0	7	2
19	441	439	2 (0.45%)	11	0	428	0	1	1
20	608	314	294 (48.35%)	1	11	392	236	26	22
21	401	276	125 (31.17%)	131	4	141	30	48	47
22	448	395	53 (11.83%)	36	3	356	11	24	18
23	472	454	18 (3.81%)	24	0	430	1	3	14
total	9'410	8'238	1'072 (11.39%)	1'212 (12.87%)	83 (0.88%)	7'233 (76.87%)	473 (5.03)	341 (3.62%)	338 (3.60%)

Sometimes, the short text available with images made it hard to judge semantic topics that required assessors to also read the annotation text. For these topics, where the user was not sure about the results and could not decide based on the image itself, we recommended selecting a partially relevant judgement.

Most of the comments and questions received from judges during the assessment process were with respect to the partially relevant relevance level. Generally, relevance and non-relevance could be determined fairly quickly, whereas they contacted us when not sure about the outcome.

3.3 Differences Per Topic

In Table 1 we can see for each topic how many double judgements were available, how many times the judges agreed and disagreed and then, how many times what kind of difference between the judges occurred. The three different section in the table are for visual topics, mixed topics and semantic topics. As notation we have + for a relevant judgement, *0* for a partially relevant judgement and − for a non–relevant judgement. Combinations such as −/+ mean that one judge judged the image relevant and another one non–relevant.

It can be seen that, fortunately, the agreement between the judges is fairly high. In our case the judges agree in 88.61% of their judgements. A more common measure for inter–judge agreement is the Kappa score. In our case the Kappa

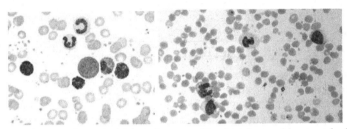

Show me microscopic pathologies of cases with chronic myelogenous leukemia.
Zeige mir mikroskopische Pathologiebilder von chronischer Leukämie (Chronic
myelogenous leukemia, CML).
Montre-moi des images de la leucémie chronique myélogène.

Fig. 2. Topic 20, where the judges disagreed the most strongly

score using three categories is 0.679, which indicates a good agreement and is
for example much higher than in the similar Genomics TREC [18] where it is
usually around 0.5.

It becomes clear that there is a difference with respect to which categories
were judged differently, when limiting ourself to only the images and topics
judged twice. From 15145 negative judgements, only 4.48% are in disagreement.
From the 3235 positive judgements, already 25.07% are in disagreement and the
worst are the partially relevant judgements, where 814 of 980 (83.06%) are not
in agreement.

When looking at topic groups (visual, mixed, semantic) it is clearly visible
that we cannot judge the semantic topics as only a single topic was judged
twice, which is statistically insufficient. The mixed topics on the other hand
have a much higher average disagreement than the visual topics. The four topics
with the highest disagreement among judges are from this category although a
few mixed topics with high agreement do exist. For topic 20, the disagreement
among relevant items is actually next to 0%, meaning that these topics will need
to be avoided in the future or additional instructions for the judges are required.

The various forms of disagreement (relevant/non–relevant, partially/relevant,
partially/non–relevant) occur in similar quantities, and underline the fact that
determining irrelevance is easy, relevance is harder, and with the partially relevant items much disagreement exists.

Another tendency that can be seen is that most topics with a very high
disagreement have a large number of relevant items. Topics with a very small
number of relevant items seem clearer defined and have less ambiguity.

3.4 Ambiguous and Non–ambiguous Topics

After having looked at the table it becomes clear that a per topic analysis needs
to be done as differences are large. Here, the two most agreed upon and the two
least agreed upon topics are discussed.

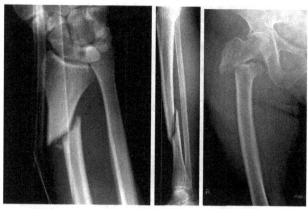

Show me all x–ray images showing fractures.
Zeige mir Röntgenbilder mit Brüchen.
Montres–moi des radiographies avec des fractures.

Fig. 3. Topic 21, where the judges disagreed the second most strongly

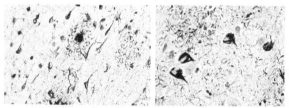

Show me microscopic pathologies of cases with Alzheimers disease.
Zeige mir mikroskopische Pathologiebilder von Fällen der Alzheimer Krankheit.
Montre-moi des images microscopiques de cas avec Alzheimer.

Fig. 4. Topic 19, where the judges agreed the most strongly

Figure 2 shows the topic with the strongest disagreement among judges. It becomes apparent that two of the experts must have interpreted this description in different ways. It is possible that one of the judges marked any case with leukemia whereas another judge marked the same sort of images with no further specification as chronic and myelogenous in the text as partially relevant. These sort of topics can profit from describing not only what is relevant but also clearly what can not be regarded as relevant.

In Figure 3 the topics the second most often disagreed upon is shown. This topic actually seems very surprising as it seems extremely well defined with very clear example images. It is only imaginable that one person actually searched the images for micro fractures or searched the text for the word fracture as well whereas the second judge only took into account very clearly visible fractures. For example, an image can show a healed fracture, when fracture appears in the text but is not anymore visible in the image.

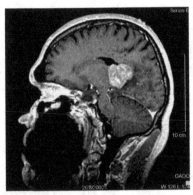

Show me sagittal views of head MRI images.
Zeige mir sagittale Ansichten von MRs des Kopfes.
Montre–moi des vues sagittales dIRMs de la tête.

Fig. 5. Topic 11, where the judges agreed the second most strongly

Figure 4 shows the least ambiguous topic. It is very clear that for this topic it was necessary to read the text and find the word Alzheimer, so no purely visual identification of relevance was possible. This finally lead to a very homogeneous judgement. The number of relevant items is also very small and thus well defined. Looking for such a simple keywords seems well–defined, and excluding non pathology images should also be quick simply by visual identification.

Figure 5 is finally the second least ambiguous topic. Again, it is very well defined as such views (sagittal) only occur on MRI and mixing up CT and MRI seems impossible in this case. The view also leads to a small number of finally relevant images.

Unfortunately, it is not easy to find a few determining factors to identify ambiguous or non-ambiguous topics. Topic creation needs to include several people to review topics and the descriptions to the judges also need to be defined extremely well to limit subjectivity in the judgement process.

3.5   Influence of Varying Judgements on the Results

When looking at the agreement table it is clear that topics with an extreme disagreement exist and we have to inspect this closer to find out whether this agreement can influence the final results. Still, for the official evaluation, only the primary judge was taken into account and all partially relevant were also regarded as relevant. We finally generated several sets of relevance judgements based on all judgements and including the double judgements. For images with a single judgement, only the primary judge was taken into account.

- strict – when the primary judge judges images as relevant, only, the final results is relevant;
- Lenient – when the primary judge says relevant or partially relevant it is relevant (default for system ranking);

- AND strict – when both judges say relevant;
- AND lenient – if both judges say relevant or partially relevant;
- OR strict – if any one judge says relevant;
- OR lenient – if any one judge says relevant or partially relevant;

The evaluations of all runs were repeated and the systems re–ranked. The absolute number of relevant items changes strongly according to this rule. It becomes very quickly clear that the absolute differences in performance occur but that the ranking of systems changes basically not at all. A few systems are ranked several positions lower but only very few systems gain more than two ranks and if they do so, the absolute differences are very small. A per topics analysis on the influence of judgements on performance is currently in preparation and would be too much for this paper.

4   Discussion and Conclusions

It becomes clear very quickly that the relevance judgement process for visual information retrieval evaluation is extremely important. Although many classification or computer vision tasks try to simulate users and automatically create judgements [22], in our opinion such a process needs to include real users. Only for very specific tasks can automatic judgements be generated, e.g. completely classified collections [23].

A few important guidelines need to be taken into account when creating new topics that are to be judged:

- a relevance judgement tool has to be easy to use, based on simple web technologies to work in every browser;
- the judgement tool could include the possibility to query visually or by text to examine also images not covered by the pools;
- the description of topics for judges needs to be as detailed as possible to accurately define the topic; it needs to also include negative examples and a description of what is regarded as partially relevant;
- trying to target a limited number of relevant images for the topics as a large number increases both the subjectivity and also increases the risk that the pool is lacking some relevant images;
- work on realistic topics as judges can more easily relate to these topics and imagine the result that they would expect;
- limit the judgement process to a certain maximum time in a row, describe how pauses should be done to have more stable and reproducible conditions for the judgement process.

Our first step to improve the judgement process is the judgement tool. The goal is to have a tool that only shows a limited number of images on screen and is thus faster to use. Access to an enlarged image and the full text of the images needs to be quick. The possibility to search for visually similar images or to search the database by keywords needs to be possible. This can improve the relevance sets by adding images that have not been in the judgement pools.

A simple change to ease evaluation after the campaign is to have the same number of topics in the three categories visual, mixed and semantic. Our goal for 2006 is to have ten topics of each category to get more of an idea about how this influences the judgement process.

When creating these new topics we have now a larger basis for creating realistic scenarios. Besides two user surveys among medical professionals, the log files of the health on the net[10] HONmedia search engine were developed to create realistic topics. This should make it easier for the judges to have an idea about the desired outcome. At the same time a clearer definition of *relevance* in our context is needed as this has been studied less for images. Along with this, a clearer topic definition for the judges is needed that does not only describe when an image must be judged as relevant, but also gives examples of non–relevant and partially relevant images. Particularly important is the partially relevant level because judges were less sure about this level which has led to lower agreement. This could be improved by a more formal definition of partially relevant. It still seems important for us to have a category for partially relevant as this can help us to identify problematic areas for a particular topic. It is important to verify afterwards that the final system ranking is not significantly influenced by the diversity of the relevance judgements. Several judgement sets for more strict or rather lenient judgements will be created for this. We still have to decide whether we really want to have stronger constraint for the judges such as a limit of one hour for judging to avoid fatigue or even choose the place for the judgements in a lab. This might improve the results but it also bears a risk to limit the motivation of the judges by giving them too many constraints.

Another very simple thing to employ is the reduction of the number of relevant items. We simply need to perform test queries ahead of topic release to make sure that the number of relevant items stays limited. A rough number of a maximum of 100 relevant items seems reasonable. Although this cannot be solved exhaustively ahead of time, some simple constraint can improve the judgement process.

It is becoming clear that evaluation of visual information retrieval system is starting to grow. Standardised evaluation and use of standard datasets is becoming increasingly common and at the main multimedia conferences systems become comparable through these standard datasets such as TRECVID. Still, to better create topics and adapt the entire evaluation process to the needs of visual data, much work is needed. Whereas text retrieval has 30 years of experience, for visual retrieval much work is still needed to better define the concepts of relevance and particularly real application scenarios than can make the techniques usable for real users.

Acknowledgements

Part of this research was supported by the Swiss National Science Foundation with grant 205321-109304/1. We also acknowledge the support of the EU FP6 project SemanticMining (IST NoE 507505).

---

[10] http://www.hon.ch/

References

1. Smeulders, A.W.M., Worring, M., Santini, S., Gupta, A., Jain, R.: Content–based image retrieval at the end of the early years. IEEE Transactions on Pattern Analysis and Machine Intelligence **22 No 12** (2000) 1349–1380
2. Cleverdon, C.W.: Report on the testing and analysis of an investigation into the comparative efficiency of indexing systems. Technical report, Aslib Cranfield Research Project, Cranfield, USA (1962)
3. Voorhees, E.M., Harmann, D.: Overview of the seventh Text REtrieval Conference (TREC–7). In: The Seventh Text Retrieval Conference, Gaithersburg, MD, USA (1998) 1–23
4. Zobel, J.: How reliable are the results of large–scale information retrieval experiments? In Croft, W.B., Moffat, A., van Rijsbergen, C.J., Wilkinson, R., Zobel, J., eds.: Proceedings of the 21st Annual International ACM SIGIR Conference on Research and Development in Information Retrieval, Melbourne, Australia, ACM Press, New York (1998) 307–314
5. Smith, J.R.: Image retrieval evaluation. In: IEEE Workshop on Content–based Access of Image and Video Libraries (CBAIVL'98), Santa Barbara, CA, USA (1998) 112–113
6. Leung, C., Ip, H.: Benchmarking for content–based visual information search. In Laurini, R., ed.: Fourth International Conference on Visual Information Systems (VISUAL'2000). Number 1929 in Lecture Notes in Computer Science, Lyon, France, Springer–Verlag (2000) 442–456
7. Müller, H., Müller, W., Squire, D.M., Marchand-Maillet, S., Pun, T.: Performance evaluation in content–based image retrieval: Overview and proposals. Pattern Recognition Letters **22** (2001) 593–601
8. Smeaton, A.F., Over, P., Kraaij, W.: TRECVID: Evaluating the effectiveness of information retrieval tasks on digital video. In: Proceedings of the international ACM conference on Multimedia 2004 (ACM MM 2004), New York City, NY, USA (2004) 652–655
9. Clough, P., Müller, H., Sanderson, M.: Overview of the CLEF cross–language image retrieval track (ImageCLEF) 2004. In Peters, C., Clough, P.D., Jones, G.J.F., Gonzalo, J., Kluck, M., Magnini, B., eds.: Multilingual Information Access for Text, Speech and Images: Result of the fifth CLEF evaluation campaign. LNCS 3491, Bath, England, Springer–Verlag (2005) 597–613
10. Clough, P., Müller, H., Deselaers, T., Grubinger, M., Lehmann, T.M., Jensen, J., Hersh, W.: The CLEF 2005 cross–language image retrieval track. In: Springer Lecture Notes in Computer Science (LNCS), Vienna, Austria (2006 – to appear)
11. Savoy, J.: Report on CLEF–2001 experiments. In: Report on the CLEF Conference 2001 (Cross Language Evaluation Forum), Darmstadt, Germany, Springer LNCS 2406 (2002) 27–43
12. Müller, H., Rosset, A., Vallée, J.P., Terrier, F., Geissbuhler, A.: A reference data set for the evaluation of medical image retrieval systems. Computerized Medical Imaging and Graphics **28** (2004) 295–305
13. Candler, C.S., Uijtdehaage, S.H., Dennis, S.E.: Introducing HEAL: The health education assets library. Academic Medicine **78** (2003) 249–253
14. Wallis, J.W., Miller, M.M., Miller, T.R., Vreeland, T.H.: An internet–based nuclear medicine teaching file. Journal of Nuclear Medicine **36** (1995) 1520–1527
15. Glatz-Krieger, K., Glatz, D., Gysel, M., Dittler, M., Mihatsch, M.J.: Web-basierte Lernwerkzeuge für die Pathologie – web–based learning tools for pathology. Pathologe **24** (2003) 394–399

16. Hersh, W., Müller, H., Gorman, P., Jensen, J.: Task analysis for evaluating image retrieval systems in the ImageCLEF biomedical image retrieval task. In: Slice of Life conference on Multimedia in Medical Education (SOL 2005), Portland, OR, USA (2005)

17. Sparck Jones, K., van Rijsbergen, C.: Report on the need for and provision of an ideal information retrieval test collection. British Library Research and Development Report 5266, Computer Laboratory, University of Cambridge (1975)

18. Hersh, W., Bhupatiraju, R.T.: Trec genomics track overview. In: Proceedings of the 2003 Text REtrieval Conference (TREC), Gaithersburg, MD, USA (2004)

19. Chevallet, J.P., Lim, J.H., Radhouani, S.: Using ontology dimentsions and negative expansion to solve precise queries in clef medical task. In: Working Notes of the 2005 CLEF Workshop, Vienna, Austria (2005)

20. Saracevic, T.: Relevance: A review of and a framework for the thinking on the notion in information science. Journal of the American Society for Information Science **November/December** (1975) 321–343

21. Schamber, L., Eisenberg, M.B., Nilan, M.S.: A re–examination of relevance: Toward a dynamic, situational definition. Information Processing and Management **26 No 6** (1990) 755–775

22. Vendrig, J., Worring, M., Smeulders, A.W.M.: Filter image browsing: Exploiting interaction in image retrieval. In Huijsmans, D.P., Smeulders, A.W.M., eds.: Third International Conference on Visual Information Systems (VISUAL'99). Number 1614 in Lecture Notes in Computer Science, Amsterdam, The Netherlands, Springer–Verlag (1999) 147–154

23. Lehmann, T.M., Schubert, H., Keysers, D., Kohnen, M., Wein, B.B.: The IRMA code for unique classification of medical images. In: Medical Imaging. Volume 5033 of SPIE Proceedings., San Diego, California, USA (2003)

An Efficient Collaborative Information Retrieval System by Incorporating the User Profile

Hassan Naderi, Béatrice Rumpler, and Jean-Marie Pinon

INSA de LYON, Bâtiment Blaise Pascal, 7, Av. Jean Capelle
F69621 Villeurbanne Cedex, France
{hassan.nadery, beatrice.rumpler, jean-marie.pinon}@insa-lyon.fr

Abstract. As the volume of information augments, the importance of the Information Retrieval (IR) increases. Collaborative Information Retrieval (CIR) is one of the popular social-based IR approaches. A CIR system registers the previous user interactions to response to the subsequent user queries more efficiently. But the goals and the characteristics of two users may be different; so when they send the same query to a CIR system, they may be interested in two different lists of documents. In this paper we deal with the personalization problem in the CIR systems by constructing a profile for each user. We propose three new approaches to calculate the user profile similarity that we will employ in our personalized CIR algorithm.

Keywords: Information retrieval, personalization, personalized collaborative information retrieval.

1 Introduction

The ultimate goal of IR is to find the documents that are useful to the user's information need expressed as a query. Much work has been done on improving IR systems, in particular in the Text Retrieval Conference series [12]. In 2000, it was decided at TREC-8 that this task should no longer be pursued within TREC, in particular because the accuracy has stagnated in the last few years [14]. We are working on a new system which learns to improve retrieval effectiveness by integrating:

1. The user characteristics (user model or user profile).
2. The characteristics of the other users (social IR, stereotypes and collaborative information retrieval).
3. The context of the research session (context modelling).

Such system may have the potential to overcome the current stagnation in ad-hoc retrieval systems. This paper concerns to two first elements: the user profile and the Collaborative Information Retrieval (CIR).

CIR is an approach which learns to improve retrieval effectiveness from the interaction of different users with the retrieval system [1]. In other words, collaborative search records the fact that a result d has been selected for query q, and then reuses this information for the next similar queries.

S. Marchand-Maillet et al. (Eds.): AMR 2006, LNCS 4398, pp. 247–257, 2007.
© Springer-Verlag Berlin Heidelberg 2007

However the goals and the characteristics of two users may be different so when they send the same query to a CIR system, they may be interested in two different lists of documents (known as **personalization problem**). Personalization is a common problem often encountered by the CIR researchers in constructing their systems. For instance Armin, who has presented three important approaches toward a CIR system in [2], declared that:

> *"We are aware of the problems of "personalization" and "context", but in our first steps towards techniques we avoid further complexity of CIR by ignoring these challenges."*

Recently Barry S. et al. implemented a significant collaborative web search technique as a search engine architecture in the form of I-SPY (*http://ispy.ucd.ie*) search engine [11]. They define collaborative web search as exploiting repetition and regularity within the query-space of a community of like-minded individuals in order to improve the quality of search results. However they state that: *"the precise nature of a community's shared interests may not be so easy to characterise"*. Because of this difficulty I-SPY can't automatically associate a user to a suitable community. So I-SPY explicitly ask the users to recognize their community among a set of predefined communities at the time of inscription. This method has several restrictions, some of them are as:

1. Finding an appropriate community is a tedious task for a user, especially when the number of communities multiplies rapidly.
2. These predefined communities are not exclusive. Thus in most of the times the user can't find an appropriate community.
3. The interests of the user change over the time while assigning a user to a predfined community is a static task.
4. A user might search different topics while he is just assigned to a community.
5. The communities are either very general or extremely specific to be helpful in retrieval process.

In this paper we create a PERsonalized CIR System (called PERCIRS) which is able to determine automatically the community of a user in order to overcome the personalization problem in CIR. Our personalized system is the first attempt toward resolving automatically the problem of personalization in the CIR systems by incorporating the user profiles.

In section 2 we will present some related works of the CIR area. The architecture of PERCIRS is presented in the section 3. In section 4 we present two formulas for calculating the similarity between two queries. We use these formulas in constructing PERCIRS. In section 5 we explain our three methods for calculating the similarity between two profiles. In section 6 we present a personalized collaborative information retrieval algorithm. We conclude our paper in section 7.

2   Related Work

[3, 5, 8, and 16] have all demonstrated how query logs can be mined to identify useful past queries that may help the current searcher. In [4, 10] a novel approach to Web search—collaborative Web search— was introduced. It combined techniques for exploiting knowledge of the query-space with ideas from social networking, to develop a Web search platform capable of adapting the needs of (ad-hoc) communities of users. In brief, the queries submitted and the results selected by a community of users are recorded and reused in order to influence the results of future searches for similar queries. Results that have been reliably selected for similar queries in the past are promoted. For example, users of an AI-related Web site might have a tendency to select case-based reasoning results in response to ambiguous queries such as 'CBR', while largely ignoring alternatives such as Google's higher-ranking 'Central Bank of Russia' or 'Comic Book Resources' results. In this instance, collaborative search will gradually adapt its result-lists to emphasise case-based reasoning results, for searches that originate from the same community.

3 PERCIRS's Architecture

This section briefly presents the technical solution and the architecture of PERCIRS (figure 1). This system makes use of a client-server architecture and is based on an object-oriented design. This system consists in two main components: content-based IR and collaborative-based IR. For the content-based IR component, we have used an efficient ad-hoc IR method such as Okapi [9]. The list of ranked documents by this ad-hoc method is represented by L_R. When a user U with profile P sends a query q to the system, the system finds the users who have a similar profile to P. For example in the figure 1, P_1 and P_N are similar to P but P_2 is not similar. The profile similarity

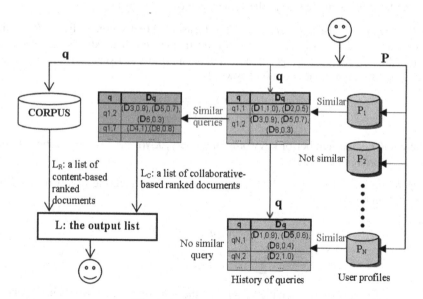

Fig. 1. Architecture of PERCIRS

calculation methods are explained in the section 5. Then the system searches in the history of queries (q, D_q) of the similar users, in order to find the queries which can be similar to q. D_q is the set of document-rank pairs, which user has selected as relevant to q. As it has been shown in the figure 1, $q_{1,2}$ and $q_{1,7}$ tied to the user profile P_1, are relevant to q; but the user with the profile P_N has not executed any relevant query to q. The methods of query similarity calculation are presented in the section 4. In the final step of collaborative ranking, a list of documents (L_C) from the relevant queries of similar users will be constructed. The rank of a document d in L_C is proportional to the three parameters:

1. The degree of similarity of P to $P_1 \dots P_N$.
2. The degree of similarity of q to $q_{i,j}$ where P_i is similar to P.
3. The rank a similar user such as U_i, has already given to d to indicate the degree of its relevancy to the query q_{ij}.

Finally, the output list to represent to user is constructed from the calculated lists L_C and L_R. The detailed procedure for calculating the collaborative rank of a document and combining the two lists L_C and L_R, are presented in the PCIR algorithm in section 6.

4   Query Similarity Calculation Methods

There have been some research studies to calculate the similarity between two different queries. With regard to the type of queries (weighted or unweighted), there are two methods to calculate the similarity between two queries [15]:

A- If the queries are not weighted: This measure directly comes from IR studies. Keywords are the words, except for words in the stop-list. All the keywords are stemmed using the Porter algorithm [13]. The similarity between two queries q_1 and q_2 is proportional to their common keywords:

$$S(q_1, q_2) = \frac{KN(q_1, q_2)}{Max(kn(q_1), kn(q_2))} \tag{1}$$

Where $kn(.)$ is the number of keywords in a query, $KN(q_1, q_2)$ is the number of common keywords in two queries.

B- If the queries are weighted: If query terms are weighted, the following modified formula can be used:

$$S(q_1, q_2) = \frac{\sum_{i=1}^{K} cw_i(q_1) \times cw_i(q_2)}{\sqrt{\sum_{i=1}^{S} w_i^2(q_1)} \times \sqrt{\sum_{i=1}^{T} w_i^2(q_2)}} \tag{2}$$

Where $cw_i(q_1)$ and $cw_i(q_2)$ are the weights of the *i-th* common keywords in the queries q_1 and q_2 respectively, and $w_i(q_1)$ and $w_i(q_2)$ are the weights of the *i-th* keywords in the queries q_1 and q_2 respectively. S and T are the number of the keywords in the queries q_1 and q_2 respectively and K is the number of common words in two queries.

5 Profiles Similarity Calculation Methods

In this section we present our initial methods for calculating the similarity between user profiles. In this project we have planed to integrate a more completed user profile which includes user's knowledge, user's preferences, and user's interests. But in this paper, to present the first step of our project, we begin with a simplified version of this profile that includes the history of the user queries. So a user profile can be presented as a set of pairs (q, D_q) in which q is a query and D_q is a set of document-rank pairs that the user has marked as relevant to q. The rank of each document is between 0 and 1 and can be explicitly provided by the user or implicitly calculated by the system from different parameters such as: the time of reading the document by the user and etc. Thus our ultimate goal is to calculate the similarity between two following sets in order to obtain the similarity between the users X and Y:

$$P(X) = \{(q_1^x, D_{q1}^x), (q_2^x, D_{q2}^x), ..., (q_N^x, D_{qN}^x)\}$$
$$P(Y) = \{(q_1^y, D_{q1}^y), (q_2^y, D_{q2}^y), ..., (q_M^y, D_{qM}^y)\}$$

Where q_i^x is the i-*th* query of the user X, and D_{qi}^x are the relevant documents (with their ranks) to q_i^x according to X's judgments. A query q is a set of keywords which can be weighted or unweighted. In what follows we describe our three Profile Similarity (PS) calculation methods: query based PS, document based PS and query-document based PS.

5.1 Query Based Profile Similarity

We believe that the users' queries can partially represent the needs and the preferences of the users because the users formally express their requirements with the queries. If we only consider the user queries in our calculation, the PS calculation problem will be reduced to the following problem: What is $S(P_q(X), P_q(Y))$ when

$$P_q(X) = \{q_1^x, q_2^x, ..., q_N^x\} \text{ and } P_q(Y) = \{q_1^y, q_2^y, ..., q_M^y\}?$$

In the above problem we have two set of queries from two different users X and Y. Thus we are required to estimate the closeness of these two sets of queries to compute the similarity between the profiles of their corresponding users.

Our first PS formula considers the queries as indissoluble objects. So the similarity between two queries is 1 if they are exactly equal and 0 otherwise. The main idea of this formula is that: the similarity between two set of queries is proportional to the number of their common queries.

$$S(P_q(X), P_q(Y)) = S(\{q_1^x, ..., q_N^x\}, \{q_1^y, ..., q_M^y\}) = \frac{|\{q_1^x, ..., q_N^x\} \cap \{q_1^y, ..., q_M^y\}|}{\log(N + M)} \quad (3)$$

According to this method if the number of common queries in the two sets of queries increases, then the similarity between these profiles increases as well. We have used the *log* function in the above formula in order to normalize the impact of $N+M$ on the PS calculation.

However two profiles may be similar while they have not so common queries (because of synonymy etc.). Thus the above formula may not be so efficient. In such cases the second formula (formula 4) which considers the queries as separable objects could be more efficient. Here the similarity between two queries is between 0 and 1 that can be calculated from formula 1 and 2 according the type of queries (weighted or not).

$$S(P_q(X), P_q(Y)) = \frac{\sum_{i=1}^{N} \sum_{j=1}^{M} s(q_i^x, q_j^y)}{N \times M} \tag{4}$$

This formula is based on the similarity between the queries which calculate the average similarity between the queries from two profiles. The $s(q_i^x, q_j^y)$ can be computed from the formula 1 or 2.

5.2 Document Based Profile Similarity

In this approach we absolutely consider the documents the user has studied or marked as pertinent to his request. When a user reads a particular document it can be judged that the user's need is related to the content of this document. By regarding purely the available documents tied to a profile, the problem of similarity calculation between two profiles can be reduced to the following problem: What is $S(P_d(X), P_d(Y))$ where

$$P_d(X) = \{d_1^x, d_2^x, ..., d_N^x\} \text{ and } P_d(Y) = \{d_1^y, d_2^y, ..., d_M^y\}?$$

Where d_i^x is the i-*th* document tied to the user X's profile of user X.

We will use the cosine formula in order to calculate the similarity between two set of documents. The first method considers each document indissoluble and doesn't deal with the content of the documents. So the similarity between two set of documents is proportional to the number of their common documents:

$$S(P_d(X), P_d(Y)) = S(\{d_1^x, ..., d_N^x\}, \{d_1^y, ..., d_M^y\}) = \frac{\left| \{d_1^x, ..., d_N^x\} \cap \{d_1^y, ..., d_M^y\} \right|}{\log(N + M)} \tag{5}$$

One of the drawbacks of this formula is that if two sets of documents are very similar but they don't have many documents in common; this formula won't be able to precisely determine their similarity. In order to overcome this difficulty we should consider the content of the documents in PS calculation as the following formula:

$$S(P_d(X), P_d(Y)) = \frac{\sum_{i=1}^{N} \sum_{j=1}^{M} s_{cosine}(d_i^x, d_j^y)}{N \times M} \tag{6}$$

In this formula, $s_{cosine}(d_i^x, d_j^y)$ is the similarity between two documents d_i^x and d_i^y, that can be calculated by the cosine formula.

5.3 Query-Document Based Profile Similarity

In the last two approaches we computed the PS respectively based on the users' queries and users' marked documents. In the formula 7 these formulas have been linearly combined in order to get profit from both methods:

$$S(P(X), P(Y)) = \alpha \times S(P_q(X), P_q(Y)) + \beta \times S(P_d(X), P_d(Y)) \tag{7}$$

where $\alpha + \beta = 1$. There is an issue concerning the setting of parameters α and β which we have planed to estimate them experimentally in our subsequent investigations.

In the above formula the mutual connection between a query and its corresponding documents has not been considered because query similarity and document similarity have been calculated separately. However we believe that there is a semantic link behind the relationship between a query and its corresponding documents which can be useful in enhancing the precision of PS calculation. In the following paragraphs we describe how we can exhaustively calculate the similarity between two profiles based on the queries, documents and their relationship. We called such approaches **Complete Profile Similarity (CPS)**. In what follows we will first explain our method for calculating the similarity between two pairs (q_1, D_{q1}) and (q_2, D_{q2}) with regard to the relationship between the queries and their corresponding documents. Then we will represent our CPS method.

The (q,Dq) similarity calculation

[6] stated that in many IR systems, similarities between two objects of the same type (say, queries) can be affected by the similarities between their interrelated objects of another type (say, documents), and vice versa. In their calculation the similarity of the documents is a function of similarity of queries and vise versa:

$$S_q(q_1, q_2) = f(S_d(D_{q_1}, D_{q_2}))$$
$$S_d(d_1, d_2) = g(S_q(q_1, q_2)), \ d_1 \in D_{q_1} \ and \ d_2 \in D_{q_2} \tag{8}$$

D_{q_1} is a list of documents the user has marked as relevant to the query q_1. They iteratively resume similarity calculation until values converge. Their method is not very effective because they consider the queries and their associated documents as two separated objects, and the convergence between the query and documents similarity is difficult to reach. In our new method we consider the queries and their associated documents as two parts of an individual compound object.

In the figure 2 we have represented a compound object as *qd* in order to represent its components: query (*q*) and document (*d*). In our *qd* similarity calculation method we use the fact that the similarity between two objects is inversely proportional to the distance between them:

$$s(o_1, o_2) = 1 / d(o_1, o_2) \tag{9}$$

So we consider a compound object as a point in the two dimensions space in which the query and the document are two axes. We use the distance formula for two points in a Cartesian space in order to calculate the distance (and consequently the similarity) between two *qd* objects.

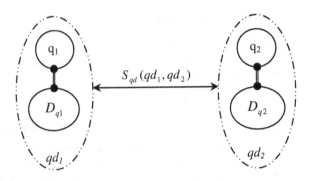

Fig. 2. The (q,d) pairs similarity

The distance between two compound objects can be calculated as the following:

$$d_{qd}(qd_1, qd_2) = \sqrt{\alpha_q \times d_q^2(q_1, q_2) + \alpha_d \times d_D^2(D_{q1}, D_{q2})} \ , \ \alpha_q + \alpha_d = 1 \tag{10}$$

Due to the difference between the units of axes x and y, we have incorporated the coefficients α_q and α_d in the distance calculating formula. Finally according to formulas 9 and 10 we will have:

$$S_{qd}((q_1, D_{q1}), (q_2, D_{q2})) = \frac{1}{d_{qd}(qd_1, qd_2)} = \frac{1}{\sqrt{\dfrac{\alpha_q}{S_q^2(q_1, q_2)} + \dfrac{1 - \alpha_q}{S_d^2(D_{q1}, D_{q2})}}}, 0 \le \alpha_q \le 1 \tag{11}$$

CPS calculation method

Now we are able to calculate the CPS between two profiles $P(X)$ and $P(Y)$ based on the (q, D_q) pairs:

$$S(P(X), P(Y)) = S(\{(q_1^x, D_{q1}^x), \ldots, (q_N^x, D_{qN}^x)\}, \{(q_1^y, D_{q1}^y), \ldots, (q_M^y, D_{qM}^y)\})$$

$$= \frac{\displaystyle\sum_{i=1}^{N}\sum_{j=1}^{M} S_{qd}((q_i^x, D_{qi}^x), (q_j^y, D_{qj}^y))}{N \times M} \tag{12}$$

D_{qi}^x is the set of documents that the user X has marked as relevant to the query q_i^x. The similarity between two compound objects (S_{qd}) can be calculated from the formula 11.

6   The Personalized CIR Algorithm

In this section we describe our personalized collaborative information retrieval algorithm. When a user U sends a query q to PERCIRS, the system uses the following procedure to create a pertinent list of documents to q (figure 3). In this algorithm (U_i, q_i, D_{qi}) describe a profile entry in which U_i is the sender of q_i and D_{qi} is the set of relevant documents to q_i according to U_i judgements. In the first step, PERCIRS selects those triples whose corresponding query has a similarity to q_i that is above some specified threshold; typically $\theta = 0.5$ according to [11]. In the current PERCIRS, ω is equal to 0.5 (we will compute the optimal value of ω in our subsequent experiments).

D_q is the set of all documents which can be pertinent to q. In the steps 3 and 4, we give a personalized collaborative rank to each document d in the D_q. $R_{PCIR}(U, d, q)$ is the rank of d, based on the other users' judgments who are similar to U. In the step 5, the rank of each document in the corpus is calculated by an efficient ad-hoc content-based retrieval algorithm. Finally in the step 6 the collaborative rank and the content-based rank are combined to obtain the final rank of each document. The value of parameters a and b will be defined during the test session.

```
//finding the similar queries to q which are sent by the similar users.
```
1. set $A = \{(U_1, q_1, D_{q1}), (U_2, q_2, D_{q2}), ..., (U_m, q_m, D_{qm})\}$ where
$$s(q, q_i) > \theta \quad \& \quad s(P(U), P(U_i)) > \omega \qquad 1 \le i \le m$$

```
//calculating the set of all documents which can be relevant to q.
```
2. set $D_q = D_{q1} \cup D_{q2} \cup ... D_{qm}$

3. for each $d \in D_q$ calculate the PCIR rank:
$$R_{PCIR}(U, d, q) = \sum_{d \in D_{qi}} s(q, q_i) \times s(P(U), P(U_i))$$

4. for each $d \notin D_q$:
$$R_{PCIR}(U, d, q) = 0$$

5. for each d in the corpus compute $R(d, q)$ with a traditional ad-hoc IR algorithm.

```
//calculating the final rank of each document in the corpus.
```
6. $R(U, d, q) = a \times R(d, q) + b \times R_{PCIR}(U, d, q)$

7. sorting decreasingly the documents by their final rank in order to constructing the output list.

Fig. 3. The personalized CIR algorithm

7 Conclusion and the Future Works

In this paper we explained the problem of personalization in the IR systems. We have also expressed that the impact of this problem on the CIR systems is more serious than on the non collaborative IR systems due to the nature of CIR systems. We proposed to integrate users' similarity in the process of CIR in order to make a more intelligent CIR system. Such a system gives a solution to the personalization problem in the CIR and more generally in the IR area. We proposed to calculate the similarity between two user profiles based on queries, documents and more precisely based on the correlation between the queries and the relevant documents. Subsequently we initiated three different methods to calculating the similarity between two user profiles.

We believe that a personalized CIR system such as PERCIRS could be successful in retrieving the more pertinent documents for a given query because:

1. A CIR system is based on the previous users' judgements.
2. Human-judgements are more efficient than machine-judgements.
3. The probability to send the same or similar queries by different users is relatively high in the search engines.
4. PERCIRS gives a solution to the personalization problem in the IR area.

In the next step toward a personalized CIR system, we will study the efficiency of the proposed PS calculation methods in this paper. We will integrate the best PS calculation method in our personalized CIR algorithm to construct the final version of PERCIRS. We will evaluate the performance of PERCIRS in relation to the other similar systems such as I-SPY [7] that are not personalized.

Acknowledgement. This research is partially supported by the French Ministry of Research and New Technologies under the ACI program devoted to Data Masses (ACI-MD), project #MD-33.

References

1. Armin H., Stefan K., Markus J., Andreas D.: Towards Collaborative Information Retrieval: Three Approaches. In: Text Mining - Theoretical Aspects and Applications. 2002.
2. Armin H.: Learning Similarities for Collaborative Information Retrieval. Proceedings of the KI-2004 workshop "Machine Learning and Interaction for Text-Based Information Retrieval", TIR-04, Germany, 2004.
3. Larry Fitzpatrick and Mei Dent.: Automatic Feedback using Past Queries: Social Searching? In Proceedings of the 20th Annual International ACM SIGIR Conference on Research and Development in Information Retrieval, pages 306–313. ACM Press, 1997.
4. Jill Freyne, Barry Smyth, Maurice Coyle, Evelyn Balfe, and Peter Briggs.: Further Experiments on Collaborative Ranking in Community-Based Web Search. Artificial Intelligence Review, 21(3–4):229–252, 2004.
5. Natalie S. Glance.: Community Search Assistant. In Proceedings of the International Conference on Intelligent User Interfaces, pages 91–96. ACM Press, 2001.

6. Gui-Rong X. et al.: Similarity spreading: a unified framework for similarity calculation of interrelated objects. Proceedings of the 13th international World Wide Web conference on Alternate track papers & posters, 2004, New York, USA

7. I-SPY search engine. Available on: http://ispy.ucd.ie, 25/02/2006.

8. Vijay V. Raghavan and Hayri Sever.: On the Reuse of Past Optimal Queries. In Proceedings of the 18th Annual International ACM SIGIR Conference on Research and Development in Information Retrieval, pages 344–350. ACM Press, 1995.

9. Robertson, S., Walker, S., Jones, S., Hancock-Beaulieu, M. M., Gatford, M.: Okapi at TREC-3, NIST Special Publication 500-225: the Third Text REtrieval Conference (TREC-3), pp. 109-126.

10. Barry Smyth, Evelyn Balfe, Peter Briggs, Maurice Coyle, and Jill Freyne.: Collaborative Web Search. In Proceedings of the 18th International Joint Conference on Artificial Intelligence, IJCAI-03, pages 1417–1419. Morgan Kaufmann, 2003. Acapulco, Mexico.

11. Smyth, B., Balfe, E. Boydell, O., Bradley, K., Briggs, P., Coyle, M., Freyne, J.: A Live User Evaluation of Collaborative Web Search. In Proceedings of the 19th International Joint Conference on Artificial Intelligence. Edinburgh, Scotland, 2005.

12. The site of TREC: Text REtrieval Conference., Aavailable on : http://trec.nist.gov/, 25/02/2006.

13. Baeza-Yates R. and Ribeiro-Neto B.: Modern Information Retrieval. Addison-Wesley, 1999.

14. Ellen M. Voorhees and Donna K. Harman.: Overview of the eighth text retrieval conference (TREC-8). NIST Special Publication 500-246, pages 1–23, 1999.

15. Wen J., Nie J., and Zhang H.: Clustering user queries of a search engine. In Proc. at 10th International World Wide Web Conference, pages 162–168. W3C, 2001.

16. Wen J.: Query clustering using user logs. ACM Transactions on Information Systems, 20(1):59–81, 2002.

The Potential of User Feedback Through the Iterative Refining of Queries in an Image Retrieval System

Maher Ben Moussa, Marco Pasch, Djoerd Hiemstra, Paul van der Vet,
and Theo Huibers

University of Twente
P.O. Box 217, 7500 AE Enschede, The Netherlands
{m.benmoussa,m.pasch,d.hiemstra,p.e.vandervet,
t.w.c.huibers}@cs.utwente.nl

Abstract. Inaccurate or ambiguous expressions in queries lead to poor results in information retrieval. We assume that iterative user feedback can improve the quality of queries. To this end we developed a system for image retrieval that utilizes user feedback to refine the user's search query. This is done by a graphical user interface that returns categories of images and requires the user to choose between them in order to improve the initial query in terms of accuracy and unambiguousness. A user test showed that, although there was no improvement in search time or required search restarts, iterative user feedback can indeed improve the performance of an image retrieval system in terms of user satisfaction.

1 Motivation

One problem of image retrieval is that users utilize inaccurate or ambiguous expressions in their queries. If a user has an image of a three story building in mind but just types in "house", the system will probably give results that satisfy the query but not the user because he will see a lot of houses that do not resemble the one he had in mind. On the other hand the word "bank" can refer to a financial institute as well as a dam protecting the country from a river or sea. Existing retrieval systems require the user to have certain knowledge about the operators the system employs and that he or she is required to use a certain precision and unambiguousness in his queries. Or as Baeza-Yates and Ribiero-Neto put it:" The user of a retrieval system has to translate his information need into a query in the language of the system" [1]. When a search result turns out insufficiently the user has to restart his search with a new, refined query. It can be a long process until the query finally matches both what the user has in mind and the representation of the retrieval system.

We assume that by implementing iterative user feedback on the result of a search we can improve the searching process. Relevance feedback helps the user refining the query without requiring sophisticated usage of the system's query language [2, 3]. Our goal is to develop a system in which the user is not required to type a very specific query. Instead the system will guide him through a number of feedback steps where he can refine his search by simply clicking on a category of items that is close

S. Marchand-Maillet et al. (Eds.): AMR 2006, LNCS 4398, pp. 258–268, 2007.

until the results are satisfactory. The user does not have to care about the phrasing of his query and simply has to click on a particular item. In terms of user friendliness, the system "forgives" errors (i.e. here: imprecise input) and this improves the usability of the image retrieval system as a whole with user satisfaction in particular.

We implement this idea by adding a categorization system on the collection of an image retrieval system. When the user types in a request the result is a number of categories that seem promising to contain the image that he is searching for. The user can then easily make a distinction for example for the word "bank" between "sea/bank" and "organization/bank". In this way, the query becomes iteratively unambiguous and more precise. As such, the approach bears some resemblance with browsing concept hierarchies [4] such as those provided by for instance the Open Directory Project [5]. A similar approach was followed successfully by Sieg et al. [6] for web search. Like Sieg et al., we use static categories, but categories might as well be taken from content classifiers as we have done recently for text search [7]. In the near future, image content classifiers will be available by collaborative efforts [8], which can be used directly in our approach to iterative user feedback.

The paper is organized as follows. In Section 2, we introduce our research questions. In Section 3 we describe our interactive image retrieval system and our approach to answer the research questions. Section 4 presents the experimental results, which are discussed further in Section 5. Finally, Section 6 concludes the paper.

2   Research Questions

In this study we investigate the potential of iterative user feedback in an image retrieval system. We think of potential here as an improvement in terms of the time needed to conduct a search, the attempts that a user has to make to conduct a search and the user's personal attitude of the retrieval system. This leads to the following research questions that we want to investigate:

1. Does iterative user feedback improve the performance of an image retrieval system in terms of the time that is needed for a search?
2. Does iterative user feedback improve the performance of an image retrieval system in terms of the results of a search and the need to restart a search?
3. Does feedback improve the quality of an image retrieval system as it is perceived by the user?

3   Methods

3.1 Prototype

In order to test our assumptions that were stated above we built a system that incorporates user feedback. For control reasons we also built a system that resembles a "traditional" image retrieval system like Google or AltaVista. Both systems feature the same search engine, built on top of Lucene of The Apache Software Foundation [9], and access the same collection. In preparation of the test we also created a domain-specific collection of image data.

Lucene is a lightweight core of a search engine, with a simple and clear API for searching and indexing information. The main disadvantage of Lucene is that it is a very light API with no API for web-crawling and that it lacks support for different file formats like images or PDF files. However, because of the simplicity of its API, it can be easily customized and support for different files can easily be added. For this study, support for image files and a lightweight web crawler have been added.

$$\text{score}(d,q) = \sum_{t \text{ in } q} tf(t \text{ in } d) \cdot idf(t) \cdot boost(t.field \text{ in } d) \cdot lengtNorm(t.field \text{ in } d)$$

Although Lucene is a lightweight search engine core it contains a reasonably sophisticated scoring algorithm. This is the score formula that is used by Lucene to determine the score for each document based on a query. An explanation of the formula is given in Table 1. The formula is taken from [9].

Table 1. Score formula of Lucene

Factor	Description
$tf(t \text{ in } d)$	Term frequency factor for the term (t) in the document (d)
$idf(t)$	Inverse document frequency of the term
$boost(t.field \text{ in } d)$	Field boost, as set during indexing
$lengthNorm(t.field \text{ in } d)$	Normalization value of a field, given the number of terms within the field. This value is computed during indexing and stored in the index

The goal of this study is not to investigate how to improve the indexing of images. We assume that there is a search engine that can index all the images perfectly with the correct keywords and the correct description. We are aware that in reality such an image search engine does not exist. For instance, the image search of Google.com has problems with indexing images with the right keywords. To realize the goal of this study the choice was made to use a test collection of images from the stock photo provider FotoSearch.com [10]. All the images in this collection have proper description and correct keywords.

The next step was to develop an indexer that would be able to index this collection. To this end a FotoSearch.com specific indexer was developed that reads a list of URLs containing an image, its description and its keywords (e.g. http://www.fotosearch.com/BNS145/fba001/) from a file and indexes it. The indexer parses a site and retrieves only the correct information about an image and ignores the rest.

For the search JSP pages are created that use the Lucene search API for searching. To get better results, the StopAnalyser class of Lucene is used to parse the user query. The StopAnalyser class removes all English stop words from the query to decrease the change for irrelevant results. After executing the Lucene search API, the results are presented to the user in a similar way as in the Google Search, in order to provide the user with an interface that he is familiar with. This search engine serves as the control condition in the experiment. Its architecture is shown in Figure 1.

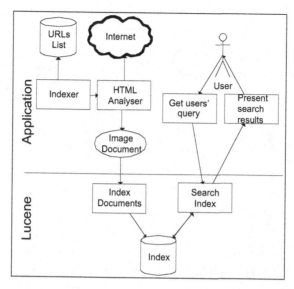

Fig. 1. Architecture of the control condition

The experimental condition was realized by extending the first prototype with support for categories. Based on the test collection of images, a category structure has been created by hand. An XML file with this category structure was built, containing category names, search queries related to these categories and images representing them. When the user types a query, the search engine does not directly pass the query to Lucene like done in the control condition, but searches in the categories XML file for the categories containing the words from this query and the words similar to them and returns the results in a list format with an image before every category that represents it. After choosing a category the user can refine his searching by continuously clicking on the desired subcategory, until he is satisfied with the results. When a (sub-) category is chosen, the search engine automatically executes the query related to this category and presents the results in the same page. The architecture of the experimental condition is shown in Figure 2.

As a test collection we created a category structure of people, with subcategories like Caucasian, Asian and African-american which have as subcategories child, teenager, young adult and older. Here the following subcategories are established by gender and the number of people in an image. To prevent confusion only images related to these categories were indexed and used by both prototypes. In total the collection consisted of 550 images. We are aware that this is a rather small collection, but we are convinced that it is sufficient for the tasks that had to be solved in the user test, which is described further below.

Another difficulty that had to be solved was that different users use different words to specify their search queries, which is also known as encoding specificity problem. Some people would use "caucasian" to search for Caucasian people, while others would use "white" for the same purpose. To solve this problem, WordNet had been

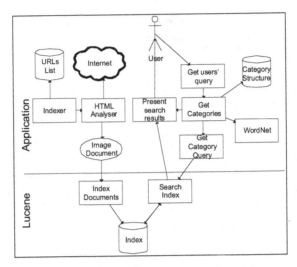

Fig. 2. Architecture of the experimental condition

integrated to the second prototype, making it possible to retrieve the category "cauca-sian" when typing "white". Although WordNet worked pretty well, there were some cases where it presented fewer alternatives than we expected. For instance, when searching for "white", "caucasian" was returned as one of the word senses. However when searching for "black", "african-american" was not between the related word senses. Although it is returned in the similarity list of the adjective "black", there was not enough time to develop a smarter application that checks all the words related in WordNet to the source word and also determines which ones are relevant and which are not. The developed prototype only uses the word senses relations in WordNet.

3.2 Design

To evaluate our approach we conducted a user study choosing a within-subjects setup, which means we use the same participants for both test conditions. The advantage of employing the within-subject setup is that we need fewer participants than with a between-subjects setup, where participants are only used for one condition. More important, this setup usually has a higher statistical power than using different partici-pants for the test conditions, as we get values for each condition from the same individuals.

There was an experimental condition with the system employing user feedback and a control condition with the system without user feedback. For both conditions the participants had to search for images that they were shown before. Those images were chosen by random. The tasks had to be assigned visually because assigning the tasks verbally would have had an influence on which keywords the participants would have used to find the images.

The participants first had to search for images in the control condition and then af-terwards with the experimental condition. Usually it is recommended to alternate the order of conditions to avoid learning effects of the participants [11]. In our case it did not appear useful to alternate the order of conditions because users can see the names of categories in the experimental condition and this could have given them cues for keywords which would have influenced the scores in the control condition. On the other hand the control condition does not give cues for working with the experimental condition. This made it possible to use the within-subject setup.

3.3 Participants

In their HCI textbook, Dix et al suggest using at least 10 participants in each condition of a user test to be able to perform statistical analysis on the results [12]. A total of 12 participants, 5 females and 7 males were recruited for this study. They were all university students, with ages ranging from 20 to 25 years.

As Dix et al further point out it is not useful to test a system that is intended for the general public on a group of computer science students because they are not representative for the common user. We coped with this by relying on students from various fields. Only one participant in our study had a background in computer science, the others came from all kinds of disciplines. All of them can be described as regular Internet users.

3.4 Procedure

Participants were asked to separately enter a room where a computer running the test systems was located. They were asked to sit in front of the computer with an observer next to them. Then they were given a short introduction what the test was about without going too much into detail to avoid giving any cues that might influence their behaviour.

Then they were shown an image and asked to search for this image with the first system. In total they had to search for three images for each system. While they were searching, notes were taken on how long it took them to search and how often they had to restart their search by entering new queries. After finishing the tasks they were asked to evaluate the two systems by describing how well they could work with each system and by assigning grades. The grades were oriented on the Dutch grading scale where a 10 represents the maximum and a 1 the minimum.

In the end a short debriefing and a short discussion about the usefulness of our approach took place. Interesting points deriving from those discussions are mentioned in the discussion section of this report.

4 Results

The first research question asked whether user feedback improves the performance of an image retrieval system in terms of the time users need to search for images. Regarding this research question we can state the following hypothesis:

H_1:   A system utilizing user feedback will be faster in use than a system without user feedback.

This leads to the null hypothesis

N_1:   There is no difference in time when using a system with or without user feedback.

During the experiment notes were taken how long it took the participants to fulfill the tasks that were given to them. Table 2 shows the results. Note that the table shows the accumulated times for the three tasks that had to be solved with each of the conditions.

Table 2. Time needed to fulfill tasks (in seconds)

Subject	Control C.	Exp. C.	Diff.	Diff.^2
1	235	120	115	13225
2	380	315	65	4225
3	180	260	-80	6400
4	80	130	-50	2500
5	80	80	0	0
6	165	90	75	5625
7	390	400	-10	100
8	120	180	-60	3600
9	120	280	-160	25600
10	240	190	50	2500
11	220	120	100	10000
12	210	120	90	8100
Sums	2420	2285	135	81875
Means	201,67	190,42	11,25	

The time needed to solve the given tasks with the system that employs user feedback was slightly shorter ($\bar{x} = 190.42$) than without feedback ($\bar{x} = 201.67$). However, when running a student's t test, the difference did not support the hypothesis that a system employing iterative user feedback is faster in use than a system without feedback since the obtained value t = 0.46 is not statistically significant at the 5% level.

The second research question was whether iterative user feedback improves the search results. This can be interpreted in many ways. In our experimental setup we think of an improvement as a reduced need to restart the search with a new query. Our hypothesis is that

H_2:   A system utilizing user feedback reduces the need to reinitiate searches than a system without user feedback.

The according null hypothesis is

N_2:   There is no difference in the number of searches that have to be carried out to fulfill a task.

Notes were taken how often participants had to enter new queries and by this reinitiate their searches. The resulting figures are given in table 3. Again the values for the three single tasks that a participant had to fulfill per condition are accumulated.

Table 3. Number of search attempts

Subject	Control C.	Exp. C.	Diff.	Diff.^2
1	7	3	4	16
2	8	7	1	1
3	3	7	-4	16
4	3	3	0	0
5	3	4	-1	1
6	5	3	2	4
7	10	9	1	1
8	4	3	1	1
9	5	5	0	0
10	5	3	2	4
11	6	4	2	4
12	7	5	2	4
Sums	66	56	10	52
Means	5,50	4,67	0,83	

The table shows that in the experimental condition less restarts took place ($\bar{x} = 4.67$) than in the control condition ($\bar{x} = 5.5$). However, when again running a t test, the difference did not support the hypothesis that the need to reinitiate searches in a system employing user feedback is smaller than with a system not utilizing user feedback as the null hypothesis could not be rejected at 5% significance level (t=1.45, degrees of freedom=11, p>0.05).

The third research question asked whether user feedback improves the quality of a system as it is perceived by the user. In other words we are interested in knowing whether users like to work with a system employing feedback. This can be rephrased into

H_3: Users rate a system utilizing user feedback higher than a system without user feedback.

The adequate null hypothesis is

N_3: There is no difference in user ratings of a system with and a system without feedback.

After the participants had worked with both systems in the experiment they were asked to rate them on a scale from 1 (low) to 10 (high). Table 4 shows these ratings.

As can be seen in the table the ratings of the experimental condition are higher ($\bar{x} = 8.25$) than those of the control condition ($\bar{x} = 7.33$). Here the difference does indeed support the hypothesis that users perceive a higher quality in a system employing iterative user feedback. The t test reaches significance at 5% significance level (t=-2.42, df=11, p>0.05). The null hypothesis is thus rejected and we can conclude that user feedback does improve the quality of a system as it is perceived by the user.

Table 4. User ratings

Subject	Control C.	Exp. C.	Diff.	Diff.^2
1	7	10	-3	9
2	8	10	-2	4
3	9	8	1	1
4	8	9	-1	1
5	8	7	1	1
6	6	8	-2	4
7	7	8	-1	1
8	6	8	-2	4
9	8	7	1	1
10	7	8	-1	1
11	7	8	-1	1
12	7	8	-1	1
Sums	88	99	-11	29
Means	7,33	8,25	-0,92	

5 Discussion

We were able to show that user feedback does improve the quality of an image retrieval system as it is perceived by the user. The majority of the participants in this study stated that they at least liked the opportunity to use the categories in addition to restart their searches. One participant even declared that he would like to solely navigate through the categories once he had started his search. This user also indicated that he liked working with similar systems like the Yahoo directories to search on the internet. Other participants said they were irritated at first, being used to minimalist interfaces like Google, but once they understood the category system most of them appreciated the extra search options offered by it.

This initial irritation when first using the system is in our opinion also the reason why no significant differences could be found in terms of speed and search restarts. We motivate this position on the fact that tendencies towards this, though not significant, could be found indeed and on the statements of some participants following the experiment. They indicated that they at first had problems in understanding the category system, but this improved with growing experience. We can also conclude from our observations that some of the participants had difficulties in distinguishing categories and images themselves.

Figure 3 shows a screenshot of our image retrieval system that employs user feedback. The first row shows the sub-categories that can be reached from the current category. Beneath this row pictures matching the current query are presented. The confusion between categories and images can be explained by their visual similarity. This can be seen as a minor flaw in our prototype and the first thing we would correct for further research.

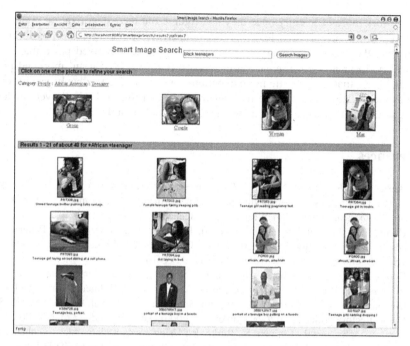

Fig. 3. Screenshot of the image retrieval system employing feedback

We do think that with an improved prototype and participants that have had more experience with retrieval systems that employ iterative user feedback it is possible to find statistically significant differences for the time users need to solve tasks and for the need to reinitiate a search, i.e. entering new queries.

Our results are confirmed by similar work done by Nemeth et al [13]. They examined methods for improving users' queries, specifically interactive and automatic query expansion, coming to the conclusion that there is a difference between users' preferences and the real performance of systems using those improvement methods. While the user satisfaction was higher with the query expansion systems, the performance did not differ significantly.

6 Conclusions

This study has shown that iterative user feedback improves the perceived quality of an image retrieval system. After a short period of getting acquainted with the categorization system users prefer the additional searching options that come with it.

A significant improvement of the performance in terms of search times and search restarts could not be found. Reason for this might be a flaw in the prototype, namely that users confused categories of images and images themselves. This was identified during the user test. Another reason might be the lack of experience of the test participants with search engines that employ iterative user feedback by means of a categorization system. Observations during the experiment show that many users were able to work more efficiently once they had figured out the categorization system, i.e. to search faster and needing less search attempts. Of course also the possibility remains that there is no necessary correlation between the perceived performance and the real performance of retrieval systems. Further research with an improved prototype and users that have a little more experience with iterative feedback systems could answer the question whether the real performance can indeed be improved analogue to the perceived user satisfaction as we were able to show in this study.

References

1. Baeza-Yates, R., Ribiero-Neto, B.: Modern Information Retrieval. Addison-Wesley (1999)
2. Salton, G., Buckley, C.: Improving retrieval performance by relevance feedback. Journal of the American Association of Information Science 41(4) (1990) 288–297
3. Harman, D.: Relevance feedback revisited. In Belkin, N., Ingwersen, P., Pejtersen, A., eds.: Proceedings of the 15th International ACM SIGIR Conference on Research and Development in Information Retrieval., ACM (1992) 1–10
4. Godin, R., Gecsei, J., Pichet, C.: Design of a browsing interface for information retrieval. In Belkin, N., Rijsbergen van, C., eds.: Proceedings of the 12th International ACM SIGIR Conference on Research and Development in Information Retrieval, ACM (1989) 32–39
5. Open directory project. http://www.dmoz.org (2006) Date retrieved: 22 March 2006.
6. Sieg, A.,Mobasher, B., Lytinen, S., Burke, R.: Using concept hierarchies to enhance user queries in web-based information retrieval. In: Proceedings of the IASTED International Conference on Artificial Intelligence and Applications. (2004)
7. Rode, H., Hiemstra, D.: Using Query Profiles for Clarification, Proceedings of the 28th European Conference on Information Retrieval ECIR, Springer (2006)
8. Lin, C.Y., Tseng, B.L., Smith, J.R.: Video Collaborative Annotation Forum: Establishing Ground-Truth Labels on Large Multimedia Datasets, Proceedings of the TRECVID video retrieval evaluation workshop (2003)
9. Hatcher, E., Gospodnetic, O.: Lucene in Action. Manning, Greenwich (2005)
10. FotoSearch Stock Photography and Stock Footage. http://www.fotosearch.com (2006)
11. Howitt, D., Cramer, D.: An Introduction to Statistics in Psychology. 2nd ed. Pearson Education Limited, Harlow (2000)
12. Dix, A., Finlay, J., Abowd, G.D., Beale, R.: Human-computer interaction. Prentice Hall, New York (2003)
13. Nemeth, Y., Shapira, B., Taeib-Maimon, M.: Evaluation of the Real and Perceived Value of Automatic and Interactive Query Expansion. SIGIR'04, Sheffield, UK. ACM (2004)

Author Index

Lecture Notes in Computer Science

For information about Vols. 1–4329

please contact your bookseller or Springer

Vol. 4378: I. Virbitskaite, A. Voronkov (Eds.), Perspectives of Systems Informatics. XIV, 496 pages. 2007.

Vol. 4377: M. Abe (Ed.), Topics in Cryptology – CT-RSA 2007. XI, 403 pages. 2006.

Vol. 4376: E. Frachtenberg, U. Schwiegelshohn (Eds.), Job Scheduling Strategies for Parallel Processing. VII, 257 pages. 2007.

Vol. 4374: J.F. Peters, A. Skowron, I. Düntsch, J. Grzymała-Busse, E. Orłowska, L. Polkowski (Eds.), Transactions on Rough Sets VI, Part I. XII, 499 pages. 2007.

Vol. 4373: K. Langendoen, T. Voigt (Eds.), Wireless Sensor Networks. XIII, 358 pages. 2007.

Vol. 4372: M. Kaufmann, D. Wagner (Eds.), Graph Drawing. XIV, 454 pages. 2007.

Vol. 4371: K. Inoue, K. Satoh, F. Toni (Eds.), Computational Logic in Multi-Agent Systems. X, 315 pages. 2007. (Sublibrary LNAI).

Vol. 4370: P.P Lévy, B. Le Grand, F. Poulet, M. Soto, L. Darago, L. Toubiana, J.-F. Vibert (Eds.), Pixelization Paradigm. XV, 279 pages. 2007.

Vol. 4369: M. Umeda, A. Wolf, O. Bartenstein, U. Geske, D. Seipel, O. Takata (Eds.), Declarative Programming for Knowledge Management. X, 229 pages. 2006. (Sublibrary LNAI).

Vol. 4368: T. Erlebach, C. Kaklamanis (Eds.), Approximation and Online Algorithms. X, 345 pages. 2007.

Vol. 4367: K. De Bosschere, D. Kaeli, P. Stenström, D. Whalley, T. Ungerer (Eds.), High Performance Embedded Architectures and Compilers. XI, 307 pages. 2007.

Vol. 4366: K. Tuyls, R. Westra, Y. Saeys, A. Nowé (Eds.), Knowledge Discovery and Emergent Complexity in Bioinformatics. IX, 183 pages. 2007. (Sublibrary LNBI).

Vol. 4364: T. Kühne (Ed.), Models in Software Engineering. XI, 332 pages. 2007.

Vol. 4362: J. van Leeuwen, G.F. Italiano, W. van der Hoek, C. Meinel, H. Sack, F. Plášil (Eds.), SOFSEM 2007: Theory and Practice of Computer Science. XXI, 937 pages. 2007.

Vol. 4361: H.J. Hoogeboom, G. Păun, G. Rozenberg, A. Salomaa (Eds.), Membrane Computing. IX, 555 pages. 2006.

Vol. 4360: W. Dubitzky, A. Schuster, P.M.A. Sloot, M. Schroeder, M. Romberg (Eds.), Distributed, High-Performance and Grid Computing in Computational Biology. X, 192 pages. 2007. (Sublibrary LNBI).

Vol. 4358: R. Vidal, A. Heyden, Y. Ma (Eds.), Dynamical Vision. IX, 329 pages. 2007.

Vol. 4357: L. Buttyán, V. Gligor, D. Westhoff (Eds.), Security and Privacy in Ad-Hoc and Sensor Networks. X, 193 pages. 2006.

Vol. 4355: J. Julliand, O. Kouchnarenko (Eds.), B 2007: Formal Specification and Development in B. XIII, 293 pages. 2006.

Vol. 4354: M. Hanus (Ed.), Practical Aspects of Declarative Languages. X, 335 pages. 2006.

Vol. 4353: T. Schwentick, D. Suciu (Eds.), Database Theory – ICDT 2007. XI, 419 pages. 2006.

Vol. 4352: T.-J. Cham, J. Cai, C. Dorai, D. Rajan, T.-S. Chua, L.-T. Chia (Eds.), Advances in Multimedia Modeling, Part II. XVIII, 743 pages. 2006.

Vol. 4351: T.-J. Cham, J. Cai, C. Dorai, D. Rajan, T.-S. Chua, L.-T. Chia (Eds.), Advances in Multimedia Modeling, Part I. XIX, 797 pages. 2006.

Vol. 4349: B. Cook, A. Podelski (Eds.), Verification, Model Checking, and Abstract Interpretation. XI, 395 pages. 2007.

Vol. 4348: S.T. Taft, R.A. Duff, R.L. Brukardt, E. Ploedereder, P. Leroy (Eds.), Ada 2005 Reference Manual. XXII, 765 pages. 2006.

Vol. 4347: J. Lopez (Ed.), Critical Information Infrastructures Security. X, 286 pages. 2006.

Vol. 4346: L. Brim, B. Haverkort, M. Leucker, J. van de Pol (Eds.), Formal Methods: Applications and Technology. X, 363 pages. 2007.

Vol. 4345: N. Maglaveras, I. Chouvarda, V. Koutkias, R. Brause (Eds.), Biological and Medical Data Analysis. XIII, 496 pages. 2006. (Sublibrary LNBI).

Vol. 4344: V. Gruhn, F. Oquendo (Eds.), Software Architecture. X, 245 pages. 2006.

Vol. 4342: H. de Swart, E. Orłowska, G. Schmidt, M. Roubens (Eds.), Theory and Applications of Relational Structures as Knowledge Instruments II. X, 373 pages. 2006. (Sublibrary LNAI).

Vol. 4341: P.Q. Nguyen (Ed.), Progress in Cryptology - VIETCRYPT 2006. XI, 385 pages. 2006.

Vol. 4340: R. Prodan, T. Fahringer, Grid Computing. XXIII, 317 pages. 2007.

Vol. 4339: E. Ayguadé, G. Baumgartner, J. Ramanujam, P. Sadayappan (Eds.), Languages and Compilers for Parallel Computing. XI, 476 pages. 2006.

Vol. 4338: P. Kalra, S. Peleg (Eds.), Computer Vision, Graphics and Image Processing. XV, 965 pages. 2006.

Vol. 4337: S. Arun-Kumar, N. Garg (Eds.), FSTTCS 2006: Foundations of Software Technology and Theoretical Computer Science. XIII, 430 pages. 2006.

Vol. 4336: V.R. Basili, D. Rombach, K. Schneider, B. Kitchenham, D. Pfahl, R.W. Selby, Empirical Software Engineering Issues. XVII, 193 pages. 2007.

Vol. 4335: S.A. Brueckner, S. Hassas, M. Jelasity, D. Yamins (Eds.), Engineering Self-Organising Systems. XII, 212 pages. 2007. (Sublibrary LNAI).

Vol. 4334: B. Beckert, R. Hähnle, P.H. Schmitt (Eds.), Verification of Object-Oriented Software. XXIX, 658 pages. 2007. (Sublibrary LNAI).

Vol. 4333: U. Reimer, D. Karagiannis (Eds.), Practical Aspects of Knowledge Management. XII, 338 pages. 2006. (Sublibrary LNAI).

Vol. 4332: A. Bagchi, V. Atluri (Eds.), Information Systems Security. XV, 382 pages. 2006.

Vol. 4331: G. Min, B. Di Martino, L.T. Yang, M. Guo, G. Ruenger (Eds.), Frontiers of High Performance Computing and Networking – ISPA 2006 Workshops. XXXVII, 1141 pages. 2006.

Vol. 4330: M. Guo, L.T. Yang, B. Di Martino, H.P. Zima, J. Dongarra, F. Tang (Eds.), Parallel and Distributed Processing and Applications. XVIII, 953 pages. 2006.